BIBLIOGRAPHY
of
DISCOGRAPHIES

BIBLIOGRAPHY
of
DISCOGRAPHIES

Volume 1

CLASSICAL MUSIC, 1925–1975

by

Michael H. Gray

and

Gerald D. Gibson

R. R. Bowker Company

New York and London, 1977

For Dottie and Emily

Published by R. R. Bowker Company
1180 Avenue of the Americas, New York, N.Y. 10036
Copyright © 1977 by Xerox Corporation
All rights reserved
Printed and bound in the United States of America

Library of Congress Cataloging in Publication Data

Gray, Michael, 1946-
    Bibliography of discographies.

    Includes indexes.
        CONTENTS: v. 1. Classical music, 1925-1975.
        1. Music—Discography—Bibliography.
I. Gibson, Gerald, 1938-   joint author.
II. Title.
ML113.G77   016.0167899'12   77-22661
ISBN 0-8352-1023-5

Contents

Foreword

As long as we need records for something more than background music we will need discographies. The proliferation of recorded sound is so great that only a devoted researcher of a composer's music on records, an artist's performing career on records, or a record company's rise and fall from the first number to the last on its list can enable us to use fully the riches that are hidden within grooves.

As long as we need discographies we will need the kind of bibliography that Michael Gray and Gerald Gibson have given us. Discographies are appearing constantly as monographs, in books, and in periodicals of such diverse origin that one wonders if any library has all of them. If one cannot find a discography, or does not know that it exists, it is useless.

This bibliography can do several things. Obviously, its first purpose is in helping to find a particular discography. It can also help a discographer to find what has already been compiled on his or her chosen subject; anyone who is going over previously plowed ground can at least improve upon preceding efforts. A word of caution: not every item that calls itself a discography includes even the most basic elements of information invariably needed by a reader. Most discographers learn by experience, profit from the insights of others in the field, and grow increasingly humble about their earliest efforts. But there is no way to keep anyone from calling any casually assembled list of a few records by this title. Before assuming that a discography listed here is adequate, evaluate it. If it falls short, see if you can do better. Finally, it is useful to note the subjects not listed in this book; discographers are hereby advised that open season is declared on all areas thus far neglected.

Gray and Gibson have tried to improve on the efforts of their predecessors in the field. Carl Bruun and John Gray are the acknowledged pioneers; in fact Mr. Bruun had recently compiled a supplement to his earlier work, which is now superseded by this bibliography. Both Lewis Foreman and David Cooper have more recently approached the subject on a broad basis. It is no denigration of their significant efforts to say that all of these works are now supplanted by this new series, which when completed will cover the entire field of discography. The compilers began from the vantage point of their adjacent desks in the Descriptive Cataloging Division of the Library of Congress, where they were in an ideal position to be aware of the great bulk of discographic material they were trying to organize, and more important to examine it firsthand. Although Michael Gray is now Music Librarian at the Voice of America and Gerald Gibson is presently Assistant Head of the Recorded Sound Section at the Library of Congress, they have not lost touch with the flow of print. Their own grasp of classical music will be complemented by collaborators in the other special fields to be covered in the succeeding volumes.

What makes the future look bright is that the compilers will continue the annual bibliography of discographies in the *Journal of the Association for Recorded Sound Collections*, where the work in progress has been appearing since 1974. In fact it will continue to be work in progress for some areas until all five volumes have been published, at which point the publisher will issue a supplement to the series.

J. F. Weber
Utica, N.Y.

Preface

This first volume of *Bibliography of Discographies*, encompassing discographies of classical music published between 1925 and 1975, begins a series of works that will eventually number five volumes devoted to discographies in all subject areas. When completed these will survey jazz (Volume 2); popular music (Volume 3); ethnic and folk music (Volume 4); and general discographies of music, as well as label lists, speech, and animal sounds (Volume 5).

In compiling this bibliography we have recognized the work of previous authors in the field—Carl Bruun and John Gray, whose pioneering bibliography was published in *Recorded Sound* in 1962—and more recent efforts by Lewis Foreman and David Cooper. We have also recognized the continuing need for a comprehensive, authoritative guide to discographies, and it is this aim that inspires our work.

We have not attempted to provide a definition of "discography," in spite of the efforts of many others to do so. Instead, our selection of citations has been guided primarily by the self-designation of a work and by its potential usefulness to the user. We hope, however, that users in search of definitions will gain some enlightenment from what we have compiled.

RESEARCH METHOD

In gathering citations we have relied almost exclusively on examination of the discographies themselves. Those not seen by us but taken from various secondary sources have been enclosed in double brackets [[ ]]. Citations of monographs are taken as closely as possible from the title page, with interpolations or other alterations enclosed in single brackets. Because of this method some citations will differ in form from those found in other bibliographies and reference sources. A number of secondary citations which could not be clarified in the time allotted to our research have been omitted and will appear after examination in a supplementary edition of this bibliography. General discographies of music, such as buyer's guides, collector's guides, and label discographies, will appear in Volume 5 of this series.

As part of the examination process we have adopted a seven-number annotative code which is used to identify elements that we believe to be important to users. These coded elements appear in double parentheses "(( ))" included in or following the citation. The symbol "((–))" is used to signify that no coded elements appear in the discography. The elements and their symbols are:

1 Noncommercial recordings
2 Not used in this volume
3 Matrix numbers
4 Index
5 Release dates
6 Take numbers
7 Place and/or date of recording

ORGANIZATION

We have divided the bibliography into two sections: the body, which contains personal names and other subjects arranged in a single-numbered alphabetical sequence; and the index, encompassing names of compilers, authors, editors, series titles, and distinctive discography titles. Surnames of compilers, authors, and editors in the body have been capitalized to facilitate identification and to make scanning entries easier. Filing of multiple listings under a given heading is by either name of the compiler of the discography, the name of the author of the work in which the discography appears, or the title of the discography. Headings for citations that are not personal names are as specific as the entry allows. For composers and their works entries have been arranged in the following manner: general discographies of the composer followed by discographies of types of works or specific works (e.g., symphonies or operas).

BEETHOVEN, LUDWIG VAN, 1770-1827

223 Phonograph records in BURK, John N.: The life and works of Beethoven. New York: Random House, [1943]: 464-478 ((–))

Works, Piano

254 GOLDSMITH, Harris: Beethoven on record: the piano music in High Fidelity, XXI/1 (January 1971): 61-66 ((–))

Sonata, Piano, Op. 57, F Minor

279 HASELAUER, Elisabeth: Diskographie in Hi Fi Stereophonie (February 1971): 114 ((5))

Discographies for performers appear in the following forms:

CARUSO, ENRICO, 1873-1921

(Journal article) → 573 DRUMMOND, H. J.: Enrico Caruso; a
chronological list of his records in
Gramophone, No. 128 (January 1934):
311-314 ((7))

(Title entry) → 574 Enrico Caruso. [Copenhagen]: Nationalmuseet, 1961. 22 leaves (Det
National Diskotek Katalog; 2) ((3,
4, 6, 7))

(Monograph) → 576 FAVIA-ARTSAY, Aida: Caruso on records. [1st ed.] Valhalla, NY: Historic
Record, [1965]: 218 pp. ((3, 4, 7))

Form of personal names and subjects in the body is based on the authority
lists of the Library of Congress; where appropriate, cross-references linking
variant subjects or name forms to those used have been made. Filing in the
body and in the index follows American Library Association filing rules.

Because no work of bibliography can ever be complete we invite readers
to submit their additions or corrections to the compilers in care of the
publisher. In making this request we also acknowledge the help and assis-
tance provided to us by these persons and institutions: Fred Bindman,
Head, and the staff of the Music Section, Descriptive Cataloging Division,
Library of Congress; James R. Smart, Reference Librarian, Recorded Sound
Section, Library of Congress; the staff of the British Institute of Recorded
Sound, London; Steve Smolian; Richard Warren, Yale University; David
Hall and Gary Gisondi, New York Public Library; J. F. Weber, Utica, New
York; John Wiser; Bill McGuire, Washington, D.C.; Bill Curtis, Boston; and
Dr. Robert Werba, Vienna.

Michael H. Gray
Gerald D. Gibson

September 1977

BIBLIOGRAPHY
of
DISCOGRAPHIES

ABBADO, CLAUDIO, 1933-

  1 Abbado discography in Records and
    Recording, XV/7 (April 1972): 28
    ((-))

  2 Discographie de Abbado in Diapason,
    No. 133 (February 1969): 13 ((-))

ABEL, KARL FRIEDRICH, 1723-1787

  3 Karl Friedrich Abels Kompositionen
    Phonographien in KNAPE, Walter:
    Bibliographisch-thematisches Ver-
    zeichnis der Kompositionen von Karl
    Friedrich Abel (1723-1787). Cuxhaven:
    W. Knape, [1972?]: 281-282 ((-))

ABENDROTH, IRENE

  4 RIEMENS, Leo: Irene Abendroth in
    Record Collector, VI/6 (April 1951):
    77-85 ((-))

ABSIL, JEAN, 1893-1974

  5 Discographie in GUIDE, Richard de:
    Jean Absil; vie et oeuvre. [Tournai]:
    Casterman, 1965: 213-214 ((-))

ACHTÉ, AINO
    See ACKTÉ, AÏNO

ACKERMANN, OTTO

  6 FISCHER, Gert: Diskografie Otto
    Ackermann in fono forum 1970 (No. 4,
    April): 219 ((-))

ACKTÉ, AÏNO, 1876-1944

  7 BRUUN, Carl L.: [Records] in Record
    News, V/3 (November 1960): 88-89
    ((3, 7))

ADAM, THEO

  8 Diskographie in Medium Schallplatte,
    No. 12 (No. 3, 1969): 4 ((-))

  9 Diskographie (in Auswahl) in Musica/
    Phonoprisma, XXII/3 (May-June 1968):
    237 ((-))

ADAMS, SUZANNE, 1872-1953

  10 FREESTONE, John: Suzanne Adams,
    1873-1953 in Gramophone, No. 361
    (July 1953): 37 ((7))

  11 [[HEVINGHAM-ROOT, L.: Discography
    in Record Collector, XIII/1-2 (March-
    April 1960)]]

AFFRE, AGUSTAELLO

  12 [[GIRARD, V.: Discography in Record
    Collector, IX/3 (March 1954]]

AGUIRRE, JULIÁN, 1869-1924

  13 Obras grabados en discos in GIA-
    COBBE, Juan Francisco: Julian
    Aguirre; ensayo sobre su vida y su
    obra en su tiempo. 2. ed. Buenos
    Aires: Ricordi Americana, [c1945]:
    96 (Músicos de America) ((-))

AGUSSOL, CHARLOTTE-MARIE

  14 [[GIRARD, V.: Discography in Record
    Collector, IX/3 (March 1954)]]

ALAIN, JEHAN, 1911-1940

  15 Discographie in Courrier Musical de
    France, No. 11 (1965): 180 ((-))

ALBANI, EMMA, 1847-1930

  16 CELLETTI, Rodolfo: Discografia di
    Emma Albani in Musica e Dischi,
    XIII (No. 129, May 1957): 60 ((-))

17 FREESTONE, John: Emma Albani in
Record News, I/5 (January 1957):
163-166 ((7))

18 HARVEY, H. Hugh: Madame Albani—
records in Gramophone, No. 354
(November 1952): 133 ((7)) [Includes
unissued records]

19 MORAN, W. R.: Emma Albani: the recordings in Record Collector, XII/4
(February-March 1959): 97-101 ((3,6,
7))

ALBENIZ, ISAAC MANUEL FRANCISCO,
1860-1909

20 [[LAPLANE, M. Gabriel: [Discography]
in Discofilia No. 7 (October 1956): 285]]

21 La musica de Isaac Albéniz en discos,
recopilación realizada por Juan Manuel
PUENTE in RAUX, Deledicque Miguel:
Albéniz; su vida inquieta y ardorosa.
[Buenos Aires]: Ediciones Peuser,
[1950]: 431-437 ((-))

ALBERT, EUGEN D', 1864-1932

22 BENKO, Gregor: Eugen d'Albert—a
discography in Antique Records, No. 1
(November 1972): 8-12 ((3))

ALDA, FRANCES, 1883-1952

23 [[FAVIA-ARTSAY, Aida: Frances Alda
in Record Collector, VI/10 (October
1951): 221-233]]

ALEXANDER, GEORGE
See WILEY, CLIFFORD ALEXANDER

ALFVÉN, HUGO, 1872-1960

24 ÅHLÉN, Carl-Gunnar: Hugo Alfven ver
också dirigent in Musik Revy, XXVII/2
(1972): 73-76 ((1, 3, 5, 7))

25 Diskografi in HEDWALL, Lennart:
Hugo Alfven; en svensk tonsättares liv
och werk. Stockholm: Norstedt, 1973:
413-416 ((-))

ALKAN, CHARLES HENRI VALENTIN, 1813-
1888

26 FRANKE, Knut: Diskografie Alkan in
fono forum 1972 (No. 4, April): 268
((-))

ALLIN, NORMAN

27 RICHARDS, J. B.: The recordings of
Norman Allin in Record Collector,

X/5-6 (October-November 1955): 122-
129 ((3))

ALONSO, ODÓN

28 [[Discography] in Discofilia (May
1957): 13]

ALSEN, ELSA

29 VESPER, Edward: Elsa Alsen in Record Collector, XV/1: 11-12 ((3, 7));
Addenda: Record Collector, XV/5-6:
142; XV/7-8: 180

ALSOP, ADA

30 [[[Discos] in Disc (Bristol) II/6
(Spring 1948): 75]]

31 Records by Ada Alsop in Disc, II/6
(Spring 1948): 75 ((-))

AMADEUS QUARTET

32 CLOUGH, F. F., and G. J. CUMING:
The Amadeus Quartet—discography
in Audio and Record Review, III/10
(June 1964): 16-17 ((-))

33 Diskographie in Phonoprisma, VI/3
(May-June 1963): 70, 76 ((-))

34 KAHLWEIT, Manfred: Diskografie in
fono forum 1961 (No. 11, November):
14 ((-))

AMATO, PASQUALE, 1878-1942

35 CELLETTI, Rodolfo: Discografia in
Musica e Dischi, IX (No. 85, October
1953): 28 ((7))

36 [[DENNIS, J. F. E.: Discography in
Record Collector, VIII/9 (September
1953)]]

37 HARDWICK, Keith: Amato discography in Record News, I/1 (September
1956): 13-15 ((7)); Addenda: Record
News, I/2 (October 1956): 76

38 KENYON, J. P., W. R. MORAN, and C.
WILLIAMS: The recordings of Pasquale
Amato in Record Collector, XXI/1-2
(May 1973): 25-47 ((1, 3, 4, 6, 7))

AMELING, ELLY

39 [[[Discography] in Disk, No. 43 (August
1970): 373]]

40 Nouveautes in Diapason, No. 154
(February 1971): 7 ((-))

AMY, GILBERT, 1936-

41 ALLVARD, Didier: Discographie in Diapason, No. 184 (February 1974): 11 ((-))

42 Discographie de Gilbert Amy in Courrier Musical de France, No. 36 (1971): 208 ((-))

ANČERL, KAREL, 1908-1973

43 Diskografie Karel Ančerl in Hi Fi Stereophonie, XII/9 (September 1973): 966-968 ((-))

44 In mémoriam K. Ančerl et H. Schmidt-Isserstedt—discographie sèlection in Diapason, No. 179 (September 1973): 9 ((-))

45 Soupis nahrávek Karla Ančerla in ŠROM, Karel: Karel Ančerl. 1. vyd. Praha: Supraphon, t.KNT 2, 1968: 70-75 (Edice Lyra) ((-))

ANCONA, MARIO, 1860-1931

46 MORAN, W. R.: The discography in Record Collector, XVI/5-6 (April 1965): 129-139 ((3, 4, 5, 6, 7)); Addenda: Record Collector, XVI/7-8 (September 1965): 188; XX/6-7 (May 1972): 164

ANDA, GEZA, 1921-1976

47 HAUSSWALD, Günter: Diskographie (Auswahl) in Musica, XXIII/5 (September-October 1969): 501 ((-))

ANDERS, PETER, 1908-1954

48 Verzeichnis der Schallplatten und Rundfunkaufnahmen mit Peter Anders in PAULI, Friedrich Wilhelm: Peter Anders. [Berlin]: Rembrandt Verlag, [1963]: 25-29 (Rembrandt-Reihe, 47) ((1, 7))

49 ROSS, A. G.: Peter Anders records in Record News, III/1 (September 1958): 8-16 ((-)); Addenda: Record News, IV/6 (February 1960): 221-223

ANDRADE, FRANCISCO
See D'ANDRADE, FRANCISCO

ANDRE, FRANZ

50 Discographie in Phono, II/3 (Spring 1956): 11 ((-))

ANDRÉ, MAURICE

51 Discographie selection in Diapason, No. 168 (June-July 1972): 10 ((-))

52 Diskographie (Auswahl) in Musica, XXIII/3 (May-June 1969): 282 ((-))

ANGELES, VICTORIA DE LOS, 1923-

53 Diskografie in BURIAN, Karel Vladimír: Victoria de Los Angeles. Praha: Supraphon, t. St 2, 1970: 44-48 (Edice Lyra) ((-))

54 CLOUGH, F. F., and G. J. CUMING: A Victoria de los Angeles discography in Audio and Record Review, II/6 (February 1963): 14-15 ((-))

55 CLOUGH, F. F., and G. J. CUMING: Victoria de los Angeles; a diskography in Gramophone Record Review, No. 83 (September 1960): 614-615 ((-))

56 Discographie de Victoria de los Angeles in GAVOTY, Bernard: Victoria de los Angeles. Genève: Éditions R. Kister, 1956: [32] (Les Grands interprètes) ((-))

57 [[SANCHEZ, M. C.: [Discography] in Discofilia, No. 10 (January-February 1957): 22]]

ANGELICI, MARTHA

58 Discographie di Martha Angelici in Disques, No. 2 (February 15, 1948): 65 ((-))

59 ROSS, A. G.: [Discography] in Record News, I/5 (January 1957): 183-187 ((-))

ANSELMI, GIUSEPPE

60 TARTONI, Guido: Discografia di Giuseppe Anselmi in Musica e Dischi, XXII (No. 239, May 15-June 15, 1966): 24 ((7))

ANSERMET, ERNEST ALEXANDRE, 1883-1969

61 Ansermet and the Suisse Romande in Audio and Record Review (April 1969): 255 ((-))

62 CLOUGH, F. F., and G. J. CUMING: Ernest Ansermet; diskography in Gramophone Record Review, No. 51 (January 1958): 228-230 ((-))

63 Diskografie in fono forum 1961 (No. 6, June): 40 ((-))

64 Plattenkatalog in GAVOTY, Bernard:
Ernest Ansermet. Genf: R. Kister,
c1961: 32-[34] (Die Grossen Interpreten) ((-))

65 HIRSCH, Nicole: Discographie
(disques Decca) in Diapason, No.
135 (April 1969): 15 ((-))

ANSORGE, CONRAD, 1862-1930

66 HOWARD, Geoffrey: Conrad Ansorge's
Parlophon recordings in 78 RPM, No.
2: 6 ((3, 7))

ANSSEAU, FERNAND

67 DE COCK, Alfred: Discography in
Record Collector, IX/1 (January 1954):
16-20 ((3, 6, 7))

APOSTOLU, GIOVANNI

68 CELLETTI, Rodolfo: Incisioni in
Musica e Dischi, XVIII (No. 188,
February 1962): 18 ((7))

ARGENTA, ATAÚLFO, 1913-1958

69 [[[Discography] in Discofilia No. 2
(April 1956): 45]]

70 Discos in FERNÁNDEZ-CID, Antonio:
Ataúlfo Argenta. [Madrid]: Biblioteca
Nueva, 1958: 208-211 ((-))

71 Discografía in FERNÁNDEZ-CID, Antonio: Ataúlfo Argenta. [Madrid]:
Dirección General de Bellas Artes,
Ministerio de Educación y Ciencia,
[1971]: 51-57 (Colección artistas
españoles contemporáneos; 4. Serie
músicos) ((-))

72 Enregistrements in GAVOTY, Bernard:
Ataúlfo Argenta. Genève: R. Kister,
c1956: [32] (Les Grands interprètes)
((-))

73 Discografía de Argenta in MONTERO
ALONSO, José: Vida apasionada de
Ataúlfo Argenta. Santander: [La
Moderna], 1959: [85]-91 (Antología de
escritores y aristas montañeses) ((-))

ARGERICH, MARTHA

74 Diskographie in Musica, XXIII/1
(January-February 1969): 56-57
((-))

75 ZURLETTI, Michelangelo: Martha
Argerich in Discoteca, No. 99 (April
1970): 14 ((-))

ARNOLDSON, SINGRID, 1861-1943

76 ÅHLÉN, Carl-Gunnar: Singrid Arnoldson (1861-1943) diskografi in Musik
Revy, XXVII/1 (1972): 38-39 (Grammofonens veteraner; 4) ((3, 5, 6, 7))

ARRAL, BLANCHE

77 FASSETT, Stephen: The Arral records
in American Record Guide, XI/8 (April
1945): 208 ((7))

ARRAU, CLAUDIO, 1903-

78 CLOUGH, F. F., and G. J. CUMING:
Claudio Arrau; diskography in Gram-
ophone Record Review, No. 76
(February 1960): 196 ((-))

79 [[Discography in Philips Music Herald
(Spring 1969)]]

80 Diskographie in Phonoprisma (March-
April 1965): 65, 67 ((-))

81 Discography in GAVOTY, Bernard:
Claudio Arrau. Geneva: R. Kister,
c1962: [30-32] (Great concert artists)
((-))

82 Plattenverzeichnis in GAVOTY,
Bernard: Claudio Arrau. Genf: R.
Kister, c1962: 33-34 (Die grossen In-
terpreten) ((-))

ARS REDIVIVA

83 HENRY-JACQUES: Ars Rediviva; une
discographie in Disques (Special Number, 1947): 6 ((-))

ASHKENAZY, VLADIMIR, 1937-

84 Discographie; disques Decca in Diapason, No. 176 (April 1973): 5 ((-))

85 REICH, Willi: Vladimir Ashkenazy in
fono forum 1966 (No. 1, January): 16
((-))

ASKENASE, STEFAN, 1896-

86 Stefan Askenase plays Chopin in Piano;
Frederic Chopin: Berceuse, op. 57.
Translated by John BELL. Zürich:
Panton Verlag; distributed by C. F.
Peters, New York, 1968: 151 [Note:
Master class lesson with accompanying
sound recording] ((-))

87 Stefan Askenase spielt Chopin in
Klavier; Frederic Chopin: Berceuse,
op. 57. Zürich: Panton Verlag, 1966:
151 [Note: Master class lesson with
accompanying sound recording] ((-))

ASMUSSEN, S.

88 [[[Discography] in L. A. Record Research, II/5 (January-February 1954): 16]]

AURIC, GEORGES, 1899-

89 Discografia in L'Approdo Musicale, No. 19-20 (1965): 187-190 ((-))

90 Discographie in GOLÉA, Antoine: Georges Auric. Paris: Ventadour, [1958]: 47 (Collection "Musiciens d'aujourd'hui") ((-))

AUSTRAL, FLORENCE, 1894-1968

91 HOGARTH, William, and Don WHITE: The records in Record Collector, XIV/1-2: 23-29 ((3, 6)); Addenda: Record Collector, XIV/7-8: 168-169 ((3, 6))

BBC RECORDED PROGRAMMES PERMA-
NENT LIBRARY
See listing for DE LARA, ADELINA.
De Lara, Adelina: Finale

BABBITT, MILTON, 1916-

92 Babbitt on records in Stereo Review, XXII/4 (April 1969): 68 ((-))

BACH, CARL PHILIP EMMANUEL, 1714-
1788

93 DOMMETT, Kenneth: Discography of keyboard works of C. P. E. Bach in BARFORD, Philip: The keyboard music of C. P. E. Bach. London: Barrie and Rockliff, 1965: [179]-180 ((-))

94 DOMMETT, Kenneth: Discography of keyboard works of C. P. E. Bach in BARFORD, Philip: The keyboard music of C. P. E. Bach. New York: October House, 1966: [179]-180 ((-))

BACH, JOHANN CHRISTIAN, 1735-1782

95 J. C. Bach on records in High Fidelity, XII/6 (June 1962): 36-37, 87 ((-))

BACH, JOHANN SEBASTIAN, 1685-1750

96 BASSO, A.: Discografia in L'Approdo Musicale, IV/14-15 (1961): 259-263 ((-))

97 Discographie critique et comparée de Jean-Sébastien Bach in BUCHET,

Édmond: Jean-Sébastien Bach, l'oeuvre et la vie. Paris: Les libraires associes, 1963: [246]-[267] ((-))

98 [[Discography in BUCHET, Édmond: Jean-Sébastien Bach après deux siècles d'études et de témoignages. Paris: Buchet-Chastel, 1968: 263-302]]

99 Discographie générale in DUFOURCQ, Norbert: Jean-Sébastien Bach; un architecte de la musique, génie allemand? génie latin? 2d. éd rev. et augm. d'une discographie générale. Paris: La Colombe, [1949, c1947]: [235]-269 ((-))

100 Discographie générale in DUFOURCQ, Norbert: Jean-Sébastien Bach, un architecte de la musique, génie allemand? génie latin? Ed. rev. et augm. d'une discographie générale entièrement mise à jour. Paris: La Colombe, [1954, c1947]: [233]-277 ((-))

101 Supplement á la discographié de 1949 in DUFOURCQ, Norbert: Jean-Sébastien Bach; un architecte de la musique, génie allemand? génie latin?. Ed. rev. et augm. d'une discographie générale entièrement mise à jour. Paris: La Colombe, [1954, c1947]: [276-288] ((-))

102 FARMER, Charles V.: A selected list of Bach recordings in [HOELTY-NICKEL, Theodore]: The little Bach book. Valparaiso, Ind.: Valparaiso University Press, [c1950]: 138-[160] ((-))

103 [[FIRMAGE, George James: Bach on LP. London: A Great Book Publication, 1968]]

104 Discografía de las obras de J. S. Bach in LEUCHTER, Erwin: Bach. Buenos Aires: Ricordi Americana, 1942: 97-[102] (Músicos célebres. No. 1) ((-))

105 Bibliografia e discografia in MALI-PIERO, Riccardo: G. S. Bach. Brescia: La Sculoa, 1948: [99]-100 ((-))

106 Suggested gramophone recordings in MANN, William S.: Introduction to the music of Johann Sebastian Bach, 1685-1750. London: D. Dobson, [1950]: [79-80] ((-))

107 Discographie in MARCEL, Luc André: Bach. [Bourges]: Éditions du Seuil, [1961]: [169-184] (Solfèges; 19) ((-))

108 MAREK, George: Bach on records. With foreword by Leopold STOKOWSKI. New York: The Four corners, [1942]: 94 pp. ((-))

109 NYS, Carl de: Catalogue des principales oeuvres de Jean-Sébastien Bach

et elements de discographie critique in Jean-Sébastien Bach. Paris: Hachette, 1963: [283]-298 ((-))

110 Selected discography in PIRRO, André: J. S. Bach. New York: Orion Press; distributed by Crown Publishers, [1957]: [257]-265 ((-))

111 Discographie in PITROU, Robert: Jean-Sébastien Bach. Paris: A. Michel, [1941]: [297]-309 ((-))

112 ROACH, G. William: The recorded works of J. S. Bach in Music Lover's Guide (August 1934): 366-369 ((-))

113 [[Service Educatif de la S. A. Gramophone: Bach—sa discographie. Bruxelles: Service, s.d. [1950?]]]

Works, Chorus

114 BRODER, Nathan: Bach: the choral works in High Fidelity, V/7 (September 1955): 79-91 ((-))

115 BRODER, Nathan: The Bach passions and oratorios; a discography in High Fidelity, XVI/7 (July 1966): 46-47, 83-85 ((-))

Works, Instrumental

116 BRODER, Nathan: Bach: the chamber and orchestral music in High Fidelity, VI/5 (May 1956): 86-99 ((-))

117 Music on record: J. S. Bach's orchestral music in Audio and Record Review, VIII/12 (August 1968): 566-567 ((-))

Works, Keyboard

118 BRODER, Nathan: Bach's keyboard music in High Fidelity, VII/10 (October 1957): 121-134 ((-))

Works, Organ

119 Discography in HENRIE, Gerald: The Baroque organ: containing an introduction to units 1-2 [and, Bach organ music] Milton Keynes [U.K.]: Open University Press, 1974: 84-86 (The Development of instruments and their music; units 1 and 2) (Arts; a third level course) ((-))

Concerti Grossi

120 HEIJNE, Ingemar von: Inspelningar av Bachs fjärde Brandenburgkonsert in Musik Revy 1965 (No. 7): 285 ((5))

121 HIGBEE, Dale: J. S. Bach's music for recorders on records: part I: The Brandenburg concerti, BWV 1046-1051 in American Recorder (Fall 1968): 116-123 ((-))

122 KROHER, Ekkehart: Diskografie in fono forum 1965 (No. 8, August): 358 ((-))

Cantatas

123 BRODER, Nathan: The Bach cantatas; a discography in High Fidelity, XII/8 (August 1962): 44-47, 116-117 ((-))

124 [No. 1-35] HALBREICH, Harry: Discographie critique in Harmonie, No. 30 (October 1967): 32-37 ((-))

125 [No. 36-66] HALBREICH, Harry: Discographie critique in Harmonie, No. 31 (November 1967): 85-88 ((-))

126 [No. 67-122] HALBREICH, Harry: Discographie critique in Harmonie, No. 33 (January 1968): 84-89 ((-))

127 [No. 123-165] HALBREICH, Harry: Discographie critique in Harmonie, No. 36 (April 1968): 85-89 ((-))

128 [No. 166-200] HALBREICH, Harry: Discographie critique in Harmonie, No. 37 (May 1968): 85-88 ((-))

129 [No. 201-217] HALBREICH, Harry: Discographie critique in Harmonie, No. 39 (August-September 1968): 86-89 ((-))

Johannespassion

130 NEUMANN, Klaus L.: Ein vergleichende Diskografie in fono forum 1970 (No. 3, March): 141 ((-))

Der Kunst der Fuge

131 [[[Discography] in CHAILLEY, Jacques: L'art de la fugue de J.-S. Bach; étude critique des sources, remise en ordre du plan, analyse de l'oeuvre. Paris: A. Leduc, 1971: 81-85]]

132 [[KLEIN, R.: Eine vergleichende Discographie in Phono, VI/2]]

Mass, S. 232, B Minor

133 Les enregistrements in Diapason, No. 141 (November 1969): 10-13 ((-))

134 FIERZ, Gerold: Die Aufnahmen in fono forum 1966 (No. 4, April): 168 ((-))

135 WIENKE, Gerhard: Bach: Hohe Messe in H-Moll; eine vergleichende Discographie in Phono, VIII/4 (March-April 1962): 79 ((-))

Matthäuspassion

136 BRENNECKE, Wilfried: Siebenmal Matthäus Passion in Phono, XII/4 (March-April 1966): 91-97 ((-))

BÄCK, SVEN ERIK, 1868-1953

137 [[BÄCK, Sven-Erik: Verkförteckning
1945-1966 in Nutida Musik, X/3-4
(1966-1967): 20, 22, 24 [Includes
discography]]]

BACKHAUS, WILHELM, 1884-1969

138 CLOUGH, F. F., and G. J. CUMING:
Wilhelm Backhaus; a diskography in
Gramophone Record Review, No. 68
(June 1959): 578-579 ((-))

139 DEPPISCH, W.: Diskografie Wilhelm
Backhaus in fono forum 1964 (No. 3,
March): 114 ((-))

140 Diskographie (Auswahl) in Phonoprisma, VII/3 (May-June 1964): 80
((-))

141 Discographie in EICHMANN, Arnold
Heinz: Wilhelm Backhaus. Genève: R.
Kister, c1958: 27-30 (Les Grands
interprètes) ((-))

BADURA SKODA, PAUL, 1927-

142 SCHWINGER, Wolfram: Diskografie
in fono forum 1962 (No. 10, October):
27 ((-))

BAKER, JANET, 1933-

143 WALKER, Malcolm: Discography in
BLYTH, Alan: Janet Baker. London:
Allan, 1973: 61-64 ((7))

144 WALKER, Malcolm: Discography in
BLYTH, Alan: Janet Baker. New York:
Drake, [1973]: 61-64 ((7))

BALLETS

145 Discography in SEARLE, Humphrey:
Ballet music: an introduction. London:
Cassell, [1958]: 210-222 ((-))

146 Discography in SEARLE, Humphrey:
Ballet music: an introduction. 2d rev.
ed. New York: Dover Publications,
[c1973]: 234-245 ((-))

147 A selective discography of ballet
music in High Fidelity, V/3 (May
1955): 111-114 ((-))

BALLIF, CLAUDE

148 Discographie in Courrier Musical de
France, No. 41 (1973): 2 ((-))

BANTOCK, SIR GRANVILLE, 1868-1946

149 FOREMAN, R. L. E.: Sir Granville
Bantock: a discography in Recorded

Sound, No. 32 (October 1968): 338-342
((1, 7))

BARBER, SAMUEL, 1910-

150 List of records in BRODER, Nathan:
Samuel Barber. New York: G.
Schirmer, [1954]: 104-107 ((-))

151 SALZMAN, Eric, and James GOOD-
FRIEND: Samuel Barber: a selective
discography in Hi Fi Stereo Review,
XVII/4 (October 1966): 88 ((-))

BARBIROLLI, SIR JOHN, 1899-1970

152 CLOUGH, F. F., and G. J. CUMING:
Sir John Barbirolli; diskography in
Gramophone Record Review, No. 66
(April 1959): 470, 479 ((-)); No. 67
(May 1959): 555-556 ((-))

153 Diskographie in Collegium Musicum
1970 (No. 2): 19 ((1))

154 The recording floor [EMI recordings,
only] in REID, Charles: John Barbirolli: a biography. London: Hamilton,
1971: 432-436 ((-))

155 The recording floor [EMI recordings,
only] in REID, Charles: John Barbirolli: a biography. New York: Taplinger Pub. Co., [1971]: 432-436
((-))

156 STONE, Ralph: The Barbirolli recordings in Le Grand Baton, VII/4
(November 1970): 31-59 ((-)); Addenda: Le Grand Baton, VIII/1 (May
1971): 33 ((-))

157 [[WALKER, John M.: [Sir John Barbi-
rolli] in Audio and Record Review
(December 1969): 833]]

158 WALKER, Malcolm: Barbirolli on
disc in Opera, XXI/3 (March 1970):
198-205 ((7))

159 WALKER, Malcolm: Barbirolli's early
recordings in Antique Records (May
1973): 28-30 ((7))

160 WALKER, Malcolm: A full discography in KENNEDY, Michael: Barbirolli; conductor laureate, the author-
ised biography, with a full discography. London: MacGibbon & Kee,
[1971]: [341]-402 ((1, 3, 7))

BARENBOIM, DANIEL, 1942-

161 BREUNIG, Christopher: The records
in Audio and Record Review (November 1969): 758 ((-))

162 FÜSSL, Karl Heinz: Barenboim-
Diskographie in Hi Fi Stereophonie,
VI/12 (December 1967): 928 ((-))

163 PLEIJEL, Bengt: Daniel Barenboim in Musik Revy, XXIV/2 (1969): 59-62 ((-))

BAROQUE MUSIC

164 BLAUKOPF, Kurt: Sehnsucht nach dem Barock? in Phono, VIII/4 (1962): 69-70 ((-))

BARTLET, JEAN

165 [[GIRARD, V.: Discography in Record Collector, IX/3 (March 1954)]]

BARTÓK, BÉLA, 1881-1945

See also listing for RAVEL, MAURICE—Odriozola, Antonio: Las grabacionnes en discos LP de seis grandes figuras de la música contemporanea....

166 Béla Bartók auf Schallplatten in Béla Bartók; [mit Beiträgen von Béla Bartók et al.]. Bonn: Boosey & Hawkes, [c1953]: 76-78 (Musik der Zeit; eine Schriftenreihe zur zeitgenössischen Musik; 3) ((-))

167 Discography in Béla Bartók; a memorial review. New York: Boosey & Hawkes, c1950: 77-82 ((-))

168 Diskographie in BARTÓK, Béla: Béla Bartók; Weg und Werk, Schriften und Briefe. Hrsg. v. Bence SZABOLCSI. Kassel, Basel, Tour, [u.a.]: Bärenreiter-Verl., [1972]: 311-323 (DTV Wissenschaftliche Reihe) ((-))

169 Orientation discographique in CITRON, Pierre: Bartók. Paris: Éditions du Seuil, 1963: 182-185 ((-))

170 CLOUGH, F. F., and G. J. CUMING: Bartók on record in Tempo (London): Béla Bartók; a memorial review including articles on his life and works, reprinted from Tempo, the quarterly review of contemporary music; a chronological listing of works; [and] Bartók on records. New York: Boosey & Hawkes, [1950]: 77-82 ((5))

171 CLOUGH, F. F., and G. J. CUMING: The works of Béla Bartók on records in Tempo, No. 13 (Autumn 1949): 39-41 ((-)); Addenda and corrigenda in Tempo, No. 14 (Winter 1949-1950): 36 ((-))

172 Discografie Béla Bartók in fono forum 1960 (No. 3, March): 34 ((-))

173 [[[Discography] in Musik und Bildung (October 1971)]]

174 FINKELSTEIN, Sidney: Béla Bartók (1881-1945); his music and the recordings in American Record Guide, XIX/1 (September 1950): 3-8; XIX/2 (October 1950): 39-43 ((-))

175 FRANKENSTEIN, Alfred: Bartók on microgroove in High Fidelity, VI/10 (October 1956): 121-130 ((-))

176 Discografie in GERAEDTS, Henri: Béla Bartók [door] Henri Geraedts en Jaap GERAEDTS. [2., geheel bijgewerkte druk]. Haarlem: J. H. Gottmer, [1961]: 171-182 (Gottmer-muziekpockets; 9) ((-))

177 Bartoks Werke auf Schallplatten in HELM, Everett: Béla Bartók in Selbstzeugnissen und Bilddokumenten. [Den Anhang besorgte der Autor]. [Reinbek b. Hamburg]: Rowohlt, [1965]: 152-153 (Rowohlts Monographien, 107) ((-))

178 [[KRAUS, Egon: Bibliographie und Diskographie: Béla Bartók in Musik und Bildung, III/10 (October 1971): 494-496]]

179 [[KRUIJFF, Jan de: [Discography] in Disk 1967 (No. 2, February): 7]]

180 Discographie in MARI, Pierette: Bartók.... Paris: Hachette, 1970: [94] (Classiques Hachette de la musique) ((-))

181 Werkverzeichnis mit Angabe der Schallplatten in MOREUX, Serge: Béla Bartók; Leben, Werk, Stil. Zürich: Atlantis Verlag, [1950]: 151-156 (Atlantis-Musikbücherei) ((-))

182 Records of Bartóks works available in England and America in MOREUX, Serge: Béla Bartók. Pref. by Arthur HONEGGER. London: Harvill Press, [1953]: 229-237 ((-))

183 [[NORDWALL, Ove: Förteckning över av Bartók inspelade grammofonskivor in Musik-Kultur, XXXII/7 (1968): 6-7]]

184 Förteckning över av Bartók inspelade grammofonskivor in NORDWALL, Ove: Béla Bartók; traditionalist—modernist. Stockholm: Nordiska musikförlaget..., 1972: 121-125 (Rondoböckerna) ((-))

185 Pour une discographie Bartók in Diapason, No. 151 (November 1970): 12-14 ((-))

186 [[SOMFAI, Laslo: [Discography] in UJFALUSSY, Jósef: Béla Bartók. Budapest: Corvina Press, 1971: 443-452]]

187 SOMFAI, László: Zusammenstellung des Schallplattenverzeichnisses in SZABOLCSI, Bence. Béla Bartók. [Auswahl und Erläuterungen der Abbildungen: Ferenc Bónis; Auswahl der Briefe Bartóks: János Demény].

Leipzig: Reclam, [1968]: 173-[193]
(Reclams Universal-Bibliothek, Bd.
341); Note: Originally published in
Hungarian under title: Bartók Béla
élete ((-))

188   Discography in STEVENS, Halsey:
The life and music of Béla Bartók.
New York: Oxford University Press,
1953: 335-343 ((5))

189   Complete list of records played by
Béla Bartók in UJFALUSSY, József:
Béla Bartók. [1st U. S. ed.] Boston:
Crescendo Pub. Co., [1972, c1971]:
444-447 ((7))

190   Diszkográfia in UJFALUSSY, József:
Bartók Béla. 2. jav. kiad. Budapest:
Gondolat, 1970: 545-[568] ((-))

191   General discography—selection in
UJFALUSSY, József: Béla Bartók.
[1st U. S. ed.] Boston: Crescendo Pub.
Co., [1972, c1971]: 447-452 ((7))

192   WEBER, Jan: Dyskografia in ZIELIŃ-
SKI, Tadeusz A.: Bartók. [Wyd. 1.]
Kraków: Polskie Wydawn. Muzyczne,
[1969]: 494-520 ((7))

193   [[ZWOL, Cornelis van: [Discography]
in Luister, No. 276 (September 1975):
8]]

Concerto for Orchestra

194   HALBREICH, Harry: Discographie
comparée in Harmonie, No. 15 (March
1966): 91-95 ((5))

BASILIDES, MARIA, 1886-1946

195   Hangle meznell é klet in MOLNÁR,
Jenö Antal: Baselides Mária. Budapest: Zenemükiadó, 1967: [70] (Nagy
magyar elöadómüvészek; 1) ((-))

BASSI, AMADEO, 1874-1949

196   CELLETTI, Rodolfo: Amedeo Bassi—
the records in Record News, I/8 (April
1957): 294 [From Musica e Dischi,
October 1953] ((7))

197   CELLETTI, Rodolfo: Dischi Bassi in
Musica e Dischi, IX (No. 85, October
1953): 26 ((7))

BASSINI, ALBERTO DE

198   CELLETTI, Rodolfo: Discografia in
Musica e Dischi, XIII (No. 128, April
1957): 52 ((7))

BASTIANINI, ETTORE

199   [[VEGETO, R.: Biscografia, [i.e., Dis-
cografia] in Corriere del Teatro,
XIX/3 (1967): 7 pp.]]

200   VEGETO, R.: Opere complete in
microsolco in Discoteca, No. 69
(April 1967): 30 ((1))

BATHORI, JANE, 1877-1970

201   BARNES, Harold M.: Discographie de
Jane Bathori in Disques, No. 6 (June-
July 1948): 171 ((-))

202   BARNES, Harold: Jane Bathori discography in Recorded Sound, I/4
(Autumn 1961): 109-110 ((3, 5))

203   Discographie in Courrier Musical de
France, No. 13 (1966): 49 ((-))

BATTISTINI, MATTIA, 1856-1928

204   DENNIS, J.: Records in Record Collector VIII/11-12 (November-December 1953): 249-265 ((3, 6, 7))

205   [[[Discography] in Record News, V/9
(May 1961)]]

206   McKENZIE, Compton: Mattia Battistini in Gramophone, IV/2 (August
1926): 97-98 ((-))

207   [[PHILLIPS, R.: Mattia Battistini in
Record Collector, II/9 (September
1947); Addenda: Record Collector,
III/5 (May 1948); IV/1 (January 1949)]]

208   VEGETO, Raffaele: Discografia di
Mattia Battistini in Musica e Dischi,
XV (No. 153, March 1959): 67 ((7))

BAX, SIR ARNOLD TREVOR, 1883-1953

209   Current recordings in Bax Society
Bulletin, No. 1 (February 1968): [7]-
[8] ((-))

210   FOREMAN, R. L. E.: Arnold Bax: a
discography in Recorded Sound, No.
29-30 (January-April 1968): 277-283
((1, 4, 7))

BAYREUTH, GER. (CITY)—FESTSPIELE

211   PERKINS, J. F., A. KELLY, and J.
WARD: The Bayreuth recordings,
1904 in Talking Machine Review, No.
37 (December 1975): 549 ((3, 7))

BEATY, LOUISE
See HOMER, LOUISE

BEECHAM, SIR, THOMAS, BART., 1879-
1961
See also listing for DELIUS, FRED-
ERICK, 1862-1934. Walker, Malcolm:
Beecham/Delius discography

212   BOTSFORD, Ward: Beecham—the
complete discography in Le Grand

Baton, VI/3-4 (August-November 1969): 1-50 ((1, 5, 7))

213   BOTSFORD, Ward: Sir Thomas and the gramophone; 1910-1960 in High Fidelity, XV/6 (June 1965): 45-48, 102-105 ((7))

214   BOTSFORD, Ward: Sir Thomas Beecham: the complete discography in American Record Guide, XXXIII/9 (May 1967): 742-747; XXXIII/10 (June 1967): 730-732; XXXIII/11 (July 1967): 1009-1012; XXXIII/12 (August 1967): 1078-1081; XXXIV/2 (October 1967): 150-151; XXXIV/3 (November 1967): 244-245; XXXIV/6 (February 1968): 506-510; XXXIV/8 (April 1968): 686-689; Addenda and corrigenda: XXXVI/4 (December 1969): 260-265, 315-316 ((1, 5, 7))

215   CLOUGH, F. F., and G. J. CUMING: Sir Thomas Beecham; diskography in Gramophone Record Review, No. 52 (February 1958): 312-315 ((-)); Addenda: No. 53 (March 1958): 438 ((-))

216   HOLMES, William A.: The Beecham recordings: project 1: the London Philharmonic revisited; discography in Le Grand Baton, I (October-December 1964): 6-31 ((-))

217   Discography in PROCTER-GREGG, Humphrey: Sir Thomas Beecham; conductor and impresario, as remembered by his friends and colleagues. Compiled and edited by Humphrey Procter-Gregg. [Windermere [(3 Oakland, Windermere, Cumbria)]: H. Procter-Gregg, 1973]: 206 ((-))

218   Sir Thomas Beecham Society: Sir Thomas Beecham discography. [Redondo Beach, Calif.]: The Society, 1975. ix, 77 pp. ((1, 3, 4, 5, 6, 7))

219   STONE, Ralph: The Beecham recordings up to 1932 in Le Grand Baton, III/2 (May 1966): 12-18 ((-))

220   [[STONE, Ralph: [Discography on microgroove] in Le Grand Baton (July-December 1966)]]

BEETHOVEN, LUDWIG VAN, 1770-1827

221   Critical appraisal of currently available recordings of Beethoven's works in BRIGGS, John: The collector's Beethoven. [1st ed.] Philadelphia: J. B. Lippincott, [c1962]. 152 pp. (Keystone books in music) ((-))

222   Contributo a un catalogo delle opere di Beethoven incise per fonografo in BRUERS, Antonio: Beethoven; catalogo storico-critico di tutte le opere. 4. ed aumentata. Roma: G. Bardi, 1951: [521]-559 ((-))

223   Phonograph records in BURK, John N.: The life and works of Beethoven. New York: Random House, [1943]: 464-478 ((-))

224   BURKE, C. G.: Beethoven up-to-date in High Fidelity, III/1 (March-April 1953): 61-72 ((-)); Orchestral addenda; sonatas in High Fidelity, III/2 (May-June 1953): 69-80 ((-))

225   BURKE, C. G.: Ludwig van Beethoven on records in High Fidelity, I/4 (Spring 1952): 33-47 ((-))

226   CALVÉ, Jacques le: Discographie critique in BOUCOURECHLIEV, André: Beethoven. Paris: Éditions du Seuil, 1963: 180-183 ((-))

227   Beethoven works and recordings in GOSS, Madeleine: Beethoven, master musician. New York: H. Holt and company, [1946]: 330-337 (Holt musical biography series) ((-))

228   [[Diszkografia in GYMES, Ferenc, and Veronika VAVRINECZ: Beethoven müvei Langlemezen. Budapest: Allami Gorkij Könyvtar, 1971]]

229   HELLER, Friedrich: Diskographie der Werke Beethovens in LEY, Stephan: Beethoven; sein Leben in Selbstzeugnissen, Briefen u. Berichten. [Erw. Neuausg.] Wien, Berlin: Neff, [1970]: 421-[432] ((-))

230   [[HOKE, Hans Gunter: Ludwig-van-Beethoven—Gesamtausgabe anlässlich der Beethoven-Erhung der Deutschen Demokratischen Republik 1970. Berlin: VEB Deutsche Schallplatten, 1970. 56 pp.]]

231   Discografía de las obras de Beethoven in LEUCHTER, Erwin: Beethoven. Buenos Aires: Ricordi Americana, [1943]: 135-149 (Músicos célebres) ((-))

232   [[[Discography] in LEY, Stephan: Beethoven; sein Leben in Selbstzeugnissen, Briefen und Berichten. Wien; Berlin: Neff, 1971: 421-432]]

233   Ludwig van Beethoven 1770-1827; complete discography [Philips records] in Philips Music Herald (Autumn 1969): between pp. 14 and 15 ((-))

234   MAREK, George: Beethoven on records. With foreword by Bruno WALTER. New York: The Four Corners, [1942]: 94 pp. ((-))

235   PANIGEL, Armand: Discographie critique des oeuvres de Ludwig van Beethoven in Beethoven. Paris: Hachette, 1961: lxxvii-lxxxvi ((-))

236   Discografie in POLS, André M.: Het leven van L. v. Beethoven. Brussel,

Amsterdam: D. A. P. Reinaert, 1965: [47] (Meesters der toonkunst; 3) ((-))

237 The Recordings of Beethoven as viewed by the critics from High Fidelity. Great Barrington, Mass., [1971]: 173 pp. [From issues of High Fidelity magazine, 1970] ((-))

238 REDFERN, Brian: Selected recordings of Beethoven's music in HUGHES, Rosemary: Beethoven; a biography with a survey of books, editions and recordings. London: Bingley, 1970: 91-105 (The Concertgoer's companions) ((-))

239 Discography in RODMAN, Selden: The heart of Beethoven by Selden Rodman [and] James KEARNS. New York: Shorewood Pub. Co., [1962]: 149-151 ((-))

240 [[SANCHEZ, M. C.: [Discography] in Discofilia, No. 6 (September 1956): 232]]

241 Diskographie in SCHMIDT-GÖRG, Joseph: Ludwig van Beethoven. [Herausgeber]: Joseph Schmidt-Görg [und] Hans SCHMIDT, [Autoren: Sieghard Brandenburg u. a.]. Bonn: Beethoven-Archiv; Hamburg: Deutsche Grammophon Gesellschaft; Braunschweig: Westermann, [1969]: 273-275 ((-))

242 [Discographic notes] in Stuttgart. Stadtbücheri: Ludwig van Beethoven zum 200. Geburtstag; Noten, Schallplatten, Bücher aus d. Beständen d. Musikabt. [Zusammengestellt von Brigitte WILLBERG.] Stuttgart: Stadbücheri, [1970]: 106 pp. ((-))

243 Soupis skladeb Ludwiga van Beethovena na čs. slouhohrajících deskách Supraphon in TEICHMAN, Josef: Ludwig van Beethoven; K tisku připr. [a pozn. opatřil] Miroslav Malura. 1. vyd. Praha: Supraphon, t. ST 2, 1968: 460-467 (Hudebni profily; 17) ((-))

244 Discographie des oeuvres de Ludwig van Beethoven in WITOLD, Jean: Ludwig van Beethoven; l'homme et son oeuvre. [Paris]: Seghers, [1964]: 181-186 (Musiciens de tous les temps; 6) ((-))

245 Schallplattenverzeichnis in Zum Beethoven-Jahr 1970. [Redakteur: Walther Siegmund SCHULTZE, et al.] Berlin: Deutscher Kulturbund, 1970: 78-85 ((-))

Works, Chamber Music

246 Beethoven: les sonates violon piano/ violon celle piano; principaux enregistrements in Diapason, No. 144 (February 1970): 6-9 ((-))

247 MARSH, Robert C.: Beethoven on record: the chamber music in High Fidelity, XX/5 (May 1970): 60-68, 100-101 ((-))

248 Trios, quintette; septuor; octuor—les enregistrements in Diapason, No. 145 (March 1970): 6-9 ((-))

Works, Chorus

249 ROBBINS-LANDON, H. C.: Beethoven on records: the choral music in High Fidelity, XX/2 (February 1970): 70-72, 103 ((-))

Works, Instrumental

250 Bagatelles; variations; Romances; l'oeuvre pour flute; enregistrements in Diapason, No. 148 (June 1970): 6-8, 37 ((-))

251 Beethoven ouvertures et musique de scene in Diapason, No. 146 (April 1970): 8-10 ((-))

252 HAMILTON, David: Beethoven on record: the orchestral music in High Fidelity, XX/7 (July 1970): 62-65, 102-103 ((-))

Works, Piano

253 ANSON, George: Beethoven: the piano music in 1970 in American Music Teacher, XX/1 (September-October 1970): 30-35 ((-)); XX/2 (November-December 1970): 30-33, 42 ((-))

254 GOLDSMITH, Harris: Beethoven on record: the piano music in High Fidelity, XXI/1 (January 1971): 61-66 ((-))

Abschulicher

255 REINOLD, Helmut: Diskographie in Phono, X/2 (November-December 1963): 31 ((1))

Concertos

256 GOLDSMITH, Harris: Beethoven on record: the concertos in High Fidelity, XX/8 (August 1970): 51-56, 60-62 ((-)); XX/9 (September 1970): 66-68 ((-))

257 [[KRUIJFF, Jan de: [Discography] in Disk, No. 22 (October 1968): 28]]

258 Pour une discographie Beethoven: les concertos in Diapason, No. 141 (November 1969): 14-17 ((-))

Concerto, Piano, No. 5, Op. 73, E-Flat Major

259 ROSTAND, Claude: Discographie comparée in Harmonie, No. 19 (September 1966): 78-81 ((-))

Concerto, Violin, Op. 61, D Major

260 Discographie comparée in Harmonie,
No. 26 (April 1967): 76-80 ((-))

261 KRAUS, Gottfried: Die Aufnahmen in
fono forum 1966 (No. 5, May): 224 ((-))

Fidelio

262 Discographie comparée in Harmonie
(October 1973): 44 ((-))

263 Fidelio; melodies in Diapason, No.
149 (July-September 1970): 18-20 ((-))

264 LORD HAREWOOD: Fidelio in Opera,
XX/3 (March 1969): 199-208 (Opera on
the gramophone; 23) ((1))

265 MOVSHON, George: Beethoven on disc:
Fidelio and the songs in High Fidelity,
XX/1 (January 1970): 81-85, 124 ((-))

Masses

266 Les messes in Diapason, No. 150
(October 1970): 18-19 ((-))

Mass, D Major, Op. 123

267 ROSTAND, Claude: Discographie
comparée in Harmonie, No. 20
(October 1966): 74-79 ((-))

Overtures

268 MATZNER, Joachim: [Diskografie] in
fono forum 1969 (No. 10, October): 658
((-))

Quartets, Strings

269 APPEL, Richard G.: Phonograph recordings in Phonograph Monthly Review, I/7 (April 1927): 292 ((-))

270 Discographie comparée in Harmonie,
No. 17 (May 1966): 84-85 ((-))

271 MORGAN, Robert P.: Beethoven on
record: the string quartets in High
Fidelity, XX/4 (April 1970): 73-76,
114 ((-))

272 Les quatuors de Beethoven. Trois
integrales in Diapason, No. 143
(January 1970): 7-9 ((-))

273 SCHUHMACHER, Gerhard: Diskographie in Musica/Phonoprisma, XXII/4
(July-August 1968): 311 ((-))

Quartets, Strings, Op. 18

274 FINSCHER, L.: Was fordet die ideale
Interpretation von Beethovens Op. 18?
Versuch einer kritischen Discographie
der Streichquartette in Phono, XI/2
(1964): 43-46 ((-))

Quartet, Strings, Op. 131

275 JUNGHANNS, Franz: Diskografie in
fono forum 1968 (No. 5, May): 263
((-))

Sonatas, Piano

276 Les enregistrements in Diapason, No.
142 (December 1969): 16-19, 45 ((-))

277 GOLDSMITH, Harris: Beethoven on
record: the piano sonatas in High
Fidelity, XX/10 (October 1970): 63-
82 ((-))

278 SCHAUMKELL, Claus-Dieter: Diskographie in KAISER, Joachim:
Beethovens 32 Klaviersonaten und
ihre Interpreten. Frankfurt: S.
Fischer, 1975: 637-650 ((-))

Sonata, Piano, Op. 57, F Minor

279 HASELAUER, Elisabeth: Diskographie
in Hi Fi Stereophonie (February 1971):
114 ((5))

Symphonies

280 APPEL, Richard G.: Recordings of
Beethoven symphonies in Phonograph
Monthly Review, I/6 (March 1927):
244-245 ((-))

281 BURKE, C. G.: The Beethoven symphonies reconsidered in High Fidelity,
VII/1 (January 1957): 95-105 ((-))

282 Integrales des symphonies de Beethoven; discographie comparée in
CHANTAVOINE, Jean: Les symphonies
de Beethoven. Paris: B. Belfond,
1970: 223-225 ((-))

283 LANG, Paul Henry: Beethoven on
record: the nine symphonies in High
Fidelity, XX/12 (December 1970):
49-68 ((-))

284 MARSH, Robert Charles: The Beethoven symphonies in stereo in High
Fidelity, X/4 (April 1960): 44-45, 85-
91 ((-))

285 Pour une discographie Beethoven in
Diapason, No. 140 (October 1969): 8-13
((-))

286 Förteckning över grammofonskivor in
RABE, Julius: Beethovens symfonier.
Stockholm: H. Geber, [1948]: 193-
[196] (Gebers musikböcker) ((-))

287 RISSIN, David: Discographie comparée
[integral versions] in Harmonie, No.
39 (August-September 1968): 21 ((-))

Symphony, No. 5, Op. 67, C Minor

288 [Eine vergleichende Discographie in
Phono, VII/2; VII/3; VII/5; VII/6]

Symphony, No. 7, Op. 92, A Major

289 MATZNER, Joachim: Diskografie in
fono forum 1962 (No. 10, October): 10
((-))

Symphony, No. 9, Op. 123, D Minor

290 [[SCHNOOR, H.: Eine vergleichende
Discographie in Phono, V/6; VI/5;
VIII/1]]

Trios, Piano and Strings

291 HARDEN, Ingo: [Diskografie] in fono
forum 1970 (No. 12, December): 937
((-))

BEHREND, SIEGFRIED

292 Diskographie in Phonoprisma (November-December 1966): 195 ((-))

BEINUM, EDUARD VAN, 1901-1959

293 Discografie in BERNET KEMPERS,
Karel Philippus: Eduard van Beinum.
Redactie. K. Ph. Bernet Kempers
[en] Marius FLOTHIUS, uitg. in
samenwerking met de Nederlandse
Vereniging Concertgebouwvrienden.
Haarlem: J. H. Gottmer, [1960?]:
109-115 ((-))

294 Diskographie in Phonoprisma, VII/2
(March-April 1964): 56 ((-))

295 Gramofoonopnamen van het Con-
certgebouworkest onder Leiting van
Ed. v. Beinum in PAAP, Wouter:
Eduard van Beinum; vijfentwintig
jaar dirigent van het Concertgebouw
orkest. Baarn: Het Wereldvenster,
[1956]: [29] ((-))

BELLEZZA, VINCENZO, 1888-1964

296 Discografia (saggio) in GIOVINE,
Alfredo: Vincenzo Bellezza; direttore
d'orchestra bitontino. Bari, 1970:
19-20 (Biblioteca dell'Archivio delle
tradizioni popolari baresi. Civiltà
musicale pugliese) ((-))

BELLICONI, GEMMA, 1864-1950

297 RICHARDS, John B.: The recordings in
Record Collector, XVI/9-10 (January
1966): 210-213 ((3, 7))

BELLINI, VINCENZO, 1801-1835

298 Music on record: Vincenzo Bellini
1801-1835 in Audio and Record Review
(October 1968): 728 ((-))

Norma

299 DECHAMPS, Eric: La Norma; discographie comparée in Diapason, No.
178 (June-July 1973): 14-15 ((-))

300 PORTER, Andrew: Norma in Opera,
IX/1 (January 1958): 12-19 (Opera
on the gramophone; 4) ((-))

301 Discographie comparée in Harmonie,
No. 38 (June-July 1968): 51-53 ((5))

I Puritani

302 [[[Discography] in L. A. Record Collector, II/5 (1947): 62-66]]

303 SHAWE-TAYLOR, Desmond: A
Puritani discography in Opera, XI/6
(June 1960): 387-395 ((-))

La Sonnambula. Vi ravviso,
o luoghi ameni

304 VEGETO, Raffaele: Nota discografica
in Discoteca, No. 49 (April 1965): 36
((-))

BELLMAN, CARL MIKAEL, 1740-1795

305 [[BRUUN, Carl L.: [Discography]
Stockholm: Radio Sweden, 1969. 26
pp.]]

BENDAZZI-GARULLI, ERNESTINA

306 CELLETTI, Rodolfo: Discografia in
Musica e Dischi, X (No. 95, August
1954): 6 ((7))

307 CELLETTI, Rodolfo: The records in
Record News, II/1-2 (September 1957):
15 [From Musica e Dischi, August
1954]; Addenda: Record News, II/3
(November 1957) ((5))

BENDER, PAUL, 1875-1904

308 DENNIS, J. F. E.: Paul Bender, discography in Record Collector, XVII/11
(April 1968): 255-256 ((3, 6, 7)); Addenda: Record Collector, XVIII/1-2
(October 1968): 46 ((-))

BERBERIAN, CATHY, 1925-

309 Discografia in Discoteca, No. 62 (July-
August 1966): 35 ((-))

BERG, ALBAN, 1885-1935

310 Discographie in Revue Musicale, No.
298-299 (1975): 135-136 ((-))

311 Music on record: Alban Berg in Audio
and Record Review, VIII/8 (April 1968):
268-269 ((-))

312 Discographie in NIJMAN, Julius:
Nieuwe oostenrijkse muziek (Schönberg, Berg, Webern). Amsterdam:
Bigot en van Rossum, n. v., [1938]:
[134] (Caecilia reeks.; 5) ((-))

313 Discography in REDLICH, Hans: Alban
Berg; the man and his music. London:
J. Calder, [1957]: 299-304 ((-))

314 Discography in REDLICH, Hans: Alban
Berg; the man and his music. New
York: Abelard-Schuman, [1957]: 299-
304 ((-))

315 Discographie in REDLICH, Hans: Alban
Berg; Versuch einer Würdigung. Wien:
Universal Edition, 1957: 339-341 ((-))

316 Diskographie in SCHERLIESS, Volker:
Alban Berg in Selbstzeugnissen und
Bilddokumenten. [1.-13. Tsd.] Reinbek
(bei Hamburg): Rowohlt, 1975: 152-
[153] (Rowohlts Monographien; 225)
((-))

317 Discographie in VOGELSANG, Konrad:
Alban Berg; Leben und Werk. Berlin-
Halensee: M. Hesse, [c1959]: 81-85
(Hesses Kleine Bücherei; 5) ((-))

318 WEBER, J. F.: Alban Berg. Utica, NY:
Weber, 1975. 16 pp. (Discography
series; 14) ((7))

Wozzeck

319 [[[Discography] in FORNEBERG, Erich:
Wozzeck von Alban Berg. Berlin: R.
Lienau, 1963. 87 pp.]]

BERGANZA, TERESA

320 Diskographie in Phonoprisma, VI/4
(July-August 1963): 97 ((-))

321 CLOUGH, F. F., and G. J. CUMING: A
Teresa Berganza discography in Audio
and Record Review, III/5 (January
1964): 18, 23 ((-))

BERIO, LUCIANO, 1925-

322 COLLINS, Dennis: Catalogue des
oeuvres; discographie in Musique en
jeu, No. 15 (September 1974): [64]-70
((-))

323 KOCH, Gerhard R.: Luciano Berio Diskographie in Hi Fi Stereophonie X/12
(December 1971): 1148 ((-))

324 ROY, Jean: Discographie in Revue
Musicale, No. 267 (1969): 29 ((-))

BERLIOZ, HECTOR, 1803-1869

See also listing for DAVIS, COLIN.
Vincent-Malettra, Françoise: Discographie Berlioz

325 Selection des enregistrements in
BARRAUD, Henry: Hector Berlioz.
[Paris]: Costard, [1955]: [275]-279
(Musiciens d'hier & d'aujourd'hui; 2)
((-))

326 Discographie in Berlioz... célébration
de son centenaire. La Traonche-
Montfleurry: "Cahiers de l'Alpe,"
1969: 137-140 (Cahiers de l'alpe; 46)
((-))

327 BURK, John N.: The Berlioz recordings
in High Fidelity, IV/5 (July 1954): 29-
31, 82-92 ((-))

328 [[CLARK, Robert S.: [Discography] in
Stereo Review, XXIII/4 (October 1969)]]

329 [[[Discography] in DELAYE-DIDIER-
DELORME, Henriette: Hector Berlioz;
ou, Le chant désespéré. Lyon: EISE,
1964. 121 pp.]]

330 Discographie in DEMARQUEZ, Suzanne:
Hector Berlioz; l'homme et son
oeuvre..., catalogue des oeuvres,
discographie.... Paris: Seghers,
1969: 183-186 (Musiciens de tous les
temps; 42) ((-))

331 Discographie in DEMARQUEZ, Suzanne:
Hector Berlioz. [Lausanne]: La Guilde
de livre, [1969]: 183-186 (Musiciens de
tous les temps) ((-))

332 Discographie Berlioz in Diapason, No.
132 (January 1969): 24-25 ((-))

333 Discographie in FESCHOTTE, Jacques:
Hector Berlioz. Paris: La Colombe,
[1951]: [142]-147 (Collection Euterpe)
((-))

334 From the discography of Hector Berlioz
(1803-1869) in Philips Music Herald
(Winter 1969): 23 ((-))

335 HALBREICH, Harry: Catalogue commenté et discographie critique in
Berlioz. Paris: Reálités Hachette,
1973: 241-[265] ((-))

336 HOFMANN, Michel R.: Discographie
d'Hector Berlioz in Journal Musical
Français, No. 179 (April 1969): 34
((-))

337 JACOBSON, Bernard: Berlioz on
records—an appraisal in High Fidelity,
XIX/3 (March 1969): 56-60, 118 ((-))

338 Discographie in KNUTTEL, F.: Hector
Berlioz. s'Gravenhage: W. P. van
Stochum, 1948: 277-282 ((-))

339 MARNAT, Marcel: Discographie in
BALLIF, Claude: Berlioz. Paris:

Éditions du Seuil, 1968: 184-187
(Collections Microcosme. Solfèges;
29) ((-))

340 Music on record: Hector Berlioz in
Audio and Record Review (March 1969):
174 ((-))

341 SCHREIBER, Ulrich: Berlioz und die
Schallplatte; eine diskografische
Skizze in Hi Fi Stereophonie, IX/2
(February 1970): 127-132 ((-))

342 Selected discography in SEROFF,
Victor: Hector Berlioz. New York:
Macmillan Co., [1967]: [162]-163
((-))

Le Damnation de Faust

343 [[MICHELSEN, K.: Eine vergleichende
Discographie in Phono, VII/4]]

Symphonie fantastique

344 Discographie in Diapason, No. 176
(April 1973): 6 ((-))

BERNAC, PIERRE, 1899-

345 HUGHES, Eric, and Patrick SAUL:
Pierre Bernac discography in Recorded Sound, No. 18 (April 1965):
322-327 ((1, 3, 4, 6, 7))

346 Discographie in Courrier Musical de
France, No. 16 (1966): 230 ((-))

BERNARD, CLAIRE
See ORCHESTRE DE CHAMBRE DE
ROUEN

BERNSTEIN, LEONARD, 1918-

347 Auswahl-Diskografie in fono forum
1966 (No. 10, October): 499 ((-))

348 Recordings by and of Leonard Bernstein in BRIGGS, John: Leonard Bernstein: the man, his work, and his world.
[1st ed.] Cleveland: World Pub. Co.,
[1961]: 259-267 ((-))

349 CLOUGH, F. F., and G. J. CUMING: A
Bernstein discography in Audio and
Record Review, II/8 (April 1963): 14-
16 ((-))

350 Diskographie in Collegium Musicum
1971 (No. 2): 26-29 ((-))

351 Discographie in Diapason, No. 111
(November 1966): 17 ((-))

352 Discographie in Diapason, No. 145
(March 1970): 13 ((-))

353 [[Recordings of Leonard Bernstein in
EWEN, David: Leonard Bernstein—a
biography. London: Allan, 1967: 166-
167]]

354 [[Recordings of Leonard Bernstein in
EWEN, David: Leonard Bernstein—a
biography. New York: Chilton, 1967:
166-167]]

355 PRAWY, Marcel: Aus der Diskografie
in fono forum 1961 (No. 11, November):
33 ((-))

356 WEBER, J. F.: Leonard Bernstein, a
composer discography in Association
for Recorded Sound Collections Journal,
VI/1 (1974): 30-39 ((5, 7))

357 WEBER, J. F.: Leonard Bernstein.
Utica, NY: Weber, 1975. 16 pp. (Discography series; 13) ((5, 7))

BEROFF, MICHEL

358 [[[Discography] in Disk (May 1972)]]

BERRY, WALTER

359 Diskographie in Collegium Musicum
1971 (No. 9): 10-11 ((-))

BERTIN, PIERRE
See BERNAC, PIERRE

BERWALD, FRANZ, 1796-1868

360 Discography in LAYTON, Robert:
Franz Berwald. With a foreword by
Gerald ABRAHAM. [London]: A. Blond,
[1959]: 185-187 ((-))

361 [[MÖRNER, Carl-Gabriel Stellan: Franz
Berwald (1796-1868). En diskografi
med anledning av jubileermsåret 1968
in Biblioteksbladet, LIII/8 (1968): 964-
967]]

362 MÖRNER, Carl-Gabriel Stellan: Diskografi in ANDERSSON, Ingvar: Franz
Berwald. Stockholm: Norstedt, 1970-
71: 78-82 (vol. II) (Svenska akademiens
minnesteckningar) ((5))

BETTENDORF, EMMY

363 WHITE, Don: The recordings of Emmy
Bettendorf in Record Collector,
XV/7-8: 158-168 ((3, 6))

BINDERHAGEL, GERTRUD

364 Discography in Program notes for
Preiser LV 89 [Sound recording]
[196-?] ((5))

BINET, JEAN, 1893-1960

365 Discographie in Schweizerisches
Musik-Archiv: Jean Binet: né le 17

octobre 1893, mort le 24 février 1960.
Zürich: Archives musicales suisses,
1970: 17 ((-))

BISPHAM, DAVID, 1857-1921

366 DENNIS, J.: David Bispham in Record
Collector, VI/1 (January 1951): 5-12
((-))

367 HEVINGHAM-ROOT, Laurie: David
Bispham (critical list) in Talking Machine Review, No. 7 (December 1970):
197-200 ((3, 6, 7)); No. 8: 209-212; No.
9: 9-12; No. 10: 33-35; No. 12: 110-113;
No. 13: 129-132; No. 14: 157-159

BIZET, GEORGES, 1838-1875

368 Discographie Bizet in Diapason, No. 197
(May 1975): 15 ((-))

369 Music on record: Georges Bizet 1838-
1875 in Audio and Record Review (November 1968): 816 ((-))

370 Discografie in POLS, André M.: Het
leven van G. Bizet. 2. druk. Brussel,
Amsterdam: D. A. P. Reinaert, 1965:
[47] (Meesters der toonkunst: 2) ((-))

Carmen

371 [[EINEM, G. von: Eine vergleichende
Discographie in Phono, VIII/2]]

372 HOPE-WALLACE, Philip: Carmen in
Opera, VIII/4 (April 1957): 221-225
(Opera on the gramophone; 2) ((-))

373 KRAUS, Gottfried: Diskografische
Angaben in fono forum 1970 (No. 10,
October): 724 ((-))

374 Tribune autour de 9 Carmen in Diapason, No. 152 (December 1970): 20-23
((-))

375 VEGETO, Raffaele: Nota discografica in
Discoteca, No. 52 (July-August 1965):
35-36 ((1))

BJÖRLING, JUSSI, 1911-1960

376 BERGQVIST, C. Hilding: Jussi Björling
in Record Research, No. 128 (July
1974): 5 ((3))

377 BRUUN, Carl L.: Discography in Record News, IV/4 (December 1959): 120-
128 ((3, 6)); IV/5 (January 1960): 176-
187 ((3, 6))

378 CLOUGH, F. F., and G. J. CUMING:
Diskography in Gramophone Record
Review, No. 55 (May 1958): 572, 633-
635 ((-)); Addenda: Gramophone Record
Review, No. 56 (June 1958): 706 ((-))

379 CLOUGH, F. F., and G. J. CUMING:
Jussi Bjoerling discography in Ameri-

can Record Guide, XII/4 (December
1945): 87-90, 95 ((-))

380 [[F. T. H.: The Bjoerling recordings—a
select discography in Le Grand Baton,
IV/1 (February 1967): 13-18]]

381 Nationaldiskoteket: Jussi Björling; a
record list. Copenhagen: Nationaldiskoteket, Hovedbygningen Brede,
1969. 84 pp. (Nationaldiskoteket Discographies; 209) ((1, 3, 4, 7))

382 PEASE, Edward: A Jussi Bjoerling discography, part one in National Association of Teachers of Singing Bulletin,
XXIX/2 (December 1972): 12-15 ((-))

383 [[SEEMUNGEL, Rupert P.: A complete
discography of Jussi Bjorling. 3d ed.
Port of Spain, Trinidad, 1964. 45 pp.]]

384 THIELEN, Hugo: Jussi Björling; Schallplattenverzeichnis in fono forum 1975
(No. 4, April): 338-343 ((1, 3, 6, 7))

BLACHER, BORIS, 1903-1975

385 Discographic references included in
STUCKENSCHMIDT, Hans: Boris
Blacher. Berlin: Bote & Bock, 1963:
45-64 ((-))

BLACHUT, BENO, 1913-

386 Snímky Beno Blachuta na deskách
Supraphon in BROŽOVSKÁ, Jarmila:
Beno Blachut. [1. vyd.] Praha: Panton,
1964: 45-49 (Umělci Národního divadla;
3) ((-))

BLACK, ANDREW, 1859-1920

387 Andrew Black's discs in Record Collector, XIV/9-10 (n.d.): 197-200 ((3, 7))

388 [[GREAVES, S. C.: Andrew Black in
Record Collector, XV/1 (n.d.): 21]]

BLISS, SIR ARTHUR, 1891-1975

389 [[Discography in THOMPSON, Kenneth
L.: The works of Sir Arthur Bliss.
London: Novello, 1966. Rev. ed., Lon-
don: Novello, 1971]]

390 THOMPSON, Kenneth L.: Catalogue of
works [Includes discographic refer-
ences] in Musical Times, CVII (No.
1482, August 1966): 666-673 ((5))

BLOCH, ERNEST, 1880-1959

391 [[LETHERER, Gary Paul: Complete
discography of Ernest Bloch. Gualala,
CA: Ernest Bloch Society, [1970?]]]

BLUM, ROBERT, 1900-

392 Diskographie in FIERZ, Gerold: Robert
Blum; Leben und Werk. Zürich:
Kommissionsverlag Hug, 1967: 41
(Neujahrsblatt der Allgemeinen Musik-
gesellschaft Zürich; 151, 1967) ((–))

BOCCHERINI, LUIGI, 1748-1805

393 Discography in GÉRARD, Yves: Thematic, bibliographical, and critical
catalogue of the works of Luigi
Boccherini. Compiled by Yves Gérard
under the auspices of Germaine de
Rothschild. London, New York: Oxford
University Press, 1969: 687-694 ((–))

BOECK, AUGUST DE, 1865-1937

394 Discografie in POLS, André M.: Het
leven van A. de Boeck. Brussel:
D. A. P. Reinaert Uitg, [1966]: 43
(Meesters der toonkunst; 5 deel) ((–))

BÖHM, KARL, 1894-

395 ASHMAN, Mike: Böhm discography in
Records and Recording, XVII/12
(September 1974): 31-32 ((–)); Supple-
ment in Records and Recording, XVIII/5
(February 1975): 8 ((–))

396 Aus der Diskografie in fono forum 1963
(No. 9, September): 329 ((–))

397 CLOUGH, F. F., and G. J. CUMING: A
Karl Böhm discography in Audio and
Record Review, III/9 (May 1964): 12-13
((–))

398 Discographie in Diapason, No. 108
(June-July 1966): 41 ((–))

399 Extrait de la discographie in Diapason,
No. 142 (December 1969): 10 ((–))

400 Diskographie in ROEMER, Margarete:
Karl Böhm (mit 39 Abbildungen).
[Berlin]: Rembrandt Verlag, [1966]:
27-31 (Rembrandt-Reihe; 54) ((–))

401 WERBA, Robert: Karl-Böhm Diskographie in Osterreichische Musikzeitschrift, XXIV/8 (1969): 489-492
((5))

BOHNEN, MICHAEL, 1886-1965

402 MÜHLEN, Theodor: Diskografie in fono
forum 1962 (No. 5, May): 12 ((–))

BOIELDIEU, FRANÇOIS ADRIEN, 1775-1834

403 Discographie in FAVRE, Georges:
Boieldieu; sa vie—son oeuvre. Paris:
E. Droz, 1944-1945: v. II [273]
(Bibliothèque de la Société des his-
toriens du théâtre, 17, 21) ((–))

BOITO, ARRIGO, 1842-1918
See also listing for PERTILE,
AURELIANO. Pertile's recordings
from Boito's "Nerone"....

Nerone

404 DENNIS, J.: Notes of the recordings
from the opera in Record Collector,
VIII/2 (February 1953): 27-41 ((–))

BONCI, ALESSANDRO, 1870-1940

405 CELLETTI, Rodolfo: Discografia in
Musica e Dischi, X (No. 93, June 1954):
8 ((–))

406 HUTCHINSON, T.: Bonci recordings in
Record Collector, XI/7 (July 1957):
153-157 ((3, 6, 7)); Addenda: Record
Collector, XI/9-10 (September-October
1957): 234-235 ((–)); XII/4 (February-
March 1959): 109 ((3))

407 MacHARG, James, Jr.: Alessandro
Bonci in Gramophone, No. 174 (November 1937): 267 ((–))

408 VEGETO, Raffaele: Discografia del
tenore Alessandro Bonci in Discoteca,
No. 53 (September 1965): 63-64 ((1, 7))

BONDON, JACQUES, 1927-

409 Discographie in Courrier Musical de
France, No. 45 (1974): 41 ((–))

BONINSEGNA, CELESTINA

410 [WILLIAMS, Clifford and John B.
RICHARDS]: Recordings in Record
Collector, XII/1-2 (January-February
1958): 27-32 ((3, 6, 7))

BORG, KIM

411 Discographie in Phono (Summer 1955):
12 ((7))

412 WERBA, Erik: Diskografie in fono
forum 1961 (No. 1, January): 27 ((–))

BORGATTI, GIUSEPPE, 1894-

413 DE BELLIS, F.: Discografia del tenore
Giuseppe Borgatti in Musica e Dischi,
VIII (No. 74, November 1952): 10 bis
((5))

BORI, LUCREZIA, 1888-1960

414 BARNES, H. M., and J. B. RICHARDS:
Lucrezia Bori's recordings in Record
Collector, IV/1 (January 1949): 5-12;
[[Addenda: Record Collector, IV/5
(May 1949)]] ((3))

415 RICHARDS, John B.: The discography in Record Advertiser, No. 2 (January-February 1971): 8-15 ((3, 6, 7))

416 RICHARDS, J. B.: The recordings of Lucrezia Bori in Record Collector, IX/5 (October 1954): 104-123 ((3, 4, 7))

417 SOBOL, Martin L.: Lucrezia Bori's records in Hobbies, LXXIX/9 (November 1974): 35-36, 121 ((3, 7))

418 VEGETO, Raffaele: Discografia di Lucrezia Bori in Musica e Dischi, XI (No. 107, July 1955): 10 ((7))

419 WILE, Raymond R.: Edison recordings by Lucrezia Bori in Record Collector, XXI/7-8 (December 1973): 169-174 ((-))

BOŘKOVEC, PAVEL, 1894-1972

420 Seznam gramofonových nahrávek díla Paula Bořkovce nahraná včs. rozhlase in KASAN, Jaroslav: Pavel Bořkovec: osobnost a dílo. [1. vyd.] Praha: Panton, 1964: 153-154 ((1))

BORODIN QUARTET
See KVARTET IMENI BORODINA

BORONAT, OLIMPIA, 1867-1934

421 VEGETO, Raffaele: Discografia in Musica e Dischi, XVI (No. 164, February 1960): 76 ((7))

422 WITTEN, Laurence C., II: A discography of Olimpia Boronat, Countess Rzewuska, 1867?-1934 in Record Collector, XX/6-7 (May 1972): 160-163 ((3, 6, 7))

BOS, COENRAAD VALENTYN, 1875-1955

423 Recordings by Coenraad V. Bos in BOS, Coenraad Valentyn: The well-tempered accompanist. Bryn Mawr: T. Presser Co., [1949]: [163] ((-))

BOSSI, MARCO ENRICO, 1861-1925

424 Dischi grammofonici in PARIBENI, Giulio Cesare: M. E. Bossi; il compositore, l'organista, l'uomo. A cura di G. C. Paribeni, L. ORSINI, E. BONTEMPELLI. Milano: Casa editrice "Erta," [1934]: 321 ((-))

BOSTON SYMPHONY ORCHESTRA

425 HELM, Everett: BSO on RCA in Musical America, LXXXII/12 (December 1962): 58 ((-))

BOUCOURECHLIEV, ANDRÉ, 1925-

426 Discographie in Courrier Musical de France, No. 31 (1970): 128 ((-))

BOULEZ, PIERRE, 1925-

427 ASHMAN, Mike: Boulez discography in Records and Recording, XVII/11 (August 1974): 19 ((-)); Supplement in Records and Recording, XVIII/5 (February 1975): 8 ((-))

428 Diskographie in BOULEZ, Pierre: Anhalts punkte: Essays. Zürich: Basler Verlag, 1975: [402]-408 ((-))

429 DERRIEN, Jean-Pierre: Discographie in Musique en jeu, No. 1 (1970): 127, 130-132 ((-))

430 Discographie in Courrier Musical de France, No. 11 (1965): 182 ((-))

431 [[[Discography] in FM Guide [New York] (July 1975)]]

BOULT, SIR ADRIAN CEDRIC, 1889-

432 ASHMAN, Mike: Boult discography in Records and Recording, XVII/7 (April 1974): 17-20 ((-)); Supplement in Records and Recording, XVIII/5 (February 1975): 7-8 ((-))

433 CLOUGH, F. F., and G. J. CUMING: Discography in The Music Yearbook, 1973-74. New York: St. Martins, 1973: 170-186 [Includes unpublished records] ((7))

434 [[CLOUGH, F. F., and G. J. CUMING: [Diskography] in Gramophone Record Review, No. 47 (September 1957)]]

435 Recommended records in Audio and Record Review (October 1968): 729 ((-))

436 WALKER, Malcolm: Sir Adrian Boult's first recordings—discography in Antique Records (October 1974): 57 ((3, 6, 7))

BRAGA, FRANCISCO, 1868-1945

437 [[[Discography] in Rio de Janeiro. Biblioteca Nacional. Exposiçao comemorativa do centenário do nascimento de Francisco Braga (1868-1945). Rio de Janeiro: Biblioteca Nacional, 1964. 84 pp.]]

BRAHMS, JOHANNES, 1833-1897

438 BAGAR, Robert C.: Brahms on records. With foreword by Dimitri MITROPOULOS. New York: The Four corners, [1942]: 91 pp. ((-))

439 Discographie in BRUYR, José: Brahms. [Paris]: Éditions du Seuil, 1965: 183-[186] (Solfèges. Collections microcosme; 25) ((-))

440 DARRELL, R. D.: The recorded works of Brahms in Music Lover's Guide, I/9 (May 1933): 258-264, 272 ((-))

441 Discographie in DELVAILLE, Bernard: Johannes Brahms; l'homme et son oeuvre. [Paris]: Seghers, [1965]: [183]-188 (Musiciens de tous les temps; 15) ((-))

442 Discographie presque completes in LAUFER, J.: Brahms. Paris: Éditions du Scorpion, [1963]: [165]-175 ((-))

443 Schallplattenaufnahmen Brahmscher Werke in MIES, Paul: Johannes Brahms; Werk, Zeit, Mensch. Leipzig: Quelle & Meyer, 1930: 127 (Wissenschaft und Bildung . . . 264) ((-))

444 Music on record: Johannes Brahms in Audio and Record Review, VIII/9 (May 1968): 346-347 ((-))

445 Discographische Notiz in NEUNZIG, Hans Adolf: Johannes Brahms in Selbstzeugnissen und Bilddokumenten. [1.-13. Tsd.] Reinbek [bei Hamburg]: Rowohlt, 1973: 137-[140] (Rororo Bildmonographien) ((-))

446 REDFERN, Brian: Selected recordings of Brahms' music in DALE, Kathleen: Brahms; a biography with a survey of books, editions & recordings. [Hamden, CT]: Archon Books, [1970]: 96-110 (The Concertgoer's companions) ((-))

447 REDFERN, Brian: Selected recordings of Brahms' music in DALE, Kathleen: Brahms; a biography with a survey of books, editions & recordings. London: Bingley, 1970: 96-110 (The Concertgoer's companions) ((-))

448 Discographie des oeuvres étudlées in ROSTAND, Claude: Brahms. Paris: Le Bon Plaisir, [1954-55]: v. I [379]-380 (Amour de la musique) ((-))

Works, Chamber Music

449 AFFELDER, Paul: The chamber music of Brahms on record. Part I: Sextets; quintets; quartets; trios in High Fidelity, IV/7 (September 1954): 75-84 ((-))

450 AFFELDER, Paul: The chamber music of Brahms on records. Part II: Sonatas, keyboard music; instrumental miscellany in High Fidelity, V/1 (March 1955): 72-82 ((-))

Works, Chorus

451 MORSE, Peter: Schubert/Schumann/Brahms choral music. Utica, NY: J. F.

Weber, 1970. 12 pp. (Discography series; 5) ((3, 4, 6, 7))

Works, Instrumental

452 BURKE, C. G.: Brahms: the orchestral music on microgroove: Part 1: Overtures; symphonies; serenades in High Fidelity, VI/4 (April 1956): 97-105 ((-))

453 BURKE, C. G.: Brahms: the orchestral music on microgroove: Part 2: Concertos; works with chorus; miscellany in High Fidelity, VI/9 (September 1956): 77-84 ((-))

454 KROHER, Ekkehart: [Diskografie] in fono forum 1968 (No. 2, February): 78 ((-))

455 [[RUFENER, R.: Eine vergleichende Discographie in Phono, V/2, V/4]]

456 [[WIENKE, Gerhard: Eine vergleichende Discographie in Phono, VII/4, VIII/1]]

Concerto, Violin, Op. 77, D Major

457 KRAUS, Gottfried: Diskografie in fono forum 1971 (No. 8, August): 559 ((-))

Concerto, Violin and Violoncello, Op. 102, A Minor

458 KONOLD, Wulf: Eine vergleichende Diskografie des Doppelkonzerts a-moll von Johannes Brahms in fono forum 1973 (No. 7, July): 606 ((-))

Ein deutsches Requiem

459 KRAUS, Gottfried: Diskografie in fono forum 1970 (No. 4, April): 217 ((-))

Songs

460 WEBER, J. F.: Brahms Lieder. Utica, NY: Weber, 1970. 20 pp. ((-))

461 WEBER, J. F.: Brahms Lieder. Utica, NY: Weber, 1971. 20 pp. (Discography series; 4) ((-))

462 [[WERBA, E.: Vier ernste Gesänge; eine vergleichende Discographie in Phono, V/3]]

Symphonies

463 HALBREICH, Harry: Discographie comparée in Harmonie, No. 41 (December 1968): 69-72 ((-))

Symphony, No. 3, Op. 90, F Major

464 JUNGHANNS, Franz: [Diskografie] in fono forum 1964 (No. 1, January): 31 ((-))

Symphony, No. 4, Op. 98, E Minor

465 JUNGHANNS, Franz: Diskografie in
fono forum 1965 (No. 3, March): 100
((-))

BRAIN, AUBREY
See listings for BRAIN, DENNIS

BRAIN, DENNIS, 1921-1957

466 CLOUGH, F. F., and G. J. CUMING:
Dennis Brain; diskography in Gramophone Record Review, No. 60 (October
1958): 953 ((7))

467 PROWSE, Martin J.: Discography
(orchestral solos) in Audio and Record
Review (October 1969): 679 ((-))

BRASS MUSIC

468 [[GLOVER, Stephen L.: Brass recordings catalog no. 3. Nashville, TN:
Brass Press, 1973. 10 pp.]]

BRENDEL, ALFRED

469 ASHMAN, Mike: Brendel discography in
Records and Recording, XVIII/6 (March
1975): 8 ((5))

470 HARDEN, Ingo: Alfred Brendel; Schallplattenverzeichnis in fono forum 1975
(No. 4, April): 330-331 ((5))

471 SCHWINGER, Wolfram: Diskografie in
fono forum 1963 (No. 2, February): 67
((-))

BRESGEN, CESAR, 1913-

472 Werkverzeichnis [includes discographical references] in LÜCK, Rudolf: Cesar
Bresgen. Wien: Lafite: Österr.
Bundesverl., 1974: 59-77 (Österreichische Komponisten des XX. Jahrhunderts; 21) ((-))

BRIAN, HAVERGAL, 1876-1972

Symphonies

473 Performance and recordings in
MacDONALD, Malcolm: The symphonies of Havergal Brian. London:
Kahn and Averill, 1974: v. 1, 206-207
((1, 7))

BRIDGE, FRANK, 1879-1941

474 [[FOREMAN, Lewis: [Discography] in
Record Advertiser, IV/3 (March-April
1974)]]

BRITTEN, BENJAMIN, 1913-1976

475 BARKER, Frank Granville: Britten on
record in Music and Musicians, XII/3
(November 1963): 41 ((-))

476 Recorded works in Boosey and Hawkes,
Inc., New York: Benjamin Britten.
[New York: Boosey and Hawkes,
1948?]: [12] ((-))

477 CLOUGH, F. F., and G. J. CUMING,
Discography of Britten as a performer
in Audio and Record Review, IV/6
(February 1965): 67-68 ((1))

478 Britten auf Schallplatten in LINDLAR,
Heinrich: Benjamin Britten. Bonn:
Boosey & Hawkes, 1954: 60 (Musik
der Zeit; 7) ((-))

479 MITCHELL, Donald: Britten on records,
part 1 in Disc, V/18 (Autumn 1951):
54-55 ((-))

480 Music on record: Benjamin Britten in
Audio and Record Review, VIII/4
(December 1967): 9, 12-13 ((-))

481 SHAWE-TAYLOR, Desmond: Discogra-
phy in MITCHELL, Donald: Benjamin
Britten; a commentary on his works
from a group of specialists, edited by
Donald Mitchell and Hans KELLER.
London: Rockliff, [1952]: 352-360 ((-))

482 SHAWE-TAYLOR, Desmond: Discography in MITCHELL, Donald: Benjamin
Britten; a commentary on his works
from a group of specialists, edited by
Donald Mitchell and Hans KELLER.
New York: Philosophical Library,
[1953, c1952]: 352-360 ((-))

483 SHAWE-TAYLOR, Desmond: Discography in MITCHELL, Donald: Benjamin
Britten; a commentary on his works
from a group of specialists, edited by
Donald Mitchell and Hans KELLER.
Westport, CT: Greenwood Press,
[1972, c1952]: 352-360 ((-))

484 WEBER, J. F.: Benjamin Britten.
Utica, NY: Weber, 1975. 58 pp. (Discography series; 16) ((5, 7))

485 List of gramophone recordings in
WHITE, Eric Walter: Benjamin Britten;
a sketch of his life and works. London,
New York: Boosey & Hawkes, [1949,
c1948]: 107 ((-))

486 Schallplatten in WHITE, Eric Walter:
Benjamin Britten; eine Skizze von
Leben und Werk. Zürich: Atlantis,
[1948]: 132-133 (Atlantis-Musikbücherei) ((-))

487 WORBS, Hans-Christoph: Diskografie
in fono forum 1961 (No. 12, December):
13 ((-))

Operas

488 PUGLIESE, Giuseppe: Discografia in
Discoteca, No. 137 (January-February
1974): 29 ((5))

BRNO ORCHESTRA
See STATNI FILHARMONIE BRNO

BROUWENSTIJN, GRE

489 Belangrijkste plaat-opnamen in
BROUWENSTIJN, Gré: Gré Brouwenstijn met en zonder make-up door
Gré van Swol-Brouwenstijn en A. C.
van Swol verteld aan J. P. M. van
Elswijk, met uittreksels uit het dagboek
van A. C. van Swol over een tournee
door de Sovjet-Unie. Bussum: Tele-
boek, [1971]: 224 ((-))

BRUCHOLLERIE, MONIQUE DE LA, 1915-
1972

490 HARDEN, Ingo: Monique de la
Bruchollerie; Schallplattenverzeichnis in fono forum 1973 (No. 1,
January): 24 [Includes unpublished
records] ((5))

BRUCKNER, ANTON, 1824-1896

491 DIETHER, Jack: Bruckner and Mahler
in the first decade of LP in Chord and
Dischord, II/8 (1958): 91-111 ((-))

492 Discografia in L'Approdo Musicale, No.
24 (1967): 294-303 ((-))

493 Discographie in Revue Musicale, No.
298-299 (1975): 101

494 Discographie in GALLOIS, Jean:
Bruckner. [Paris]: Éditions du Seuil,
[1971]: 187-189 (Collections Microcosme. Solfèges; 32) ((-))

495 Discographie in LANCELOT, Michel:
Anton Bruckner; l'homme et son
oeuvre. [Paris]: Seghers, [1964]: 183-
188 (Musiciens de tous les temps; 13)
((-))

496 LITTLE, Paul Hugo: Bruckner and
Mahler on records in Chord and Dischord, II/7 (1954): 44-60 ((-))

497 Schallplatten in NOWAK, Leopold: Anton
Bruckner; Musik und Leben. Wien:
Österreichischer Bundesverlag, [1964]:
97-100 ((-))

498 PFLUGER, Rolf: Diskographie Anton
Bruckner (1824-1896) in Österreichische Musikzeitschrift, XXIX/12 (December 1974): 645-651 ((-))

499 TAISHOFF, Saul: Bruckner on microgroove in High Fidelity, VIII/3 (March
1958): 89-97 ((-))

500 TRIGO DE SOUSA, António: Mahler e
Bruckner em discos in Arte Musical,
XXVIII/9 (1960): 251-252 ((-))

501 WALKER, Arthur D.: Bruckner scores
[includes information on recordings] in
Audio and Record Review, VIII/3 (November 1967): 15-16 ((-))

502 WEBER, J. F.: Bruckner. Utica, NY:
Weber, 1971: 20 pp. ((1, 5, 7))

503 WEBER, J. F.: Bruckner. 2d ed.
Utica, NY: Weber, 1971: 34 pp. (Discography series; 10) ((1, 5, 7))

Symphony, No. 8, C Minor

504 [[ROBBINS-LANDON, H. C.: Eine vergleichende Discographie in Phono,
VIII/3]]

BUDAPEST QUARTET

505 BREH, K.: Diskographie zum Buda-
pester Streichquartett in Hi Fi
Stereophonie, I/11 (November 1962):
486 ((-))

506 CLOUGH, F. F., and G. J. CUMING:
Budapest Quartet—discography in
Audio and Record Review, III/3 (No-
vember 1963): 16-17 ((-))

507 SMOLIAN, Steve: Four decades of the
Budapest Quartet—a discography,
1926-1966 in American Record Guide,
XXXVII/4 (December 1970): 220-227
((7))

BUMBRY, GRACE, 1937-

508 SCHWINGER, Wolfram: Diskografie
in fono forum 1963 (No. 4, April): 147
((-))

BURGUNDIAN MUSIC

509 WIDMAIER, Karl: Diskographie in
Phonoprisma (May-June 1966): 69 ((-))

BURIAN, KARL
See BURRIAN, KARL

BURKE, EDOUARD

510 [[MORAN, W. R.: Discography in Record Collector, XIX/3-4 (June 1970)]]

BURKE, TOM

511 [[JARRETT, Jack: [Discography] in
Record Advertiser, IV/1 (November-
December 1973)]]

512 WINSTANLEY, S.: Tom Burke: a discography in 78 RPM, No. 8 (November 1969): 33-34 ((3, 6, 7))

BURKHARD, WILLY, 1900-1955

513 Schallplattenverzeichnis in Willy-Burkhard-Gesellschaft: Willy Burkhard, 17. April 1900-18. Juni 1955. [Liebefeld: Willy-Burkhard-Gesellschaft, 1968]: 32 ((-))

BURMEISTER, ANNELIES

514 Diskographie in Medium Schallplatte, No. 12 (No. 3, 1969): 5 ((-))

BURMESTER, WILLI, 1869-1933

515 JARRETT, Jack: Willi Burmester in Record Advertiser, I/4 (May-June 1971): 11 ((3, 7))

BURNSTEIN, GEORGE
See LONDON, GEORGE

BURRIAN, KARL, 1870-1924

516 BREW, Dennis, and George SOVA: Karel Burian in Record Collector, XVIII/7 (July 1969): 156-164 ((3, 7))

517 WILHELM, Paul: [Discography] in Record News, IV/7 (March 1960): 243-244; Addenda: Record News, IV/8 (April 1960): 311 ((5, 7))

BURZIO, EUGENIA

518 VEGETO, Raffaele: Discografia di Eugenia Burzio in Musica e Dischi, XIII (No. 136, November 1957): 40 ((-))

BUSCH, ADOLF GEORG WILHELM, 1891-1952

519 DELALANDE, J.: Adolf Busch (8.8.1891-9.6.1952) sein tönendes Erbe; eine Diskographie in Hi Fi Stereophonie, V/5 (May 1966): 334-335 ((1, 7)); Fortsetzung in Hi Fi Stereophonie, V/6 (June 1966): 404 ((1, 7)); Schluss in Hi Fi Stereophonie, V/8 (August 1966): 536-537 ((1, 7))

520 Historiche Aufnahmen mit Adolf, Hermann und Fritz Busch in In Memoriam Adolf Busch. Dahlbruch [Krs. Siegen]: Brüder-Busch-Gesellschaft e. V., 1966: 62-63 ((-))

BUSCH, FRITZ, 1890-1951
See also BUSCH, ADOLF GEORG WILHELM. In Memoriam Adolf Busch

521 DELALANDE, Jacques: Fritz Busch tönendes Erbe; eine Diskographie in Hi Fi Stereophonie, IV/2 (February 1965): 104-106 ((1, 7)); Fortesetzung in Hi Fi Stereophonie, IV/3 (March 1965): 164-166 ((1, 7)); Fortesetzung und Schluss in Hi Fi Stereophonie, IV/5 (May 1965): 290-292 ((1, 7))

522 DELALANDE, Jacques: Tönen des Erber—ein Diskographie in BUSCH, Grete: Fritz Busch; Dirigent. [Frankfurt am Main]: S. Fischer, [1970]: 334-[354] ((1))

523 A catalog of the phonotapes in De-LERMA, Dominque-René: The Fritz Busch collection: an acquisition of Indiana University. Bloomington: Indiana University Libraries, 1972: 40-46 (Lilly Library publication; 15) ((1,7))

BUSCH, HERMANN
See BUSCH, ADOLF GEORG WILHELM. In Memoriam Adolf Busch

BUSH, GEOFFREY, 1920-

524 Tape recordings of music by Geoffrey Bush in the collection of the British Institute of Recorded Sound in Recorded Sound, No. 40 (October 1970): 694-695 ((1, 7))

BUSONI, FERRUCCIO, 1866-1924

525 ÅHLÉN, Carl-Gunnar: Ferruccio Busoni (1866-1924) in Musik Revy, XXVI/5 (1971): 300-301 (Grammofonens veteraner; 2) [Includes music played by Busoni pupils Egon Petri, Edward Steuermann, and Michael von Zadora] ((1, 3, 7))

526 [[[Discography] in Busoni's pupils play Busoni compositions. [Sound recording] International Piano Library IPL-104]]] [Includes recordings by Egon Petri, Edward Weiss, and Michael von Zadora]

527 SAUL, P.: Gramophone records played by Busoni in Recorded Sound, I/8 (Autumn 1962): 258 ((3)); Records by people who were associated with Busoni in Recorded Sound, I/8 (Autumn 1962): 258 ((-)); Selected list of records of works by Busoni not included above in Recorded Sound, I/8 (Autumn 1962): 260-261 ((-)); Miscellaneous in Recorded Sound, I/8 (Autumn 1962): 261 ((-))

528 VEGETO, Raffaele: Busoni come interprete; Ferruccio Busoni autore; nota discografica in Discoteca, No. 45 (November 1964): 24 ((-))

BUTT, CLARA, 1873-1936

529 JARRETT, Jack: Clara Butt—the
     records in Record Advertiser, II/1
     (November-December 1971): 4-8
     ((3, 7)); II/2 (January-February 1972):
     2-9 ((3, 7)); II/5 (July-August 1972)
     ((-))

BUTTERWORTH, GEORGE, 1885-1916

530 THOMPSON, Kenneth L.: A Butter-
     worth catalogue [Includes discographic
     references] in Musical Times, CVII
     (No. 1483, September 1966): 771-772
     ((5))

CBS RECORDS
     See listing for ENTREMONT,
     PHILIPPE

CABALLÉ, MONSERRAT

531 Diskographie in Musica, XXIII/2
     (March-April 1969): 171 ((-))

CABANILLES, JUAN, 1644-1712

532 Schallplattenaufnahmen in GARCÍA
     FERRERAS, Arsenio: Juan Bautista
     Cabanilles; sein Leben und sein Werk.
     Regensburg: G. Bosse, 1973: 179 (Köl-
     ner Beiträge zur Musikforschung; 70)
     ((-))

CAGE, JOHN, 1912-

533 GOODFRIEND, James: Cage on disc in
     Stereo Review, XXII/5 (May 1969): 69
     ((-))

534 Recordings in John Cage. New York:
     Henmar Press, c1962: 44 (Edition
     Peters) ((-))

535 Recordings in KOSTELANETZ, Rich-
     ard: John Cage. New York: Praeger,
     [1970]: 215-217 ([Documentary mono-
     graphs in modern art]) ((-))

CALLAS, MARIA, 1923-1977

536 Chronology [includes recording ses-
     sions] in Callas: the art and the life, by
     John ARDOIN. The great years, by
     Gerald FITZGERALD. 1st ed. New
     York: Holt, Rinehart and Winston,
     [1974]: [265]-275 ((7))

537 CLOUGH, F. F., and G. J. CUM-
     ING: Maria Meneghini Callas; a micro-
     groove diskography in Gramophone
     Record Review, No. 43 (May 1957):
     534-535 ((-))

538 [[[Discography] in After Dark (Febru-
     ary, 1974)]]

539 Diskographie in Collegium Musi-
     cum 1971 (No. 8): 16-17 ((-))

540 [[Discography in GALATOPOULOS,
     Stelios: Callas—La Divina, art that
     conceals art. Elmsford, NY; Lon-
     don: House & Maxwell, 1970. 218
     pp.]]

541 Recordings in GALATOPOULOS,
     Stelios: Callas; la Divina, art that
     conceals art. Revised and enlarged
     [ed.] London: Dent, 1966: 198-208 ((7))

542 Discographie in GARA, Eugenio:
     Maria Callas. Genève: R. Kister,
     c1957: [32] (Les Grands inter-
     prètes) ((-))

543 HAMILTON, David: A Callas discogra-
     phy in High Fidelity, XXIV/3 (March,
     1974): 46-48 ((1, 7))

544 The Callas discography, 1960 in JEL-
     LINEK, George: Callas; portrait of a
     prima donna. New York: Ziff-Davis
     Pub. Co., [1960]: 341-346 ((7))

545 The Callas discography, 1960 in JEL-
     LINEK, George: Callas; portrait of a
     prima donna. Freeport, NY: Books for
     Libraries Press, [1971, c1960]: 341-
     346 (Biography index reprint series)
     ((7))

546 JELLINEK, George: A Callas discogra-
     phy in Saturday Review (October 27,
     1956): 7 ((-))

547 PASI, Mario: I dischi della Callas in
     CEDERNA, Camilla: Callas. Milano:
     Longanesi, 1968: [147]-149 (Chi e?
     "Gente famosa," 11) ((5))

548 VEGETO, Raffaele: Discografia in Dis-
     coteca, No. 71 (June 1967): 27-31
     ((1, 5))

549 Discography of private recordings in
     WISNESKI, Henry: Maria Callas: the
     art behind the legend; with performance
     annals, 1947-1974, [includes recording
     sessions] by Arthur GERMOND.
     [[251]-384] Garden City, NY: Double-
     day, 1975: [385]-396 ((1, 7))

CALVÉ, EMMA, 1858-1942

550 BARNES, Harold, and William MORAN:
     Emma Calvé: a discography in Re-
     corded Sound, No. 59 (July 1975): 450-
     452 ((3, 4, 6, 7))

551 COURT, H. P.: Discography in Record
     News, II/3 (November 1957): 82-85 ((7))

552 [[HEVINGHAM-ROOT, L.: Discography
     in Record Collector, XIII/1-2 (March-
     April 1957)]]

CALVET, ROSSA EMMA
     See CALVÉ, EMMA

CAMPOLI, ALFREDO

553 [[[Diskographie] in fono forum 1975
No. 5, May): 438]]

CANTATE RECORDS
See listing for CHURCH MUSIC. Dürr,
Alfred: Evangelische Kirchenmusik

CANTELLI, GUIDO, 1920-1956

554 A Cantelli discography. [Dumas, Tex:
Arturo Toscanini Society, 1974]: 4 pp.
((1, 7))

555 Discografie in COLONNA, Luigi: Presenza di Guido Cantelli. Navara: [n.p.],
1962: 97-98 ((−))

556 List of works recordet [sic] by Guido
Cantelli between 1946 and 1956 in
COLONNA, Luigi: Presenza di Guido
Cantelli. Navara: [n.p.], 1962: 99 ((−))

557 GOLDSMITH, Harris: Guido Cantelli—
his legacy on records in Le Grand
Baton, III/1 (January-March, 1966):
3-14 ((7))

CAPLET, ANDRÉ, 1878-1925

558 Discographie in Courrier Musical de
France, No. 16 (1966): 232 ((−))

CARACCIOLO, JUANITA

559 VEGETO, Raffaele: Discografia di Juanita Caracciolo in Musica e Dischi, XIV
(No. 140, February 1958): 53 ((−))

CARELLI, EMMA

560 DENNIS, J.: The records in Record
Collector, XI/8 (August 1957): 179-183
((1, 3, 6, 7))

CARSONE, RENATO

561 [[[Discography] in Discofilia (September 1957): 336]]

CARTER, ELLIOT COOK, 1908-

562 TRIMBLE, Lester: A Carter discography in Stereo Review, XXIX/6 (December 1972): 71 ((−))

CARUSO, ENRICO, 1873-1921

563 BOLIG, John Richard: The recordings
of Enrico Caruso; a discography. Dover: Eldridge Reeves Johnson Memorial, Delaware State Museum, 1973:
88 pp. ((3, 4, 6, 7))

564 [[BRUUN, Carl L.: Enrico Caruso in
Record Collector, IV/5 (May, 1949):
82-95; IV/6 (June 1949); Addenda: Record Collector, IV/9 (September 1949);
V/3 (March 1950)]]

565 Caruso recordings; a discography in
CARUSO, Dorothy Park: Enrico Caruso;
his life and death. [New York]: Simon
and Schuster, [1945]: 289-301 ((3, 7))

566 A complete list of Caruso's records in
CARUSO, Dorothy Park: Enrico Caruso;
his life and death. London: T. W. Laurie, ltd., [1946]: 289-310 ((3, 7))

567 Caruso. Auswahldiskografie in Hi Fi
Stereophonie, X/8 (August 1971): 624
((−))

568 Caruso—Discographie 1900-1908 in
Phono (Winter 1954-1955): 16 ((−))

569 CELLETTI, Rodolfo: Discografia di
Caruso in Musica e Dischi, XVII (No.
175, January 1961): 50 ((7)); XVII (No.
177, March 1961): 80 ((7)); XVII (No.
178, April 1961): 86 ((3, 7))

570 DECHAMPS, Eric: Discographie in
Diapason, No. 176 (April 1973): 15 ((−))

571 [[DENNIS, J. F. E.: Discography in Record Collector, IV/5 (May 1949)]]

572 DRUMMOND, Canon H. J.: The seven
Zonophone records in Gramophone, No. 196 (September 1939): 140-
143 ((5))

573 DRUMMOND, H. J.: Enrico Caruso; a
chronological list of his records in
Gramophone, No. 128 (January 1934):
311-314 ((7))

574 Enrico Caruso. [Copenhagen]: Nationalmuseet, 1961. 22 leaves (Det
Nationale Diskotek Katalog; 2) ((3,
4, 6, 7))

575 Enrico Caruso in Discoteca, No. 116
(December 1971): 25-29 ((7))

576 FAVIA-ARTSAY, Aida: Caruso on records. [1st ed.] Valhalla, NY: Historic
Record, [1965]: 218 pp. ((3, 4, 7))

577 FREESTONE, John, and H. J. DRUM-
MOND: A Caruso anniversary [G. & T.
1902, Zonophone] in Gramophone, No.
346 (March 1952): 238 ((3, 7))

578 FREESTONE, John: Enrico Caruso; his
recorded legacy, by J. Freestone and
H. J. DRUMMOND. London: Sidgwick
and Jackson, [1960]: 130 pp. ((3, 4, 7))

579 FREESTONE, John: Enrico Caruso; his
recorded legacy, by J. Freestone and
H. J. DRUMMOND. Minneapolis: T. S.
Denison, [1961]: 130 pp. ((3, 4, 7))

580 Discographie de Caruso in MOUCHON,
Jean Pierre: Enrico Caruso; 1873-1921,

sa vie et sa voix, étude psycho-physio-
logique, physique, phonétique et esthé-
tique.... Langres: Impr. du Petit-
Cloître, 1966: 95-102 ((3))

581 SECRIST, John B.: Caruso discography
in Record Collector, VI/11-12 (November 1951): 245-280 ((3, 7)); Corrections
in Record Collector, VII/6-7 (June-
July 1952): 159-161 ((–))

582 [[SECRIST, John: Discography in
ROBINSON, Francis: Caruso: his life in
pictures. New York: Crowell, 1957.
160 pp.]]

583 TEUCHTLER, Roland: Diskografie (Alle
Aufnahmen auf Telefunken) in fono
forum 1961 (No. 11, November): 13 ((–))

CASA, LISA DE LA
See DELLA CASA, LISA

CASADESUS, ROBERT MARCEL, 1899-1972

584 BERTHOUMIEUX, Serge: Discographie
in Diapason, No. 171 (November 1972):
17 ((–))

585 Diskographie in Collegium Musicum
1971 (No. 1): 5 ((–))

586 Discography in Robert Casadesus; a
tribute to a great artist [Sound record-
ing]. Columbia M 3 32135, [1974]: 9-10
of program notes inserted in container
((1, 7))

587 SCHREIBER, U.: Diskographie Robert
Casadesus in Hi Fi Stereophonie, IV/3
(March 1965): 158-159 ((–))

CASALS, PABLO, 1876-1973

588 BAUMANN, Peter: Pablo Casals und die
Schallplatten in KAHN, Albert E.: Pablo
Casals. [n.p.]: Fischer Taschenbuch
Verlag, 1974: 226-235 ((5))

589 Casals—Discographie in Phono (Winter
1954-1955): 6 ((–))

590 CLOUGH, F. F., and G. J. CUMING: Pau
Casals; diskography in Gramophone
Record Review, No. 49 (November
1957): 30-31 ((–))

591 Complete Casals discography in Pablo
Casals [Sound recording] Columbia M5
30069, [1970]. 5 leaves ((–))

592 Discographie in Diapason, No. 182
(December 1973): 13 ((–))

593 [[[Discography] in Stereo (Spring
1974): 90-91]]

594 Discographie in GAVOTY, Bernard:
Pablo Casals. Genève: R. Kister,
c1955: [32] (Les Grands interprètes)
((–))

595 Recordings by Pablo Casals in GA-
VOTY, Bernard: Pablo Casals. Geneva:
R. Kister, c1956: [32] (Great concert
artists) ((–))

596 [Discography] in GINZBURG, Lev Solo-
monovich: Pablo Kazal's. Izd 2, dop.
Moskva: "Muzyka," 1966: [211]-219
((–))

597 A list of Casals recordings in LITTLE-
HALES, Lillian: Pablo Casals. [Rev.
and enl. ed.] New York: W. W. Norton,
[1948]: 225-228 ((–))

598 A list of Casals recordings in LITTLE-
HALES, Lillian: Pablo Casals. Westport, CT: Greenwood Press, [1970,
c1929]: 225-228; Note: A reprint of the
2d edition, 1948 ((–))

599 Discographie in MÜLLER-BLATTAU,
Joseph: Casals. [Berlin]: Rembrandt
Verlag, [c1964]: 28-31 (Rembrandt-
Reihe; 49) ((–))

600 Diskographie in SEILER, Alexander J.
P.: Casals. [Olten: Walter, 1956]: 112-
115 ((–))

601 TOWE, Teri Noel: Discography in
KIRK, H. L.: Pablo Casals; a biography.
[1st ed.] New York: Holt, Rinehart and
Winston, [1974]: 568-625 ((7))

CASANOVA, ANDRÉ, 1919-

602 Discographie in Courrier Musical de
France, No. 33 (1971): 52 ((–))

CASELLA, ALFREDO, 1883-1947

603 Discografia in AMICO, Fedele d': Alfredo Casella, a cura di Fedele d'Amico
e Guido M. GATTI. [Milano]: Ricordi,
[1958]: 209-211 (Symposium; collana
di studi musicali, 1) ((1))

604 Discografia in L'Approdo Musicale,
I/1 (January-March 1958): 95-99 [In-
cludes piano rolls] ((–))

605 HUGHES, Eric: Alfredo Casella: a
discography in Recorded Sound, No. 28
(October 1967): 237-239 ((1, 7))

CASTERÈDE, JACQUES

606 Discographie in Courrier Musical de
France, No. 43 (1973): 123 ((–))

CATLEY, GWEN

607 [[[Discos] in Disc (Bristol) III/11
(Autumn 1949): 152]]

608 Some records by Gwen Catley in Disc,
III/12 (Autumn 1949): 152 ((–))

ČESKÉHO KVARTETA
See CZECH QUARTET

CHABRIER, EMMANUEL, 1841-1894

609 Discographie in Courrier Musical de
France, No. 13 (1966): 52-53 ((-))

610 Music on record: Emmanuel Chabrier
1841-1894 in Audio and Record Review
(January 1969): 14 ((-))

611 Some recommended records in MYERS,
Rollo: Emmanuel Chabrier and his cir-
cle. London: Dent, 1969: 170 ((-))

612 Some recommended records in MYERS,
Rollo: Emmanuel Chabrier and his cir-
cle. Rutherford, N. J.: Fairleigh Dick-
inson University Press, 1970: 180 ((-))

613 Discographie in ROBERT, Frédéric:
Emmanuel Chabrier; l'homme et son
oeuvre, catalogue des oeuvres, discographie. [Paris]: Seghers, [1970]:
[183]-186 (Musiciens de tous les temps;
43) ((-))

CHAÏKOVSKIÍ, PETR IL'ICH, 1840-1893

614 BLASL, Franz: Werke von Tschaikov-
sky auf Langspielplatten in Musikziehung, XIV/1 (September 1960): 36-
40 ((-))

615 BRITZIUS, K. E.: Recorded works in
Phonograph Monthly Review, I/7 (April
1927): 304-306 ((-))

616 Discographie in ERISMANN, Guy: Piotr
Illitch Tchaïkovski; l'homme et son
oeuvre. [Paris]: Seghers, [1964]: 183-
188 (Musiciens de tous les temps; 9)
((-))

617 HALLIDAY, John: Tchaikovsky on records. With foreword by Artur RODZIN-
SKI. New York: The Four corners,
[1942]: 89 pp. ((-))

618 Discographie critique in HOFMANN,
Rostislav: Tchaikovski. Paris, Éditions
du Seuil, 1969: 179-184 ((-))

619 A selected discography from Great Britain and America in HOFMANN, Rostislav: Tchaikovsky. London: J. Calder,
[1962]: 183-185 (Illustrated Calderbook,
CB. 59 ((-))

620 Pour une discographie Tchaikovski in
Diapason, No. 136 (May 1969): 8-9 ((-))

621 Discografie in RAEDT, Paul de: Het
leven en werk van P. I. Tsjaikofski.
Brussel: D. A. P. [De Arbeiderspers.],
[1972]: 45-48 (Meesters der toonkunst;
19) ((-))

Works, Instrumental

622 INDCOX, J. F.: Tchaikovsky recordings
on microgroove. Part I: Symphonies,

concertos in High Fidelity, IV/6 (August 1954): 55-61 ((-))

623 INDCOX, J. F.: Tchaikovsky recordings
on microgroove. Part II: Ballet, symphonic program music, orchestral miscellany in High Fidelity, IV/8 (October
1954): 89-99 ((-))

624 INDCOX, J. F.: Tchaikovsky recordings
on microgroove. Part III: Orchestral
suites, chamber music, opera in High
Fidelity, V/3 (May 1955): 85-89 ((-))

Concerto, Piano, No. 1, B-Flat Minor, Op. 23

625 Enregistrements in Diapason, No. 151
(November 1971): 36-39 ((-))

626 MEYER-JOSTEN, J.: Diskografie in
fono forum 1965 (No. 9, September):
379 ((-))

Concerto, Violin, Op. 35, D Major

627 KONOLD, Wulf: Probestück mit Flit-
ter—Peter Tchaikovskys Violinkonzert
und 19 Aufnahmen: Ein vergleichende
Diskografie in fono forum 1973 (No. 9,
September): 800-801 ((-))

Eugene Onegin

628 SEMEONOFF, Boris: Eugene Onegin: a
synopsis and discography in Record
Collector, VII/6-7 (June-July 1952):
141-149 ((-))

Manfred

629 KEY, Clyde J.: Tchaikovsky's Manfred:
an opera without human voices in Le
Grand Baton, IV/4 (November 1967):
9-14 ((-))

Symphonies

630 [[[Discography] in HAMBURGER, Povl:
Tjajkovskij som symfoniker. Udg. af
Folkeuniversitatsforeningen i Køben-
havn. Kobenhavn: Rhodos, 1962: 89]]

Symphony, No. 6, B Minor, Op. 74

631 WIENKE, Gerhard: Tskaikovsky Symphonie Nr. 6: eine vergleichende Discographie in Phono, IX/2 (November-
December 1962): 32-35 ((-))

CHAILLEY, JACQUES, 1910-

632 Discographie in Courrier Musical
de France, No. 16 (1966): 236 ((-))

CHALIAPINE, FÉODOR
See SHALIÂPIN, FEDOR IVANOVICH

CHAMBER MUSIC

633 [[Discography in Catalogue of chamber
music available on loan from the Library of the Canadian Music Centre.
Toronto: The Centre, 1967. 288 pp.]]

Czechoslovakia

634 VORKURA, Klaus Alexander: Tsche-
chische Kammermusik auf Schallplatten
in Phono, XII/5 (May-June 1966): 124-
126 ((–))

CHAMINADE, CÉCILE, 1857-1944

635 [[CAPES, S. J.: [Discography] in British Institute of Recorded Sound Bulletin,
No. 3 (Winter 1956)]]

CHANTS (PLAIN, GREGORIAN, ETC.)
See also CHURCH MUSIC

636 Discographie in BESCOND, Albert-
Jacques: Le chant grégorien. [Paris]:
Buchet/Chastel, [1972]: 312-313 ((–))

637 Discography in The Gregorian chant
manual of the Catholic music hour, by
Bishop Joseph SCHREMBS, Sister Alice
MARIE, [and] Gregory HUEGLE; a
practical method of integrating the
study of Gregorian chant and modern
music, the teaching procedure in accor-
dance with approved educational thought.
New York: Silver Burdett, [c1935]: 304-
311 (The Catholic music hour) ((–))

CHAPUIS, MICHEL

638 GALLOIS, Jean: Discographie in Diapason, No. 189 (September 1974): 8-9 ((–))

CHARPENTIER, JACQUES, 1933-

639 Discographie in Courrier Musical de
France, No. 30 (1970): 90 ((–))

640 GALLOIS, Jean: Discographie in Diapason, No. 183 (January 1974): 17 ((–))

CHATSCHATURIAN, ARAM
See KHACHATURIAN, ARAM IL'ICH

CHAUSSON, ERNEST, 1855-1899

641 Discographie in GALLOIS, Jean: Ernest Chausson; l'homme et son oeuvre..., catalogue des oeuvres, discographie.... Paris: Seghers, 1967:
[189] (Musiciens de tous les temps; 34)
((–))

CHÁVEZ, CARLOS, 1899-

642 Discografía in GARCÍA MORILLO, Roberto: Carlos Chávez; vida y obra. [1.

ed.] México: Fondo de Cultura Econó-
mica, [1960]: 228-230 ((–))

CHAYNES, CHARLES

643 Discographie in Courrier Musical de
France, No. 38 (1972): 110 ((–))

CHEREPNIN, ALEKSANDR NIKOLAEVICH,
1899-

644 Schallplatten in REICH, Willi: Alexander Tscherepnin. Bonn: M. P. Belaieff,
[1961]: 71 ((–))

CHERKASSKY, SHURA, 1911-

645 Diskographie in Phonoprisma (May-
June 1965): 87 ((–))

CHOEUR DE CHAMBRE "MADRIGAL"

646 COSMA, Viorel: Discographie in
Muzica, XXIII/6 (June 1973): 47 ((–))

CHOPIN, FRYDERYK FRANCISZEK, 1810-
1849

647 AGUETTANT, Robert: Catalogue commenté et discographie critique in
Chopin. Paris: Hachette, 1965: [257]-
[283] ((–))

648 Discography from Great Britain and
America in BOURNIQUEL, Camille:
Chopin. New York: Grove Press,
[1960]: 182-191 (Evergreen profile
book, 8) ((–))

649 Verzeichnis der Werke, mit Angabe
über die Wiedergabe auf Schallplatten
in CHERBULIEZ, Antoine Élisée
Adolphe: Fryderyk Chopin; Leben und
Werk. Rüschlikon-Zürich: A. Müller,
[1948]: 188-194 (Meister der Musik im
19. und 20. Jahrhunderts) ((–))

650 CLARKE, Cyril: Discography in
CORTOT, Alfred: In search of Chopin.
London, New York: P. Nevill, [1951]:
231-268 ((–))

651 Discography in CORTOT, Alfred: In
search of Chopin. Westport, CT:
Greenwood Press, [1975] c1952: 231-
268 ((–))

652 [[[Discography] in Discofilia (May
1956): 86]]

653 Discographie in GAUTHIER, André:
Frédéric Chopin. Paris: Editions
Hermès, 1967: 205-207 (W, 14. Figures)
((–))

654 Discographie de l'oeuvre de Frédéric
Chopin in GRENIER, Jean Marie:
Frédéric Chopin; l'homme et son

oeuvre. [Paris]: Seghers, [1964]:
[173]-179 (Musiciens de tous les
temps, 10) ((-))

655 Discographie de l'oeuvre de Frédéric
Chopin in GRENIER, Jean Marie:
Frédéric Chopin. Lausanne: La Guilde
du livre, [1967]: [173]-179 (Musiciens
de tous les temps) ((-))

656 [[HOLCMAN, Jan: The honor roll of recorded Chopin in Saturday Review (February 27, 1960): 44-45]]

657 Schallplattenverzeichnis in IWAS-
ZKIEWICZ, Jarosław: Chopin. Berlin:
Henschelverlag, 1958: 236-[245] ((-))

658 Discographie générale in PANIGEL,
Armand: L'oeuvre de Frédéric Chopin;
discographie générale. Introd. et notes
de Marcel BEAUFILS. [1. éd.] Paris:
La Revue de Disques, [1949]: 253 pp.
(Archives de la musique enregistrée
UNESCO. Ser. A: Musique occidentale;
1) ((4, 5))

659 SCHONBERG, Harold C.: The collec-
tor's Chopin and Schumann. [1st ed.]
Philadelphia: Lippincott, [1959]: 256 pp.
(Keystone books, KB-8) ((-))

660 SCHONBERG, Harold: Frédéric Chopin
in High Fidelity, V/4 (June 1955): 78-
89 ((-))

661 Selected discography in SEROFF, Victor: Frederic Chopin. New York: Macmillan Co., [1964]: [113]-115 ((-))

662 Discography in WALKER, Alan: Frédéric Chopin; profiles of the man and the
musician. London: Barrie & Rockliff,
[1968]: [301]-321 ((-))

663 Discography in WALKER, Alan: Frederic Chopin; profiles of the man and the
musician. [1st American ed.] New
York: Taplinger Pub. Co., [1967]:
[301]-321 ((-))

Sonata, No. 2, Op. 35, B Minor

664 LEWINSKI, Wolf-Eberhard von: [Disko-
grafie] in fono forum 1967 (No. 4,
April): 191 ((-))

665 [[OLTNER, H.: Eine vergleichende
Discographie in Phono, VIII/3]]

Waltzes

666 [[BLAUKOPF, K.: Eine vergleichende
Discographie in Phono, VII/4]]

CHORAL MUSIC

667 Recommended gramophone records in
JACOBS, Arthur: Choral music: a
symposium. Baltimore: Penguin Books,
[1963]: [427]-436 (Pelican books) ((-))

668 KIRCHBERG, Klaus: Der Männechor—
eine Discographie in Musikhandel,
XIII/5 (1962): 219 ((-))

669 [[MILLER, Philip L.: A Guide to recordings of 'standard' choral works;
part I: Renaissance and baroque in
American Choral Foundation Memos,
No. 20 (January 15, 1961)]]

670 [[MILLER, Philip L.: A Guide to recordings of 'standard' choral works;
part II: Classical, romantic and modern
in American Choral Foundation Memos,
No. 21 (February 15, 1961)]]

CHORAL MUSIC, ENGLISH
See listing for COMPOSERS, ENGLISH.
List of gramophone recordings in Man-
ning, Rosemary Joy: From Holst to
Britten

CHOSTAKOVITCH, DMITRI
See SHOSTAKOVICH, DMITRIĬ
DMITRIEVICH

CHRISTOFF, BORIS, 1918-

671 CLOUGH, F. F., and G. J. CUM-
ING: Boris Christoff—discography in
Audio and Record Review, IV/1 (Sep-
tember 1964): 73-74 ((-))

CHURCH MUSIC
See also CHANTS (PLAIN, GRE-
GORIAN, ETC.)

672 [[DÜRR, Alfred: Evangelische Kirchenmusik auf Schallplatten. Zur Produktion der "Cantate" Schallplatten in
Die Musikforschung, XIII (1960): 60-
62]]

673 Discographie in HUOT-PLEUROUX,
Paul: Histoire de la musique religieuse
des origines à nos jours. [1. éd.] Paris:
Presses universitaires de France,
1957: [373]-439 ((-))

674 International Catholic Association for
Radio and Television: Catalogue du
disque de musique religieuse. Fri-
bourg, [1956]: 300 pp. ((-))

675 Royal School of Church Music: A selected list of church music recordings.
Croydon: Royal School of Church Music,
1967: 12 pp. ((-))

676 SATCHER, Herbert Boyee: A church
music discography in Phonograph
Monthly Review, V/1 (October 1930):
6-9 ((-))

Eastern Orthodox

677 [[LAADE, Wolfgang: Die Geschichte
der liturgischen Musik der Ostkirchen

auf Schallplatten in Schallplatte und Kirche, XXXIX/5 (September-October 1969): 109-114; XL/3 (May-June 1970): 225-233]]

Russian

678 [[GARDNER, Johann von: Zur Diskographie des russischen Kirchengesangs in Ostkirchliche Studien, IX (1960): 265-292]]

679 [[GARDNER, Johann von: Zur Diskographie des russischen Kirchengesangs in Ostkirchliche Studien, X (1961): 136-155]]

680 [[GARDNER, Johann von: Diskographie des russischen Kirchengesangs in Ostkirchenliche Studien, XII (1963): 39-60]]

681 [[GARDNER, Johann von: Diskographie des russischen Kirchengesangs in Ostkirchliche Studien, XIII (1964): 282-309]]

682 [[GARDNER, Johann von: Diskographie des russischen Kirchengesangs in Ostkirchliche Studien, XVIII (1969): 23-42]]

20th Century

683 Discography in ROUTLEY, Erik: Twentieth century church music. New York: Oxford University Press, 1964: 235-239 (Studies in church music) ((-))

CILEA, FRANCESCO, 1866-1950

Adriana Lecouvreur. Poveri fiori, gemme de prati

684 VEGETO, Raffaele: Nota discografica in Discoteca, No. 66 (January 1967): 32 ((1))

CIORTEA, TUDOR, 1903-

685 Discographie in Muzica, XX/9 (September 1970): 43 ((-))

CISNEROS, ELEANORA DE, 1878-1934

686 [[GANDIA, Roberto de: [Discography] in Discofilia, No. 5 (July-August 1956): 189]]

ČIURLIONIS, MIKALOJUS KONSTANTINAS, 1857-1911

687 [Discography] in LANDSBERGIS, Vytautas: Tvorchestvo Chiurlenisa: sonata vesnyl. lzd. 2-e, dop. Leningrad: Muzyka, Leningrad. otd-nie, 1975: 314-315 ((-))

CLARINET MUSIC

688 Literatura-diskografija in EBERST, Anton: Klarinet i klarinetisti. Novi Sad, [Yugoslavia]: Forum, [1963]: [117]-150 ((-))

689 GILBERT, Richard: The clarinetists' solo repertoire: a discography. New York: Grenadilla Society, [1972]: ii, 100 pp. ((-))

690 The recordings in GILBERT, Richard: The clarinetists' discography II. New York: Grenadilla Society, 1975: 2-44 ((-))

691 Discography in GILLESPIE, James E.: Solos for unaccompanied clarinet: an annotated bibliography of published works. Detroit: Information Coordinators, 1973: 79 (Detroit studies in music bibliography; 28) ((-))

692 WALKER, Bonnie Hicks: Recordings for the clarinet and the recording artists. Augusta, GA: Walker, 1969: v, 63 leaves ((-))

CLAVICHORD MUSIC

693 [[Discography in WAGNER, Lavern J.: The clavichord today in Periodical of the Illinois State Music Teachers Association, VI/1 (Spring 1968): 20-38; VII/1 (Summer 1969): 1-16]]

CLEMENT, EDMOND, 1867-1928

694 FASSETT, Stephen: Edmond Clement— lyric tenor in American Music Lover, X/4 (December 1943): 105-106 ((7))

CLEMENTI, MUZIO, 1752-1832

Sonatas, Piano

695 Catalogo tematico [includes discographical references] in ALLORTO, Riccardo: Le sonate per pianoforte di Muzio Clementi: studio critico e catalogo tematico. Firenze: L. S. Olschki, 1959: [65]-138 (Historiae musicae cultores. Biblioteca; 12) ((-))

CLEVELAND ORCHESTRA

696 Discography in MARSH, Robert C.: The Cleveland Orchestra. New York: World, 1967: [189]-[200] ((-))

697 Recordings of the Cleveland Symphony Orchestra in Phonograph Monthly Review, II/12 (September 1928): 440 ((-))

CLIBURN, VAN, 1934-

698 Diskographie (sämtliche Aufnahmen RCA) in Phonoprisma, VII/4 (July-August 1964): 119 ((-))

CLICQUOT, FRANÇOIS HENRI, 1732-1790

699 Discographie in L'oeuvre de François-Henri Clicquot, facteur d'orgues du roy (1732-1790). Études autour du grand-orgue F.-H. Clicquot de la cathédrale de Poitiers. [Laval]: Impr. Barnéoud, 1973: 235 ((-))

CLUYTENS, ANDRÉ, 1905-1967

700 Enregistrements réalises sous la direction d'Andre Cluytens in GAVOTY, Bernard: André Cluytens. Genève: R. Kister, c1955: 30-[32] (Les Grands interprètes) ((-))

701 Recordings by Andre Cluytens in GAVOTY, Bernard: André Cluytens. Geneva: R. Kister, c1956: 30-[32] (Great concert artists) ((-))

702 VEGETO, Raffaele: Andre Gluytens [i.e., Cluytens] discografia in Disco-teca, No. 73 (September 1967): 26-27 ((-))

COATES, ALBERT, 1882-1953

703 DYMENT, Christopher: Albert Coates discography in Recorded Sound, No. 57-58 (January-April 1975): 386-405 ((3, 4, 6, 7)); Errata in Recorded Sound, No. 59 (July 1975): 464 ((3, 6))

COATES, ERIC, 1886-1957

704 BROWN, Nathan E.: A Coates discography in Le Grand Baton, VI/1 (February 1969): 4-15 ((-))

COATES, JOHN, 1865-1941

705 [[John Coates—the recordings in Record Advertiser, II/3 (March-April 1972): 4-6; II/5 (July-August 1972)]]

COLE, BELLE

706 [[MOYER, K.: Discography in Record Collector, XXI/7-8 (December 1973)]]

COLUMBIA RECORDS
See listings for FREMSTED, OLIVE; GEDDA, NICOLAI. Diskographie; GIESEKING, WALTER. Gavoty, Bernard; YSAŸE, EUGÈNE

COMPOSERS

707 Recordings in ANGOFF, Charles: Fathers of classical music. New York: Beechhurst Press, [1947]: 153-161 ((-))

708 Discography in ANGOFF, Charles: Fathers of classical music. Freeport, NY: Books for Libraries Press, [1969, c1947]: 153-161 (Essay index reprint series) ((-))

709 Basic works for the record library in CROSS, Milton: Encyclopedia of the great composers and their music, by Milton Cross and David EWEN. New rev. ed. Garden City, NY: Doubleday, 1962: [919]-926 ((-))

710 Basic works for the record library in CROSS, Milton: The Milton Cross new encyclopedia of the great composers and their music, by Milton Cross and David EWEN. Rev. and expanded. Garden City, NY: Doubleday, 1969: [1185]-1192 ((-))

711 DOUGLAS, John R.: The composer and his music on record in Library Journal, XCII/6 (March 15, 1967): 1117-1121 ((-))

712 Guide to recorded music in EWEN, David: Pioneers in music. New York: Thomas Y. Crowell Co., 1940: 247-250 ((-))

713 Guide to recorded music in EWEN, David: Pioneers in music. Freeport, NY: Books for Libraries Press, [1972]: 247-250 (Essay index reprint series) ((-))

714 [[MALIPIERO, Riccardo: Guida disco-grafica alla musica sinfonica. Milano: Messaggerie musicali, [1957]: 62 pp.]]

715 [[MÜLLER VON ASOW, Hedwig: Komponistinen-Discographie. Berlin: Internationales Musiker-Brief-Archiv, 1962. 231 pp.]]

716 [Discographies included] in RANGE, Hans Peter: Von Beethoven bis Brahms: einführung in die konzertanten Klavier-werke der Romantik. Lahr/Schwarzw.: Schauenburg, [1967]: 233 pp. ((-))

20th Century

717 Discographie in HODIER, André: La musique depuis Debussy. [1. ed.] Paris: Presses universitaires de France, 1961: [213]-214; Note: Includes discographies for Barraqué, Berg, Berio, Boulez, Henze, Messiaen, Nono, Philippot, Pousseur, Stockhausen, Varèse, and Webern ((-))

COMPOSERS, AMERICAN

718 Discographies in COHN, Arthur: The collector's twentieth-century music in the Western Hemisphere. New York: Da Capo Press, 1972, c 1961. 256 pp. ((-))

719 The newest "new festival"; a discography of music by Alliance composers in Bulletin of the American Composers Alliance, IX/2 (1960): 13-17; IX/3 (1960): 19-25 ((-))

720 TRIGO DE SOUSA, António: Discografia seleccionada de compositores americanos in Arte Musical, XXXIII/25-26 (1967): 83-88 ((-))

COMPOSERS, AUSTRALIAN

721 Discography of music by Australian composers in Studies in Music, No. 7 (1973): 91-93 ((-))

722 Discographies in MURDOCH, James: Australia's contemporary composers. Melbourne: Macmillan, 1972. 223 pp. ((-))

723 Discographies in MURDOCH, James: Australia's contemporary composers. Melbourne: Sun Books, 1975. 223 pp. ((-))

724 PLUSH, Vincent: Discography of music by Australian composers in Studies in Music, No. 6 (1972): 68-75 ((1, 4, 7))

COMPOSERS, BELGIAN

725 Brief list of recordings in Centre belge de documentation musicale, Brussels: Music in Belgium: contemporary Belgian composers. Brussels: A. Manteau, c1964: 141-158 ((-))

COMPOSERS, BRITISH
See COMPOSERS, ENGLISH

COMPOSERS, CANADIAN

726 Discographical references in Contemporary Canadian composers. Edited by Keith MacMILLAN and John BECKWITH. Toronto; New York: Oxford, 1975. 248 pp. ((-))

COMPOSERS, CZECH

20th Century

727 Recordings of contemporary Czech and Slovak music in GARDAVSKÝ, Čeněk: Contemporary Czechoslovak composers. Prague: Panton, 1965: 539-562 ((-))

COMPOSERS, DANISH
See also COMPOSERS, SCANDINAVIAN

20th Century

728 List of the records of Danish music in KAPPEL, Vagn: Contemporary Danish composers against the background of Danish musical life and history. [Copenhagen]: Danske Selskab, 1948: 95-108 (Danes of the present and past) ((-))

729 List of records of Danish music in KAPPEL, Vagn: Contemporary Danish composers against the background of Danish musical life and history. [2d, rev. ed. Copenhagen]: Danske Selskab, 1950: 97-113 (Danes of the present and past); Note: The 3d edition of this book, published in 1967, did not contain a discography ((-))

COMPOSERS, ENGLISH

730 Discography in British music now: a guide to the work of younger composers. Edited by Lewis FOREMAN. London: P. Elek, 1975: 216-237 ((-))

731 Discography in FRANK, Alan: Modern British composers. London: D. Dobson, [1953]: 112 pp. (The Student's music library); Note: Includes discographies of Vaughan-Williams, Ireland, Bax, Bliss, Benjamin, Moeran, Rubbra, Walton, Berkeley, Tippett, Rawsthorne, Lambert, Britten, Searle, Frankel, Alan Bush, and Fricker ((-))

732 List of gramophone recordings in MANNING, Rosemary Joy: From Holst to Britten: a study of modern choral music. London: Workers' Music Association, 1949: vii ((-))

20th Century

733 [Discographies included in each listing] in FLUCK, Alan: The sour, sweet music: a beginner's guide to contemporary music. London: Putnam, 1957. 141 pp. ((-))

COMPOSERS, FINNISH
See COMPOSERS, SCANDINAVIAN

COMPOSERS, FLEMISH

Medieval

734 Verzeichnis von Schallplatten mit Werken Niederländischen Meister und ihrer Zeitgenossen in WOLFF, Hellmuth Christian: Die Musik der alten

Niederländer (15. und 16. Jahrhundert).
Leipzig: Breikopf & Härtel, 1956: 253-
255 ((-))

COMPOSERS, FRENCH

735 Discography in DAVIES, Laurence:
The gallic muse. London: Dent, 1967:
207-218 ((-))

736 Discography in DAVIES, Laurence: The
gallic muse. [1st American ed.] South
Brunswick: A. S. Barnes, [1969]: 207-
218 ((-))

737 Platenlijst in MOORTGAT, Gabriël:
XVIe [i.e. Zestiende] XVIIe & XVIIIe
eeuwse Franse orgelmeesters. Brugge:
Verbeke-Loys, [1963]: 103-107; Includes discographies of Titelouze,
Marchand, Clerambaylt, Claude
d'Aquini, Du Mage, and DeGrigny ((-))

20th Century

738 [Discography included after each
sketch] in ROY, Jean: Présences con-
temporaines: musique française - Satie,
Koechlin, Roussel, Schmitt, Varèse,
Migot, Honegger, Milhaud, Poulenc,
Jaubert, Sauguet, Jolivet, Lesur, Messiaen, Ohana, Dutilleux, Nigg, Jarre,
Boulez, Bondon, avec un index des
oeuvres et des disques. Paris: Nou-
velles Éditions Debresse, [1962]:
488 pp. ((-))

COMPOSERS, GERMAN

739 [[[Discographies] in DUPONT, Wilhelm:
Werkausgaben Nürnberger Komponisten
in Vergangenheit und Gegenwart. Nürnberg: Selbstverlag der Stadtbibliothek
Nürnberg, 1971. 378 pp.]]

COMPOSERS, HUNGARIAN

20th Century

740 Discography in Contemporary Hungar-
rian composers. Budapest: Editio
Musica, 1970: 144-156 ((-))

741 [Discographies] in Contemporary Hungarian composers. 3d. ed. Budapest:
Editio Musica, 1974: 176 pp. ((-))

COMPOSERS, JEWISH

742 [List of recordings at end of each chap-
ter] in LANDAU, Anneliese: The contribution of Jewish composers to the
music of the modern world. Cincinnati:
National Federation of Temple Sister-
hoods, [1946]: 94 leaves ((-))

COMPOSERS, NEW ZEALANDER

743 MUZ, Peter: Discography of music by
New Zealand composers in Studies in
Music, No. 8 (1974): 110-112 ((-))

COMPOSERS, NORWEGIAN
See COMPOSERS, SCANDINAVIAN

COMPOSERS, SCANDINAVIAN
See also, COMPOSERS, DANISH

744 Composers gallery in YOELL, John:
The Nordic sound. Boston: Crescendo
Pub. Co., [1974]: 240-259 ((-))

745 Selective international discography in
YOELL, John: The Nordic sound. Boston: Crescendo Pub. Co., [1974]: [231]-
259 ((-))

20th Century

746 Bibliografier och grammofonlistor in
Ny musik i Norden. [Stockholm]: KFs
bokförlag i distribution, [1953]: 117-
138 (Nordens serie; 27) (Norden, svensk
förening för nordiskt samarbete.
Norden serie, 27) ((-))

COMPOSERS, SWEDISH
See also COMPOSERS, SCANDINAVIAN

747 [Discographies] in BERGENDAL,
Göran: 33 [i.e. Trettiotre] svenska
komponister. Stockholm: Lindblad,
1972. 255 pp. (Lindblads nutidsböcker)
((-))

748 Diskografi in CONNOR, Herbert: Samtal
med tonsättare. Stockholm: Natur och
Kultur, 1971: 194-218 ((-))

749 HEDMAN, Frank: Diskografie in fono
forum 1965 (No. 2, February): 56 ((-))

20th Century

750 Tonsättarna och deras verk; biografi,
verkförteckning, bibliografi, och diskografi i urval in CONNOR, Herbert:
Samtal med tonsättare. Stockholm:
Natur och kultur, 1971: 193-218 ((-))

COMPOSERS, SWISS

751 [[Discographies in Verein Schweizer-
ischer Tonkünstler: 40 contemporary
Swiss composers. Amriswil: Bodensee-
Verlag, 1956. 222 pp.]]

752 [Discographie at end of biography] in
Schweizerischer Tonkünstlerverein: 40
[i.e. Vierzig] Schweizer Komponisten
der Gegenwart = 40 compositeurs
suisses contemporains. Amriswil:
Bodensee-Verlag, 1956. 236 pp. ((-))

COMPOSERS, WOMEN

753 [[MÜLLER VON ASOW, Hedwig: Kom-
ponistinnen-Discographie. Berlin:
Internationales Musiker-Brief-Archiv,
1962. 4 pp.]]

754 MÜLLER VON ASOW, Hedwig: Kom-
ponistinnen-Discographie in Musiker-
ziehung, XV/2 (1964): 94-96 ((-))

CONCENTUS MUSICUS

755 Diskographie in Collegium Musicum
1971 (No. 11): 11-12 ((-))

CONCERTGEBOUW ORKEST
See BEINUM, EDUARD VAN

CONCERTOS

756 DARRELL, R. D.: Recorded concertos
in Music Lover's Guide, I/11 (July
1933): 324-326; 331 ((-)); I/12 (August
1933): 362-365 ((-))

757 [[Discography in DELDEN, Lex van: Het
concert. Bilthoven: H. Nelissen [1957]:
61-64]]

758 Gramofonové závody, Prague: Instru-
mentálnf koncerty na československých
gramofonových deskách. Praha: Gra-
mafonové závody, [1957]: 47 pp. ((-))

759 Discography in VEINUS, Abraham: The
concerto. Garden Park, NY: Doubleday,
1944: 285-294 ((-))

760 Discography in VEINUS, Abraham: Victor book of concertos. [New York]:
Simon and Schuster, 1948: 441-450 ((-))

761 Discography in VEINUS, Abraham: The
concerto. London: Cassell, [1948]:
295-306 ((-))

762 Index of works and recordings in
YOUNG, Percy M.: Concerto. Boston:
Crescendo Publishers, [1968]: 155-162
(Phoenix music guides; 1) ((-))

CONCERTOS, PIANO

763 GOLDSMITH, Harris: The romantic
piano concerto; a discography in High
Fidelity, XI/5 (May 1961): 64-69 ((-));
XI/6 (June 1961): 65-68 ((-))

CONDUCTORS

764 Gramophone records in BLAUKOPF,
Kurt: Great conductors. [1st ed.] London: Arco Publishers, 1955: 168-192
((-))

765 Schallplatten in BLAUKOPF, Kurt:
Grosse Dirigenten. Teufen: A. Niggli

und W. Verkauf, [1953]: 177-199
(Bücher der Weltmusik) ((-))

766 Schallplatten in BLAUKOPF, Kurt:
Grosse Dirigenten. [2. erweiterte und
ergänzte Aufl.] Teufen: Niggli, [1957]:
183-206 (Bücher der Weltmusik) ((-))

767 Select discography in WOOLDRIDGE,
David: Conductor's world. London:
Barrie & Rockcliff, the Cresset P.,
1970: 349-363 ((-))

768 Select discography in WOOLDRIDGE,
David: Conductor's world. New York:
Praeger, 1970: 349-363 ((-))

CONSTANT, MARIUS

769 Discographie in Courrier Musical de
France, No. 8 (1964): 262 ((-))

770 Discographie in Diapason, No. 151
(November 1970): 5 ((-))

CONSTANTINESCU, PAUL, 1909-1963

771 DRĂGONI, Constantin: Disques in
Muzica, XIX/12 (December 1969): 47
((-))

772 Creatieri [includes discographical ref-
erences] in TOMESCU, Vasile: Paul
Constantinescu. Bucureşti: Editura
Muzicală, 1967: 488-[499] ((-))

CONTEMPORARY MUSIC

773 Discographie in Revue Musicale, No.
244: 61 ((-))

COPELAND, GEORGE

774 MOORE, Jerrold: George Copeland discography in Recorded Sound, No. 25
(January 1967): 142-147 ((1, 3, 4, 5, 6,
7))

COPLAND, AARON, 1900-

775 List of records in BERGER, Arthur:
Aaron Copland. New York: Oxford University Press, 1953: 107-112 ((5))

776 List of records in BERGER, Arthur:
Aaron Copland. Westport, CT: Greenwood Press, [1971, c1953]: 107-112
((5))

777 BERGER, Arthur: An Aaron Copland
discography in High Fidelity, V/5 (July
1955): 64-69 ((-))

778 FLANAGAN, William: Aaron Copland:
recommended recordings in Hi Fi
Stereo Review, XVI/6 (June 1966): 53
((-))

779 HAMILTON, David: Aaron Copland: a discography of the composer's performances in Perspectives of New Music, IX/1 (Fall-Winter 1970): 149-154 ((7))

780 HAMILTON, David: The recordings of Copland's music in High Fidelity, XX/11 (November 1970): 64-72, 116 ((-))

781 List of recordings in SMITH, Julia: Aaron Copland: his work and contribution to American music. [1st ed.] New York: Dutton, 1955: [312]-318 ((-))

COPPOLA, PIERO, 1888-1971

782 HOLMES, William A.: A Piero Coppola discography in Le Grand Baton, X/3-4 (September-December 1973): 49-76 ((3, 6, 7))

CORNELIUS, PETER, 1824-1874

783 Peter Cornelius. [Copenhagen]: Nationmuseet, 1965. 20 pp. (Det Nationale Diskotek Katalog; 4) ((3, 4, 5))

784 ZACHS, Jean: The records in Record News, II/5 (January 1958): 160-164 ((5)); Record News, II/6 (February 1958): 203-206

CORTIS, ANTONIO

785 LÉON, J. A., and J. DENNIS: Antonio Cortis discography in Record Collector, XX/3 (October 1971): 63-69 ((3, 5, 6, 7))

CORTOT, ALFRED, 1877-1962

786 Alfred Cortot e i suoi dischi in Musica e Dischi, XVIII (No. 193, July 1962): 45 ((-))

787 CLOUGH, F. F., and G. J. CUMING: A Cortot diskography in Gramophone Record Review, No. 50 (December 1957): 135-136 ((-))

788 Sämtliche Aufnahmen von Alfred Cortot in "Les gravures illustres" in fono forum 1963 (No. 3, March): 92 ((-))

COTOGNI, ANTONIO

789 CELLETTI, Rodolfo: Discografia di Antonio Cotogni in Musica e Dischi, XIII (No. 131, July 1957): 51 ((7))

COUPERIN, FRANÇOIS, 1668-1733

790 Recordings of François Couperin in CAUCHIE, Maurice: Thematic index of the works of François Couperin. Monaco: Lyrebird Press, [c1949]: 71-[77] ((-))

791 Discographie in CHARLIER, Henri: François Couperin. Lyon: Éditions et impr. du Sud-Est, 1965: 121 (Nos amis les musiciens) ((-))

792 Les disques in CITRON, Pierre: Couperin. [Bourges?]: Éditions du Seuil, [1956]: 191 (Solfèges; 1) ((-))

793 CLOUGH, F. F. and G. J. CUMING: Recordings of François Couperin's works in BRUNOLD, Paul: François Couperin. Monaco: Lyrebird Press, [c1949]: 71-[77] ((-))

794 A Couperin discography in Hi Fi Stereo Review, XXI/5 (November 1968): 64 ((-))

795 HALBREICH, Harry: Discographie critique in Harmonie, No. 40 (October 1968): 28-31 ((-))

796 Gramophone records of works by Couperin in MELLERS, Wilfrid: François Couperin and the French classical tradition. London: D. Dobson, [1950]: 390-394 ((-))

COWELL, HENRY, 1897-1965

797 The music of Cowell: a selective discography in Stereo Review, XXXIII/6 (December 1974): 80 ((-))

CRABBÉ, ARMAND, 1883-1947

798 [[MORAN, W. R.: Armand Crabbé in Record News, IV/1 (September 1959)]]

799 [[MORAN, W. R.: [Discography] in Record News, IV/2 (October 1959); Addenda: Record News, IV/3 (November 1959)]]

CRASS, FRANZ

800 SCHNEIDER, Günter: Aus der Diskografie in fono forum 1962 (No. 3, March): 27 ((-))

CRESPIN, RÉGINE

801 HAMON, Jean: Discographie in Diapason, No. 100 (October 1965): 32 ((-))

CROIZA, CLAIRE

802 SAUL, Patrick: Records of Claire Croiza in British Institute of Recorded Sound Bulletin, No. 1 (Summer 1956): 26-29 ((-))

CROOKS, RICHARD, 1900-1972

803 MORGAN, Charles I.: Discography in
Record Collector, XII/6 (May 1959):
135-142 ((1, 3, 6, 7)); Addenda: Record
Collector, XII/10-11 (December 1959-
January 1960): 260-261 ((-))

804 [[MORGAN, Charles I.: [Discography]
in Record Advertiser, II/6 (September-
October 1972): 8-12; III/1 (November-
December 1972): 2-16; III/2 (January-
February 1973): 17]]

805 SHELDON, Scott: Richard Crooks discography in Record News, II/9 (May
1958): 310-320 ((-))

CROTCH, WILLIAM, 1775-1847

806 Discography in RENNERT, Jonathan:
William Crotch (1775-1847): composer,
artist, teacher. Lavenham, [Eng.]: T.
Dalton, 1975: 111 ((-))

CULP, JULIA, 1880-1970

807 PORTE, J. F.: Julia Culp: a great
lieder singer in Gramophone, V/4
(September 1927): 164-165 ((-))

808 [[RIEMENS, L.: Julia Culp in Record
Collector, II/7 (July 1947)]]

CURTIS-VERNA, MARY

809 [[Mary Curtis-Verna in Record Collector, II/6 (February 1948)]]

CURZON, CLIFFORD, 1907-

810 CLOUGH, F. F., and G. J. CUMING,
Discography in Audio and Record Review, III/11 (July 1964): 14 ((-))

811 HAUSSWALD, Günter: Diskographie in
Musica, XXIII/4 (July-August 1969):
391 ((-))

CZECH QUARTET
See also listing for SUK, JOSEF.
Enregistrements historiques réalisés
par le Quatuor Tchéque; Historic gramophone recordings made by the Czech
Quartet; Historické gramofonové
snímky Ceského kvarteta

812 Gramofonové nahrávky Ceského
Kvarteta deskách in Kńiha, Prague:
Josef Suk; výběrová bibliografie. Sest.
Ratibor BUDIŠ. Odpovědný redaktor:
Ratibor Budiš a Feodor POKORNÝ.
Praha: Kńiha, 1965: 81-87 ((-))

CZIFFRA, GYÖRGY, 1921-

813 COSSÉ, Peter: György Cziffra: voll-
ständiges Schallplattenverzeichnis in
fono forum 1975 (No. 1, January): 24
((-))

D'ALBERT, EUGEN
See ALBERT, EUGEN D'

DALLAPICCOLA, LUIGI, 1904-1975

814 Catalogue des oeuvres; discographie
in Musique en jeu, No. 21 (November
1975): [77]-79 ((-))

815 Discografia di Luigi Dallapiccola in
Quaderni della Rassegna Musicale 1965
(No. 2): [155]-156 ((-))

816 Luigi-Dallapiccola Diskographie in
Revue Musicale Suisse, CXV/4 (July-
August 1975): 212 ((-))

DAL MONTE, TOTI
See MONTE, TOTI DAL

DAMASE, JEAN-MICHEL, 1928-

817 Discographie in Courrier Musical de
France, No. 18 (1967): 117 ((-))

DA MOTTA, JOSE VIANNA, 1868-1948

818 HOWARD, Geoffrey: Jose Vianna da
Motta's Pathé recordings in 78 RPM,
No. 2: 6 ((7))

D'ANDRADE, FRANCISCO, 1859-1921

819 WILHELM, Paul: Francisco D'Andrade
in Record News, III/7 (March 1959):
233-237 ((-))

DANIEL-LESUR, 1908-

820 Discographie in Courrier Musical de
France, No. 7 (1964): 183 ((-))

DANISH STATE RADIO SYMPHONY ORCHES-
TRA

821 POTTS, J. E.: Records by the Danish
State Radio Symphony Orchestra in
Disc, II/8 (Autumn 1948): 164 ((-))

DARCLÉE, HARICLEA

822 CELLETTI, Rodolfo: Hariclea Darclée
in Musica e Dischi, VIII (No. 74, November 1952): 10 bis ((5))

DAVIES, BEN, 1854-1943

823 [[Ben Davies—the records in Record
Advertiser, No. 5 (July-August 1971):
4-9]]

DAVIES, FRANCES
See ALDA, FRANCES

DAVIES, TUDOR

824 [[The Tudor Davies discography in
Record Advertiser, II/4 (May-June
1972): 19-21; II/5 (July-August 1972):
1-9; IV/1 (November-December 1973)]]

DAVIS, COLIN, 1927-

825 Colin Davis on record—a listing of
some available LPs in Audio and Record Review, VIII/10 (June 1968): 431
((-))

826 Discographie in Diapason, No. 148
(June 1970): 5 ((-))

827 Recommended records in Audio and
Record Review (March 1969): 174-175
((-))

828 VINCENT-MALETTRA, Françoise:
Discographie Berlioz—Colin Davis in
Diapason, No. 135 (April 1969): 7 ((-))

829 WALKER, Malcolm: Discography in
BLYTH, Alan: Colin Davis. London:
Allan, 1973: 60-64 ((7))

830 WALKER, Malcolm: Discography in
BLYTH, Alan: Colin Davis. New York:
Drake Publishers, [1973]: 60-64 ((7))

DEBUSSY, CLAUDE, 1862-1918

831 Vaerkfortegnelse med diskografi in
BALZER, Jürgen: Claude Debussy: en
kritisk studie. København: Jespersen
og Pio, 1949: 196-205 ((-))

832 Discographie in BARRAQUÉ, Jean:
Debussy. [Paris]: Éditions du Seuil,
[1962]: 183-189 (Solfèges; 22) ((-))

833 COBB, Margaret G.: Discographie de
l'oeuvre de Claude Debussy. Genève:
Minkoff, 1975. 127 pp. ((5))

834 Schallplattenverzeichnis in DANCKERT,
Werner: Claude Debussy. Berlin: W. de
Gruyter, 1950: 217 ((-))

835 Discographie sélective de Claude
Debussy in Courrier Musical de
France, No. 24 (1968): 235 ((-))

836 Diskografie in fono forum 1962 (No. 8,
August): 13 ((-))

837 Discographie in Duran et Cie, Paris:
Catalogue de l'oeuvre de Claude

Debussy. Paris: Durand, c1962:
[113]-123 ((-))

838 FISHER and BRITZIUS: Recorded
music of Debussy in Gramophone,
III/12 (May 1926): 563 ((-))

839 FRANKENSTEIN, Alfred: Debussy:
orchestral and vocal music in High
Fidelity, VIII/1 (January 1958): 79-
86 ((-))

840 GOLDSMITH, Harris: Debussy on
microgroove in High Fidelity, XII/9
(September 1962): 66-69, 120-129 ((-))

841 Catalogue analytique des oeuvres de
Claude Debussy et discographie in
GOLÉA, Antoine: Claude Debussy:
l'homme et son oeuvre, liste...
discographie.... [Paris]: P. Seghers,
1965: [173]-184 (Musiciens de tous les
temps; 23) ((-))

842 HALBREICH, Harry: Catalogue
commenté et discographie critique
in Debussy. Paris: Réalités
Hachette, 1972: 235-[258] ((-))

843 HALBREICH, Harry: Une discotheque
Debussy in Harmonie, No. 34 (February
1968): 26-31 ((-))

844 HART, Philip: Debussy on records in
Music Magazine, CLXIV/7 (August
1962): 37 ((-))

845 Recordings of Debussy's works in
HARVEY, Harry B.: Claude of France:
the story of Debussy. New York: Allen,
Towne & Heath, [1948]: 177-184 ((-))

846 Discographie abrégée des oeuvres de
Debussy in INGHELBRECHT, Ger-
maine: Claude Debussy, [par] Ger-
maine et D. E. INGHELBRECHT.
[Paris]: Costard, [1953]: [293]-301
(Musiciens d'hier et d'aujourd'hui; 1)
((-))

847 HOLCMAN, Jan: Debussy on disc in
Saturday Review (August 25, 1962): 34-
35 ((-))

848 LEYDI, R.: Discografia delle opere di
Claude Debussy in L'Approdo Musicale,
II/7-8 (July-September 1959): 160-170
((-))

849 Discografia in MALIPIERO, Riccardo:
Debussy. [2. ed. rev.] [Brescia]: La
Scuola, [1959]: 126 (Note: Includes no
record numbers) ((-))

850 [[MOLES, E.: [Discography] in Discofilia (January-February 1957): 5]]

Works, Chamber Music

851 GOLDSMITH, Harris: Debussy on
microgroove. Part 2: Chamber music
in High Fidelity, XII/10 (October 1962):
98-99 ((-))

Works, Piano

852 Les integrales du piano de Debussy in
     Harmonie, No. 34 (February 1968): 36-
     39 ((-))

Works, Vocal

853 MORSE, Peter: Debussy and Ravel
     vocal music. Utica, NY: Weber, 1973:
     38 pp. (Discography series; 11) ((5))

854 OSBORNE, Conrad L.: Debussy on
     microgroove. Part 3: Vocal music in
     High Fidelity, XII/11 (November 1962):
     84-90, 144, 149 ((-))

Le Martyre de Saint Sebastien

855 Discographie in Revue Musicale, No.
     234 (1957): 81 ((-))

Pelléas et Mélisande

856 APRAHAMIAN, Felix: Pelléas et
     Mélisande in Opera, XX/12 (Decem-
     ber 1969): 1008-1016 (Opera on the
     gramophone; 26) ((-))

DECCA RECORDS
     See listings for FERRIER, KATHLEEN—
     Records made by Kathleen Ferrier for
     the Decca Record Company and
     FERRIER, KATHLEEN—Records made
     for the Decca Record Company; WIL-
     SON, STEUART

DEGENHARDT, FRANZ JOSEF, 1931-

857 Discographie in ARNOLD, Heinz
     Ludwig: Franz Josef Degenhardt:
     politische Lieder 1964-1972. München:
     R. Boorberg, c1972: 159-166 ((-))

DE GOGORZA, EMILIO EDUARDO
     See GOGORZA, EMILIO EDUARDO DE

DE KLERK, ALBERT

858 SPINGEL, Hans Otto: Diskografie in
     fono forum 1962 (No. 12, December):
     16 ((-))

DELALANDE, MICHEL RICHARD
     See LALANDE, MICHEL RICHARD DE

DE LARA, ADELINA, 1872-1961

859 List of recordings by Adelina de Lara
     in DE LARA, Adelina: Finale. [London]
     Burke, [1955]: 219-220 ((-))

860 List of recordings by Adelina de Lara
     in DE LARA, Adelina: Finale. St. Clair
     Shores, MI: Scholarly Press, 1972: 219-
     220; Note: Reprint of the 1955 ed. ((-))

861 Recordings in BBC Recorded Pro-
     grammes Permanent Library of
     Adelina de Lara in DE LARA, Adelina:
     Finale. [London]: Burke, [1955]: 221-
     222 ((1))

862 Recordings in BBC Recorded Pro-
     grammes Permanent Library of
     Adelina de Lara in DE LARA, Adelina:
     Finale. St. Clair Shores, MI: Scholarly
     Press, 1972: 221-222; Note: Reprint of
     the 1955 ed. ((1))

DELIUS, FREDERICK, 1862-1934

863 Gramophone recordings of Delius's
     works in HUTCHINGS, Arthur: Delius.
     London: Macmillan, 1948: 192-193
     ((-))

864 MAYES, Stanley H.: Frederick Delius,
     a man of genius; a discography in Le
     Grand Baton, II/1 (January-March
     1965): 3-15 ((-))

865 UPTON, Stuart: Frederick Delius: a
     discography, compiled by Stuart Upton
     & Malcolm WALKER. [Edgware,
     Middlesex: Delius Society, 1969]: 42 pp.
     ((1, 3, 6, 7)); Additions and corrections
     in Delius Society Newsletter, No. 24
     (September 1969); No. 26 (Winter 1970):
     15-18 ((1, 3, 6, 7)); No. 30 (Spring
     1971): 15-16 ((1, 3, 6, 7))

866 WALKER, Malcolm: Beecham/Delius
     discography in BEECHAM, Thomas, Sir:
     Frederick Delius. [Revised ed.] [Lon-
     don]: Severn House, 1975: [231]-[243]
     ((3, 6, 7))

DELLA CASA, LISA

867 Diskographie in Collegium Musicum
     1973 (No. 1-2): 10 ((-))

DELLER, ALFRED, 1912-

868 Discography in HARDWICK, Michael:
     Alfred Deller: a singularity of voice,
     by Michael and Mollie HARDWICK,
     with a foreword by Sir Michael
     TIPPETT. London: Cassell, 1968: 181-
     190 ((-))

869 Discography in HARDWICK, Michael:
     Alfred Deller: a singularity of voice,
     by Michael and Mollie HARDWICK,
     with a foreword by Sir Michael Tippett.
     New York: F. A. Praeger, [1969,
     c1968]: 181-190 ((-))

DEL MONACO, MARIO
See MONACO, MARIO DEL

DELNA, MARIE, 1875-1932

870 [[[Discography] in Record News, VI/5
(February 1961)]]

871 [[Marie Delna in Record Collector,
VI/5 (February 1951)]]

DE LOS ANGELES, VICTORIA
See ANGELES, VICTORIA DE LOS

DE LUCA, GIUSEPPE, 1876-1952

872 [[FAVIA-ARTSAY, Aida: Giuseppe de
Luca in Record Collector, V/ (March
1950): 56-58]]; Addenda: Record
Collector, VI/7 (July 1951): 151-153
((-))

873 [[FAVIA-ARTSAY, Aida: The speeds
of De Luca's acoustical Victor[s] in
Hobbies, XLIX (February 1955): 24-
25]]

874 VEGETO, Raffaele: Discografia in
Musica e Dischi, XI (No. 111, November 1955): 42 ((7)); Addenda: Musica
e Dischi, XIII (No. 128, April 1957): 52
((-))

DE LUCIA, FERNANDO

875 [[[Discografia] in Musica e Dischi, XI
(No. 103 bis, April 1955)]]

876 [WILLIAMS, Clifford]: Discography in
Record Collector, XI/6 (June 1957):
131-140 ((7))

DE MURO, BERNARDO

877 [[Discography in Gramophone, No. 173
(October 1937)]]

878 LEÓN, J. A.: Bernardo de Muro-dis-
cography in Record Collector, XVIII/
3 (November 1968): 62-65 ((3, 6, 7));
Addenda: Record Collector, XVIII/11-
12 (December 1969): 274; XIX/3-4
(June 1970): 92-95; XX/6-7: 166

DE MURO LOMANTO, ENZO, 1902-1952

879 Discografia (Saggio) in GIOVINE,
Alfredo: (Tenore) Enzo De Muro
Lomanto. Bari: [s.n.], 1970: 20 (Biblioteca dell'Archivio delle tradizioni
popolari baresi. Civiltà musicale
pugliese) ((-))

DEMUTH, LEOPOLD

880 NORTON-WELSH, Christopher: Leopold
Demuth, 1861-1910 in Record Collector,
XXI/11-12 (March 1974): 262-268
((3, 7))

DE NEGRI, GIOVANNI BATTISTA

881 CELLETTI, Rodolfo: [Discography]
in Gramophone, No. 351 (August 1952):
52; [From Musica e dischi, April 1952]
((5))

882 CELLETTI, Rodolfo: Giovanni Battista
de Negri in Musica e Dischi, VIII (No.
67, April 1952): 21 ((5))

883 CELLETTI, Rodolfo: The records in
Record News, III/2 (October 1958): 65;
[From Musica e Dischi] ((5))

DE RESZKE, EDOUARD
See RESZKE, EDOUARD DE

DERMOTA, ANTON

884 [[Discography of A. Dermota in
Vienna. Nationalbibliothek. Musik-
sammlung: Sammlung Anton Dermota:
Sonderausstellung, 11. Juni-31. Aug.
[Abfassung des Katalogtextes; Agnes
Ziffer]. [Wien: Österr. Nationalbiblio-
thek, 1971]: 30]]

DE SABATA, VICTOR, 1892-1967

885 CLOUGH, F. F., and G. J. CUMING:
Victor de Sabata; diskography in
Gramophone Record Review, No. 64
(February 1958): 269 ((-))

886 VINCENTINI, Mario: Discografia di
Victor de Sabata in Discoteca alta
Fedelta, No. 153 (September 1975):
[97] ((-))

887 WEIHER-WAEGE, H.: Diskografie in
fono forum 1962 (No. 5, May): 14 ((-))

DESARZENS, VICTOR

888 Enregistrements de disques in
Hommage à Victor Desarzens.
Lausanne: Éditions L'Age d'homme,
[1973]: 44-46 ((-))

DÉSORMIÈRE, ROGER, 1898-1963

889 Principaux registrements in MAYER,
Denise: Roger Désormière et son
temps: textes en hommage, réunis par
Denise Mayer et Pierre SOUVTCHIN-
SKY. Monaco: Éditions du Rocher,
[1966]: 174-185 (Domaine musical)
((1, 7))

DESSAU, PAUL, 1894-

890 Diskographie in Medium Schallplatte,
No. 12 (No. 3, 1969): 7 ((–))

891 Discographie in HENNENBERG, Fritz:
Paul Dessau. Leipzig: VEB Deutscher
Verlag für Musik, 1965: 153-155 ((–))

892 Diskographie in Paul Dessau aus
Gesprächen. Leipzig: VEB Deutscher
Verlag für Musik, 1974: 264-[267] ((–))

DESTINN, EMMY, 1878-1930

893 DENNIS, J.: Emmy Destinn discography in Record Collector, XX/1-2 (July
1971): 29-47 ((3, 4, 5, 6, 7)); Addenda:
Record Collector, XX/4 (December
1971): 93-94 ((–))

894 HARVEY, H. Hugh: List of records in
Gramophone, No. 190 (March 1939):
448-451 ((3, 7)); Addenda: Gramophone,
No. 192 (May 1939): 545 ((–))

895 MEADMORE, W. S.: Emmy Destinn in
Gramophone, No. 83 (April 1930): 493-
494 ((–)); Addenda: Gramophone, No.
88 (September 1930): 194 ((–))

896 Discografie in POSPÍŠIL, Miloslav:
Veliké srdce: Život a umění Emy
Destinnové. 1. vyd. Praha: Supra-
phon, t.ST 4, 1974: 158-172 ((3, 6, 7))

897 SCHUBERT, Antonín: Přehled gramofonových nahrávek Demy Destinnové in
HOLZKNECHT, Vaclav: Ema Destin-
nová: Ve slovech i obrazech. 1. vyd.
Praha: Panton, t. PG 3, 1972: 283-297
((3))

DEUTSCHE GRAMMOPHON RECORDS
See listings for FOLDES, ANDOR.
Diskographie (Auswahl); KEMPFF,
WILHELM. Discographie de Wilhelm
Kempff; MAAZEL, LORIN. Diskogra-
phie; SCHLUSNUS, HEINRICH;
SCHNEIDERHAN, WOLFGANG

DICKIE, MURRAY

898 ROSS, A. G.: Murray Dickie in Record
News, I/7 (March 1957): 261-262 ((–))

DIDUR, ADAMO, 1874-1946

899 DENNIS, J.: Didur discography in
Record Collector, XVI/1 (July 1964):
21-23 ((3, 5, 6, 7))

DI GIOVANNI, EDOARDO
See JOHNSON, EDWARD

DIKSHITAR, MUTHUSWAMY, 1776-1835

900 A selective discography of Muttuswami
Dikshitar's works in Muttuswami
Dikshitar. 1st ed. Bombay: National
Centre for the Performing Arts, 1975:
51-54 ((–))

DISTLER, HUGO, 1908-1942

901 SCHWINGER, Wolfram: Diskografie in
fono forum 1963 (No. 2, February): 51
((–))

DIXON, DEAN, 1915-1976

902 SCHAEFER, Hans Joachim: Diskographie in Musica, XXIV/2 (March-April
1970): 204 ((–))

DOHNÁNYI, ENRÖ, 1877-1960

903 Discography of the works of Ernst von
Dohnanyi in RUETH, Marion Ursula:
The Tallahassee years of Ernst von
Dohnányi. Tallahassee: Robert Manning
Strozier Memorial Library, Florida
State University, 1962: 246-257 ((5))

904 Lemezjegyzék in VÁZSONYI, Bálint:
Dohnányi Erno. Budapest: Zenemükiado,
1971: 241-243 ((–))

DONALDA, PAULINE, 1882-1970

905 Discography in BROTMAN, Ruth C.:
Pauline Donalda: the life and career of
a Canadian prima donna. Montreal:
Eagle Pub., 1975: 112 ((3, 7))

906 [[GLASSFORD, A. A.: Pauline Donalda
in Record Collector, II/9 (September
1947)]]

907 [KNIGHT, Arthur E.]: The Donalda
records in Record Collector, X/12
(November 1956): 273-274 ((3, 7))

DONIZETTI, GAETANO, 1797-1848

Don Pasquale

908 ROSENTHAL, Harold: Don Pasquale in
Opera, XXIV/3 (March 1973): 203-215
(Opera on the gramophone; 34) ((–))

Lucia di Lammermoor

909 DUNLOP, Lionel: Lucia di Lammermoor in Opera, X/2 (February 1959):
86-92 (Opera on the gramophone; 8)
((–))

Lucia di Lammermoor.
Verranno a te sull' aure

910 VEGETO, Raffaele: Nota discografica in
Discoteca, No. 51 (June 1965): 36-37
((-))

Lucrezia Borgia

911 RICHARDS, John B.: Lucrezia Borgia:
the Brindisi, Il segreto per esser felice
(Orsini's Ballata) in Record Collector,
XX/11-12 (December 1972): 270-275
((7))

Lucrezia Borgia.
Il segreto per esser felice

912 VEGETO, Raffaele: Nota discografica
in Discoteca, No. 48 (March 1965): 40
((-))

DORATI, ANTAL, 1908-

913 ASHMAN, Mike: [Discography] in
Records and Recording, XVIII/2 (November 1974): 14-16, 97 ((-)); Supplement in Records and Recording
XVIII/5 (February 1975): 8 ((-))

914 CLOUGH, F. F., and G. J. CUMING: A
Dorati discography in Gramophone
Record Review, No. 79 (May 1960): 391,
431-432 ((-))

915 CLOUGH, F. F., and G. J. CUMING: An
Antal Dorati discography in Audio and
Record Review, II/4 (December 1962):
19-22 ((-))

916 HELM, Everett: Diskografie Antal
Dorati (Auswahl) in fono forum 1965
(No. 2, February): 58 ((-))

917 PFOB, Karl: Antal Dorati in fono
forum 1960 (No. 11, November): 14
((-))

DOUATTE, ROLAND

918 Roland Douatte a enregistré avec les
soloistes et l'orchestre du Collegium
Musicum de Paris in Harmonie, No.
26 (April 1967): 29 ((-))

DOUBLE-BASS MUSIC

919 Bass recordings, orchestral in
ELGAR, Raymond: Introduction to
the double bass. [1st ed.] Sussex:
[Elgar], 1960: 123-124 ((-))

DREYFUS, HUGUETTE

920 Diskographie in Phonoprisma (May-
June 1966): 92 ((-))

DROLC-QUARTET

921 SCHWINGER, Wolfram: Aus der
Diskografie in fono forum 1961 (No.
8, August): 27 ((-))

DRZEWIECKI, ZBIGNIEW, 1890-1971

922 Dyskografia in KISIELEWSKI, Stefan:
Zbigniew Drzewiecki. [Wyd. 1.
Kraków]: Polskie Wydawn. Muzyczne,
1973: 63 ((-))

DUBOIS, PIERRE-MAX, 1930-

923 Discographie in Courrier Musical de
France, No. 22 (1968): 148 ((-))

DUKAS, PAUL, 1865-1935

924 Discographie in Courrier Musical de
France, No. 8 (1964): 264 ((-))

925 ROY, Jean: Discographie in Diapason,
No. 100 (October 1965): 37 ((-))

DUMITRESCU, GHEORGHE

926 DRĀGONI, Constantin V.: Disques in
Muzica, XX/7 (July 1970): 47 ((-))

DUMITRESCU, ION

927 DRĀGONI, V.: Disques in Muzica,
XX/5 (May 1970): 47 ((-))

DUNNAEVSKIĬ, ISAAK OSIPOVICH, 1900-
1955

928 [Discography] in PERSON, David
Mikhaĭlovich: I.O. Dynaievskiĭ. Noto-
bibliogr. spravochnik. Sost. D.M.
Person. Moskva: Sov. kompositor,
1971: 199-[206] ((-))

DUPARC, HENRI, 1848-1933

929 Discographie in Courrier Musical de
France, No. 18 (1967): 120 ((-))

930 HENRY-JACQUES: Henri Duparc; une
discographie in Disques, No. 3 (March
15, 1948): 90 ((-))

Songs

931 List of gramophone recordings in
NORTHCOTE, Sydney: The songs of
Henri Duparc. London: D. Dobson,
[1949]: 120-122 ((-))

DUPRÉ, MARCEL, 1886-1971

932 Reconstruction and recordings of
improvisations by Marcel Dupré in

DUPRÉ, Marcel: Recollections. Melville, NY: Belwin-Mills Pub. Corp., c1975: 148-149 ((-))

933 Recordings by Dupré in DUPRÉ, Marcel: Recollections. Melville, NY: Belwin-Mills Pub. Corp., c1975: 150-158 ((-))

DUREY, LOUIS, 1888-

934 Discographie in Courrier Musical de France, No. 8 (1964): 268 ((-))

935 Discographie in ROBERT, Frédéric: Louis Durey: l'ainé des six. Paris: Les Éditeurs français réunis, 1968: [219]-220 ((-))

DURUFLÉ, MAURICE, 1902-

936 Discographie in Courrier Musicale de France, No. 29 (1970): 52 ((-))

DUTILLEUX, HENRI, 1916-

937 Discographie in Diapason, No. 102 (December 1965): 38 ((-))

DVOŘÁK, ANTONÍN, 1841-1904
See also listing for SMETANA, BEDŘICH, 1824-1884. Discothek in Boese, Helmut: Zwei Urmusikanten: Smetana, Dvořak

938 La liste des oeuvres d'Antonín Dvořák [includes discographies] in BURGHAUSER, Jarmil: Antonín Dvořák. Praha: Státni hudební vydavatelství, 1966: 63-68 ((-))

939 List of works and list of recordings in BURGHAUSER, Jarmil: Antonín Dvořák. Praha: Státni hudební vydavatelství, 1967: 57-78 ((-))

940 DARRELL, R. D.: Dvořák's recorded works in Phonograph Monthly Review, III/8 (May 1929): 259 ((-))

941 Discographie in ERISMANN, Guy: Antonin Dvořak: l'homme et son oeuvre..., catalogue des oeuvres, discographie.... Paris: Seghers, 1966: [186]-190 (Musiciens de tous les temps; 29) ((-))

942 Recommended recordings of Dvořák's works in FLES, Barthold: Slavonic rhapsody. New York: Allen, Towne and Heath, 1948: 215-218 ((-))

943 Výbeiz čes kosloven ských gramofonových desek od. r. 1960 in MARIÁNKOVÁ, Jana: Antonín Dvořák: 8.9.1841-1.5.1904. Kladno: Kraj. knihovna, 1974: 50-51 (Edice KK Kladno. Bibliografie. Malá řada; 39) ((-))

944 SCHONBERG, Harold C.: A Dvořak discography in High Fidelity, V/10 (December 1955): 101-110 ((-))

945 Dvořáks Werke auf Supraphon Langspielplatten 33 1/3 in ŠOUREK, Otakar: Antonín Dvořák: sein Leben und sein Werk. Praha: Artis, [1953]: 211-[212] ((-))

946 SVOBODA, Otakar: Seznam gramofonových nahrávek skladeb Antonína Dvořáka in BURGHAUSER, Jarmil: Antonín Dvořák: thematický katalog, bibliografie, přehled života a díla. [1. vyd.] Praha: Státní nakl. krásné literatury, hudby a umění, 1966: [687]-785 ((-))

947 VOJAN, J. E. S.: Dvořak recordings in Phonograph Monthly Review, I/8 (May 1927): 332-333 ((-))

Symphony, No. 9, Op. 95, E Minor

948 [[BLAUKOPF, K.: Eine vergleichende Discographie in Phono, VIII/3]]

EMI RECORDS
See listing for BARBIROLLI, SIR JOHN. Reid, Charles: John Barbirolli

EAMES, EMMA, 1865-1952

949 MIGLIORINI, Louis: The records in Record Collector, VIII/4 (April 1953): inside cover, 79-96 ((1, 3, 4)); Addenda: Record Collector, VIII/6 (June 1953): 139-142 ((-))

950 SMOLIAN, Steven: Emma Eames—a discography in American Record Guide, XXIX/3 (November 1962): 215-217 ((3, 4, 6, 7))

EASTON, FLORENCE, 1884-1955

951 STRATTON, John: Florence Easton discography in Record News, IV/10 (June 1960): 373-377 ((1, 3)); Addenda: Record News, V/4 (December 1960): 141-142

952 STRATTON, John: The recordings of Florence Easton in Record Collector, XXI/9-10 (January 1974): 221-230 ((1, 3, 6, 7))

953 STRATTON, John: The recordings of Florence Easton; Addenda: Record Collector, XXI/11-12 (March 1974): 286 ((1, 3, 6, 7))

EDISON RECORDS
See listings for HEMPEL, FRIEDA. Wile, Raymond; KASCHMANN, GIUSEPPE. Wile, Raymond; MARTI-

NELLI, GIOVANNI. Wile, Raymond;
MUZIO, CLAUDIA. Wile, Raymond R.;
WALKER, EDYTH. Wile, Raymond

EDVINA, MARIE LOUISE

954 HARVEY, H. Hugh: Marie Louise
Edvina—records in Gramophone, No.
349 (June 1952): 7 ((7))

EGK, WERNER, 1901-

955 Schallplatten in KRAUSE, Ernst:
Werner Egk: Oper und Ballett.
Wilhelmshaven: Heinrichshofen's
Verlag, 1971: 222 ((5))

EISLER, HANNS, 1898-1962

956 Schallplattenverzeichnis in BROCK-
HAUS, Heinz Alfred: Hanns Eisler.
Leipzig: Breitkopf & Härtel, 1961:
187-[189] (Musikbücherei für Jeder-
mann; 10) ((-))

957 Schallplatten (Langspielplatten) mit
Werken von Hanns Eisler in KLEMM,
Eberhardt: Hanns Eisler: 1898-1962.
Berlin: Kulturbund der DDR, 1973:
102-111 ((-))

958 KOCH, G. R.: Eisler—Diskographie-
Bibliographie in Hi Fi Stereophonie,
XI/9 (September 1972): 800 ((-))

959 MARKOWSKI, Liesel: Diskographie in
Medium Schallplatte, No. 7 (No. 2,
1968): 5-6 ((-))

960 NIERMANN, Franz: Kommentierte
Diskographie Hanns Eisler in Hanns
Eisler. 1. - 4. Tsd. Berlin: Argument-
Verlag, 1975: 302-327 (Argument-
Sonderbände; 5) ((-))

961 Verzeichnis der Komponisitimen von
Hanns Eisler in Deutschen Schall-
plattenproduktionen in NOTOWICZ,
Nathan: Hanns Eisler: Quellennach-
weise. Leipzig: Deutscher Verlag für
Musik, [1966]: 141-173 ((-))

962 Das musikalische Werk Hanns Eislers
in Schallplattenaufnahmen in TISCH-
MEYER, Margot: Hanns Eisler:
[Anlässlich des 75. Geburtstages von
Hanns Eisler am 6. Juli 1973] Berlin:
Berliner Stadtbibliothek, 1973: 20-27
(Bibliographische Kalenderblätter.
Sonderblatt; 38) ((-))

ELECTROLA RECORDS
See listings for GÉCZY, BARNABÁS
VON; GEDDA, NICOLAI. Diskographie

ELECTRONIC MUSIC
See also listing for MUSIC, EXPERI-
MENTAL. Discographie in Prieberg,
Fred K.: Musica ex machina

963 Discography in APPLETON, Jon H.:
The development and practice of electronic music. Editors: Jon H. Appleton, Ronald C. PERERA. Englewood
Cliffs, NJ: Prentice-Hall, 1975: 344-
366 ((-))

964 DAVIES, Hugh: A discography of electronic music and musique concrète in
Recorded Sound, No. 14 (April 1964):
205-224 ((1, 4)); Supplement in Recorded Sound, No. 22-23 (April-July
1966): 69-78 ((1, 4))

965 Discography/Discographie in DAVIES,
Hugh: Repertoire international des
musiques electroacoustics. International electronic music catalog. A co-
operative publication of le Groupe de
recherches musicales de l'O. R. T. F.,
Paris, and the Independent Electronic
Music Center, New York. Cambridge,
MA: distributed by MIT Press, 1968:
242-275 ((-))

966 Discography/discographie in Electronic
Music Review, No. 2-3 (April-July
1967): 242-275 ((1))

967 Gramophone records on electronic
music produced at the Institute of
Sonology—Utrecht State University
in Sonorum Speculum, No. 52 (1973):
23 ((-))

968 KRELLMANN, Hanspeter: Elektron-
ische Musik und Schallplatte in Musica,
XXIII/5 (September-October 1969): 450
((-))

969 Suggestions for listening in ORAM,
Daphne: An individual note: of music,
sound, and electronics. London:
Galliard Ltd., 1972: 129-136 (A Galliard
Paperback) ((-))

970 Suggestions for listening in ORAM,
Daphne: An individual note: of music,
sound, and electronics. New York:
Galaxy Music Corporation, 1972: 129-
136 ((-))

971 Discography in RUSSCOL, Herbert: The
liberation of sound: an introduction to
electronic music. Englewood Cliffs,
NJ: Prentice-Hall, 1972: 243-264 ((-))

972 Discography in SCHWARTZ, Elliott:
Electronic music: a listener's guide.
New York: Praeger Publishers [1973]:
293-298 ((-))

973 Discography in SCHWARTZ, Elliott:
Electronic music: a listener's guide.
Rev. ed. New York: Praeger, [1975]:
293-298 ((-))

Swedish

974 [Discographic notes included in]
"Works" in JOHNSON, Bengt Emil:
Electronic music in Sweden, by Bengt
Emil Johnson & Knut WIGGEN.
Stockholm: STIM (Tegnérlunden 3),
1972: 53-64 ((1))

ELGAR, EDWARD WILLIAM, SIR, 1857-1934

975 ÅHLÉN, Carl-Gunnar: Sir Edward
Elgar, Bart., OM, K. C. V. O. (1857-
1934 in Musik Revy, XXVIII/6 (1973):
399-402 (Grammofonens veteraner; 8)
((7))

976 Works by Elgar in English gramophone
catalogue at the time of writing in
ANDERSON, William Robert: Introduction to the music of Elgar. London: D.
Dobson, [1949]: [69-70]; [Note: No record numbers] ((-))

977 [[[Discography] in British Institute of
Recorded Sound Bulletin, No. 5 (Summer 1957)]] [as conductor]

978 Recordings conducted by Elgar in
KENNEDY, Michael: Portrait of Elgar.
London, New York, [etc.]: Oxford Uni-
versity Press, 1968: 302-305 ((7))

979 Gramophone records of Elgar's works
in MAINE, Basil: Elgar: his life and
works. London: G. Bell & sons, ltd.,
1933: v. 2, 315-317 ((-))

980 Gramophone records of Elgar's works
in MAINE, Basil: Elgar: his life and
works. Bath: Chivers, 1973: v. 2, 315-
317; Reprint of the 1933 ed. ((-))

981 MOORE, Jerrold N.: An Elgar discography. [London]: British Institute of
Recorded Sound, [196-?, c1963]: iv,
48 pp. [Note: Reprinted from Recorded
Sound] ((3, 4, 6, 7))

982 MOORE, Jerrold N.: An Elgar discography in Recorded Sound, II/9 (January
1963): 7-17 ((-)); Elgar's recording
sessions in Recorded Sound, II/9 (January 1963): 18-42 ((3, 4, 6, 7))

983 MOORE, Jerrold Northrop: Elgar on
record: the composer and the gramophone. London, New York: Oxford
University Press, 1974: vi, 244 pp.
((3, 4, 5, 6, 7))

984 Music on record: Sir Edward Elgar in
Audio and Record Review, VIII/5
(January 1968): 12-13; VIII/6 (Febru-
ary 1968): 100-101 ((-))

985 [[STONE, Ralph: [Discography] in Le
Grand Baton, III/3-4]]

986 [[UPTON, S.: [Discography] in Commo-
dore, No. 3 (September 1971): 8]]

Organ Music

987 Verzeichnis der Orgelwerke und der
Werke mit Orgelpart [includes disco-
graphical references] in FANSELAU,
Rainer: Die Orgel im Werk Edward
Elgars. Kassel: Bärenreiter-
Antiquariat [in Komm.], 1973: 338-
343 (Göttinger musikwissenschaftliche
Arbeiten; 5) ((-))

ELIZABETHAN MUSIC

988 DARRELL, R. D.: The recorded music
of Elizabethan composers in Music
Lover's Guide, II/1 (September 1933):
11-14, 19-20 ((-))

ELMO, CLOE

989 CAPUTO, Pietro: Discografia di Cloe
Elmo in Musica e Dischi, XVIII (No.
193, July 1962): 8 ((-))

990 HIRSCH, Howard J.: Cloe Elmo on disc
in Le Grand Baton, XI/1 (March 1974):
[17] ((-))

ELOY, JEAN-CLAUDE, 1938-

991 Discographie in Courrier Musical de
France, No. 46 (1974): 82 ((-))

ELSNER, JÓZEF KSAWERY, 1769-1854

992 Nagrania utwory in NOWAK-ROMANO-
WICZ, Alina: Józef Elsner: monografia.
[wyd. 1. Warszawa]: Polskie Wydawn.
Muzyczne, [1957]: 333-334 ((-))

ELWES, GERVASE, 1866-1921

993 HYDE, J. N.: The recordings of
Gervase Elwes in Record Collector,
XVII/8 (December 1967): 190-191;
Addenda: Record Collector, XVIII/1-2
(October 1968): 47 [Includes notes on
playing speeds] ((3, 7))

EMMANUEL, MAURICE, 1862-1938

994 Discographie in Courrier Musical de
France, No. 6 (1964): 114 ((-))

ENDRÈZE, ARTHUR

995 BARNES, H. M., and Victor GIRARD:
Arthur Endrèze (barytone): a discography in Recorded Sound, No. 27 (July
1967): 207-208 ((3, 6, 7))

ENESCO, GEORGES, 1881-1955

996 FONI, Fernanda: Discografia George
     Enescu in Academia Republicii
     Populare Romîne. Institutul de
     Istoria Artei: George Enescu.
     Bucuresti: Editura Muzicala a Uniunii
     Compozitorilor din R. P. R., 1964:
     [353-375] ((-))

997 Discographie in GAVOTY, Bernard:
     Les souvenirs de Georges Enesco.
     Paris: Flammarion, [1955]: [185]-
     190 ((-))

998 The same recordings realized by
     Georges Enesco and Yehudi Menuhin
     in GAVOTY, Bernard: Yehudi Menuhin
     and Georges Enesco. Geneva: R.
     Kister, c1955: [32] ((-))

ENESCU, GEORGE
     See ENESCO, GEORGES

ENGEL, CARL

999 SCHWINGER, Wolfram: Diskografie in
     fono forum 1961 (No. 6, June): 27 ((-))

ENGLISH SINGERS

1000 The English Singers: discography in
      Recorded Sound, No. 20 (October 1965):
      380-381 ((1, 3, 6, 7))

ENTREMONT, PHILIPPE, 1934-

1001 Philippe Entremont a enregistré chez
      C.B.S. in Harmonie, No. 23 (January
      1967): 26 ((-))

ERDMANN, EDUARD, 1896-1958

1002 Schallplatten- und Rundfunkaufnahmen
      in Begegnungen mit Eduard Erdmann.
      Darmstadt: Agora, 1972: 350-[363] ((1))

ESCHENBACH, CHRISTOPH

1003 Diskographie in Phonoprisma (Novem-
      ber-December 1965): 182 ((-))

ESPLÁ, OSCAR, 1886-1976

1004 Discografia in IGLESIAS, Antonio:
      Oscar Esplá. [Madrid: Servicio de
      Publicaciones del Ministerio de
      Educación y Ciencia, Secretaría
      General Técnica], 1973: 59-60
      (Artistas españoles contemporáneos;
      56. Serie Músicos) ((-))

ESTA RECORDS
     See listing for MUSIC, CZECH.
     Gramofonové zavody, Prague

EURODISC RECORDS
     See listing for SVETLANOV, EVGENY
     FEDOROVITCH

EXPERIMENTAL MUSIC

1005 [[Discography in LINCOLN, Harry B.:
      Uses of the computer in music compo-
      sition and research in Advances in
      Computers, XII (1972): 73-114]]

1006 An incomplete discography of experi-
      mental music in InterAmerican Music
      Bulletin, No. 14 (November 1959): 3
      ((-))

FABINI, EDUARDO, 1883-1950

1007 [[MUTTONI, E. J.: [Discography] in
      Recorded Sound, I/2 (June 1961)]]

FALKNER, DONALD KEITH, 1900-

1008 [[TURNER, W.: Sir Keith Falkner in
      Record Collector, XIX (1970): 149-171]]

FALLA, MANUEL DE, 1876-1946
     See also listing for RAVEL, MAURICE,
     1875-1937. Odriozola, Antonio: Las
     grabacionnes en discos LP de seis
     grandes figuras de la música con-
     temporanea....

1009 Discographie critique in CAMPO-
      NONICO, Luis: Falla. Paris, Édi-
      tions du Seuil, 1959: 182-183 ((-))

1010 [[[Discography] in Discofilia No. 2
      (April 1956): 41]]

1011 Discographie in FALLA, Manuel de:
      Spanien und die neue Musik: ein
      Lebensbild in Schriften, Bildern,
      Erinnerungen. Zürich: Verlag Die
      Arche, 1968: 175-178 ((-))

1012 Discographie in GAUTHIER, André:
      Manuel de Falla: l'homme et son
      oeuvre; catalogue des oeuvres,
      discographie.... Paris: Seghers,
      1966: 185-[188] (Musiciens de tous les
      temps; 27) ((-))

1013 MARINELLI, Carlo: Discografia in
      MILA, Massimo: Manuel de Falla.
      [Milano]: Ricordi, [1962]: 237-346
      (Symposium; 3) ((-))

1014 MARSH, Robert Charles: A selective
      discography of Manuel de Falla in
      High Fidelity, VII/7 (July 1957): 63-66
      ((-))

FALÚ, EDUARDO

1015 Discografia in SÁBATO, Ernesto R.:
      Eduardo Falú. Madrid: Ediciones
      Júcar, c1974: [183]-190 (Los Juglares;
      11) (Colección Los Poetas) ((-))

FARNETI, MARIA

1016 CELLETTI, Rodolfo: Discografia in
      Musica e Dischi, X (No. 88, January
      1954): 19 ((7))

FARQUHAR, DAVID, 1926-

1017 [[List of recorded works in HEENAN,
      Ashley David Joseph: NZBC Schola
      Musicum: [a commentary & some
      personal reminiscences on the NZBC
      orchestral trainee scheme] Wellington:
      New Zealand Broadcasting Corporation,
      1974]] [Lists of published and recorded
      works of Douglas Lilburn, Ronald
      Tremain, David Farquhar, and Larry
      Pruden in pocket]

FARRAR, GERALDINE, 1882-1967

1018 Geraldine Farrar. [Copenhagen]:
      Nationalmuseet, 1962: 10 pp.
      (National Diskotek Katalog; 18) ((3,
      4, 6, 7))

1019 Geraldine Farrar sings/plays in
      Record Collector, XIII/9-10 (n.d.):
      193-240 ((3, 6, 7)); Corrections and
      addenda: Record Collector, XIV/7-8:
      172-173 ((-))

1020 HARVEY, H. Hugh: List of records in
      Gramophone, No. 204 (May 1940): 428-
      430 ((3, 7))

1021 [Harvey discography] Corrections [in
      correspondence] in Gramophone, No.
      205 (June 1940): 26 ((-))

1022 McLENAN-BURROS, H.: Gramophone
      celebrities—17 in Gramophone, V/1
      (June 1927): 7 ((-))

1023 SELTSAM, William Henry: A Farrar
      discography in Phonograph Monthly
      Review, V/4 (January 1931): 113 ((7))

FAURÉ, GABRIEL URBAIN, 1845-1924

1024 Discographie in FAURÉ-FRÉMIET,
      Philippe: Gabriel Fauré. Nouv. éd.,
      suivie de Réflexions sur la confiance
      fauréenne et de Notes sur l'interpré-
      tation des oeuvres. Paris: A. Michel,
      [1957]: [197]-231 ((-))

1025 Gabriel Fauré et le disque in Gabriel
      Fauré. Paris: Publications techniques
      et artistiques, c1946: [42] ((-))

1026 Catalogue des oeuvres et discographie
      in NECTOUX, Jean Michel: Fauré.
      [Paris]: Éditions du Seuil, [1972]: 178-
      187 (Collections microcosme. Solfeges;
      33) ((-))

1027 SMOLIAN, Steve: Discography in
      VUILLERMOZ, Émile: Gabriel Fauré.
      [1st American ed.] Philadelphia:
      Chilton Book Co., [c1969]: [173]-259
      ((5))

1028 Discographie selective in VUAILLAT,
      Jean: Gabriel Fauré. [Lyon]: E. Vitte,
      [1973]: 129-130 ((-))

FELDMAN, LUDOVIC

1029 DRĀGONI, C.: Discographie in Muzica,
      XXI/2 (February 1971): 46 ((-))

FERRANI, CESIRA, 1863-1943

1030 CELLETTI, Rodolfo: Discografia in
      Musica e Dischi, XI (No. 103, March
      1955): 21 ter. ((5))

1031 CELLETTI, Rodolfo: The records in
      Record News, III/5 (January 1959): 156;
      [From Musica e Dischi, March 1955]
      ((5))

1032 WITTEN, Laurence C., II: A discogra-
      phy of Cesira Ferrani, soprano, 1863-
      1943 in Record Collector, XX/6-7
      (May 1972): 157-159 ((3, 7))

FERRAS, CHRISTIAN

1033 Une discographie Ferras in Diapason,
      No. 117 (May 1967): 40 ((-))

FERRIER, KATHLEEN, 1912-1953

1034 Records made by Kathleen Ferrier for
      the Decca Record Company in CARDUS,
      Neville: Kathleen Ferrier: a memoir.
      London: Hamilton, 1954: 120-125 ((-))

1035 Records made by Kathleen Ferrier for
      the Decca Record Company in CARDUS,
      Neville: Kathleen Ferrier: a memoir.
      New York: Putnam, [1955]: 120-125
      ((-))

1036 Records made for the Decca Record
      Company in CARDUS, Sir Neville:
      Kathleen Ferrier: a memoir. London:
      Hamilton, 1969: 120-122 ((-))

1037 CLOUGH, F. F., and G. J. CUMING:
      Kathleen Ferrier; diskography in
      Gramophone Record Review, No. 48
      (October 1957): 975, 1027-1028 ((-))

1038 Discographie K. Ferrier in Disques,
      VI/59 (September-October 1953): 587
      ((-)); Addenda: Disques, VI/60 (Christ-
      mas 1953): 729 ((5))

1039 Diskographie in Collegium Musicum
      1971 (No. 7): $\overline{21}$ ((–))

1040 GLUTH, Walter: Diskografie in fono
      forum 1961 (No. 4, April): 14 $\overline{7}$(–))

1041 PORTER, Andrew: The records of
      Kathleen Ferrier in Gramophone, No.
      369 (February 195$\overline{4}$): 325-326 ((5, 7));
      Corrections, etc. in Gramophone, No.
      380 (January 1955)$\overline{:}$ 372 ((7))

1042 REUTER, Evelyn: Discographie Kath-
      leen Ferrier in Revue Musicale, No.
      223 (1953-195$\overline{4}$): 28-29 ((5))

FIBICH, ZDENĚK, 1850-1900

1043 BOHÁČEK, Ludvík: Regstřík skladeb
      sestavil [includes discographical ref-
      erences] in JIRÁNEK, Jaroslav:
      Zdeněk Fibich. [1. vyd.] Praha:
      Státní hudební vydavatelství, 1963:
      268-280 (Hudební profily; 10) ((–))

1044 Soupis snímků nahraných v lentech
      1950-1952 gramofonovými závody in
      REKTORYS, Artuš: Zdeněk Fibich:
      sborník dokumentů a studií o jeho
      živote a díle. [Praha]: Orbis, 1951-
      52: 463-468 ((–))

FIEDLER, ARTHUR, 1894-

1045 Discography in MOORE, Robin: Fiedler:
      the colorful Mr. Pops; the man and his
      music. [1st ed.] Boston: Little, Brown,
      [1968]: [293]-364 ((3, 7))

1046 Current RCA Victor records by Arthur
      Fiedler in WILSON, Carol: Arthur
      Fiedler: music for the millions; the
      story of the conductor of the Boston
      Pops Orchestra. New York: Evans Pub.
      Co., [1968]: 221-223 ((–))

FIELD, JOAN

1047 Diskografie in fono forum 1961 (No. 2,
      February): 2$\overline{7}$ ((–))

FIELD, JOHN, 1782-1837

1048 DOSCHER, David: A John Field discog-
      raphy in International Piano Library
      Bulletin, II/2-3 (September 1968): 34-
      36 ((–))

FIERSOHN, REBA
      See GLUCK, ALMA

FINE ARTS QUARTET

1049 CLOUGH, F. F., and G. J. CUMING:
      Fine Arts Quartet—discography in
      Audio and Record Review, III/1
      (September 1963): 16-17 ((–))

FINKE, FIDELIO F., 1891-1968

1050 Die Wichtigsten Werke [includes disco-
      graphical references] in KOERTH,
      Manfred: Fidelio F. Finke: Wichtigste
      Werke. Berlin: Verband deutscher
      Komponisten und Musikwissenschaftler,
      Musikinformationszentrum, 1967: [6]
      (Komponisten der DDR) ((–))

FISCHER, ANNIE

1051 SPINGEL, Hans Otto: Diskografie in
      fono forum 1963 (No. 3, March): 10$\overline{7}$
      ((–))

FISCHER, EDWIN, 1886-1960

1052 BADURA-SKODA, Paul: Diskographie
      in HAID, Hugo: Dank an Edwin Fischer.
      Wiesbaden: F. A. Brockhaus, 1962,
      [c1961]: 157-161 ((5))

1053 Enregistrements (microsillons)
      réalisés par Edwin Fischer in
      GAVOTY, Bernard: Edwin Fischer.
      Genève: R. Kister, c1954: [32] (Les
      Grands interprètes) ((–))

1054 Bandaufnahmen in HAID, Hugo: Dank an
      Edwin Fischer. Wiesbaden: F. A.
      Brockhaus, 1962, [c1961]: 162 ((7))

1055 HUGHES, Eric: Edwin Fischer discog-
      raphy in Recorded Sound, I/5 (Winter
      1961-19$\overline{6}$2): 158-163 ((–))

1056 OLSEN, Henning Smidth: Edwin Fischer:
      a discography. København: Danmarks
      Biblioteksskole, 1974: 40 pp. (Studier
      fra Danmarks Biblioteksskole; 5)
      (Copenhagen. Danmarks biblioteks-
      skole. Studier; 5) ((1, 3, 4, 5, 6, 7))

FISCHER-DIESKAU, DIETRICH, 1925-

1057 Diskographie in DEMUS, Jörg: Dietrich
      Fischer-Dieskau. Berlin: Rembrandt
      Verlag, [1966]: 83-88 ((–))

1058 Discographie Fischer-Dieskau in
      Diapason, No. 102 (December 19$\overline{6}$5):
      13 ((–))

1059 VEGETO, Raffaele: Discografia del
      baritono Fischer-Dieskau in Discoteca,
      No. 80 (May 1968): 65-71 ($\overline{(4}$, 5))

1060 WOLFE, Linda: A Fischer-Dieskau
      discography in Saturday Review (June
      30, 1962): 35 $\overline{(}$(–))

FLAGSTAD, KIRSTEN, 1895-1962

1061 CLOUGH, F. F., and G. J. CUMING:
      Diskography in Gramophone Record
      Review, No. 5$\overline{3}$ (March 1958): 391-392,
      438 ((–))

1062 DENNIS, J.: [Discography] in Record
Collector, VII/8 (August 1952): 180-
190 ((3, 5, 7))

1063 HARVEY, H. Hugh: The Flagstad pre-
war records in Gramophone, No. 366
(November 1953): 181 ((5))

1064 Kirsten Flagstad—Discographie in
Musikhandel, XIV/1 (January 1963):
12 ((-))

1065 Grammofoninnspillinger: 1914-1959 in
REIN, Aslaug: Kirsten Flagstad. Oslo:
Mortensen, 1967: [272]-277 ((-))

FLESCH, CARL

1066 WILE, R.: The Edison recordings of
Carl Flesch in Talking Machine Review,
No. 37 (December 1975) 511-515 ((3, 6,
7))

FLETA, MIGUEL

1067 LEÓN, Jacques Alain: Miguel Fleta
discography in Record Collector, XV/
5-6 (n.d.): 104-108 ((3, 6))

1068 VEGETO, Raffaele: Discografia di
Miguel Fleta in Musica e Dischi, XIII
(No. 134, September 1957): 66 ((7))

1069 VEGETO, R.: Discografia operistica
del tenore Miguel Fleta in Discoteca,
No. 41 (June 1964): 21-22 ((5))

FLUTE

1070 Discography in BERGER, Melvin: The
flute book. New York: Lothrop, Lee
and Shepard Co., [1973]: [120]-122 ((-))

FLUTE MUSIC

1071 Discography in BALLANTINE, Bill:
The flute: an introduction to the instrument. New York: F. Watts, [1971]:
[115]-122 ((-))

1072 Discographie in GIRARD, Adrien:
Historie et richesses de la flûte.
Paris: Librarie Grund, 1953: 129-134
((-))

1073 [[Discography in LASCOKI, David
Ronald Graham: The baroque flute
and its role today in Recorder and
Music Magazine, II/4 (February 1967):
96, 99, 100, 104]]

FOERSTER, JOSEF BOHUSLAV, 1859-1951

1074 SVOBODA, Otakar: Soupis skladeb
Josefa Bohuslava Foerstra na čs.
gramofonových deskách do r. 1961 in
PALA, František: Josef Bohuslav
Foerster. [1. vyd.] Praha: Stántí

hudební vydavatelství, 1962: 27-30
((-))

FOLDES, ANDOR, 1913-

1075 Diskographie (Auswahl)—sämtlich
Deutsche Grammophon in Phonoprisma,
VI/6 (November-December 1963): 168
((-))

1076 GLUTH, Walter: Diskografie in fono
forum 1960 (No. 11, November): 27
((-))

FONOTIPIA RECORDS
See listing for KRISMER, GIUSEPPE

FORNIA, RITA, 1878-1922

1077 MORAN, W. R.: The recordings of Rita
Fornia in Record Collector, X/1-2
(September-October 1956): 232-237
((3, 6, 7))

FORSELL, JOHN, 1868-1941

1078 BRUUN, Carl L.: John Forsell [discog-
raphy] in Record News, IV/7 (March
1960): 256-263 ((3)); IV/8 (April 1960):
292-296 ((-))

1079 LILIEDAHL, Karleric: John Forsell: a
discography. [Trelleborg, Sweden]:
Liliedahl, 1972: 22 leaves ((1, 3, 4, 7))

FOULDS, JOHN, 1880-1939

1080 Discography in MacDONALD, Malcolm:
John Foulds: his life in music. Rick-
mansworth, [Eng.]: Triad Press, 1975:
103 ((-))

FOURNIER, PIERRE, 1906-

1081 Discographie in Diapason, No. 123
(February 1968): 7 ((-))

1082 Folgende Schallplatten...in fono
forum 1961 (No. 4, April): 27 ((-))

1083 Discographie in GAVOTY, Bernard:
Pierre Fournier. Genève: R. Kister,
c1955: [32] (Les Grands interprètes)
((-))

1084 List of recordings in GAVOTY,
Bernard: Pierre Fournier. Geneva:
R. Kister, c1956: [32] (Great concert
artists) ((-))

FRANÇAIX, JEAN, 1912-

1085 Discographie in Courrier Musical de
France, No. 15 (1966): 170 ((-))

1086 Principaux enregistrements phono-
      graphiques in LANJEAN, Marc: Jean
      Françaix: musicien français. Paris:
      Contact Éditions, [1961]: [92]-[93]
      (Élites de notre temps. Musique) ((-))

FRANCK, CÉSAR AUGUSTE, 1822-1890

1087 AFFELDER, Paul: César Franck on
      microgroove in High Fidelity, VII/3
      (March 1957): 93-101 ((-))

1088 Gramophone records in ANDRIESSEN,
      Hendrik: César Franck. Stockholm:
      Continental Book Co., [194-]: 60 ((-))

1089 Discographie in BUENZOD, Emmanuel:
      César Franck: l'homme et son
      oeuvre...; catalogue des oeuvres,
      discographie. Paris: Seghers, 1966:
      185-187 (Musiciens de tous les temps,
      28) ((-))

1090 Discographie in DUFOURCQ, Norbert:
      César Franck: le milieu, l'oeuvre,
      l'art. Paris: Colombe, 1949. [111]-
      112 (Euterpe, no. 5) (Collections
      Euterpe. Paris, 5) ((-))

1091 Discographie in GALLOIS, Jean:
      Franck. Paris: Éditions du Seuil,
      1966: 187-189 (Solfèges, 27 ((-))

1092 Schallplattenverzeichnis in MOHR,
      Wilhelm: César Franck. 2., erg.
      Aufl. Tutzing: H. Schneider, 1969:
      197-201 ((-))

1093 Discographie in MONNIKENDAM,
      Marius: César Franck. Haarlem:
      J. H. Gottmer, [1966]: 242-248
      (Componistenserie, 5) ((-))

FRANÇOIS, SAMSON, 1924-1970

1094 BERTHOUMIEUX, Serge: Discographie
      in Diapason, No. 152 (December 1970):
      19 ((-))

1095 Discographie de Samson François in
      GAVOTY, Bernard: Samson François.
      Genève: R. Kister, c1955: [32] (Les
      Grands interprètes) ((-))

1096 List of recordings in GAVOTY, Ber-
      nard: Samson François. Geneva: R.
      Kister, c1956: [32] (Great concert
      artists) ((-))

1097 HAMON, Jean: Samson François in
      Diapason, No. 122 (January 1968): 7
      ((-))

FRANZ, PAUL

1098 [[Discographie in Disques, III/25
      (July 1950)]]

FRANZ, ROBERT, 1815-1892

1099 WEBER, J. F.: Loewe and Franz.
      Utica, NY: Weber, 1971: 20 pp. (Dis-
      cography series, 8) ((5))

FREITAS BRANCO, PEDRO DE, 1890-1955

1100 CASSUTO, Alvaro: Discografia de
      Pedro de Freitas Branco in Arte
      Musical, 3d Series, No. 20-22 (July-
      November 1963; March 1964): 379-383
      ((-)); Addenda: Arte Musical, 3d Series,
      No. 23 (July 1964): 641 ((3, 7))

FREMSTED, OLIVE, 1871-1951

1101 DENNIS, J.: Columbia tricolor label
      records in Record Collector, VII/2
      (February 1952): 53-65 ((3, 5))

FRENCH HORN

1102 UGGEN, Stuart: A French horn dis-
      cography in Instrumentalist, XXIV
      (March 1970): 59-61 ((-))

FRENI, MIRELLA, 1935-

1103 LÖBL, Karl: Diskografie Mirella Freni
      in fono forum 1965 (No. 4, April): 151
      ((-))

FRESCOBALDI, GIROLAMO ALESSANDRO,
1583-1643

1104 Discographie in MACHABEY, Armand:
      Gerolamo Frescobaldi Ferrarensis
      (1583-1643). Paris: La Colombe,
      [1952]: [150] (Collection Euterpe) ((-))

FRICSAY, FERENC, 1914-1963

1105 CLOUGH, F. F., and G. J. CUMING: A
      Fricsay diskography in Gramophone
      Record Review, No. 81 (July 1960):
      510-512 ((-))

1106 Diskographie in HERZFELD, Friedrich:
      Ferenc Fricsay: ein Gedenkbuch.
      Berlin: Rembrandt, [c1964]: 110-114
      ((-))

1107 WERNER, Arnold: Ferenc Fricsay;
      Schallplattenverzeichnis in fono forum
      1973 (No. 9, September): 806-809 ((7))

FRIEDHEIM, ARTHUR, 1859-1932

1108 BENKO, Gregor: Arthur Friedheim—a
      discography in Antique Records (No-
      vember 1973): 14-16 ((3, 6, 7))

FRIEDMAN, IGNAZ

1109 MASON, D., and Gregor BENKO: Ignaz
Friedman—discography in International
Piano Library Bulletin, II/4 (December
1968): 12-19 ((3, 6, 7))

1110 MASON, D. H., and Gregor BENKO:
Ignaz Friedman; a discography in 78
RPM, No. 3 (1968): 9-12 ((3, 6, 7));
No. 4 (February 1969): 11-14 ((3, 6, 7));
No. 5 (April 1969): 6-11 ((3, 6, 7))

FRIJSH, POVLA, d. 1960

1111 [[MILLER, P.: [Discography] in Record News, V/12 (August 1961)]]

FRIND, ANNI

1112 The recordings of Anni Frind in Record
Collector, XIV/7-8: 149-158 ((3)); Addenda: Record Collector, XIV/11-12:
284 ((3))

FUGÈRE, LUCIEN, 1848-1935

1113 GIRARD, Victor: Discography in Record
Collector, VIII/5 (May 1953): 106-109
((3, 7))

FURTWÄNGLER, WILHELM, 1886-1954

1114 CLOUGH, F. F., and G. J. CUMING:
Diskography in Gramophone Record
Review, No. 54 (April 1958): 475-476
((-))

1115 Essai de discographie de W. Furtwängler (25-I-1886—30-XI-1954) in Disques, No. 69 (January 1955): 48-49 ((-))

1116 Enregistrements in GAVOTY, Bernard:
Wilhelm Furtwängler. Genève: R.
Kister et Union européenne d'éditions,
c1954: [32] (Les Grands interprètes)
((-))

1117 Some recordings by Wilhelm Furtwängler in GAVOTY, Bernard: Wilhelm
Furtwängler. Geneva: R. Kister, c1956:
29 (Great concert artists) ((-))

1118 Furtwängler on record in GILLIS,
Daniel: Furtwängler recalled. Zürich:
Atlantis Verlag, [c1965]: 185-221 ((-))

1119 Diskographie in HÖCKER, Karla:
Wilhelm Furtwängler: Dokumente,
Berichte und Bilder. [Berlin]: Rem-
brandt Verlag, [1968]: 146-147 ((-))

1120 Tonbandverzeichnis in HÖCKER, Karla:
Wilhelm Furtwängler: Dokumente,
Berichte und Bilder. [Berlin]: Rem-
brandt Verlag, [1968]: 148-149 ((-))

1121 JUNGHANNS, Franz: Diskografie in
fono forum 1964 (No. 11, November):
436 ((-))

1122 MATZNER, Joachim: Diskographie
Furtwängler in fono forum 1970 (No.
12, December): 939 ((-)

1123 OLSEN, Henning Smidth: Wilhelm
Furtwängler: a discography. Copenhagen: Nationaldiskoteket, 1970: 95 pp.
(Nationaldiskoteket. Discographies,
211) ((3, 4, 5, 6, 7))

1124 OLSEN, Henning Smidth: Wilhelm
Furtwängler: a discography. [2d rev.
ed.] [n.p.]: L. Schipper and the North
American Wilhelm Furtwaengler
Society, 1973: vi, 71 pp.; Note: world
distribution: Moe's Books, Berkeley,
California ((1, 3, 4, 5, 6, 7))

1125 SHARPE, Geoffrey: Furtwängler's
records in Music Review, XVI (February 1955): 3-4 ((-))

1126 VINCENTINI, Mario: Discografia in
Discoteca alta Fedelta, No. 148
(March 1975): 41-42 ((1, 7))

1127 Was Furtwängler hinterlassen hat in
Phono, XI/2 (1964): 38-39 ((-))

G & T RECORDS
See listing for CARUSO, ENRICO.
Freestone, John, and H. J. Drummond:
A Caruso anniversary

GABBI, ADALGISA

1128 CELLETTI, Rodolfo: Discografia in
Musica e Dischi, XIII (No. 128, April
1957): 52 ((7))

GADSKI, JOHANNA, 1872-1932

1129 RIDLEY, N. A.: Discography in Record
Collector, XI/9-10 (September-Octo-
ber 1957): 199-201 ((1, 7)); Addenda:
Record Collector, XI/11-12 (November-
December 1957): 276-285 ((-))

GAILHARD, PIERRE, 1848-1918

1130 FREESTONE, John: Collectors' corner
in Gramophone, No. 355 (December
1952): 159 ((-))

1131 RICHARD, Jean-Roger: [Discographie]
in Disques, No. 6 (June-July 1948): 186
((-))

GALEFFI, CARLO, 1884-1961

1132 TIBERI, Maurzio and SCHIAVONI,
Fidia: Discografia in MARCHETTI,

Arnaldo: Carlo Galeffi: una vita per il canto. Roma, 1973: 99-101 ((7))

GALLI-CURCI, AMELITA, 1889-1963

1133 Amelita Galli-Curci. [Copenhagen] Nationalmuseet, [1961]: 10 pp. (Det National Diskotek Katalog, 10) ((3, 4))

1134 CASKETT, James: Galli-Curci records in Gramophone, I/2 (June 1923): 30 ((-))

1135 [[FAVIA-ARTSAY, Aida: Amelita Galli-Curci in Record Collector, IV/ (October 1949): 163-179]]; Addenda: Record Collector, V/4 (April 1950): 78 ((-))

1136 Galli-Curci records in LE MASSENA, C. E.: Galli-Curci's life of song. New York: The Paebar Co., [1945]: 333-336 ((-))

1137 MARCHINGTON, Bryan: Amelita Galli-Curci: her career and records: Part 2: the twelve inch recordings in Hill and Dale News, No. 20 (August 1974): 71-72 ((-)); Part 3: the ten-inch recordings in Hill and Dale News, No. 21 (October 1964): 82-83 ((-)); Part 4: miscella- neous in Hill and Dale News, No. 22 (December 1964): 100-101 ((-))

GARDEN, MARY, 1874-1967

1138 List of recordings in BARNES, Harold: Mary Garden on records. San Angelo, TX: Holcombe-Blanton Printery, 1947: [18]-20 ((5))

1139 WHELAN, Gordon: The recorded art of Mary Garden in Gramophone, No. 347 (April 1952): 248-249 ((3, 7))

GARDNER, JOHN, 1917-

1140 John Gardner recordings in Recorded Sound, No. 44 (October 1971): 803-804 ((1, 7))

GARULLI, ALFONSO

1141 CELLETTI, Rodolfo: Discografia in Musica e Dischi, X (No. 94, July 1954): 10 ((7))

1142 CELLETTI, Rodolfo: Discography in Record News, I/11 (July 1957): 388; [From Musica e Dischi, July 1954]; Addenda: Record News, II/3 (November 1957): 113 ((-))

1143 VEGETO, Raffaele: Discografia del tenore Alfonso Garulli in Musica e Dischi, XV (No. 162, December 1959): 84 ((7))

GAUK, ALEXSANDR VASIL'EVICH, 1893-1963

1144 [Discography] in Memaury, izbrannye stat'i, vspominania sovremennikov. Moskva: Sov. kompositor, 1975: 243-250 ((-))

GÉCZY, BARNABÁS VON, 1897-

1145 Barnábas von Géczy auf Electrola- musikplatten in SCHNOOR, Hans: Barnabás von Géczy: aufstieg einer kunst; rhapsodie in zehn sätzen. Dres- den: Verlag der Dr. Güntzschen stiftung, [1937]: [60]-[62] ((-))

GEDDA, NICOLAI, 1925-

1146 Diskographie in Collegium Musicum 1972 (No. 1): 10-12 ((-))

1147 Diskographie (sämtlich Electrola/ Columbia) in Phonoprisma, VII/6 (November-December 1964): 184, 192 ((-))

1148 HAUSSWALD, Günter: Diskographie in Musica, XXIV (January-February 1970): [65] ((-))

1149 WOLFF, Egon: Diskografie in fono forum 1961 (No. 3, March): 27 ((-))

GENCER, LEYLA

1150 VEGETO, Raffaele: Nota discografica del soprano Leyla Gencer in Discoteca, No. 117 (January-February 1972): 20 ((1))

GENDRON, MAURICE

1151 SPINGEL, Hans Otto: Diskografie in fono forum 1963 (No. 6, June): 229 ((-))

GEORGESCU, GEORGE, 1887-1964

1152 [[HOFFMANN, A.: Interpretationsstile in der Kunst des Dirigierens: George Georgescu (Bezüglich seiner Letzten internationalen Tournees) in Revue Roumaine d'Histoire de l'Art, I/1 (1964): 139-150]]

1153 [[HOFFMANN, A.: Stiluri dirijorale: George Georgescu in Istoria Artei, XII/1 (1965): 37-38]]

GERHARDT, ELENA, 1883-1961

1154 SHAWE-TAYLOR, Desmond: Elena Gerhardt and the gramophone in GER- HARDT, Elena: Recital. London: Methuen, [1953]: [168]-180 ((3, 7))

1155 SHAWE-TAYLOR, Desmond: Elena
Gerhardt and the gramophone in GER-
HARDT, Elena: Recital. London:
Methuen; St. Clair Shores, Mich.
Scholarly Press, 1972: [168]-180 ((3, 7))

1156 SHAWE-TAYLOR, Desmond: List of
Mme. Gerhardt's records in Gramophone, No. 114 (November 1932): 205
((-))

GERMAN, SIR EDWARD, 1898-1937

1157 [[PLANT, R. M.: The British composer
on 78 rpm in Record Advertiser, III/6
(September-October 1973): 11-]]

GERSHWIN, GEORGE, 1898-1937

1158 A Gershwin discography in ARMITAGE,
Merle: George Gershwin: man and leg-
end. [1st ed.] New York: Duell, Sloan
and Pearce, [1958]: 186-188 ((-))

1159 A Gershwin discography in ARMITAGE,
Merle: George Gershwin: man and leg-
end. Freeport, NY: Books for Libraries Press, [1970, c1958]: 186-188 (Biography index reprint series) ((-))

1160 Records in ARMITAGE, Merle: George
Gershwin. New York, London: Long-
mans, Green & Co., 1938: 250 ((-))

1161 Discografia essenziale in CHALUPT,
Renè: Gershwin. [Milano]: Nuova
accademia editrice, [1959]: 193-198
(Le Cite dei musicisti) ((-))

1162 DASHIELL, Alan: A selected Gershwin
discography in GOLDBERG, Isaac:
George Gershwin: a study in American
music. [New ed.] New York: F. Ungar
Pub. Co., [1958]: 357-370 ((-))

1163 Discografia in L'Approdo Musicale,
I/4 (October-December 1958): 54-57
((-))

1164 Gershwin records in EWEN, David: The
story of George Gershwin. New York:
H. Holt and Company, [1943]: 187-195
((-))

1165 Recommended recordings of Gershwin's
music in EWEN, David: A journey to
greatness. New York: Holt, 1956: 356-
362 ((-))

1166 JABLONSKI, E.: Gershwin after 20
years [Includes discography] in Hi-Fi
Music at Home, III (July-August 1956):
22-23 ((-))

1167 JABLONSKI, Edward: George Gershwin:
a selective discography in Hi Fi Stereo
Review, XVIII/5 (May 1967): 60 ((-))

1168 An informal discography in JABLONSKI,
Edward: The Gershwin years, by Edward Jablonski and Lawrence D. STEW-

ART. [2d ed.] Garden City, NY: Doubleday, 1973: 389-395 ((-))

1169 Selected Gershwin discography in
JABLONSKI, Edward: George Gershwin.
New York: Putnam, [1962]: 161-177
(Lives to remember) ((-))

1170 Discography in KIMBALL, Robert: The
Gershwins, by Robert Kimball and Al-
fred SIMON. [1st ed.] New York:
Antheneum, 1973: [281]-285 ((-))

1171 Discography in KIMBALL, Robert: The
Gershwins, by Robert Kimball and Alfred SIMON. London: Cape, 1974:
[281]-285 ((-))

1172 Dyskografia in KYDRYŃSKI, Lucjan:
Gershwin. Wyd. 1. Kraków: Polskie
Wydawn Muzyczne, [1962]: 195-196
((-))

1173 Discography in RUSHMORE, Robert:
The life of George Gershwin. New
York: Crowell-Collier Press, [1966]:
[167]-171 (America in the making) ((-))

1174 Discography in SCHWARTZ, Charles:
George Gershwin: a selective bibliog-
raphy and discography. Detroit: Pub-
lished for the College Music Society by
Information Coordinators, 1974: 91-118
(Bibliographies in American music, 1
((-))

1175 A selected George Gershwin discography in SCHWARTZ, Charles: Gershwin:
his life and music. Indianapolis: Bobbs-
Merrill Co., [1973]: 353-365 ((-))

1176 [[WATT, Peter: Select discography in
PAYNE, Robert: Gershwin. London:
Hall, 1962: 119-122]]

1177 [[WATT, Peter: Selected discography
in Payne, Robert: Gershwin. New York:
Pyramid, 1960: 119-122]]

GERSHWIN, IRA, 1896-
See listing for GERSHWIN, GEORGE.
Discography in Kimball, Robert: The
Gershwins

GERSTER, OTTMAR, 1897-1969

1178 Schallplatten in LAUX, Karl: Ottmar
Gerster: Leben und Werk. [1. Aufl.]
Leipzig: P. Reclam Jun., [1961]: 109-
[110] ((-))

GERVILLE-REACHE, JEANNE, 1882-1915

1179 MORAN, W. R.: The recordings of
Jeanne Gerville-Reache in Record Collector, XXI/3-4 (July 1973): 73-79
((3, 4, 6, 7))

GESTKY, SYLVIA

1180 Diskographie in Medium Schallplatte, No. 12 (No. 3, 1969): 9 ((-))

GHEDINI, GIORIO FEDERICO, 1892-1965

1181 [[SALVETTI, Guido: Symphonia. Opera posthuma di G. F. Ghedini in Musicalia, I/1 (September 1970): 13-16]]

GHIAUROV, NICOLAI, 1929-

1182 Diskographie in Phonoprisma (July-August 1965): 113 ((-))

1183 LÖBL, Karl: Diskografie in fono forum 1964 (No. 12, December): 512 ((-))

GIANNINI, DUSOLINA, 1902-

1184 MORAN, W. R.: Dusolina Giannini and her recordings in Record Collector, IX/2 (February 1954): 50-51 ((1, 3, 6)); Additions: Record Collector, XIV/3-4: 94 ((3))

GIEBEL, AGNES

1185 SCHWINGER, Wolfram: Aus der Diskografie in fono forum 1962 (No. 6, June): 14 ((-))

GIESEKING, WALTER, 1895-1956

1186 CLOUGH, F. F., and G. J. CUMING: Walter Gieseking; a microgroove diskography in Gramophone Record Review, No. 45 (July 1957): 703-704, 707 ((-))

1187 [[Discographie générale de Walter Gieseking in Disques, No. 83-84 (December 1956): 892-893]]

1188 Enregistrements réalisés par W. Gieseking in GAVOTY, Bernard: Walter Gieseking. Genève: R. Kister, c1954: [32] (Les Grands interprètes) ((-))

1189 Walter Gieseking exclusive Columbia recordings in GAVOTY, Bernard: Walter Gieseking. Geneva: R. Kister, c1955: [32] (Great concert artists) ((-))

1190 Bandaufnahmen in GIESEKING, Walter: So wurde ich Pianist. Wiesbaden: F. A. Brockhaus, 1963: 141-144 ((1))

1191 HAJMÁSSY, Imre: Discographie zusammengestellt in GIESEKING, Walter: So wurde ich Pianist. Wiesbaden: F. A. Brockhaus, 1963: 136-140 ((-))

GIESEN, HUBERT

1192 MAYER, Ute: Ausgievahlte diskographie in GIESEN, Hubert: Am Flügel; Hubert Giesen; meine Lebenserinnerungen. [Frankfurt am Main]: S. Fischer, [c1972]: 281-[288] ((-))

GIGLI, BENIAMINO, 1890-1957

1193 Beniamino Gigli. [Copenhagen]: Nationalmuseet, [1961]: 19 pp. (Det Nationale Diskotek Katalog, 6) ((3, 4, 7))

1194 CRONSTROM, Anne-Marie, and Gustave CRONSTROM: Beniamino Gigli: a discography in Record Collector, IX/9-10 (February-March 1955): 221-240 ((3, 6, 7)); Addenda: Record Collector, IX/11-12 (April-May 1955): 247-269 ((3, 6, 7)); XIII/7-8 (September-October 1960): 184-188 ((3, 6))

1195 HILLIER, Arthur D.: Beniamino Gigli— a supplementary discography in Record Advertiser, III/2 (January-February 1973): 2-16 ((-)); III/3 (March-April 1973): 2-18 ((-)); III/4 (May-June 1973): 2-7; [LP and EP records only] ((-))

1196 RICALDONE, Mark: A Gigli discography in GIGLI, Beniamino: Memoirs. London: Cassell, [1957]: 233-270 ((3, 4, 7))

1197 SMITH, French Crawford: Beniamino Gigli (including a complete discography) in American Record Guide, XXIV/6 (February 1958): 240, 277-278, 282 ((-))

1198 Unpublished Gigli records in Record News, I/10 (June 1957): 374-375 ((3, 7)) [From Musica e Dischi, April 1957]

1199 VEGETO, Raffaele: Beniamino Gigli's complete discography in Musica e Dischi, XIII (No. 137, December 1957): 42 [Includes unpublished records] ((3, 7))

1200 VEGETO, Raffaele: La discografia completa di Beniamino Gigli in Musica e Dischi, XII (No. 114, February 1956): 35 ((7)); Addenda: Musica e Dischi, XIII (No. 128, April 1957): 52 ((-))

1201 VEGETO, Raffaele: Discografia completa di Beniamino Gigli in Musica e Dischi, XVI (No. 173, November 1960): 96 [Includes unpublished records] ((3, 7))

GILBERT, WILLIAM SCHWENCK, SIR, 1836-1911

1202 Discography in HARDWICK, Michael: The Osprey guide to Gilbert and Sullivan. Reading: Osprey, 1972: [271]-279 ((-))

GILELS, EMIL, 1916-

1203 Diskografie in JIRÍK, Marián: Emil
Gilels. Praha: Editio Supraphon, 1974:
55-58 ((-))

1204 [Discography] in KHENTOVA, Sof'ía
Mikhaĭlovna: Emil' Gilel's. Moskva:
Gos.Musykal'noye Izd-vo, 1959: 175-
180 ((7))

1205 SPINGEL, Hans Otto: Diskografie in
fono forum 1961 (No. 1, 1961): 14 ((-))

GILLY, DINH

1206 HARVEY, H. Hugh: Dinh Gilly: the records in Record Collector, V/7 (July
1950): 152-154 ((-))

1207 HARVEY, H. Hugh: Records in Gramophone, No. 206 (July 1940): 34 ((5))

GINASTERA, ALBERTO EVARISTO, 1916-

1208 Discografia in MARIZ, Vasco: Alberto
Ginastera: en adhesión a la fecha
nacional argentina. Rosario: Cursos
Libres de Portugués y Estudios Bra-
sileños, Sección Publicaciones, 1954
[i.e. 1955]: 36 ((-))

1209 Discografia in SUÁREZ URTUBEY,
Pola: Alberto Ginastera. [Buenos
Aires]: Ediciones Culturales Argen-
tinas, [1967]: 158-159 (Serie Argen-
tinos en las artes) ((-))

GINSTER, RIA, 1898-

1210 JONES, Robert: Ria Ginster discography in Recorded Sound, No. 20 (October
1965): 383-388 ((1, 3, 4, 6, 7))

GIORDANO, UMBERTO, 1867-1948

1211 VEGETO, Raffaele: Discografia giorda-
niana in MORINI, Mario: Umberto
Giordano. Milano: Casa musicale
Sonzogno, 1968: xlv-lxxiii ((1, 5))

Andrea Chenier

1212 MANN, William: Andrea Chénier in
Opera, X/9 (September 1959): 565-571
(Opera on the gramophone, 8 [sic])
((-))

Feodora

1213 SCHAUMKELL, Claus-Dieter: Diskografie in fono forum 1970 (No. 8, August): 505 ((1))

GIOVANNI, EDOARDO DI
See JOHNSON, EDWARD

GIRALDONI, EUGENIO, 1871-1924

1214 CELLETTI, Rodolfo: Discografia in
Musica e Dischi, X (No. 89, February
1954): 23 ((-))

1215 CELLETTI, Rodolfo: Discography in
Record News, I/12 (August 1957): 424
((-)) [From Musica e Dischi, February
1954]; Addenda: Record News, II/3
(November 1957): 113 ((-))

GIULINI, CARLO MARIA

1216 A Giulini discography in Records and
Recording, XVI/5 (February 1973): 23
((-))

1217 MATZNER, Joachim: Carlo Maria
Giulini; Schallplattenverzeichnis in fono
forum 1972 (No. 9, September): 679 ((5))

1218 SCHWINGER, Wolfram: Diskografie in
fono forum 1962 (No. 4, April): 14 ((-))

GLUCK, ALMA, 1884-1938

1219 EKE, Bernard T.: Alma Gluck in
Record Collector, VI/2 (February
1951): 33-45 ((-))

1220 WRATTEN, B. D.: Madame Alma Gluck
in Gramophone, II/12 (May 1925): 471
((-))

GLUCK, CHRISTOPH WILLIBALD, RITTER
VON, 1714-1787

1221 Discografía de las obras de Gluck in
SUFFERN, Carlos: Gluck. Buenos
Aires: Ricordi Americana, [1943]:
183-186 (Músicos célebres) ((-))

Alceste

1222 [[REHM, Wolfgang: Eine vergleichende
Discographie in Phono, VI/3]]

GOBBI, TITO, 1915-

1223 STEANE, John: Tito Gobbi: a discography in JACOBS, Arthur: British music
yearbook, 1975. New York; London:
Bowker, 1975: 13-21 ((1, 3, 4, 7))

GOETHALS, LUCIEN

1224 Discografie in SABBE, Herman:
Komponist Lucien Goethals. [Moorsele:
H. Verlinde, Clerck'sstraat 46, 1974]:
150 ((-))

GOGORZA, EMILIO EDUARDO DE, 1874-1949

1225 KLEIN, Herman: De Gogorza records in
Gramophone, IV/I (July 1926): 52 ((-))

GOLDBERG, SZYMON, 1909-

1226 Discographie in Disques, II/11 (January-February 1949): 299 ((-))

1227 Discography in GAVOTY, Bernard:
Szymon Goldberg. Geneva: R. Kister,
[1960]: [32] (Great concert artists)
((-))

GOMES, ANTONIO CARLOS, 1836-1896

Il Guarany

1228 LÉON, Jacques Alain: A discography of
"Il Guarany" in Record Collector,
XIII/6 (August 1960): 137-139 ((-))

GOOSSENS, SIR EUGENE, 1893-1962

1229 Recorded works in Phonograph Monthly
Review, II/7 (April 1928): 247 ((-))

GOSSEC, FRANÇOIS JOSEPH, 1734-1829

1230 OEuvres de Gossec. Discographie in
PROD'HOMME, Jacques Gabriel: Fran-
çois-Joseph Gossec, 1734-1829: la vie,
les oeuvres, l'homme et l'artiste.
Paris: La Colombe, 1949: 111-112
(Euterpe, 8) (Collection Euterpe,
Paris, 8) ((-))

1231 Les disques in THIBAUT, Walter:
François-Joseph Gossec: chantre de la
Révolution française. [Gilly]: Institut
Jules Destrée pour la défense et l'il-
lustration de la Wallonie, 1970: 75
(Chaussée de Châtelet, 42) ((-))

GOTTSCHALK, LOUIS MOREAU, 1829-1869

1232 FRANKE, Knut: Louis Moreau Gottschalk, Diskografie in fono forum 1972
(No. 2, February): 93 ((-))

1233 OFFERGELD, Robert: Gottschalk on
records in Hi Fi Stereo Review, XXI/3
(September 1968): 67 ((-))

GOULD, GLENN, 1932-

1234 COSSÉ, Peter: Glenn Gould; Schallplattenverzeichnis in fono forum 1973
(No. 4, April): 332 ((5)); Addenda: fono
forum 1973 (No. 7, July): 594; 1973
(No. 10, October): 920 ((-))

GOUNOD, CHARLES FRANÇOIS, 1818-1893

1235 Music on record: Charles Gounod in
Audio and Record Review (February
1969): 94 ((-))

GRAINGER, PERCY ALDRIDGE, 1882-1961

1236 HUGHES, Eric: The recorded works of
Percy Grainger in Recorded Sound, 45-
46 (January-April 1972): 38-43 ((1))

1237 HUGHES, Eric: The recorded works of
Percy Grainger in SLATTERY,
Thomas C.: Percy Grainger: the inveterate innovator. Evanston, Ill.: Instrumentalist Co., [1974]: 245-250
((1, 3, 4, 6, 7))

1238 LAWRENCE, A. F. R.: Records of
Percy Grainger as an interpreter in
Recorded Sound, No. 45-46 (January-
April 1972): 43-48; [Includes unpub-
lished records] ((1, 3, 4, 6, 7))

1239 LAWRENCE, A. F. R.: Records of
Percy Grainger as an interpreter in
SLATTERY, Thomas C.: Percy
Grainger: the inveterate innovator.
Evanston, Ill.: Instrumentalist Co.,
[1974]: 250-255 ((1, 3, 4, 6, 7))

GRANFORTE, APOLLO

1240 COURT, H. P.: The records in Record
News, I/2 (October 1956): 65-67 ((-));
Addenda: Record News, I/4 (December
1956): 157-158 ((-))

1241 DELICATA, A. G.: Apollo Granforte:
discography in Record Collector,
XII/8-9 (November-December 1959):
180-194 ((3, 6, 7)); Errata in Record
Collector, XII/10-11 (December 1959-
January 1960): 258 ((3, 6, 7)); XIII/3
(May 1960): 71 ((-))

GREEF, ARTHUR DE, 1862-1940

1242 ANDERSON, H. L.: The recording sessions of Arthur de Greef in Recorded
Sound, No. 29-30 (January-April 1968):
284-291 [Includes piano rolls] ((3, 4, 6,
7))

GREEF-ANDRIESSEN, PELAGIE, 1860-1937

1243 MOORE, Jerrold N.: Pelagie Greef-
Andriessen discography in Antique
Records (May 1973): 24 ((3, 7))

GREENE, HARRY PLUNKET, 1865-1936

1244 [[[Discography] in Record Advertiser
(September-October 1971]]

1245 Plunket Greene discography in Recorded Sound, No. 32 (October 1968):
329-330 ((3, 6, 7))

GREGORIAN CHANTS
   See CHANTS (PLAIN, GREGORIAN,
   ETC.)

GRIEG, EDVARD HAGERUP, 1843-1907

1246 ÅHLÉN, Carl-Gunnar: Edvard Grieg
      (1843-1907) in Musik Revy, XXVIII/3
      (1972): 155-157 (Grammofonens
      veteraner, 6) ((3, 5, 7))

1247 [[[Discografie] in CUYPERS, Jules:
      Edvard Grieg. Haarlem: J. H. Gottmer,
      [1967]]]

1248 Discografie in POLS, André M.: Het
      leven van E. Grieg. Brussel: Reinaert
      Uitgaven, [1971]: 44-47 (Meesters der
      toonkunst, 16) ((-))

GRIFFES, CHARLES TOMLINSON, 1884-1920

1249 Recordings of Griffes's works in
      MAISEL, Edward M.: Charles T.
      Griffes: the life of an American com-
      poser. New York: A. A. Knopf, 1943:
      346-347 ((-))

1250 Recordings of Griffes' works in
      MAISEL, Edward M.: Charles T.
      Griffes: the life of an American com-
      poser. New York: Da Capo Press,
      1972: 346-347 (Da Capo Press music
      reprint series) ((-))

GROZĂVESCU, TRAIAN

1251 Discografie in DEMETER-GROZĂ-
      VESCU, Mira: Traian Grozăvescu, [de]
      Mira Demeter-Grozăvescu [si] I.
      VOLEDI. Bucureşti: Editura Muzicală
      a Uniunii Compozitorilor din R. P. R.,
      1965: 261 ((-))

GRÜMMER, ELISABETH

1252 Diskografie in fono forum 1960 (No. 9,
      September): 25 ((-))

GRUMIAUX, ARTHUR, 1921-

1253 Diskographie in Phonoprisma, VI/1
      (January-February 1963): 20 ((-))

1254 From the discography of Arthur
      Grumiaux in Philips Music Herald
      (Summer 1969): 23 ((-))

GRUMIAUX TRIO

1255 From the discography of Arthur
      Grumiaux in Philips Music Herald
      (Summer 1969): 23 ((-))

GUEDEN, HILDE, 1917-

1256 CLOUGH, F. F., and G. J. CUMING:
      Hilde Gueden diskography in Gramo-
      phone Record Review, No. 58 (August
      1958): 810, 813 ((-))

GUI, VITTORIO, 1885-1975

1257 VINCENTINI, Mario: Vittorio Gui e il
      disco in Discoteca alta Fedelta, No.
      156 (December 1975): 15 ((-))

GUILLAUME DE MACHAUT, d. 1377

1258 Records in LEVARIE, Siegmund:
      Guillaume de Machaut. New York:
      Sheed and Ward, 1954: 114 (Great reli-
      gious composers) ((-))

1259 Records in LEVARIE, Siegmund:
      Guillaume de Machaut. New York: Da
      Capo Press, 1969 [c1954]: 114 (Da
      Capo Press music reprint series) ((-))

GULBRANSON, ELLEN, 1863-1947

1260 HEGERMANN-LINDENCRONE, Knudde:
      [Collector's corner] in Gramophone,
      No. 185 (October 1938): 223 ((-))

GULDA, FRIEDRICH, 1930-

1261 Diskographie in GEITEL, Klaus: Fragen
      an Friedrich Gulda: Anmerkungen zu
      Musik und Gesellschaft. Berlin: Rem-
      brandt Verlag, [1973]: 53 ((-))

1262 Schallplatten-Verzeichnis in JANTSCH,
      Erich: Friedrich Gulda: die Verant-
      wortung des Interpreten. London: J.
      Weinberger, [1953]: 56 (Musiker, die
      der Welt gehören, 1) ((-))

GUNTHER, INGEVONK
   See IVOGÜN, MARIA

GURIDI, JESÚS, 1886-1961

1263 [[MOLES, E.: [Discography] in Disco-
      filia, No. 4 (June 1956): 138]]

HMV RECORDS
   See listing for NEVEU, GINETTE.
   Ronze-Nevey, Marie-Jeanne

HACKETT, CHARLES, 1889-1942

1264 HOLDRIDGE, Lawrence F.: The re-
      cordings of Charles Hackett in Record
      Collector, XXII/8-9 (February 1975):
      202-214 ((1, 3, 6, 7)); Addenda: Record
      Collector, XXII/10-11 (April 1975):
      257 ((-))

HADLEY, PATRICK ARTHUR SHELDON,
1899-1973

1265 [[HUGHES, Eric: Discography in
TODDS, Walter: Patrick Hadley; a
memoir. London: Triad Press, 1974:
17-18]]

HAEBLER, INGRID

1266 SPINGEL, Hans Otto: Ingrid Haebler in
fono forum 1960 (No. 7, July): 25 ((−))

1267 WORBS, Hans Christoph: Diskographie
(Auswahl) (sämtliche Aufnahmen bei
Philips) in Musica, XXIV/3 (May-June
1970): 295 ((−))

HAEFLIGER, ERNST

1268 KOEGLER, Horst: Ernst Haefliger in
fono forum 1960 (No. 10, October): 12
((−))

HÄNDEL, GEORG FRIEDRICH, 1685-1759

1269 ALLORTO, R., and R. EWERHART:
Discografia ragionata delle musiche
italiane di Haendel in L'Approdo
Musicale, III/12 (October-December
1960): 47-72 ((−))

1270 BURKE, C. G.: The records of Handel
in High Fidelity, II/2 (September-
October 1952): 60-68 ((−))

1271 Discografie in POLS, André M.: Het
leven van G. F. Haendel. Brussel:
Reinaert Uitgaven, [1970]: 43-48
(Meesters der toonkunst, 15) ((−))

1272 REDFERN, Brian: Selected recordings
of Handel's music in CUDWORTH,
Charles: Handel: a biography, with a
survey of books, editions, and recordings. London: Bingley, 1972: 90-101
(The Concertgoer's companions) ((−))

1273 REDFERN, Brian: Selected recordings of
Handel's music in CUDWORTH, Charles:
Handel: a biography, with a survey of
books, editions, and recordings. [Ham-
den, CT]: Linnet Books, [1972]: 90-101
(The Concertgoer's companions) ((−))

1274 Discographie in ROLLAND, Romain:
Haendel. [Nouv. éd.] Paris: Michel,
[1951]: [295]-311 ((−))

1275 Discography in SADIE, Stanley:
Handel. London: J. Calder, [1966]:
189-192 ((−))

1276 SASSE, Konrad: Verzeichnis der
Schallplatten mit Werken von Georg
Friedrich Händel in Deutschland für
die Jahre 1952-1954 in Händel Jahrbuch, VII (1955): [139]-[150] ((−))

1277 SASSE, Konrad: Verzeichnis von
Schallplatten aus der Produktion in

de sozialistischen Ländern mit Werken
von Georg Friedrich Händel. Halle:
[s.n.], [1964]: 15 pp. ((−))

1278 Werke von Georg Friedrich Händel auf
Langspielplatten in Musikziehung,
XII/4 (June 1959): 231-232 ((−)); XIII/1
(September 1959): 36-37 ((−))

Messiah

1279 MANNONI, Gérard: Messiah: discographie comparée in Harmonie (February
1973): 92-97 ((−))

HAHN, REYNALDO, 1875-1947

1280 BARNES, H. M., and V. GIRARD:
Reynaldo Hahn discography in Recorded Sound, No. 21 (January 1966):
16-18 ((1, 3, 6, 7))

1281 Discographie in Courrier Musical de
France, No. 19 (1967): 175 ((−))

1282 GALTAT, Claude: Reynaldo Hahn; un
essai de discographie in Disques, No. 7
(August-September 1948): 194-195 ((−))

HAITINK, BERNARD JOHAN HERMAN, 1929-

1283 A Haitink discography in Records and
Recording, XV/12 (September 1972):
23 ((−))

1284 SCHWINGER, Wolfram: Diskografie in
fono forum 1964 (No. 6, June): 224 ((−))

HALFFTER JIMÉNEZ, CRISTOBAL, 1930-

1285 Discografia in MARCO, Tomás:
[Cristóbal Halffter]. [Madrid: Servicio
de Publicaciones del Ministerio de
Educación y Ciencia], 1972: 85-86
(Artistas españoles contemporáneos,
34. Serie músicos) ((−))

HALLE ORCHESTRA
See HARTY, SIR HAMILTON

HALLER, HERMANN, 1914-

1286 Plattenaufnahmen in LARESE, Dino:
Hermann Haller eine Lebensskizze.
Amriswil: Amriswiler Bücherei, 1975:
46 ((−))

HAMMERKLAVIER MUSIC
See PIANO MUSIC

HAMMOND, JOAN, 1912-

1287 Discography in HAMMOND, Joan: A
voice, a life: autobiography. London:
Gollancz, 1970: [249]-256 ((−))

HARASIEWICZ, ADAM, 1932-

1288 BURG, To: Diskografie in fono forum 1963 (No. 9, September): 347 ((-))

HARNONCOURT, NIKOLAS
See CONCENTUS MUSICUS

HARP

1289 Harp News reference record list—1950-1960 in Harp News, III/2 (1960): 11-16 ((-))

HARP MUSIC

1290 Composers, compositions and recordings in RENSCH, Roslyn: The harp: its history, technique and repertoire. London: Duckworth, 1969: [183]-210 ((-))

1291 Composers, compositions and recordings in RENSCH, Roslyn: The harp: its history, technique and repertoire. New York: Praeger Publishers, [1969]: [183]-210 ((-))

HARTMANN, KARL AMADEUS, 1905-1963

1292 RUPPEL, Karl Heinz: Diskografie in fono forum 1961 (No. 1, January): 10 ((-))

1293 SCHUMANN, Karl: Diskografie in fono forum 1964 (No. 1, January): 5 ((-))

HARTY, SIR HAMILTON, 1879-1941

1294 Recordings by Sir Hamilton Harty and the Halle Orchestra in Phonograph Monthly Review, I/8 (May 1927): 338 ((-))

HASKIL, CLARA, 1895-1960

1295 Clara Haskil; Schallplattenverzeichnis in fono forum 1973 (No. 10, October): 950 ((7))

1296 Diskographie in GAVOTY, Bernard: Clara Haskil. Genf: R. Kister, c1962: 30, 32 (Die Grossen Interpreten) ((-))

1297 LEWINSKI, Wolf-Eberhard von: Clara Haskil, eine Diskografie in fono forum 1961 (No. 9, September): 30-31, 40 ((-))

1298 MANN, Carl-Heinz: Clara Haskil in fono forum 1961 (No. 2, February): 39 ((-))

1299 Discographie in SPYCKET, Jérôme: Clara Haskil. Lausanne: Payot, c1975: 265-267 ((-))

1300 Discographie in WOLFENSBERGER, Rita: Clara Haskil. 1. Aufl. Bern: Scherz, 1961: [163]-166 ((-))

HAYDN, JOSEPH, 1732-1809

1301 Haydn et le disque in BARBAUD, Pierre: Haydn. [Paris]: Éditions du Seuil, [1957]: 186-191 (Solfèges, 6) ((-))

1302 A selected discography from Great Britain and America in BARBAUD, Pierre: Haydn. New York: Grove Press, [1959]: 186-190 ((-))

1303 BURKE, C. G.: The collector's Haydn. Philadelphia: Lippincott, [1959]: 316 pp. (Keystone books in music, KB-7) ((-))

1304 Discografia in L'Approdo Musicale, III/11 (July-September 1960): 164-190 ((-))

1305 Discography of discarded Haydn in Saturday Review (February 25, 1961): 63-64 ((-))

1306 Selected recordings of Haydn's music in REDFERN, Brian: Haydn: a biography, with a survey of books, editions & recordings. London: Bingley, 1970: 85-104 (The Concertgoer's companions) ((-))

1307 Selected recordings of Haydn's music in REDFERN, Brian: Haydn: a biography, with a survey of books, editions & recordings. [Hamden, CT]: Archon Books, 1970: 85-104 (The Concertgoer's companions) ((-))

1308 Discographie de Haydn in VIGNAL, Marc: Franz-Joseph Haydn: l'homme et son oeuvre. [Paris]: Seghers, [1964]: 180-188 (Musiciens de tous les temps, 3) ((-))

1309 Werke von Joseph Haydn auf Langspielplatten in Musikziehung, XII/3 (March 1959): 159-163 ((-))

Works, Instrumental

1310 BURKE, C. G.: The music of Joseph Haydn on microgroove records. Part I: Orchestral works in High Fidelity, II/3 (November-December 1952): 70-78 ((-))

1311 BURKE, C. G.: Haydn on L.P. Part II: Concertos and chamber works in High Fidelity, II/4 (January-February 1953): 71-80 ((-))

1312 BURKE, C. G.: Haydn on microgroove. Part III: Keyboard, vocal works, addenda in High Fidelity, III/1 (March-April 1953): 72-80 ((-))

Die Schöpfung

1313 Discographie comparée in Harmonie, No. 30 (October 1967): 76-79 ((-))

Symphonies

1314 BOLLERT, Werner: Die besprochenen
Aufnahmen in fono forum 1967 (No. 9,
September): 512 ((-))

1315 The Haydn symphonies on disc in
Stereo Review, XXXIII/3 (September
1974): 81 ((-))

1316 HODGSON, Antony, and R. J. DEAR-
LING: Joseph Haydn—the London symphonies. A critical assessment of the
microgroove recordings in Haydn
Yearbook/Haydn Jahrbuch, IX (1975):
126-188 ((-))

1317 HODGSON, A., R. J. DEARLING, and K.
WARSOP: Joseph Haydn—the pre-
London symphonies. A critical assessment of the microgroove recordings in
Haydn Yearbook/Haydn Jahrbuch, VII
(1970): 169-252 ((-)); Supplementary
discography—78 rpm recordings: 252-
253 ((-))

1318 MARSH, Robert Charles: The symphonies of Haydn; discography in High
Fidelity, XI/10 (October 1961): 54-56,
136-140 ((-))

1319 [[ROBBINS-LANDON, H. C.: Eine
vergleichende Discographie in Phono,
VIII/1]] [Symphonies no. 99-101]

1320 [[ROBBINS-LANDON, H. C.: Eine
vergleichende Discographie in Phono,
VIII/2]] [Symphony no. 102]

1321 [[ROBBINS-LANDON, H. C.: Eine
vergleichende Discographie in Phono,
VIII/4]] [Symphony no. 103]

1322 [[ROBBINS-LANDON, H. C.: Eine
vergleichende Discographie in Phono,
VIII/6]] [Symphony no. 104]

HAYES, ROLAND, 1887-1976

1323 [KNIGHT, Arthur E.]: Roland Hayes
discography in Record Collector, X/2
(July 1955): 38-45 ((1, 3, 7)); Addenda:
Record Collector, XII/8-9 (November-
December 1959): 215 ((3, 6))

HEDENBLAD, IVAN EGGERT, 1851-1908

1324 ÅHLÉN, Carl-Gunnar: OD och Ivan Eg-
gert Hedenblad (1851-1908) in Musik
Revy, XXVII/4 (1972): 218 (Grammofonens veteraner, 7) ((3, 6, 7))

HEIFETZ, JASCHA, 1901-

1325 Diskographie in Collegium Musicum
1971 (No. 1): 12-13 ((-))

1326 HARTNACK, Joachim W.: Diskografie
Jascha Heifetz in fono forum 1971
(No. 2, February): 93-94 ((5))

1327 Jascha Heifetz in Gramophone, III/6
(November 1925): 278-279 ((-))

1328 Jascha Heifetz recommended records
in Audio and Record Review (May
1969): 331 ((-))

1329 MALTESE, John Anthony: A Jascha
Heifetz discography in Le Grand
Baton, XXII/1-2 (March-June 1975):
24-53 ((1, 4, 7))

1330 SPINGEL, Hans Otto: Diskografie in
fono forum 1961 (No. 9, September):
14 ((-))

HEINRICH SCHÜTZ CHOIR

1331 Grammofoonplaten van het Heinrich
Schütz Choir (& Chorale) op Argo: in
Festival of Flanders, Louvain, 1972:
Heinrich Schütz-herdenking, 1672-
1972. Ed. Karel AERTS. Leuven:
[s.n.], 1972: 100 ((-))

HELENA, EDITH

1332 FAVIA-ARTSAY, Aida: Discography of
Edith Helena in Hobbies, LIX/11
(January 1955): 22 ((7))

1333 KNIGHT, Arthur E.: The Edith Helena
heritage in Record Collector, IX/7
(December 1954): 162-165 ((7)); IX/11-
12 (April-May 1955): 271 ((-))

HELMUTH, OSVALD, 1894-1966

1334 ANDREASEN, Axel: Osvald Helmuth og
grammofonen en discografi, af Axel
Andreasen, Jens HANSEN [og] Emil
MAROTT. København: Axel Andreasen,
(Hothers Plads 23/1), 1972: 108 pp.
((3, 4, 6, 7))

HEMPEL, FRIEDA, 1885-1955

1335 STONE, Barbara F.: Discography of
Mme. Frieda Hempel in Record Collector, X/3 (August 1955): 65-71
((1, 3, 6, 7))

1336 WILE, Raymond: The Edison discs of
Frieda Hempel in Association for
Recorded Sound Collections Journal,
III/2-3 (Fall 1971): 47-52 ((4, 6, 7))

HENKEMANS, HANS, 1913-

1337 Discographie in Phono, II/1 (Fall 1955):
3 ((-))

HENRY, PIERRE, 1925-

1338 ROY, Jean: Discographie in Revue
Musicale, No. 267 (1969): 29-30 ((-))

HEROLD, WILHELM

1339 STUBINGTON, Kenneth: [Discography]
in Record News, I/10 (June 1957): 350-
351 ((-))

1340 Vilhelm Herold. [Copenhagen]:
Nationalmuseet, [1961]: 19 pp. (Det
National Diskotek Katalog, 8)
((4, 5, 7))

HESELTINE, PHILIP, 1894-1930

1341 [[MARVIN, Keith, and C. P. MILLS: An
inventory of Peter Warlock recordings
in The Peter Warlock Society Newsletter, No. 1 (1966): 10-11]]

1342 Discography in TOMLINSON, Fred: A
Peter Warlock handbook. London:
Triad Press, 1974: 46-49 ((4, 5))

HESS, ERNST, 1912-1968

1343 Diskographie in GRAF, Harry: Ernst
Hess. Zürich: Kommissionsverlag
Hug, 1970: 43 (Neujahrsblatt der
Allgemeinen Musikgesellschaft
Zürich auf das Jahr 1970, 154) ((-))

HESS, MYRA, 1890-1965

1344 CLOUGH, F. F., and G. J. CUMING:
Myra Hess discography in Recorded
Sound, No. 24 (October 1966): 104-106;
[Includes unpublished records] ((1, 4,
5, 7))

1345 CLOUGH, F. F., and G. J. CUMING:
Discography in LASSIMONNE, Denise:
Myra Hess. London: H. Hamilton,
1966: 112-119 ((-))

1346 CLOUGH, F. F., and G. J. CUMING:
Discography in LASSIMONNE, Denise:
Myra Hess. New York: Vanguard
Press, [1966]: 114-121 ((-))

HEWARD, LESLIE HAYS, 1897-1943

1347 Leslie Heward's records in BLOM,
Eric: Leslie Heward, 1897-1943: a
memorial volume. [2d ed.] Birming-
ham, Eng.: Cornish Bros., [1946]:
92-94 ((-))

HILDA, BERNARD

1348 [[[Discography] in Discofilia, No. 11
(March 1957): 105]]

HINDEMITH, PAUL, 1895-1963
See also listing for RAVEL, MAURICE,
1875-1937. Odriozola, Antonio: Las
grabacionnes en discos LP de seis
grandes figuras de la música contemporanea....

1349 DELALANDE, Jacques: Diskographie
in Hi Fi Stereophonie, III/3 (March
1964): 143-149 ((-))

1350 Deutsches Rundfunkarchiv: Paul
Hindemith, 16.11.1895-28.12-1963: als
Dirigent und Solist im Rundfunk.
Frankfurt am Main: Deutsches Rund-
funkarchiv, 1965: xii, 85 leaves ((1,
4, 7))

1351 Discografia in L'Approdo Musicale,
I/3 (July-September 1958): 63-69 ((-))

1352 Discographie de Paul Hindemith in
Revue des Disques, No. 133 (February 1965): 187-188 ((-))

1353 Discographie des oeuvres de Hindemith
etablie au 31 mars 1973 in Revue Musicale de Suisse Romande, XXVI/2
(1973): 42 ((-))

1354 Discographie in Hommage à Paul
Hindemith: 1895-1963, l'homme et
l'oeuvre. Yverdon: Éditions de la
Revue Musicale de Suisse Romande,
[1973]: 187-190 ((-))

1355 [Discography] in LEVAÎA, Tamara
Nikolaevna: Paul Hindemith: Zhizn i
Tvorchestvo. Moskva: "Muzyka,"
1974: 435-[446] ((-))

1356 [Discographic information included] in
RÖSNER, Helmut: Paul Hindemith:
Katalog seiner Werke, Diskographie,
Bibliographie, Einführung in das
Schaffen. Frankfurt am Main: Städt-
ische Musikbibliothek, [1970]: 60 pp.
((-))

1357 [[Schallplatten in Paul Hindemith—
Werkverzeichnis. Mainz: Schott
[1965]: 55-59]]

1358 SCHUMANN, Karl: Diskografie in fono
forum 1964 (No. 2, February): 52-53
((-))

1359 Gramophone records by Paul Hindemith
in SKELTON, Geoffrey: Paul Hindemith:
the man behind the music; a biography.
London: Gollancz, 1975: 308-310 ((-))

1360 Alphabetical list of recorded works in
STONE, Kurt: Paul Hindemith: catalogue of published works and recordings, November 1954. New York: Associated Music Publishers, 1954: 44-52
((-))

1361 [[Werke von Paul Hindemith auf Schallplatten in Musik und Bildung, VI (June
1974): 381-382]]

HISLOP, JOSEPH

1362 ENGLUND, Björn: Joseph Hislop's recordings in Talking Machine Review,
No. 4 (June 1970): 109-110 ((7))

1363 Joseph Hislop: a discography in 78
RPM, No. 4 (February 1969): 4-8
((3, 7))

HOENGEN, ELISABETH

1364 Konzert und Rundfunkaufnahmen in
WURM, Ernst: Elisabeth Höngen: ein
Künstlerbild. Wien; München: Österreichischer Bundesverlag, [1966]: 67-
68 ((1, 7))

1365 Schallplatten in WURM, Ernst: Elisabeth Höngen: ein Künstlerbild. Wien;
München: Österreichischer Bundesverlag, [1966]: 69-71 ((-))

HOFFMAN, LUDWIG

1366 GRÄTER, Manfred: Diskografie in fono
forum 1960 (No. 10, October): 25 ((-))

HOFMANN, JOSEF, 1876-1957

1367 [[CAPES, S. J.: [Discography] in
Phonographiana (September-October
1956)]]

1368 KANSKI, J.: Hofmann na płytach gramo-
fonowych (Jozef Hofmann) in Ruch
Muzyczny, VI/4 (1962): 4-5 ((-))

1369 LAWRENCE, A. F. R., and Gregor
BENKO: Josef Hofmann discography in
International Piano Library Bulletin,
I/2 (Summer 1967): 9-16 ((3, 5, 6, 7));
I/3-4 (Fall-Winter 1967): 11-18;
II/1 (May 1968): 3-8; II/4 (December
1968): 3-5 ((3, 5, 6, 7))

1370 WEBER, Jan: Legenda utrwalona na
płytach wznowionych nagraniach Jozefa
Hofmanna in Ruch Muzyczny, XVIII/12
(1974): 6-7 ((7)); XVIII/14 (1974): 14-
15 ((7))

HOLBROOKE, JOSEF CHARLES, 1878-1958

1371 FOREMAN, Lewis, and Graham PAR-
LETT: Discography in Antique Records
(October 1974): 22-26 ((1, 3, 6, 7))

1372 List of gramophone records, piano and
organ rolls in Josef Holbrooke: Various
appreciations. London: Rudall Carte &
Co. and [Holbrooke Society], 1937: 183-
188 ((-))

HOLLIGER, HEINZ, 1939-

1373 Grammofoninspelning in Nutida Musik,
VIII/2 (1964-1965): 70 ((-))

HOLLWEG, ILSE

1374 Schallplattenaufnahmen in RUHRBERG,
Karl: Ilse Hollweg. [1. Aufl.] Duisburg:
W. Braun, [1971]: 71-72 ((-))

HOLMBOE, VAGN, 1909-

1375 Complete discography in RAPOPORT,
Paul: Vagn Holmboe: a catalogue of his
music, discography, bibliography, essays. London: Triad Press, 1974: 69-
74 (Triad Press bibliographical
series, 2) ((-))

HOLST, GUSTAV, 1874-1934

1376 HUGHES, Eric: The music of Gustav
Holst: a discography in Recorded
Sound, No. 59 (July 1975): 441-446
((1))

1377 Music on record: Gustav Holst in Audio
and Record Review, VIII/10 (June 1968):
426-427; VIII/11 (July 1968): 499 ((-))

1378 List of music, including discography in
SHORT, Michael: Gustav Holst, 1874-
1934: a centenary documentation.
London; New York: White Lion Publishers, 1974: 285 pp. ((1, 5, 7))

HOMER, LOUISE, 1871-1947

1379 REUTLINGER, Dale: Louise Homer: a
discography in Maestro, IV-V (1972-
1973): 62-65 ((7))

HONEGGER, ARTHUR, 1892-1955

1380 Discographie in BRUYR, José:
Honegger et son oeuvre. Paris:
Corrêa, [1947]: 255-257 (Collection
"Musique") ((-))

1381 CALVÉ, Jacques de: Discographie
critique in LANDOWSKI, Marcel:
Honegger. Bourges: Éditions du
Seuil, 1957: 181-191 ((-))

1382 Discographie des oeuvre d'Arthur
Honegger in DELANNOY, Marcel
François Georges: Honegger. Paris:
P. Horay, [1953]: [233]-239 ((-))

1383 Essai de discographie générale de
Honegger in Disques, No. 75-76 (December 1955): 898-899 ((-))

1384 Discographie d'Arthur Honegger in
FESCHOTTE, Jacques: Arthur
Honegger: l'homme et son oeuvre...,
catalogue des oeuvres, discographie.
Paris: Seghers, 1966: [171]-[177]
(Musiciens de tous les temps, 30)
((-))

1385 Discographie d'Arthur Honegger in
FESCHOTTE, Jacques: Arthur

Honegger. [Lausanne]: La Guilde du livre, [1970]: 173-[177] (Musiciens de tous les temps) ((-))

1386 Discographie in GAUTHIER, André: Arthur Honegger. Lyon: Éditions et imprimeries du Sudest, [1957]: [95]-[96] (Collection Nos amis les musiciens) ((-))

1387 Discographie d'Arthur Honegger in GUILBERT, Yves: Arthur Honegger. Paris: Apostolat de la presse, [1959]: [125]-[143] (Caritas) ((-))

1388 HOÉRÉE, Arthur: Discographie in Arthur Honegger. Paris: Publications techniques, 1943?: [34] (Collection comaedia-Charpentier, [5]) ((-))

1389 ROY, Jean: Discographie in Diapason, No. 100 (October 1965): 39 ((-))

1390 Diszkografia in SZÖLLÖSY, András: Arthur Honegger. Budapest: [Gondolat Kiadó], 1960: 361-[366] (Kis zenei könyvtáz, 16) ((-))

1391 Schallplattenverzeichnis in TAPPOLET, Willy: Arthur Honneger. Zürich; Leipzig: Gebrüder Hug & Co., 1933: 265-266 ((-))

1392 Musique enregistrée: liste des disques in TAPPOLET, Willy: Arthur Honegger. Neuchâtel: Éditions de la Baconnière, [1938]: [300]-301 ((-))

HOPPE, HEINZ

1393 Diskographie in HOPPE-LINZEN, Carla: Willst du dein Herz mir schenken. Mein Leben mit Heinz Hoppe. Emsdetten: Lecthe, 1972: 137-151 ((-))

HORENSTEIN, JASCHA, 1898-1973
See also KERTÉSZ, ISTVÁN

1394 DIETHER, Jack: A Horenstein discography in High Fidelity, XXIII/10 (October 1973): 80-83 ((-))

HOROWITZ, VLADIMIR, 1904-

1395 ALDER, Caine: Horowitz on records in High Fidelity, XXIII/7 (July 1973): 53-56 ((5))

1396 CLOUGH, F. F., and G. J. CUMING: A Horowitz discography in Audio and Record Review, V/5 (January 1966): 9-10 ((-))

1397 CLOUGH, F. F., and G. J. CUMING: Vladimir Horowitz; a microgroove diskography in Gramophone Record Review, No. 42 (April 1957): 442-445 ((-))

1398 MOHR, Wolfgang: Vladimir Horowitz; Schallplattenverzeichnis in fono forum 1974 (No. 10, October): 945-950 ((5, 7))

1399 Recommended records in Audio and Record Review (November 1968): 817 ((-))

HOTTER, HANS, 1909-

1400 Diskographie in WESSLING, Berndt: Hans Hotter. Bremen: Schünemann, [1966]: [141] ((-))

HUBERMAN, BRONISLAW, 1882-1947

1401 GLASPOLE, Raymond: Bronislaw Huberman—a discography in Record Advertiser (November-December 1970): 5-7 ((-))

IBERT, JACQUES, 1890-1962

1402 Liste des disques microsillons des oeuvres de Jacques Ibert in FESCHOTTE, Jacques: Jacques Ibert. Paris: Ventadour, [1958]: [44]-46 (Collection "Musiciens d'aujourd'hui") ((-))

1403 Discographie in MICHEL, Gérard: Jacques Ibert l'homme et son oeuvre..., catalogue des oeuvres. Paris: Seghers, 1968: [183]-185 (Musiciens de tous les temps, 37) ((-))

IMPRESSIONISM

1404 Discography and films in HARDER, Paul O.: Bridge to 20th century music: a programmed course. [Boston: Allyn and Bacon, 1973]: 271-277 ((-))

IMPROVISATION (MUSIC)
See listing for ORGAN MUSIC. Records in Conely, James: A guide to improvisation: an introductory handbook for church organists

IRELAND, JOHN, 1879-1962

1405 [[CHAPMAN, Ernest: Discography in The John Ireland Charitable Trust: A Catalogue of published works and recordings. London: Boosey & Hawkes, 1968: 37-42]]

1406 HUGHES, Eric: John Ireland discography in Recorded Sound, No. 53 (January 1974): 258-262 ((1, 7))

IRWIN, ROBERT

1407 Records by Robert Irwin in Disc, III/10 (Spring 1949): 74 ((-))

ISLANDI, STEFÁN, 1907-

1408 Skrayfir hljómplötur in INDRIDI, G.:
Áfram veginn: sagan um Stefán Islandi.
Akureyri: Björnsson, 1975: [251]-252
((-))

ISSERSTEDT, HANS SCHMIDT
See SCHMIDT-ISSERSTEDT, HANS

IVES, CHARLES EDWARD, 1874-1954

1409 A list of the compositions of Charles
Edward Ives [including discographical
references] in COWELL, Henry:
Charles Ives and his music, by Henry
Cowell and Sidney COWELL. New
York: Oxford University Press, 1955:
207-233 ((-))

1410 A list of recorded compositions of
Charles Edward Ives in COWELL,
Henry: Charles Ives and his music, by
Henry Cowell and Sidney COWELL.
London; New York: Oxford University
Press, [1969, c1955]: 228-243 (A
Galaxy book) ((5))

1411 Phonorecord index [includes discographical notes] in DE LERMA,
Dominique-René: Charles Edward
Ives, 1874-1954: a bibliography of his
music. [1st ed. Kent, OH]: Kent
State University Press, [1970]: 189-
205 ((-))

1412 HALL, David: Charles Edward Ives: a
discography in Hi Fi Stereo Review
(October 1964): 102-106 ((-)); (November 1964): 142-146 ((-)); (December
1964): 92-96 ((-))

1413 Ives in sound and print in Music Edu-
cators Journal, LXI (October 1974):
71, 103-109 [Discography only] ((-))

1414 MORGAN, Robert P.: The recordings
of Charles Ives's music in High Fidelity, XXIV/10 (October 1974): 72-76
((-))

1415 VINCENT-MALETTRA, F.: Discographie in Diapason, No. 134 (March 1969):
19 ((-))

1416 WARREN, Richard: Charles E. Ives:
discography. New Haven: Historical
Sound Recordings, Yale University
Library, [1972]: xii, 124 pp. (The
Historical sound recordings publi-
cation series, 1) ((1, 3, 4, 6, 7))

1417 Select discography in WOOLDRIDGE,
David: From the steeples and moun-
tains: a study of Charles Ives. [1st
ed.] New York: Knopf, 1974: [330]-
342 ((-))

IVOGÜN, MARIA, 1891-

1418 DENNIS, J.: Maria Ivoguen, discography in Record Collector, XX/5 (January 1972): 114-119; Addenda: Record
Collector, XX/11-12 (December 1972):
283-284 ((3, 4, 6, 7))

1419 MÜHLEN, Theodor: Diskografie in fono
forum 1962 (No. 10, October): 32 ((-))

JACOBS, HOWARD

1420 WALKER, Steve: The recordings of
Howard Jacobs in Talking Machine
Review, No. 6 (October 1970): 168-
169 ((7))

JADLOWKER, HERMANN, 1878-1953

1421 COURT, H. P.: [Discography] in
Record News I/1 (September 1956):
30-36; Addenda: Record News, I/2
(October 1956): 63; I/4 (December
1956): 158; I/11 (July 1957): 412-413
((-))

1422 KAUFMAN, Tom, and Dennis BREW:
Hermann Jadlowker in Record Collector, XIX/1-2 (March 1970): 11-32
((3, 4, 6, 7))

1423 VEGETO, R.: Discografia in Discoteca,
No. 63 (September 1966): 35-36 ((5))

JANÁČEK, LEOŠ, 1854-1928

1424 [[BARTOŠ, Jaroslav: Diskografie Leoše
Janáčka in Tempo, XX/9-10: 250-252]]

1425 Seznam skladeb [includes discographical references] in ČERNOHORSKÁ,
Milena: Leoš Janáček. [1. vyd.] Praha:
Státní hudební vyd., 1966: 72-80 (Editio Supraphon) ((-))

1426 FELLEGARA, Vittorio: Discografia in
L'Approdo Musicale, III/11 (April-June
1960): 104-108 ((-))

1427 Janáčkova hudba na gramofonových
deskách in Brünn. Universita.
Knihovna: Leoš Janáček, 1854-1928:
výběrová bibliografie. V Brně, 1958:
43-49 ((-))

1428 [[PROCHÁZKA, Jaroslav: Janáčkovská
diskografie na deskách Ultraphon.
Prague, 1943]]

1429 Leoš Janáček: soupis snímků na gramofonových deskách československé
výroby, v red. Jaroslava PROCHÁZKY.
V Praze: Centrogram, [1950]: unpaged
((-))

1430 [[[Discography] in RACEK, Jan: Leoš
Janáček. Leipzig: Reclam, 1962: 205-
[210]]]]

1431 Schallplattenverzeichnis in RACEK,
Jan: Leoš Janáček. Leipzig: Reclam,
1971: 253-[265] ((-))

1432 Skladby [Janáčkovy tvorby] na čs.
gramofonových deskách in ŠEDA,
Jaroslav: Leoš Janáček. [1. vyd.]
Praha: Státní hudební vydavatelství,
1961: 416-426 (Hudební profily, 8)
((-))

1433 SILVERBERG, Robert: Janáček; a
selective discography in High Fidelity,
XIII/3 (March 1963): 57 ((-))

1434 [[ŠTĚDROŇ, Bohumír: Dilo Leoše
Janáčeka; abecední seznam Janáčkových
skladeb a úprav. Bibliografie a diskografie. Prague: [s.n.], 1959]]

JANÁČKOVO KVARTETO

1435 Discografie in VRATISLAVSKÝ, Jan:
Janáčkovo kvarteto. 1. vyd. Praha:
Supraphon, 1975: 55-56 (Edice Lyra)
((-))

JANIS, BYRON, 1928-

1436 MAYER, Martin: Diskografie in fono
forum 1963 (No. 11, November): 451
((-)); Additions and corrections: fono
forum 1964 (No. 2, February): 88 ((-))

JANOWITZ, GUNDULA

1437 Discographie in Diapason, No. 138
(July-August, 1969): 6 ((-))

1438 HÖSLINGER, Clemens: Diskografie in
fono forum 1965 (No. 3, March): 104
((-))

1439 PIPER-ZIETHEN, Herta: Gundula
Janowitz; Verzeichnis der Schall-
plattenaufnahmen in fono forum 1972
(No. 5, May): 362 ((5))

JANSSEN, HERBERT, 1895-1965

1440 HART, Ted: Herbert Janssen; discography in Record Collector, XVI/11-12
(May 1966): 256-263; [Includes unpublished records] ((1, 3, 5, 6, 7))

JÁRDÁNYI, PÁL, 1920-

1441 Diszkográfia in KECSKEMÉTI, István:
Járdányi, Pál. Budapest: Zenemükiadó,
1967: 30 (Mai magyar zeneszerzök) ((5))

JAUBERT, MAURICE, 1900-1940

1442 Discographie in Courrier Musical de
France, No. 9 (1965): 59 ((-))

1443 Archives in PORCILE, François: Maurice Jaubert; musicien populaire ou
maudit? Paris: Les Éditeurs français
réunis, [1971]: [257]-262 ((1))

1444 Discographie in PORCILE, François:
Maurice Jaubert: musicien populaire ou
maudit? Paris: Les Éditeurs français
réunis, [1971]: [253]-256 ((-))

JAUNET, ANDRÉ

1445 Schallplattenverzeichnis /Schallplatten
in Flute: W. A. Mozart: Andante in
C-dur, KV 285e (315) Zürich: Panton
Verlag, 1966: 119 [Note: Master class
lesson with accompanying sound re-
cording] ((-))

JEFFERSON, JOSEPH

1446 GARDNER, M. L.: Joseph Jefferson
discography in 78 RPM, No. 6 (June
1969): 12 ((7))

JENKINS, FLORENCE FOSTER

1447 Melotone recordings by Florence Foster Jenkins in BENDINER, Milton:
Florence Foster Jenkins. New York:
The Melotone Recording Studio, [1946]:
11 ((-))

1448 Discography: Melotone recordings by
Florence Foster Jenkins in Record
Collector, VIII/9 (September 1953):
214 ((-))

JEREMIÁŠ, OTAKAR, 1892-1962

1449 Dirigentskí vykony Otakara Jeremiáše
na gramofonových deskách in PLAVEC,
Josef: Národní umélec Otakar Jeremiáš.
[Vyd. 1.] Praha: Státní nakl. krásné
literatury a umění, 1964: 161-[164]
(Knižnice národních umělců československých) ((-))

JEUNESSE, MARIE LA
See ALBANI, EMMA

JIRÁK, KAREL BOLESLAV, 1891-1972

1450 Recordings and tapes of Jirák music in
TISCHLER, Alice: Karel Boleslav
Jirák: a catalog of his work. Detroit:
Information Coordinators, 1975: 67
(Detroit studies in music bibliography,
32) ((1, 5))

JOACHIM, IRÈNE

1451 BARNES, Harold M.: Discographie
Irène Joachim in Disques, No. 6 (June-
July 1948): 171 ((-))

JOACHIM, JOSEPH, 1831-1907

1452 WARREN, Richard, Jr.: Joseph Joachim (1831-1907); a discography of
his recordings in Antique Records
(October 1974): 58 ((3))

JOCHUM, EUGEN, 1902-

1453 BREH, K.: Gesamtaufnahmen—
Kassettenausgaben in Hi Fi Stereophonie, I/11 (November 1962): 491-
494 ((-))

1454 Eugen Jochum; Schallplattenverzeichnis
in fono forum 1972 (No. 11, November):
948-949 ((5))

1455 HAMON, Jean: Discographie de Eugen
Jochum in Diapason, No. 107 (May
1966): 40-41 ((-))

JOHNSON, EDWARD, 1878-1959

1456 CELLETTI, Rodolfo: The records in
Record News, II/6 (February 1958):
199-201; [From Musica e Dischi, June
1956]; Addenda: Record News, II/7
(March 1958): 265 ((-))

1457 Edward Johnson records [in corres-
pondence] in Gramophone, No. 72 (May
1929): 556 ((-))

1458 FASSETT, Stephen: Edward Johnson
discography in Opera News, XIV/23
(April 17, 1950): 27 ((5))

1459 VEGETO, Raffaele: Discografia di
Edward Johnson (Edoardo di Giovanni)
in Musica e Dischi, XII (No. 118, June
1956): 8 ((7)); Addenda: Musica e
Dischi, XIII (No. 128, April 1957): 52
((-))

JOLIVET, ANDRÉ, 1905-1974

1460 Disques in DEMARQUEZ, Suzanne:
André Jolivet. Paris: Ventadour,
[1958]: 42-44 (Collection "Musiciens
d'aujourd'hui") ((-))

1461 Discographie in Diapason, No. 101
(November 1965): 37 ((-))

1462 Discographie André Jolivet in Diapason,
No. 194 (February 1975): 14-15 ((-))

JONES, SISSIERETTA

1463 [[DAUGHTRY, Willia E.: Sissieretta
Jones: profile of a black artist in Musical Analysis, I/1 (Winter 1972): 12-18]]

JURINAC, SENA, 1921-

1464 Schallplatten in TAMUSSINO, Ursula:
Sena Jurinac. Augsburg: Schroff-Druck
Verlagsgesellschaft, [c1971]: 205-206
((-))

JURJEWSKA, ZINAIDA

1465 Discography in Program notes for
Preiser LV 89 [Sound recording]
[196-?] ((5))

JYLHÄ, KOUSTA, 1910-

1466 Konstaja Koustisen Purppuripelimannit
äänilevy in HELISTÖ, Paavo: Konstan
parempi valssi: Konsta Jylhä ja
suomalainen kansanmusiikki. Helsinki:
Tammi, 1972: 179-[182] ((-))

KABALEVSKIĬ, DMITRIĬ BORISOVICH, 1904-

1467 [Discography] in NAZAREVSKIĬ, Pavel
Petrovich: D. B. Kabalevskii. Moskva:
Sov. kompozitor, 1969: 151-[162] ((-))

KAGEL, MAURICIO

1468 Discographie in SCHNEBEL, Dieter:
Mauricio Kagel: Musik, Theater, Film.
[Köln]: M. DuMont Schauberg, [c1970]:
332 (DuMont Dokumente) ((-))

KAMMERORCHESTER, LAUSANNE
See DESARZENS, VICTOR

KARAJAN, HERBERT VON, 1908-

1469 BREUNIG, Christopher, and Robert
BOAS: Karajan on record in Audio
and Record Review (June 1969): 395
((-))

1470 CLOUGH, F. F., and G. J. CUMING:
Herbert von Karajan; diskography in
Gramophone Record Review, No. 65
(March 1959): 348-349 ((-))

1471 Diskographie in Auswahl in Musica/
Phonoprisma, XXII/2 (March-April
1968): 149 ((-))

1472 Diskographie in GAVOTY, Bernard:
Herbert von Karajan. Genève: R.
Kister, c1955: [32] (Les Grands
interprètes) ((-))

1473 Recordings made by Herbert von
Karajan in GAVOTY, Bernard: Herbert
von Karajan. Geneva: R. Kister, c1956:
[32] (Great concert artists) ((-))

1474 PUGLIESE, Giuseppe: La discografia
completa di Herbert von Karajan in
Discoteca, No. 114 (October 1971):
31, x-xix ((7))

1475 SURTEES, Bruce: Discography in
ROBINSON, Paul: Karajan. Toronto:
Lester and Orpen, c1975: 125-152
(The Art of the conductor) ((-))

1476 WERBA, Robert: Diskographie in
HAEUSSERMANN, Ernst: Herbert von

Karajan: Biographie. [Gütersloh]: C. Bertelsmann, [1968]: 303-[316] ((-))

1477 WERBA, Robert: Karajan—Diskographie in Österreichische Musikzeitschrift, XXII/4 (April 1967): 233-243 ((-))

KASCHMANN, GIUSEPPE

1478 CELLETTI, Rodolfo: Il baritono Giuseppe Kaschmann in Musica e Dischi, VIII (No. 70, July 1952): 9 ((5))

1479 CELLETTI, Rodolfo: Discografia del baritono Giuseppe Kaschmann in Musica e Dischi, XV (No. 154, April 1959): 54 ((7))

1480 [[CELLETTI, Rodolfo: The Kaschmann records in Record News, IV/3 (November 1959)]] [From Musica e Dischi, April 1959]

1481 CELLETTI, Rodolfo: Records in Record News, II/12 (August 1958): 444 [From Musica e Dischi]

1482 FREESTONE, John: Collectors' corner in Gramophone, No. 355 (October 1952): 159 ((-))

1483 VEGETO, Raffaele: Discografia del baritono Giuseppe Kaschmann in Discoteca, No. 54 (October 1965): 37 ((5))

1484 WILE, Raymond: Edison disc recordings of Giuseppe Kaschmann in Association for Recorded Sound Collections Journal, III/2-3 (Fall 1971): 52-53 ((6, 7))

KATCHEN, JULIUS, 1926-1969

1485 Discographie française de Julius Katchen in Diapason, No. 137 (June 1969): 4 ((-))

1486 Recommended records in Audio and Record Review (July 1969): 468 ((-))

KATUL'SKAÍÁ, ELENA KLIMENT'EVNA, 1888-

1487 [Discography] in Elena Kliment'evna Katul'skaía. Moskva: Sov. kompozitor, 1973: 286-[308] ((-))

KEILBERTH, JOSEPH, 1908-1968

1488 Discographie in Phono, II/1 (Fall 1955): 7 ((-))

1489 FREYSE, Renate: Discographie in Neue Zeitschrift für Musikwissenschaft, CXXIV/11 (1963): 439 ((-))

KEMPE, RUDOLF, 1910-1976

1490 Diskographie Rudolf Kempe (Auswahl) in Phonoprisma, VI/5 (September-October 1963): 138 ((-))

KEMPFF, WILHELM, 1895-

1491 Discographie de Wilhelm Kempff chez Deutsche Grammophon in Diapason, No. 109 (August-September 1966): 39 ((-))

1492 Enregistrements reálises par Wilhelm Kempff in GAVOTY, Bernard: Wilhelm Kempff. Genève: R. Kister, c1954: [32] (Les Grands interprètes) ((-))

1493 PURKYT, Robert: Wilhelm Kempff auf Schallplatten in Phono, XII/2 (November-December 1965): 36-38 ((-))

KERTÉSZ, ISTVÁN, 1929-1973

1494 Discographie de J. Horenstein, I. Kertész et P. Kletski in Diapason, No. 178 (June-July 1973): 8-9 ((-))

1495 Diskographie in Collegium Musicum 1971 (No. 3): 7 ((-))

1496 Discographie in RICHTER, Karl: István Kertész. Augsburg: Schroff-Druck Verlaggesellschaft, 1974: 171-173 ((-))

KEYBOARD MUSIC
        See also ORGAN MUSIC; PIANO MUSIC

1497 [[LE HURAY, Peter: Early keyboard music on the gramophone in Music and Letters, XLI (1960): 46-52]]

KHACHATURÍÁN, ARAM IL'ICH, 1903-

1498 [Discography] in SADOVNIKOV, E. L.: A. I. Khachaturíyan; Notograficheskii i bibliograficheskii spravochnik. I izd. Moskva: "Muzyka," 1967: 104-[108] ((-))

1499 Discographie in STRELLER, Friedbert: Aram Chatschaturian. Leipzig: Deutscher Verlag für Musik, 1968: 210-214 ((-))

KHACHATURÍÁN, KAREN SURENOVICH, 1920-

1500 [Discography] in DOLINSKÍÁ, Elena Borisovna: Karen Khachaturian. Moskva: Sov. kompozitor, 1975: 139-[140] ((-))

KIEPURA, JAN, 1902-1966

1501 VEGETO, R.: Discografia in Discoteca, No. 65 (December 1966): 40 ((1, 5))

1502 Nagrania ptytowe Jana Kiepury in
WALDORFF, Jerzy: Jan Kiepura.
Wyd. 1. Krakow: Polskie Wydawn.
Muzyczne, 1974: 89-93 ((5))

KIPNIS, ALEXANDER, 1896-

1503 A Kipnis discography in Stereo Review,
XXVI/1 (January 1971): 73 ((-))

1504 DENNIS, J.: Alexander Kipnis discography in Record Collector, XXII/3-4
(July 1974): 65-79 ((1, 3, 4, 6, 7))

KIRKBY-LUNN, LOUISE, 1873-1930

1505 RICHARDS, John B.: The discography
in Record Collector, XIX/5-6 (August
1970): 120-143 ((3, 4, 5, 6, 7))

1506 RICHARDS, John B.: The Kirkby-Lunn
recordings in Record Collector,
XIX/7-8 (November 1970): 172-188
((-))

KIRKPATRICK, RALPH, 1911-

1507 SPINGEL, Hans Otto: Diskografie in
fono forum (No. 8, August): 307 ((-))

KLEIBER, ERICH, 1890-1956

1508 CLOUGH, F. F., and G. J. CUMING:
Erich Kleiber; a diskography in
Gramophone Record Review, No. 74
(December 1959): 117, 121 ((-))

1509 ROSENBERG, W.: Diskographie Erich
Kleiber in Hi Fi Stereophonie, V/3
(March 1966): 255-256 ((1))

1510 List of recordings by Erich Kleiber
available in Great Britain in RUSSELL,
John: Erich Kleiber: a memoir.
[London]: A. Deutsch, [1957]: [247]
((-))

KLEMPERER, OTTO, 1885-1973

1511 Aufnahmen mit Otto Klemperer
(Auswahl) in Phonoprisma (May-June
1965): 69 ((-))

1512 CLOUGH, F. F., and G. J. CUMING:
Discography in KLEMPERER, Otto:
Minor recollections. London: D. Dob-
son, [1964]: [103]-117 ((-))

1513 CLOUGH, F. F., and G. J. CUMING:
Otto Klemperer—discography in Audio
and Record Review, III/12 (August
1964): 61-62 ((-))

1514 HIRSCH, Nicole: Klemperer: hommage
et discographie in Diapason, No. 179
(September 1973): 7 ((-))

1515 KRELLMANN, Hanspeter: Otto
Klemperer; Schallplattenverzeichnis
in fono forum 1974 (No. 7, July): 604-
606 ((7))

1516 WALKER, Malcolm: Discography in
HEYWORTH, Peter: Conversations with
Klemperer. London: Gollancz, 1973:
[105]-122 ((-))

KLERK, ALBERT DE
See DE KLERK, ALBERT

KLETZKI, PAUL
See listing for KERTÉSZ, ISTVÁN

KNAPPERTSBUSCH, HANS

1517 CLOUGH, F. F., and G. J. CUMING:
Hans Knappertsbusch; a diskography in
Gramophone Record Review, No. 85
(November 1960): 18 ((-))

KOCH, HELMUT

1518 Diskographie in Medium Schallplatte,
No. 12 (No. 3, 1969): 8 ((-))

1519 SPIELER, Heinrich: Diskographie in
Medium Schallplatte, No. 11 (No. 2,
1969): 12-13 ((-))

KOCHAN, GÜNTER

1520 Die Wichtigsten Werke [includes discographical notes] in KYNASS, Hans-
Joachim: Günter Kochan. Berlin:
Verband deutscher Komponisten und
Musikwissenchaftler, Musikinforma-
tionszentrum, 1967: [n.p.] (Komponisten der DDR) ((-))

KOCHANSKA, MARCELLA
See SEMBRICH, MARCELLA

KODÁLY, ZOLTÁN, 1882-1967

1521 BARNA, István: A Qualiton márkájú
mikrobarázdás hanglemezek
diszkográfiája in Magyar Zene,
VIII/2 (1967): 185-188 ((-))

1522 FÁBIÁN, Imre: Kódaly auf ungarischen
Schallplatten in Österreichische
Musikzeitschrift, XXIII/1 (January
1968): 56-58 ((-))

1523 GREENFIELD, Edward: Kodály on
records in Tempo, No. 63 (Winter
1962-1963): [41]-43 ((-))

1524 PLOEGER, Roland: Diskografie
(Auswahl) in fono forum 1962 (No. 12,
December): 15 ((-))

1525 SKALICZKI, Józsefné: Kódaly müveinak hanglemezjegyzéke: diskográfia, [by] Skaliczki Józsefné, TÓTH Ferencné. Szeged: Somogyi Könyvtár, 1974: 46 pp. (A Somogyi-Könyvtár kiadványai) ((4))

1526 Recordings in YOUNG, Percy M.: Zoltán Kodály: a Hungarian musician. London: E. Benn, [1964]: 218-220 ((-))

KOECHLIN, CHARLES LOUIS EUGENE, 1867-1950

1527 Discographie in L'Oeuvre de Charles Koechlin: catalogue. Paris: M. Eschig, 1975: 43-45 ((1))

KOGAN, LEONID BORISOVICH, 1924-

1528 Diskografie Leonid Kogan in fono forum 1964 (No. 9, September): 363 ((-))

1529 Diskographie in Phonoprisma (July-August 1967): 124 ((-))

1530 [Discography] in GRIGOR'EV, Vladimir: Leonid Kogan. Moskva: Muzyka, 1975: 172-175 ((-))

KÓKAI, REZSÖ, 1906-

1531 Diszkográfià in HAMBURGER, Klára: Kókai Rezsö. Budapest: Zenemükiadó, 1968: 32 (Mai magyar zeneszerzök) ((-))

KONWITSCHNY, FRANZ, 1901-1962

1532 Verzeichnis der von Franz Konwitschny Dirigierten Schallplattenaufnahmen (auswahl) in Vermächtnis und Verpflichtung: Festschrift für Franz Konwitschny zum 60. Geburtstag. Leipzig: Deutscher Verlag für Musik, 1961: 91-[92] ((-))

KORJUS, MILIZA

1533 Miliza Korjus [in correspondence] in Gramophone, No. 152 (January 1936): 353 ((-))

1534 PEARMAIN, J.: Miliza Korjus discography in Record Collector, XVI/2 (September 1964): 39-45 ((3, 5, 6, 7)); Addenda: Record Collector, XVI/7-8 (September 1965): 188-189 ((-))

KOSHETZ, NINA, 1894-1965

1535 LIFF, Vivian: Nina Koshetz, discography in Record Collector, XVII/3 (March 1967): 58-60 ((3, 7)); Corrections: Record Collector, XVIII/1-2 (October 1968): 43

KOUSSEVITZKY, SERGIEǏ See KUSSEVITSKIǏ, SERGIEǏ ALEK-SANDROVICH

KOZUB, ERNST

1536 Diskographie in Phonoprisma, VII/1 (January-February 1964): 23 ((-))

1537 SCHUNCK, Gisela: Diskografie in fono forum 1964 (No. 1, January): 29 ((-))

KRAMÁŘE, FRANTIŠKA See KROMMER, FRANZ

KRÁSOVÁ, MARTA, 1901-

1538 Snímky Marty Krásové na deskách Supraphon in ŠOLÍN, Vladimír: Marta Krásová: [Ze života velké pěvkyně]. Praha: Panton, [1960]: 32-37 (Umělci Národního divadla, 1) ((-))

KRAUSS, CLEMENS HEINRICH, 1893-1954

1539 Clemens Krauss—Discographie in Phono (Winter 1954): 6 ((-))

1540 Discografia in Musica e Dischi, X (No. 93, June 1954): 13 ((-))

1541 GLUTH, Walter: Diskografie in fono forum 1961 (No. 6, June): 14 ((-))

1542 HÖSLINGER, Clemens: Clemens Krauss; Schallplattenverzeichnis in fono forum 1973 (No. 4, April): 326-327 ((5)); Addenda: 1973 (No. 7, July): 594 ((-)); 1973 (No. 10, October): 920 ((-))

1543 KENDE, Götz Klaus: Nachlass von Clemens Krauss in Phono, XII/3 (January-February 1966): 65-66 ((-))

1544 Performances by Clemens Krauss: non-commercial recordings in the archives of the West German Radio and the Clemens Krauss-Archiv, Vienna in Recorded Sound, No. 42-43 (April-July 1971): 743-746 ((1, 7))

KREISLER, FRITZ, 1875-1962

1545 Discography in LOCHNER, Louis: Fritz Kreisler. New York: Macmillan, 1950: 417-428 ((-))

1546 Discography in LOCHNER, Louis: Fritz Kreisler. New York: Macmillan, 1951, [c1950]: 417-428 ((-))

1547 Discography in LOCHNER, Louis: Fritz Kreisler. London: Rockliff, [1951, c1950]: 413-432 ((-))

1548 Discographie in PINCHERLE, Marc: Fritz Kreisler. Genève: R. Kister,

c1956: [32] (Les Grands interprètes)
((-))

KRENEK, ERNST, 1900-

1549 [[KRENEK, Ernst: Skladatchl a deska in Hudební Rozhledy, XIX (1966): 744-746]]

KRENZ, JAN, 1926-

1550 Dyskografia in KYDRYŃSKI, Lucjan: Jan Krenz. Wyd. 1. Kraków: Polskie Wydawn. Muzyczne, [1960]: 41-42 ((-))

KRIPS, JOSEF, 1902-1974

1551 NYS, Carl de: Discographie Krips in Diapason, No. 191 (November 1974): 19 ((-))

KRISMER, GIUSEPPE

1552 GUALERZI, Giorgio: Giuseppe Krismer; elenco delle incisioni "Fonotipia" in Discoteca, No. 27 (December 1962): 29 ((-))

KROMBHOLC, JAROSLAV

1553 ECKSTEIN, Pavel: Diskografie in fono forum 1962 (No. 3, March): 14 ((-))

KROMMER, FRANZ, 1759-1831

1554 Gramofonové desky se skladbami Františka Kramáře Universitní Knihovné in Brünn. Universita. Krihova: František Vincene Kramář (François Krommer): 1759-1959, výběrová bibliografie. V Brně: [s.n.], 1950: 11 ((7))

KRUSZELNICKA, SALOMEA

1555 AUTREY, R. L.: Kruszelnicka discography in Record Collector, XVIII/4 (February 1969): 83-88 ((3, 6, 7))

1556 CELLETTI, Rodolfo: Discografia in Musica e Dischi, IX (No. 86, November 1953): 16 ((-))

KUBELÍK, RAFAEL, 1914-

1557 Discographie in Diapason, No. 110 (October 1966): 30 ((-))

KUENTZ, PAUL, 1937-

1558 Discographie in Diapason, No. 177 (May 1973): 11 ((-))

KULLMAN, CHARLES, 1903-

1559 MORGAN, C. I.: Charles Kullmann—discography in Record Collector, XX/11-12 (December 1972): 250-258 ((3, 5, 6, 7))

KUNZ, ERICH

1560 Discographie in Phono, II/2 (Winter 1955-1956): 7 ((-))

KURZ, SELMA, 1875-1933

1561 KNIGHT, Arthur E.: Selma Kurz discography in Record Collector, XIII/3 (May 1960): 53-66 ((3))

KUSSEVITSKIĬ, SERGIEĬ ALEKSANDROVICH, 1874-1951

1562 MOSTYN, Kevin P.: Serge Koussevitsky—a brief list of commercial recordings in Views and Reviews, III/2 (Fall 1971): 67-68 ((7)); III/3: 74-75 ((7)); III/4: 87-88 ((7))

1563 MOSTYN, Kevin P.: Serge Koussevitsky: a brief list of commercial recordings. [Boston]: Koussevitsky Recordings Association, [1970] ((7))

1564 Koussevitsky recordings (through June 1946) in SMITH, Moses: Koussevitsky. New York: Allen, Towne & Heath, Inc., 1947: 378-382 ((-))

KUZHEUOBA, MARIJA NIKOLAEVNA See KUZNECOVA, MARIJA NIKOLAEVNA

KUZNECOVA, MARIJA NIKOLAEVNA

1565 BARNES, Harold: [Discography] in Record Collector, XII/7 (October 1959): 156 ((-))

KVARTET IMENI BORODINA

1566 [Discography] in ÍAKUBOV, Manashir Abramovich: Kvartet imeni Borodina. K 25letiyu tvorch. deyatel'nosti. Moskva: "Sov. Kompositor," 1971: 63-[71] ((-))

KWRENKO, MARIA

1567 KNIGHT, Arthur E.: The records in Record Collector, VIII/10 (October 1953): 224-226 ((-))

LABIA, MARIA, 1880-1953

1568 CELLETTI, Rodolfo: Discografia in Musica e Dischi, IX (No. 79, April 1953): 17 ((-))

1569 CELLETTI, Rodolfo: The records in Record News, III/1 (September 1958): 34 [From Musica e Dischi]

LA JEUNESSE, MARIE
See ALBANI, EMMA

LALANDE, MICHEL RICHARD DE, 1657-1726

1570 Discographie in DUFOURCQ, Norbert: Notes et références pour servir à une histoire de Michel-Richard Delalande, surintendant, maître et compositeur de la musique de la chambre du roi. Paris: A. & J. Picard, 1957: 277-278 (La Vie musicale en France sous les rois Bourbons) ((-))

LAMBERT, CONSTANT, 1905-1951

1571 List of records in SHEAD, Richard: Constant Lambert. London: Simon Publications, 1973: 175-192 ((-))

LANDOWSKA, WANDA, 1877-1959

1572 CLOUGH, F. F., and G. J. CUMING: Wanda Landowska (1879-1959); a discography in Gramophone Record Review, No. 72 (October 1959): 850-851 ((-))

1573 [[[Discography] in British Institute of Recorded Sound Bulletin, No. 15-16 (Spring 1960)]]

1574 Wanda Landowska—recordings in GAVOTY, Bernard: Wanda Landowska. Geneva: R. Kister, c1957: 30-[32] (Great concert artists) ((-))

1575 KIPNIS, Igor: The legacy of Landowska—a discography in American Record Guide, XXVI/4 (December 1959): 239, 295-301 ((7))

1576 Landowska discography in LANDOWSKA, Wanda: Landowska on music, collected, edited, and translated by Denise Restout, assisted by Robert Hawkins. New York: Stein and Day, [1964]: 411-422 ((7))

LANDOWSKI, MARCEL, 1915-

1577 Discographie in BAIGNÈRES, Claude: Marcel Landowski. Paris: Ventadour, [1959]: [45] (Collection "Musiciens d'aujourd'hui") ((-))

1578 Discographie in Courrier Musical de France, No. 9 (1965): 62 ((-))

1579 Discographie in GOLÉA, Antoine: Marcel Landowski: l'homme et son oeuvre..., catalogue des oeuvres, discographie. Paris: Seghers, 1969: [179]-182 (Musiciens de tous les temps, 41) ((-))

LARA, ADELINA DE
See DE LARA, ADELINA

LARRIEU, MAXENCE

1580 Principaux enregistrements in Diapason, No. 153 (January 1971): 7 ((-))

LARSSON, LARS ERIK VILNER, 1908-

1581 Kompositionen inspelade på grammofon in WALLNER, Bo: Lars-Erik Larsson: och hans concertinor. [Stockholm]: Radiotjänst, [1957]: 152-153 ((-))

LASSALLE, JEAN-LOUIS, 1847-1909

1582 FREESTONE, John: Collectors' corner in Gramophone, No. 355 (December 1952): 160 ((-))

1583 FREESTONE, John: [Jean Lassalle Pathes] in Gramophone, No. 339 (August 1951): 52 ((-))

1584 HEGERMANN-LINDENCRONE, Knudde: [Collectors corner] in Gramophone, No. 185 (October 1938): 223 ((-))

LAURI-VOLPI, GIACOMO, 1892-

1585 MORAN, William: Giacomo Lauri-Volpi in Record Collector, XX/8-10 (August 1972): 239 [Odeon-Nacional records] ((7))

1586 NATAN, Alex: Diskothek in fono forum 1966 (No. 1, January): 9 ((-))

1587 VEGETO, Raffaele: Discografia...in Musica e Dischi, XIV (No. 149, November 1958): 70 [Includes unpublished records] ((3, 7))

1588 VEGETO, Raffaele: Discografia del tenore Giacomo Lauri Volpi in Discoteca, No. 50 (May 1965): 36-37 ((1, 7))

1589 WILLIAMS, Clifford, and Tom HUTCHINSON: Recordings in Record Collector, XI/11-12 (November-December 1957): 263-272 ((1, 3, 6, 7)); Addenda: Record Collector, XII/3 (March 1958): 66-67 ((3, 6, 7)); XII/4 (February-March 1959): 108 ((3, 6, 7))

LAUTENBACHER, SUSANNE

1590 SPINGEL, Hans Otto: Diskografie in fono forum 1964 (No. 3, March): 115 ((-))

LAZARO, HIPOLITO

1591 RICHARDS, J. B.: The recordings in
Record Collector, XVI/3-4 (November-
December 1964): 72-94 ((1, 3, 5, 6, 7))
[Includes unpublished records]; Ad-
denda and corrigenda: Record Collec-
tor, XVI/9-10 (January 1966): 226-228
((-)); XVI/5-6 (April 1965): 130, 143
((-)); XVIII/11-12 (December 1969):
280-281 ((-))

1592 RICHARDS, J. B.: The Spanish recordings of Hipolito Lazaro in Record Collector, XV/3-4: 88-91 ((3, 5, 6, 7))

LEAR, EVELYN, 1930-

1593 Discographie Evelyn Lear in Diapason,
No. 102 (December 1965): 13 ((-))

LECLAIR, JEAN MARIE, 1697-1764

1594 Discographie in PINCHERLE, Marc:
Jean Marie Leclair: l'aîné. Paris: La
Colombe, [1952]: [131] (Collection
Euterpe) ((-))

LEHÁR, FERENC, 1870-1948

1595 Selective discografie in RAEDT, Paul
de: Het leven en werk van F. Lehar.
Brussel: D. A. P. [De Arbeiderspers],
Reinaert Uitgaven, 1973: 39-40
(Meesters der toonkunst, 20) ((-))

LEHMANN, LILLI, 1848-1929

1596 FREESTONE, John: Collectors' corner
in Gramophone, No. 355 (December
1952): 160 ((-))

LEHMANN, LOTTE, 1888-1976

1597 COURT, H. P.: Lotte Lehmann (Discography) in Record News, IV/12 (August
1960): 440-455 ((3, 6)); V/1 (September
1960): 20-31 ((3, 6)); Addenda and corrections: Record News, V/5 (January
1961): 181-184 ((-))

1598 COURT, H. P., rev. Clyde J. KEY: A
Lotte Lehmann discography in Maestro,
III (1971): 16-20 [Reprinted with revi-
sion from Record News, IV/12, V/1,
and V/5] ((3, 6))

1599 Diskographie in WESSLING, Berndt W.:
Lotte Lehmann...; mehr als eine
Sängerin. Salzburg: Residenz Verlag,
1969: 194-203 ((-))

LEIDER, FRIDA, 1888-1975

1600 BARNES, H. M.: Frida Leider: discography in British Institute of Recorded

Sound Bulletin, No. 7 (Winter 1957): 14-
19 ((3, 7))

1601 BARNES, Harold: Frida Leider discography in LEIDER, Frida: Playing my
part. New York: Meredith Press,
[1966]: 211-214 ((3, 5, 6))

1602 [[BURROS, H.: [Discography] in Record
News, II/10 (June 1958)]]

1603 [[BURROS, Harold: Frida Leider discography in LEIDER, Frida: Das war
mein Teil. Berlin-Grunewald: Herbig,
1959]]

1604 BURROS, Harold: Frida Leider [dis-
cography] in LEIDER, Frida: Playing
my part. London: Calder & Boyars,
1966: 211-214 ((3, 5, 6))

1605 RIEMANS, Leo: Frida Leider; some
notes on her career and a discography
in American Record Guide, XV/4 (December 1948): 101-103 ((-))

LEINSDORF, ERICH, 1912-

1606 HELM, Everett: Diskografie in fono
forum 1963 (No. 10, October): 371 ((-))

1607 HIRSCH, Nicole: Discographie RCA in
Diapason, No. 124 (March 1968): 45
((-))

LEIPZIG GEWANDHAUSORCHESTER

1608 RUDOLPH, Eberhard: Diskographie in
Medium Schallplatte, No. 8 (No. 3,
1968): 5-6 ((-))

LEIPZIG THOMANER CHOR

1609 SCHWINGER, Wolfram: Diskografie in
fono forum 1962 (No. 9, September): 9
((-))

LEMNITZ, TIANA

1610 SEELIGER, Ronald, and Bill PARK:
Tiana Lemnitz discography in Record
Collector, XV/1: 37-43 ((3, 5, 6, 7))

LENO, DAN

1611 JARRETT, Jack: Dan Leno in Record
Advertiser, No. 4 (May-June 1971): 4
((3, 5))

LENYA, LOTTE

1612 Lotte Lenya Diskografie in fono forum
1971 (No. 10, October): 788 ((-))

LEONI, EVA

1613 NYKLICEK, George: Eva Leoni in
Record Collector, XX/11-12 (December 1972): 282 ((3))

LESUR, DANIEL
See DANIEL-LESUR

LHÉVINNE, JOSEF, 1874-1944

1614 ANDERSON, Harry L.: Josef Lhévinne
discography in Recorded Sound, No. 44
(October 1971): 791-796 ((1, 3, 4, 6, 7))

LHÉVINNE, ROSINA, 1880-1976

1615 ANDERSON, Harry L.: Rosina Lhévinne
discography in Recorded Sound, No. 44
(October 1971): 797 ((1, 7))

LIEDER, GERMAN

1616 CLARK, Robert S.: A basic library of
German lieder in Stereo Review,
XXII/6 (June 1969): 67-72 ((-))

LIETUVOS KVARTETAS

1617 SARASAS, M.: Lietuvos kvarteto
Plokštelių i šleistų iki 1970 in KATKUS,
Donatas: Lietuvos kvartetas. Vilnius:
Vaga, 1971: 126-[127] ((-))

LIETUVOS TSR KAMERINIS ORKESTRAS

1618 Discography in PALIONYTĚ, Dana:
Lietuvos TSR kamerinis orkestras.
Vilnius: Vaga, 1972: 59-61 ((-))

LIGETI, GYÖRGY, 1923-

1619 List of works 1957-1972 by György
Ligeti [Includes discographic refer-
ences] in Numus-west (February
1972): 16 ((-))

1620 SZERSNOVICZ, Patrick: Catalogue des
oeuvres; discographie in Musique en
Jeu, No. 15 (September 1974): [120]-
123 ((-))

LILBURN, DOUGLAS
See listing for FARQUHAR, DAVID

LILL, JOHN

1621 Diskographie in Musica, XXIV/6
(November-December 1970): 606
((-))

LIPATTI, DINU, 1917-1950

1622 BĂRGĂUANU, Grigore: Discografie
Dinu Lipatti in Muzica, XIV/5-6 (May-
June 1964): 87 ((7))

1623 Discographie in Muzica, XXI/1 (January 1971): 38-39 ((-))

1624 Discographie in 1970 [i.e. Dix-neuf
cent soixante-dix];, in memoriam Dinu
Lipatti. Genève: Editions Labor et
Fides, 1970: 125-126 ((-))

1625 GLUTH, Walter: Diskografie in fono
forum 1960 (No. 12, December): 14
[As pianist and composer] ((-))

1626 Discographie in Hommage à Dinu
Lipatti. Genève: Labor & Fides,
[1952]: 89-90 ((-))

1627 Discographie in LIPATTI, Anna: Dinu
Lipatti la douleur de ma vie. [Genève]:
Perret-Gentil, [1967]: 80-90 ((-))

1628 REUTLINGER, Dale: A Dinu Lipatti
discography in Maestro, IV-V (1972-
1973): 72-74 ((7))

1629 Records in TĂNĂSESCU, Dragos:
Lipatti. Bucharest: Meridiane Pub.
House, 1965: 95-98 ((1))

1630 Discographie in TĂNĂSESCU, Dragoş:
Dinu Lipatti. Bucureşti: Editura
musicală, 1971: 195-208 ((1, 7))

LISZT, FRANZ, 1811-1886

1631 Liszt Werke auf Schallplatten in HELM,
Everett: Franz Liszt in Selbstzeug-
nissen und Bilddokumenten. Reinbeck
bei Hamburg: Rowohlt, 1972: 155-156
(Rororo-Bildmonographien) (Rowohlts
Monographien, 185) ((-))

1632 Discografía in HURTADO, Leopoldo:
Liszt. Buenos Aires: Ricordi Americana, [1944]: 133-147 (Músicos
célebres) ((-))

1633 JACOBSON, Bernard: Liszt on records
in High Fidelity, XVIII/4 (April 1968):
51-55 ((-))

1634 Discographie in LEROY, Alfred: Franz
Liszt l'homme et son oeuvre. [Paris]:
Seghers, [1964]: 183-187 (Musiciens
de tous les temps, 5) ((-))

1635 Discographie in LEROY, Alfred: Franz
Liszt. [Lausanne]: La Guilde du livre,
1967: 183-187 (Musiciens de tous les
temps) ((-))

1636 Recordings of compositions of Franz
Liszt in LINGG, Ann M.: Mephisto
waltz: the story of Franz Liszt. [1st
ed.] New York: Holt, [1951]: [295]-296
((-))

1637 Discographie in MOUTHIER, Paul G.:
Franz Liszt. [2. éd.] Molenbeek-

Bruxelles: Editions du Trefle à quatre feuilles, [1945]: [79]-85 ((−))

1638 RAJBEN, Bernard: Catalogue commenté et discographie critique in Liszt. Paris: Hachette, 1967: [271]-[287] ((−))

1639 Sélection discographique in ROSTAND, Claude: Liszt. [Paris]: Éditions du Seuil, [1960]: 183-186 (Collections Microcosme. Solfèges, 15) ((−))

1640 Selected discography in SEROFF, Victor: Franz Liszt. New York: Macmillan Co., [1966]: [147]-149 ((−))

1641 Selected discography in SEROFF, Victor: Franz Liszt. Freeport, NY: Books for Libraries Press, [1970, c1966]: [147]-149 (Biography index reprint series) ((−))

1642 A selection of recordings in WALKER, Alan: Liszt. London: Faber and Faber, 1971: 102-104 (The Great composers) ((−))

1643 Discographie in WESSLING, Berndt W.: Franz Liszt: ein virtuoses Leben. München; Zürich: Piper, [1973]: 203-305 ((−))

Concertos, Piano

1644 MEYER-JOSTEN, Jürgen: Die besprochenen Aufnahmen in fono forum 1968 (No. 9, September): 505 ((−))

LITVINNE, MME. FÉLIA, 1863-1936

1645 BARNES, H. M., and Victor GIRARD: Discography in Record Collector, VIII/6 (June 1953): 130-132 ((3, 7))

1646 CELLETTI, Rodolfo: Discografia in Musica e Dischi, XV (No. 156, June 1959): 65 ((5)); VEGETO, Raffaele: Discografia in Musica e Dischi, XV (No. 157, July 1959): 66 ((−))

1647 CELLETTI, Rodolfo: The records in Record News, IV/6 (February 1960): 212-213 [From Musica e Dischi, June 1959] ((5))

1648 WITTEN, Laurence C., II: A discography of Felia Litvinne in Record Collector, XX/6-7 (May 1972): 147-156 ((3, 6, 7)); Addenda: Record Collector, XX/11-12 (December 1972): 283 ((−))

LLOYD, EDWARD

1649 FREESTONE, John: Collectors' corner in Gramophone, No. 355 (December 1952): 160 ((−))

1650 JARRETT, Jack, Michael REDDY, and John B. RICHARDS: The recorded art of Edward Lloyd in Record Collector,

XII/10-11 (December 1959-January 1960): 230-236 ((3, 6, 7))

LOCKE, MATTHEW, 1632-1677

1651 Some gramophone records in HARDING, Rosamond E. M.: A thematic catalog of the works of Matthew Locke: with a calendar of the main events of his life. Oxford: R. E. M. Harding, distributed by Blackwell, 1971: 148-149 ((−))

LOEWE, KARL, 1796-1869

1652 ELSON, James: Carl Loewe and the nineteenth century German ballad—discography in National Association of Teachers of Singing Bulletin, XXVIII/1 (October 1971): 19 ((−))

1653 WEBER, J. F.: Loewe and Franz. Utica, NY: Weber, 1971: 20 pp. (Discography series, 8) ((5))

LOMANTO DE MURO, ENZO
See DE MURO LOMANTO, ENZO

LOMBARDI, GIANNINA ARANGI

1654 VEGETO, Raffaele: Discografia in Musica e Dischi, XII (No. 113, January 1956): 8 ((7))

LONDON, GEORGE, 1920-

1655 KRAUS, Gottfried: Diskografie in fono forum 1964 (No. 4, April): 137 ((−))

1656 SCHWINGER, Wolfram: Aus der Diskografie in fono forum 1961 (No. 10, October): 27 ((−))

LONDON PHILHARMONIC ORCHESTRA
See listing for BEECHAM, SIR, THOMAS, BART. Holmes, William A.: The Beecham recordings: project 1: the London Philharmonic

LONG, KATHLEEN

1657 The records of Kathleen Long in Disc, I/4 (Autumn 1947): 172-173 ((−))

LONG, MARGUERITE, 1878-1966

1658 BARBIER, Jean-Joel: Enregistrements de M. Long et J. Thibaud in Revue Musicale, No. 245 (1959): 34-37 ((−))

1659 Discographie in Courrier Musical de France, No. 7 (1964): 186 ((−))

1660 HAMON, Jean: Discographie in Diapason, No. 105 (March 1966): 11 ((−))

LORENGAR, PILAR

1661 Diskographie (Auswahl) in Phonoprisma
(September-October 1967): 160, 166
((-))

LOTHAR, MARK, 1902-

1662 Verzeichnis der Werke [includes disco-
graphical notes] in OTT, Alfons: Mark
Lothar: ein Musikporträt. München:
Süddeutscher Verlag, [1968]: 201-221
((-))

LOUCHEUR, RAYMOND

1663 Discographie in Courrier Musical de
France, No. 6 (1964): 117 ((-))

LOUVIER, ALAIN

1664 BRAS, Jean-Yves: Discographie in
Diapason, No. 187 (May 1974): 19 ((-))

LUBIN, GERMAINE, 1890-

1665 BARNES, Harold: Germaine Lubin discography in Recorded Sound, No. 19
(July 1965): 367 ((3, 6, 7))

1666 Discographie in CASANOVA, Nicole:
Isolde 39: Germaine Lubin. Paris:
Flammarion, [1974]: 249-[250] ((-))

LUCA, GIUSEPPE DE
See DE LUCA, GIUSEPPE

LUCIA, FERNANDO DE
See DE LUCIA, FERNANDO

LUDWIG, CHRISTA, 1928-

1667 ASHMAN, Mike: Ludwig discography in
Records and Recording, XVII/9 (June
1974): 24 ((-))

LUDWIG, LEOPOLD

1668 Verzeichnis der im deutschen Schallplatten Handel in WESSLING, Berndt
W.: Leopold Ludwig. Bremen: Sohüne-
mann, 1968: 130 ((-))

LULLY, JEAN BAPTISTE DE, 1639-1687

1669 Discographie in BORREL, Eugène:
Jean-Baptiste Lully; le cadre, la vie,
l'oeuvre, la personnalité, le reyonne-
ments, les oeuvres, bibliographie.
Paris: La Colombe, 1949: [109]
(Euterpe, 7) ((-))

LUNDSTEN, RALPH

1670 ÅHLÉN, Carl-Gunnar: Ralph Lundsten
på skiva in Nutida Musik, XV/3 (1971-
1972): 25-26 ((-))

LUNN, LOUISE KIRKBY
See KIRKBY-LUNN, LOUISE

LUSSAN, ZÉLIE DE, 1862-1949

1671 DENNIS, J.: The records in Record
Collector, XVII/8 (December 1967):
181-182 ((7))

1672 [[HURST, P. G.: [Discography] in
Gramophone, No. 321 (February 1960)]]

LUTE

1673 MILLER, Carl: The lute on discs in
Guitar Review, No. 27 (October 1963):
22-26 ((-))

LUTOSLAWSKI, WITOLD, 1913-

1674 Diskografie in fono forum 1961 (No. 6,
June): 11 ((-))

LUTYENS, ELISABETH, 1906-

1675 HUGHES, Eric, and Sylvia JUNGE: Recorded music by Elisabeth Lutyens in
Recorded Sound, No. 38 (April 1970):
599-600 ((1, 7))

LYMPANY, MOURA

1676 Discography in Disc, I/2 (Spring 1947):
81 ((-))

MAAZEL, LORIN, 1930-

1677 BLAUKOPF, K.: Diskographie Lorin
Maazel in Hi Fi Stereophonie, V/2
(February 1966): 119-120 ((-))

1678 CHERIERE, Georges: Discographie in
Diapason, No. 103 (January 1966): 11
((-))

1679 Diskographie (sämtliche Aufnahmen
Deutsche Grammophon Gesellschaft,
wenn nicht anders angegeben) in
Phonoprisma (September-October
1965): 153 ((-))

1680 Lorin Maazel discographie in GELENG,
Ingvelde: Lorin Maazel: Monographie
eine Musikers. Berlin: Rembrandt
Verlag, [c1971]: 130-133 ((-))

1681 KRAUS, Gottfried: Diskografie in fono
forum 1963 (No. 11, November): 428
((-)); Additions and corrections: fono
forum 1964 (No. 2, February): 88 ((-))

MACCHI, MARIA DE

1682 CELLETTI, Rodolfo: Discografia in Musica e Dischi, XVIII (No. 194, August 1962): 8 ((-))

MCCORMACK, JOHN, 1884-1945

1683 BUSCEMI, John: John McCormack—the man with the voice of an angel in The New Amberola Graphic, No. 3 (Winter 1968): 3, 13 ((-)); No. 4 (July 1969): 8-9 ((-)); No. 5 (Spring 1973): [5] ((-)); No. 6 (Summer 1973): 6 ((-)); No. 8 (Winter 1974): 7 ((-)); No. 10 (Summer 1974): 7 ((-))

1684 [[[Discography] in Record News, I/6 (May 1947)]] [Irish issues]

1685 McKENZIE, Compton: John McCormack in Gramophone, II/5 (October 1924): 153-155 ((-))

1686 [[MORBY, P.: Brown wax to blue amberol—and the McCormack cylinders in Record Collector, XVIII/1-2 (1968): 5-42]]

1687 RODEN, Philip F.: Recordings by John McCormack in Gramophone, No. 283 (December 1946): 99-100; No. 284 (January 1947): 115-116; No. 287 (April 1947): 169-170; No. 288 (May 1947): 187-189 ((7))

1688 RODEN, Philip F.: A McCormack discography in McCORMACK, Lily: I hear you calling me. Milwaukee: Bruce Pub. Co., [1949]: 190-201 ((-))

1689 RODEN, Philip F.: A McCormack discography in McCORMACK, Lily: I hear you calling me. Westport, CN: Greenwood Press, 1975, c1949: 190-201 ((-))

1690 RODEN, Philip F.: The McCormack Odeons in Record Collector, XI/1 (January 1957): [5]-18 ((3, 6, 7))

1691 ROE, Leonard F. X. McDermott: John McCormack: the complete discography. London: C. Jackson, 1956: 93 pp. ((3, 4, 6, 7))

1692 ROE, Leonard F. X. McDermott: The John McCormack discography. [Lingfield, Eng.]: Oakwood Press, 1972 [c1971]: 93 pp. ((3, 4, 6, 7))

1693 A list of John McCormack's records in STRONG, L. A. G.: John McCormack; the story of a singer. New York: Macmillan Co., 1941: 297-301 ((-))

1694 List of John McCormack's records in STRONG, L. A. G.: John McCormack; the story of a singer. London: Methuen & Co., [1941]: 289-[292] ((-))

1695 List of John McCormack's records in STRONG, L. A. G.: John McCormack. London: P. Nevil, [1949]: 305-309 ((-))

1696 WEBSTER, Robert L.: Matrix listing of the McCormack Odeons in Record Collector, XI/1 (January 1957): 16-18 ((3, 6, 7)); Addenda: Record Collector, XIV/3-4: 95 ((-)); XIV/9-10: 234 ((3))

1697 WOOD, Denis: Records by McCormack in Gramophone, No. 195 (August 1939): 129-133 ((-))

MACDOWELL, EDWARD ALEXANDER, 1861-1908

1698 LOWENS, Irving, and Margery L. MORGAN: Edward MacDowell: a selective discography in Hi Fi Stereo Review, XIX/6 (December 1967): 70 ((-))

MACEWAN, SYDNEY

1699 [[[Discography] in Disc (Bristol) III/9 (Winter 1948): 29]]

MCGUCKIN, BARTON

1700 FREESTONE, John: Collectors' corner in Gramophone, No. 356 (January 1953): 192 ((-))

MACHAUT, GUILLAUME DE
See GUILLAUME DE MACHAUT

MACHE, FRANÇOIS-BERNARD

1701 Discographie in Courrier Musical de France, No. 49 (1975): 42 ((-))

MACLENNAN, FRANCIS, 1879-1935

1702 MACLENNAN, John W.: [Discography] in Record Collector, XXII/3-4 (July 1974): 91 ((3, 7))

MAHLER, GUSTAV, 1860-1911

1703 Discografie in BĂLAN, George: Gustav Mahler sau cum exprima muzica idei. [Ediţit 1.] Bucareşti: Editura Muzicală a Uniunii Compozitorilor din R. P. R., 1964: 193-[195] ((-))

1704 [[Bibliographie: Gustav Mahler in Musik und Bildung, V (November 1973): 632-636]]

1705 BLAUKOPF, Kurt: Gustav Mahler— Diskographie in Hi Fi Stereophonie, X/4 (April 1971): 364-366 ((-))

1706 BRUUN, Carl L.: Gustav Mahler—a discography in Record News, IV/10 (May 1960): 353-368 ((-))

1707 [[COMMAULT, Roger: Discographie Gustav Mahler 1860-1911. Paris: [s.n.], 1951]]

1708 DIETHER, Jack: Bruckner and Mahler in the first decade of LP in Chord and Dischord, II/8 (1958): 91-111 ((-))

1709 [[DIETHER, J.: Mahler: a musical existentialist? in New York times, 109/12 (March 13, 1960): section 12]]

1710 Discographie in Revue Musicale, No. 298-299 (1975): 163 ((-))

1711 Discographie critique in Harmonie, No. 29 (August-September 1967): 29-33 ((-))

1712 [[[Discography] in Discofilia, No. 49 (June 1960): 304]]

1713 Discografia in DUSE, Ugo: Gustav Mahler. Torino: G. Einaudi, 1973: [383]-387 ((-))

1714 Discografia in DUSE, Ugo: Gustav Mahler: introduzione allo studio della vita e delle opere. Padova: Marsilio, [1962]: 268-270 ((-))

1715 HALL, David: A Mahler discography in Hi Fi Stereo Review (September 1960): 45-[47] ((-))

1716 LITTLE, Paul Hugo: Bruckner and Mahler on records in Chord and Dischord, II/7 (1954): 44-60 ((-))

1717 A Mahler discography in Views and Reviews, I/1 (Summer 1969): 53-59 ((-))

1718 MARSH, Robert Charles: A Mahler discography on historical principles in High Fidelity, VII/5 (May 1957): 81-87 ((-))

1719 MARTINOTTI, Sergio: Discografia in L'Approdo Musicale, No. 16-17 (1963): 188-195 ((-))

1720 Discographie in MATTER, Jean: Connaissance de Mahler: documents, analyses et synthèses. Lausanne: Éditions L'Age d'homme, [1974]: 417-424 ((-))

1721 MITCHELL, Donald: Mahler on the gramophone in Music and Letters, XLI/2 (1960): 156-160 ((-))

1722 Mahlers Werke auf Schallplatten in SCHREIBER, Wolfgang: Gustav Mahler in Selbstzeugnissen und Bilddokumenten. [Reinbek bei Hamburg]: Rowohlt, [1971]: 183-[186] ((-))

1723 Nahrávky z díla na deskách Supraphon in ŠÍP, Ladislav: Gustav Mahler. 1.vyd. Praha: Supraphon, t. ST 4, 1973: 211-212 ((-))

1724 TRIGO DE SOUSA, António: Mahler e Bruckner em discos in Arte Musical, XXVIII/9 (1960): 251-252 ((-))

1725 Orientation discographie in VIGNAL, Marc: Mahler. [Paris]: Éditions du Seuil, [1966]: [185]-187 ((-))

1726 WEBER, J. F.: Mahler. Utica, NY: Weber, 1971. 38 pp. (Discography series, 9) ((1, 4, 5, 7))

1727 WEBER, J. F.: Mahler. 2d ed. Utica, NY: Weber, 1974. 47 pp. (Discography series, 9) ((1, 4, 5, 7))

1728 Diskographie in WESSLING, Berndt W.: Gustav Mahler: ein Prophet; Leben. 1.-7.Tsd. Hamburg: Hoffmann und Campe, 1974: 347-357 ((-))

1729 Diskographie in WORBS, Hans Christoph: Gustav Mahler. Berlin-Halensee: M. Hesses Verlag, [c1960]: 94-98 ((-))

Das Lied von der Erde

1730 [[HAMBURG, O.: Eine vergleichende Discographie in Phono, VII/3]]

1731 [[RESTAGNO, Enzo: Das Lied von der Erde in Musicalia, I/1 (September 1970): 55-59]]

1732 SCHREIBER, Wolfgang: Diskografie in fono forum 1973 (No. 5, May): 428 ((-))

Symphonies

1733 FIERZ, Gerold: Gustav Mahler: eine Diskographie seiner Sinfonien in Schweizerische Musikzeitung, C/3 (1960): 185-188 ((-))

1734 JACOBSON, Bernard: The Mahler symphonies on records in High Fidelity, XVII/9 (September 1967): 55-59 ((-))

1735 SCHUMANN, Karl: Besprochene Aufnahmen in fono forum 1966 (No. 10, October): 505 ((-)); Addenda: fono forum 1966 (No. 12, December): 666 ((-))

1736 VINCENTINI, Mario: Le sinfonie di Gustav Mahler; cinquant'anni di incisioni discografiche in Discoteca alta Fedelta, No. 150 (May 1975): 28-30 ((5))

Symphony, No. 1, D Major

1737 Discographie in Diapason, No. 154 (February 1971): 9 ((-))

Symphonies, No. 1-2

1738 [[HAMBURG, O.: Eine vergleichende Discographie in Phono, VII/5]]

Symphony, No. 4

1739 [[HAMBURG, O.: Eine vergleichende Discographie in Phono, VIII/1]]

Symphony, No. 5

1740 [[HAMBURG, O.: Eine vergleichende
Discographie in Phono, VIII/5]]

MAINARDI, ENRICO, 1897-1976

1741 Diskographie in Phonoprisma (March-
April 1966): 60 ((-))

1742 KRAUS, Gottfried: Enrico Mainardi;
verzeichnis der Schallplattenaufnahmen
in fono forum 1972 (No. 5, May): 366
((5))

MALCOLM, GEORGE

1743 Diskografie in fono forum 1961 (No. 12,
December): 27 ((-))

MAŁCUŻYŃSKI, WITOLD, 1914-1977

1744 List of recordings in GAVOTY, Bernard:
Witold Małcużyński. Geneva: R. Kister,
1957: [32] ((-))

MALIPIERO, RICCARDO, 1914-

1745 Discografia in L'Approdo Musicale,
III/9 (January-March 1960): 205-206
((-))

MANTELLI, EUGENIA

1746 WOLF, Albert: Eugenia Mantelli: a
discography in Record Collector,
IV/4 (April 1949): 69-71 ((-))

1747 ZIERING, R. M.: Eugenia Mantelli: a
discography in Record Collector,
XIV/11-12 (n.d.): 279-284 ((3))

MARCEL, LUC-ANDRÉ

1748 Discographie in Courrier Musical de
France, No. 37 (1972): 51 ((-))

MARCHESI, BLANCHE, 1863-1940

1749 FREESTONE, John L. C.: Blanche
Marchesi in Gramophone, No. 193
(June 1939): 39 ((-))

MARCHETTI, GIANNI

1750 STRONA, Oscar: Marchetti (Ruy Blas)
in Discoteca, No. 97 (January-February 1970): 16 ((-))

MARCO, TOMÁS

1751 Discografía in GÓMEZ AMAT, Carlos:
Tomás Marco. Madrid: Dirección

General de Bellas Artes, 1974: 113
((-))

MARCOUX, VANNI, 1877-1962

1752 BARNES, Harold M.: Vanni Marcoux: a
discography in Recorded Sound, No.
29-30 (January-April 1968): 269-272
((3, 6, 7))

MARESCOTTI, ANDRÉ FRANÇOIS, 1902-

1753 Discographie in GOLÉA, Antoine:
André-François Marescotti: biographie,
études analytiques. Paris: Société des
Editions Jobert, [1963]: 18 ((-))

MARIE, JEAN-ETIENNE

1754 Discographie in Courrier Musical de
France, No. 32 (1970): 166 ((-))

MARKEVITCH, IGOR, 1912-

1755 Enregistrements réalisés sous le
direction d' Igor Markévitch in
GAVOTY, Bernard: Igor Markévitch.
Genève: R. Kister et Union européene
d'éditions, c1954: [32] ((-))

1756 Igor Markevitch in fono forum 1960
(No. 3, March): 11 ((-))

MAROS, RUDOLF, 1917-

1757 Diszkográfia in VÁRNAI, Péter: Maros
Rudolf. Budapest: Zenemukiadó, 1967:
[32] ((-))

MARRINER, NEVILLE

1758 McLACHLAN, Don: A Marriner discography in Records and Recording,
XV/9 (June 1972): 23 ((-))

MARTELLI, HENRI, 1895-

1759 Discographie in Courrier Musical de
France, No. 21 (1968): 80 ((-))

MARTIN, FRANK, 1890-1974

1760 Verzeichnis der im Jahre 1970 erhältlichen Schallplatten in BILLETER,
Bernhard: Frank Martin: ein Aussen-
seiter der neuen Musik. Frauenfeld,
Stuttgart: Huber, [1970]: 185-187 ((-))

1761 Discographie actuelle in Diapason, No.
193 (January 1975): 21 ((-))

1762 Discographie in MARTIN, Bernard:
Frank Martin; ou La réalité du rêve.
Neuchâtel: [Editions de] La Baconnière,
[1973]: [221]-224 ((-))

1763 Discographie in MARTIN, Frank: Entretiens sur la musique. Neuchâtel: la Baconnière, [1967]: 127-129 ((-))

MARTINELLI, GIOVANNI, 1885-1969

1764 AYLWARD, Derek: Martinelli on LP records in Recorded Sound, I/8 (Autumn 1962): 239-241 ((-))

1765 HÖSLINGER, Clemens: Diskografie in fono forum 1969 (No. 8, August): 497 ((1))

1766 Recordings of broadcasts by Martinelli in Recorded Sound, I/8 (Autumn 1962): 241 ((1, 7))

1767 REUTLINGER, Dale: Giovanni Martinelli—a discography in Maestro, II (January-December 1970): 66-69 ((7))

1768 [[RICHARDS, J. B.: Giovanni Martinelli in Record Collector, V/ (August 1950): 173-193]]; Addenda: Record Collector, VII/6-7 (June-July 1952): 139-140 ((1, 3, 7))

1769 RICHARDS, John B.: A Martinelli discography in Hobbies, LVII/3 (May 1952): 20-21 ((7))

1770 WILE, Raymond: The Edison recordings of Giovanni Martinelli in Association for Recorded Sound Collections Journal, III/2-3 (Fall 1971): 42-45 ((3, 6, 7))

1771 WILLIAMS, Clifford: The "private off the air" recordings of Giovanni Martinelli in Record Collector, X/10-11 (September-October 1956): 241-242 ((1, 7)); Addenda: Record Collector, XI/9-10 (September-October 1957): 233 ((1, 7))

MARTINET, JEAN-LOUIS, 1916-

1772 Discographie in Courrier Musical de France, No. 44 (1973): 166 ((-))

MARTINON, JEAN, 1910-1976

1773 Discographie [as composer] in Courrier Musical de France, No. 26 (1969): 143 ((-))

MARTINŮ, BOHUSLAV, 1890-1959

1774 ECKSTEIN, Pavel: Diskografie in fono forum 1964 (No. 3, March): 97 ((-))

1775 Zusammenfassende Diskographie aller zurzeit Verfügbaren Schallplatten in HALBREICH, Harry: Bohuslav Martinů: Werkverzeichnis, Dokumentation und Biographie. [Zürich, Freiburg i. Br.]: Atlantis-Verlag, [1968]: 345-348 ((-))

1776 Seznam děl [includes discographical references] in MIHULE, Jaroslav:

Bohuslav Martinů. [1. vyd.] Praha: Státní hudební vydavatelství, 1966: 59-78 ((-))

1777 Přehled dila a diskografies in MIHULE, Jaroslav: Bohuslav Martinů: profil života a díla. 1.vyd. Praha: Supraphon, 1974: 212-228 ((-))

1778 Skladby Bohuslava Martinů vydaré na čs. dlouhoh rajících deskách in NEDBAL, Miloslav: Bohuslav Martinů; několik pohledů na život a dílo velkého českého skladatele našeho století. [1. vyd.] Praha: Panton, 1965: 72-78 ((-))

1779 Gramofonové desky in Prague Státní pedagogická knihovna Komenského: Bohuslav Martinů. Praha, 1960: 1-3 ((-))

MARX, JOSEPH, 1882-1964

1780 WEBER, J. F.: Pfitzner and Marx. Utica, NY: Weber, 1975: 18 pp. (Discography series, 15) ((3, 5, 6, 7))

MARX, KARL, 1897-

1781 [[Schallplattenverzeichnis in Festschrift Karl Marx zum 70 Geburtstag dargebracht von seinen Schülern. Stuttgart: Ichtys Verlag, 1967: 118-119]]

MASCAGNI, PIETRO, 1863-1945

1782 CELLETTI, Rodolfo: Discografia internazionale opere complete di Mascagni in Musica e Dischi, XIX (No. 200, February 1963): 50 ((-)); XX (No. 212, February 1964): 39 ((-))

1783 CELLETTI, Rodolfo: Il teatro di Mascagni attraverso il disco in Comitato nazionale delle onoranze a Pietro Mascagni nel primo centenario della nascita: Pietro Mascagni; contributi alla conoscenza della sua opera nel 1° centenario della nascita. Livorno, diciembre 1963: [389]-557 ((-))

1784 VEGETO, Raffaele: Discografia mascagnana in MORINI, Mario, ed.: Pietro Mascagni. Milano: Casa Musicale Sonzogno di Piero Ostali, [c1964]: [235]-280 ((1, 5))

Cavalleria Rusticana

1785 GOLDSTEIN, Joachim M.: Aus der Diskografie in fono forum 1963 (No. 12, December): 507 ((-))

Iris

1786   Mascagni's Iris: Addenda in Record
Collector, III/8 (August 1948): 75-79
((−))

MASON, EDITH

1787   [KNIGHT, Arthur E.]: The Edith Mason
records in Record Collector, X/4
(September 1955): 85-86 ((7))

MASS

1788   JOHNSON, David: The mass since Bach
in High Fidelity, VIII/4 (April 1958):
81-92 ((−)); VIII/5 (May 1958): 85-90
((−))

MASSENET, JULES ÉMILE FRÉDÉRIC,
1842-1912

1789   Discographie in COQUIS, André: Jules
Massenet; l'homme et son oeuvre.
[Paris]: Éditions Seghers, [1965]: 181-
182 (Musiciens de tous les temps, 20)
((−))

Manon

1790   BLYTH, Alan: Manon in Opera, XV/2
(February 1974): 105-114 (Opera on the
gramophone, 35) ((−)); XXV/3 (March
1974): 200-208 ((−))

MAST, EDWARD CY

1791   [[WILE, Ray: [Discography] in Talking
Machine Review, No. 13 (December
1971): 125-128]]

MATHIS, EDITH, 1938-

1792   Diskographie Edith Mathis (Auswahl) in
Phonoprisma (May-June 1967): 89 ((−))

MATTHAY, TOBIAS, 1858-1945

1793   SAUL, Patrick: Tobias Matthay discography in Recorded Sound, I/5
(Winter 1961-1962): 143 ((1, 7))

MATZENAUER, MARGARET, 1881-1963

1794   FAVIA-ARTSAY, Aida: Margaret
Matzenauer's discography in Hobbies,
LXV (September 1960): 32 ((1, 3, 6, 7));
Corrections in Hobbies, LXV (January
1961): 31, 60 ((−))

MAUREL, VICTOR, 1848-1923
See also GAILHARD, PIERRE

1795   CELLETTI, Rodolfo: Discografia in
Musica e Dischi, IX (No. 87, December
1953): 23 ((7))

1796   FASSETT, Stephen: The Maurel records
in American Music Lover, X/6 (February 1944): 158 ((−))

MEDTNER, NIKOLAĬ KARLOVICK, 1880-1951

1797   [Discography] in DOLINSKAĬA, Elena
Borisovna: Nikolaĭ Metner; Monografi-
cheskii ocherk. Moskva: Muzyka, 1966:
190-191 ((−))

1798   Gramophone recordings of Medtner's
works in HOLT, Richard, ed.: Nicolas
Medtner, 1879 [i.e. 1880]-1951; a
tribute to his art and personality. London: D. Dobson, [1955]: 237-238 ((−))

MEHTA, ZUBIN, 1936-

1799   Diskographie in Phonoprisma (September-October 1966): 155 ((−))

MEI-FIGNER, MEDEA

1800   BRY, Michel de, and J.-R. RICHARD:
Medea Mei-Figner, une discographie
in Disques, No. 2 (February 15, 1948):
80 ((7))

1801   DENNIS, J.: Medea Mei-Figner: the
records in Record Collector, IV/3
(March 1949): 53 ((−))

MEISTER, KARL, 1903-

1802   Verzeichnis der Tonbänder des
Bayerischen Rundfunks in PESCHECK,
Jürgen: Von und über Karl Meister.
München; Würzberg; Bern: Relief-
Verl. Eilers, 1968: [28-29] ((1))

MEISTERSINGER
See MINSTRELS

MELBA, NELLIE, 1861-1931

1803   GOODBODY, T. E.: Dame Melba in
Gramophone I/10 (March 1924): 196
((−))

1804   [[HARVEY, H. H.: Discography in
Record Collector, IV (December
1949): 203-215]]

1805   ROTHERMEL, Henry McK.: The recorded art of Nellie Melba in Gramophone, No. 104 (January 1932): 349-352
((7))

MELCHIOR, LAURITZ, 1890-1973

1806   Discographie in Diapason, No. 177 (May
1973): 17 ((−))

1807 HANSEN, Hans: Lauritz Melchior: a
discography. Copenhagen: Nationaldiskoteket, 1965: 44 pp. ((1, 3, 4,
5, 6, 7))

1808 HANSEN, Hans: Lauritz Melchior: a
discography. Copenhagen: Nationaldiskoteket, 1972: 40 pp. (Nationaldiskoteket. Discographies, 205)
((1, 3, 4, 5, 6, 7))

1809 HÖSLINGER, Clemens: Melchior auf
der Platte in fono forum 1970 (No. 12,
December): 933 ((-))

1810 Lauritz Melchior. [Copenhagen]:
Nationalmuseet, [1961]: 22 pp. (Det
National Diskotek Katalog, 11)
((3, 4, 7))

1811 MORTENSEN, Erik B., and Jean
ZACHS: A Lauritz Melchior discography in Record News, III/12 (August
1959): 433-441 ((3, 5)); IV/1 (September 1959): 12-21 ((3, 5)); IV/2 (October
1959): 49-58 ((3, 5)); Addenda: Record
News, IV/4 (December 1959): 155 ((-))

MELCHISSÈDEC, LÉON, 1843-1925

1812 FREESTONE, John: Collectors' corner
in Gramophone, No. 360 (May 1953):
316 ((-))

1813 WITTEN, Laurence C., II: Léon
Melchissèdec in Antique Records
(May 1973): 32-33 ((3, 6, 7))

MELIS, CARMEN, 1885-1967

1814 VEGETO, Raffaele: Discografia di
Carmen Melis in Musica e Dischi,
XII (No. 121, September 1956): 8 ((7));
Addenda: Musica e Dischi, XIII (No.
128, April 1957): 52 ((-))

MELKUS, EDWARD

1815 Recordings with Edward Melkus in
The University of Georgia presents six
evenings of baroque music for strings
[Program book] Athens, Ga.: University of Georgia, Music Dept., 1974:
18-20 ((-))

MELOTONE RECORDING STUDIO
See listing for JENKINS, FLORENCE
FOSTER

MENDELSSOHN-BARTHOLDY, FELIX, 1809-
1847

1816 List of Mendelssohn recordings in
ERSKINE, John: Song without words;

the story of Felix Mendelssohn. New
York: J. Messner, [c1941]: [193]-196
((-))

1817 List of Mendelssohn works and recordings in HUMPHREYS, Dena: On
wings of song; the story of Mendelssohn.
New York: H. Holt and Co., [1944]: 252-
267 ((-))

1818 Schallplattenverzeichnis in KÖHLER,
Karl Heinz: Felix Mendelssohn-
Bartholdy. Leipzig: Reclam, [1966]:
253-[258] ((-))

1819 Schallplattenverzeichnis in KÖHLER,
Karl Heinz: Felix Mendelssohn-
Bartholdy. [2., veränd. Aufl.]. Leip-
zig: Reclam, 1972: 248-[256] ((-))

1820 Discographie in RICHMOND, Bruno L.:
Félix Mendelssohn. Bruxelles: Éditions
du Trefle à quatre feuilles, [194-]: 136-
139 ((-))

1821 Discographie sommaire des oeuvres de
Mendelssohn in TIÉNOT, Yvonne:
Mendelssohn; musicien complet. Paris:
H. Lemoine, [1972]: 241-246 (Pour
mieux connaître) ((-))

1822 WORBS, Hans Christoph: Diskographie
in Phonoprisma (July-August 1967):
100 ((-))

Works, Vocal

1823 [[MORSE, Peter: Mendelssohn vocal
music. Utica, NY: J. F. Weber, 1970:
13 pp. (Discography series, 6)]]

1824 MORSE, Peter: Mendelssohn vocal
music. Utica, NY: J. F. Weber, 1973:
30 pp. (Discography series, 6) ((3, 4,
5, 6, 7))

Concerto, Violin, E Minor, Op. 64

1825 KROHER, Ekkehart: Die Aufnahmen in
fono forum 1966 (No. 9, September):
432 ((-))

Symphony, No. 4, Op. 90, A Major

1826 [[AHLERS, N.: Eine vergleichende
Discographie in Phono, VI/5, VII/2]]

1827 Discographie in Diapason, No. 156
(April 1971): 36 ((-))

MENGELBERG, WILLEM, 1871-1951

1828 Grammofoon plaat opnamen in
BYSTERUS HEEMSKERK, E.: Over
Willem Mengelberg, 1871-1951:
illustraties en documentatie uit het
archief van Willem Mengelberg en
persoonlijke herinneringen. Amsterdam: Heuff, [c1971]: 153-155 ((-))

1829 DØSSING, Bo: Willem Mengelberg: a discography. [Slagelse]: Slagelse Centralbibliotek, 1975: 27 pp. ((4, 5))

1830 HARDIE, R. H.: The recordings of Willem Mengelberg: a discography. Nashville: Hardie, 1972: iv, 44 pp. ((1, 3, 5, 6, 7))

1831 Recorded works by Willem Mengelberg in Phonograph Monthly Review, I/4 (January 1927): 186 ((-))

1832 WOLF, Robert: The Mengelberg recordings; a discography in Le Grand Baton, VIII/2-3 (August-November 1971): 40-54 ((-))

MENOTTI, GIAN CARLO, 1911-

1833 PATRONITE, Thomas E.: Gian-Carlo Menotti on disc—a select discography in Le Grand Baton, VI/2 (May 1969): 32 ((-))

1834 Discographie in TRICOIRE, Robert: Gian Carlo Menotti, l'homme et son oeuvre...; Catalogue des oeuvres, discographie. Paris: Seghers, 1966: [185]-186 (Musiciens de tous les temps, 26) ((-))

Operas

1835 Recordings in GRIEB, Lyndal: The operas of Gian Carlo Menotti, 1937-1972: a selective bibliography. Metuchen, NJ: Scarecrow Press, 1974: 20-21 ((-))

MENUHIN, HEPHZIBAH
See listing for MENUHIN, YEHUDI. Clough, F. F., and G. J. Cuming: Yehudi and Hephzibah Menuhin

MENUHIN, YEHUDI, 1916-
See also listing for ENESCO, GEORGES. Same recordings realized by Georges Enesco and Yehudi Menuhin

1836 CLOUGH, F. F., and G. J. CUMING: Yehudi and Hephzibah Menuhin—a joint discography in Audio and Record Review, II/10 (June 1963): 17 ((-))

1837 CLOUGH, F. F., and G. J. CUMING: A Yehudi Menuhin discography in Audio and Record Review, V/12 (August 1966): 11-16 ((-)); VI/1 (September 1966): 11-12 ((-))

1838 CLOUGH, F. F., and G. J. CUMING: Yehudi Menuhin; diskography in Gramophone Record Review, No. 61 (November 1958): 21-24 ((-))

1839 Quelques enregistrements réalises par Georges Enesco et Yehudi Menuhin in

GAVOTY, Bernard: Yehudi Menuhin et Georges Enesco. Genève: R. Kister, c1955: [32] ((-))

1840 Recordings by Yehudi Menuhin in MAGIDOFF, Robert: Yehudi Menuhin; the story of the man and the musician. Garden City, NY: Doubleday, 1955: [299]-308 ((7))

1841 Recordings by Yehudi Menuhin in MAGIDOFF, Robert: Yehudi Menuhin; the story of the man and the musician. Westport, Conn.: Greenwood Press, [1973]: [299]-308 ((7))

1842 Recordings by Yehudi Menuhin in MAGIDOFF, Robert: Yehudi Menuhin; the story of the man and the musician. 2d ed. London: Hale, 1973: 324-340 ((7))

1843 SCHWINGER, Wolfram: Aus der Diskografie in fono forum 1962 (No. 1, January): 14 ((-))

1844 Diskographie in SPINGEL, Hans Otto: Yehudi Menuhin. [Berlin]: Rembrandt Verlag, [c1964]: 28-31 (Rembrandt-Reihe, 50) ((-))

MERLI, FRANCESCO

1845 VEGETO, Raffaele: Discografia in Discoteca, No. 71 (June 1967): 35-37 ((5))

MERRICK, FRANK, 1886-

1846 Frank Merrick discography in Recorded Sound, No. 18 (April 1965): 340-341 ((1, 7))

MERRILL, ROBERT, 1917-

1847 [[ROSENTHAL, Harold: Robert Merrill in Gramophone, No. 374 (July 1954): 55]]

MESPLÉ, MADY

1848 Discographie in Diapason, No. 182 (December 1973): 11 ((-))

MESSAGER, ANDRÉ CHARLES PROSPER, 1853-1929

1849 Discographie in AUGÉ-LARIBÉ, Michel: André Messager: musicien de théâtre. Paris: La Colombe, [1951]: [235]-238 (Collection Euterpe) ((-))

1850 Discographie in Courrier Musical de France, No. 15 (1966): 175 ((-))

MESSIAEN, OLIVIER, 1908-

1851 Discographie d'Olivier Messiaen in
GOLÉA, Antoine: Rencontres avec
Olivier Messiaen. Paris: R. Julliard,
[1961], c1960: [283] ((-))

1852 GOLÉA, Antoine: Diskografie in fono
forum 1960 (No. 11, November): 11 ((-))

1853 Discographie in MARI, Pierrette:
Olivier Messaien: l'homme et son
oeuvre. [Paris]: Éditions Seghers,
[1965]: 187-188 (Musiciens de tous les
temps, 21) ((-))

1854 Discographie in MARI, Pierrette:
Olivier Messaien: l'homme et son
oeuvre. Liste complète des oeuvres,
discographie. 2e édition mise à jour.
Paris: Seghers, 1970: 186-188
(Musiciens de tous les temps, 21)
((-))

1855 Olivier Messiaen in the surrealistic
context; a bibliography in Brio, XI/1
(Spring 1974): 2-11; [Includes dis-
cographies] ((-))

1856 Discographie in ROSTAND, Claude:
Olivier Messaien. Paris: Ventadour,
[1957]: 46-47 (Collection "Musiciens
d'aujourd'hui") ((-))

1857 Discographie in SAMUEL, Claude:
Entretiens avec Olivier Messiaen.
Paris: P. Belfond, 1967: 227-231
(Collection "Entretiens") ((-))

1858 Disques 1947-1948-1949 in ZINKE-
BIANCHINI, Virginie: Olivier
Messiaen: compositeur de musique
et rythmicien. [Paris: L'Eman-
cipatrice, 1949]: 18 ((-))

MEYER, ERNST HERMANN, 1905-

1859 Diskographie in Medium Schallplatte,
No. 12 (No. 3, 1969): 14 ((-))

MEYERBEER, GIACOMO, 1791-1864

Les Huguenots

1860 BEBB, Richard, and Vivian LIFF: Les
Huguenots in Opera, XX/7 (July 1969):
580-586 ((-)); XX/8 (August 1969):
678-684 (Opera on the gramophone, 24)
((-))

Les Huguenots. Bianca al par di neue alpina

1861 VEGETO, Raffaele: Nota discografica
in Discoteca, No. 45 (November 1964):
40 ((-))

MICHAILOVA, MARIA

1862 BARNES, Harold: Maria Michailova: a
discography in Recorded Sound, No. 33
(January 1969): 366-380 ((3, 4, 6, 7))

MICHELANGELI, ARTURO BENEDETTI,
1920-

1863 Discographie in Diapason, No. 166
(April 1972): 19 ((-))

1864 MEYER, Martin: Arturo Benedetti
Michelangeli; Schallplattenverzeichnis
in fono forum 1975 (No. 6, June): 530-
531 ((1, 5))

MIGOT, GEORGES, 1891-

1865 Discographie in Courrier Musical de
France, No. 19 (1967): 181 ((-))

MIHALOVICI, MARCEL, 1898-

1866 Discographie in Courrier Musical de
France, No. 15 (1966): 180 ((-))

1867 DRAGONI, Constantin: Discographie in
Muzica, XX/8 (August 1970): 47 ((-))

MILANOV, ZINKA, 1906-

1868 Aus der Diskografie in fono forum 1961
(No. 9, September): 13 ((-))

1869 EINSTEIN, Edwin K., Jr.: Zinka
Milanov: a complete discography in
Le Grand Baton, V/2 (May 1968):
7-16, 21 ((-))

MILHAUD, DARIUS, 1892-1974

1870 Discographie in BECK, Georges Henri:
Darius Milhaud; étude suivie du catalogue chronologique complet de son
oeuvre. Paris: Heugel, [1949]: [131]-
135 ((-))

1871 Discographie in BECK, Georges Henri:
Darius Milhaud; étude suivie du catalogue chronologique complet de son
oeuvre. Supplément; oeuvres compo-
sées de novembre 1949 à avril 1956.
Paris: Heugel, [c1956]: [22]-29 ((-))

1872 BLOCH, Francine: Discographie des
oeuvres de Darius Milhaud in
MILHAUD, Darius: Ma vie heureuse.
Paris: Belfond, [1974]: [317-344] (Les
Bâtisseurs du XXe siècle) ((-))

1873 Discographie in Courrier Musical de
France, No. 12 (1965): 229-230 ((-))

1874 Discographie des oeuvres de Darius
Milhaud in Bulletin de la Phonotheque
nationale, Supplément spécial No. 1
(January-June 1964): 47 pp. ((5))

1875 Skladby Daria Milhauda na deskách
      Supraphon in MILHAUD, Darius:
      Notivy bez tónу. Praha: Editio
      Supraphon, 1972: 291 ((-))

1876 PRÉTESEILLE, Jean: Darius Milhaud
      et le disque in Diapason, No. 169
      (September 1972): 38 ((-))

1877 Discographie in ROY, Jean: Darius
      Milhaud; l'homme et son oeuvre....
      Catalogue des oeuvres, discographie.
      Paris: Seghers, 1968: [183]-185
      (Musiciens de tous les temps, 39)
      ((-))

1878 ROY, Jean: Discographie in Diapason,
      No. 189 (September 1974): 10-11 ((-))

MILSTEIN, NATHAN, 1904-

1879 Diskographie in Collegium Musicum
      1971 (No. 5): 14 ((-))

1880 Diskographie zu Nathan Milstein in
      Phonoprisma (January-February 1967):
      32 ((-))

1881 Discographie in GAVOTY, Bernard:
      Nathan Milstein. Genève: Éditions R.
      Kister, 1956: [32] (Les Grands
      interprètes) ((-))

1882 Recordings made by Milstein in
      GAVOTY, Bernard: Nathan Milstein.
      Geneva: R. Kister, c1956: [32] (Great
      concert artists) ((-))

MINGHINI-CATTANEO, IRENE

1883 DELICATA, A. A.: Irene Minghini-
      Cattaneo in Record Collector, XIII/7-8
      (September-October 1960): 165-172
      ((3, 5))

MINSTRELS

1884 Discography in GOLDRON, Romain:
      Minstrels and masters. [n.p.]: H. S.
      Stuttman Co., distributed by Doubleday,
      [1968]: 5-8 (History of music, 3) ((-))

MITROPOULOS, DIMITRI, 1896-1960

1885 Discography in CHRISTOPOULOU,
      Maria: Dēmētrēs Mētropoulos: zoē
      kai ergo. Athens: Yannoukakis, 1971:
      245 ((-))

1886 CLOUGH, F. F., and G. J. CUMING:
      Dimitri Mitropoulos; a diskography in
      Gramophone Record Review, No. 88
      (February 1961): 192-193 ((-))

1887 Folgende Aufnahmen...in fono forum
      1961 (No. 11, November): 11 ((-))

MÖDL, MARTHA

1888 Diskografie in SCHÄFER, Walter Erich:
      Martha Mödl. Velber b. Hannover:
      Friedrich Verlag, [1967]: 98-99 ((-))

MOERAN, EDWARD JOHN, 1894-1950

1889 FOREMAN, Lewis: Discography in
      WILD, Stephen: E. J. Moeran. London:
      Triad Press, 1973: 23-31 ((1, 4))

MÖRIKE, EDUARD

1890 CHISLETT, W. A.: Eduard Mörike in
      Gramophone, III/4 (September 1925):
      167-168 ((-))

MOFFO, ANNA, 1932-

1891 Diskographie in Musica/Phonoprisma,
      XXII/4 (July-August 1968): 323 ((-))

1892 Diskographie (Auswahl) in Musica,
      XXIV/4 (July-August 1970): 404 ((-))

1893 HELM, Everett: Diskografie in fono
      forum 1966 (No. 2, February): 53 ((-))

MOMPOU Y DENCAUSSE, FEDERICO, 1893-

1894 Discografía in JANÉS, Clara: La vida
      callada de Federico Mompou. Bar-
      celona: Editorial Ariel, 1975: [276]-
      277 ((-))

MONACO, MARIO DEL, 1915-

1895 Diskografie in BURIAN, Karel Vladimír:
      Mario del Monaco. Praha: Supraphon,
      t. ST 2, 1969: 54-56 (Edice Lyra) ((-))

1896 ROSENTHAL, Harold: Del Monaco re-
      cordings in Gramophone, No. 372 (May
      1954): 468 ((-))

MONIUSZKO, STANISLAW, 1819-1872

1897 ARCHETTI, Enzo: List of recorded
      works in Music Lover's Guide, II/8
      (April 1934): 238 ((-)); II/9 (May 1934):
      297-299 ((-))

1898 MICHAŁOWSKI, Kornel: Dyskografia
      in RUDZIŃSKI, Witold: Moniuszko.
      Wyd. 3. Kraków: Polskie Wydawn.
      Muzyczne, [1969]: 245-274 ((5))

1899 MICHAŁOWSKI, Kornel: Dyskografia
      in RUDZIŃSKI, Witold: Moniuszko.
      Wyd. 4. Kraków: Polskie Wydawn.
      Muzyczne, [1972]: 245-273 ((5))

1900 Dyskografia in PROSNAK, Jan: Stanis-
      ław Moniuszko. Wyd. 2. Kraków:
      Polskie Wydawn. Muzyczne, 1968: 185-
      [199] ((-))

1901 Works of Stanislaw Moniuszko on Muza
Records in Polish Music, VII/2 (1972):
17-[23] ((-))

MONTE, TOTI DAL

1902 [[RENTON, A. C.: Toti dal Monte in
Record Collector, IV/ (September
1949): 147-150]]

1903 REUTLINGER, Dale: The recordings in
Maestro, I/3-4 (July-December 1969):
3-4 ((7))

MONTEUX, PIERRE, 1875-1964

1904 CLOUGH, F. F., and G. J. CUMING: A
Monteux discography in Audio and Record Review, II/5 (January 1963): 23-24
((-))

1905 Diskographie in Phonoprisma, VIII/1
(January-February 1965): 24 ((-))

1906 KUNZEL, Erich: Discography of
Pierre Monteux in MONTEUX, Doris:
It's all in the music. New York:
Farrar, Straus and Giroux, [1965]:
233-263 ((1))

1907 KUNZEL, Erich: Discography of
Pierre Monteux in MONTEUX, Doris:
It's all in the music. London: Kimber,
1966: 225-249 ((1))

1908 Platten in Hi Fi Stereophonie, IV/9
(September 1965): 533-534 ((-))

MONTEVERDI, CLAUDIO, 1567-1643

1909 [[CÈ, Nivia: Saggio di discografia
monteverdiana in Congresso internazionale sul tema Claudio Monteverdi
e il suo tempo. Venezia, Mantova,
Cremona. 3-7 maggio 1968. Relazioni
e communicazioni. Ed. Raffaello
MONTEROSSO. Verona: Stamperia
Valdoneza, 1969: 543-556]]

1910 HAGG, Walter: Monteverdi-Diskogra-
phie in Österreichische Musikzeitschrift, XXVI/8 (1971): 468-471 ((-))

1911 HALBREICH, Harry: Monteverdi—
discographie critique in Harmonie,
No. 28 (June-July 1967): 23-31 ((-))

1912 KOEGLER, Horst: Diskografie in fono
forum 1962 (No. 7, July): 33 ((-))

1913 Discographie in LE ROUX, Maurice:
Claudio Monteverdi. Paris: Éditions
du Coudrier, [1951]: [186]-189 ((-))

1914 RAUGEL, Felix: Claudio Monteverdi;
une discographie in Disques, No. 2
(February 15, 1948): [64] ((-))

1915 Discographie in ROCHE, Maurice:
Monteverdi. [Paris]: Éditions du

Seuil, [1960]: 173-177 (Collections
Microcosme. Solfèges, 14) ((-))

1916 [[SOMMERFIELD, David: A Monteverdi
discography in Current Musicology, No.
9 (1969): 215-232]]

1917 Discographie in TELLART, Roger:
Claudio Monteverdi. [Lausanne]: La
Guilde du livre, [1970]: 181-184
(Musiciens de tous les temps) ((-))

1918 WESTERLUND, Gunnar: Music of
Claudio Monteverdi: a discography, [by]
Gunnar Westerlund & Eric HUGHES.
London: British Institute of Recorded
Sound, 1972: viii, 72 pp. ((4))

MOORE, GERALD, 1899-

1919 CLOUGH, F. F., and G. J. CUMING:
Gerald Moore: sketch for a discography
in Audio and Record Review, IV/3
(November 1964): 81-84 ((-))

MORRISSON, LOUIS

1920 HAESEN, Franck: Louis Morrisson discography in Record Collector, XIX/3-4
(June 1970): 66-75 ((3, 6, 7))

MOSER, EDDA

1921 PIPER-ZIETHEN, Herta: Edda Moser;
Verzeichnis der Schallplattenaufnahmen
in fono forum 1972 (No. 12, December):
1061 ((-))

MOTTA, JOSE VIANNA DA
See DA MOTTA, JOSE VIANNA

MOZART, JOHANN CHRYSOSTOM WOLF-
GANG AMADEUS, 1756-1791

1922 BURKE, C. G.: Mozart on records; a
selective discography in High Fidelity,
VI/1 (January 1956): 93-106 ((-))

1923 Discographie (succincte) des oeuvres
de Mozart in CADIEU, Martine: Wolfgang Amadeus Mozart l'homme et son
oeuvre. Liste complète des oeuvres,
discographie. [Paris]: Seghers, 1966:
[181]-189 (Musiciens de tous les temps,
25) ((-))

1924 Catalogue des principales oeuvres et
discographie critique in Mozart.
Paris: Hachette, 1964: [271]-[294] ((-))

1925 CELLETTI, Rodolfo: Discografia in
Mozart: la vita. [Milano]: Edizioni
della Scala, [1955]: [279]-296 ((-))

1926 [[[Discography] in Discofilia, No. 11
(March 1956): 7]]

1927 Discographie in FLOTHIUS, Marius:
W. A. Mozart. s'Gravenhage: J. P.
Kruseman, [1940]: 113-120 (De Muziek,
IX) ((-))

1928 Schallplatten-Archiv in HECKMANN,
Elenore: Wolfgang Amadeus Mozart,
1756-1791. [Frankfurt am Main:
Maindruck, 1956]: [33]-39 ((-))

1929 Schallplattenverzeichnis in HENNEN-
BERG, Fritz: Wolfgang Amadeus
Mozart. Leipzig: Reclam, 1970: 344-
[363] (Reclams Universal-Bibliothek,
455) ((-))

1930 Mozart par le disque in HEVESY,
André de: Vie de Mozart. Paris: Les
Editions de Portiques, [1934]: [243-249]
((-))

1931 Discographie anthologique in HOC-
QUARD, Jean Victor: Mozart. [Paris]:
Éditions du Seuil, [1958]: 179-[191]
(Solfèges, 8) ((-))

1932 [[[Discography] in HOCQUARD, Jean
Victor: Mozart. Nouv. ed. Paris:
Éditions du Seuil, 1970: 180-186]]

1933 KOLODIN, Irving: Mozart on records,
with a foreword by Lily PONS. New
York: The Four corners, [1942]: 94 pp.
((-))

1934 LINDLAR, Heinrich: Kleine Mozart-
Diskographie in Phonoprisma, V/2
(March-April 1962): 33-34 ((-))

1935 [[Mozart by a mile in Audio, LIII
(April 1969): 18]]

1936 PIRIE, Peter J.: A bibliography of
Mozart records (available in England)
in Music Review, XVII (February
1956): [71]-86 ((-))

1937 REDFERN, Brian: Selected recordings
of Mozart's music in KING, Alexander
Hyatt: Mozart; a biography with a
survey of books, editions & recordings.
London: Bingley, 1970: 88-105 (The
Concertgoer's companions) ((-))

1938 Discographie in REINOLD, Helmut:
Der italienische Mozart. [Freiburg i.
Br.: Fono-Verlagsgesellschaft, 1962]:
26-31 (Zugänge; Texte, Schallplatten,
Diskographien, 1) ((-))

1939 Selected discography in SEROFF, Victor: Wolfgang Amadeus Mozart. New
York: Macmillan Co., [1965]: [115]-121
((-))

1940 A Mozart record library in STEARNS,
Monroe: Wolfgang Amadeus Mozart;
master of pure music. New York: F.
Watts, [1968]: 240-243 (Immortals of
music) ((-))

1941 ULANOV, Barry: The recorded music
of Mozart: a discography, with an introduction by José ITURBI. [New York:
The Resonance Publishing Corporation,
1941]: 15 pp. ((-))

1942 Das Musikalische Werk Mozarts Schallplattenaufnahmen in Wolfgang Amadeus
Mozart zum 175. Todestag zm 5.
Dezember. [Berlin]: Berliner Stadtbibliothek, 1966: 22-39 (Bibliographische Kalenderblätter, Sonderblatt, 19)
((-))

Works, Chamber Music

1943 [[BRIERLEY, Peter: [Discography] in
Disc (Bristol) III/12 (Autumn 1949):
166-169]]

1944 BURKE, C. G.: Mozart on microgroove.
Part V: Miscellaneous orchestral;
chamber music in High Fidelity, III/6
(January-February 1954): 76-88 ((-))

Works, Instrumental

1945 [[BRIERLEY, Peter: [Discography] in
Disc (Bristol) III/11 (Summer 1949):
117-118]]

1946 BURKE, C. G.: Mozart on microgroove:
Symphonies and violin concertos in
High Fidelity III/2 (May-June 1953): 61-
68 ((-))

1947 BURKE, C. G.: Mozart on microgroove.
Part II: Concertos; overtures in High
Fidelity, III/3 (July-August 1953): 65-
72 ((-))

1948 BURKE, C. G.: Mozart on microgroove.
Part IV: Divertimentos; serenades,
cassations, and church music in High
Fidelity, III/5 (November-December
1953): 60-64, 122-124 ((-))

1949 BURKE, C. G.: Mozart on microgroove.
Part VI: Sonatas; instrumental addenda;
postscript in High Fidelity, IV/1 (March
1954): 72-85 ((-))

Works, Organ

1950 Diskografie in fono forum 1966 (No. 8,
August): 413 ((-))

Works, Vocal

1951 [[BRIERLEY, Peter: [Discography] in
Disc (Bristol) IV/14 (Summer 1950):
71-73]]

1952 [[BRIERLEY, Peter: [Discography] in
Disc (Bristol) IV/15 (Autumn 1950):
116-118]]

1953 BURKE, C. G.: Mozart on microgroove.
Part III: Concert arias; opera; songs in
High Fidelity, III/4 (September-October
1953): 81-96 ((-))

Concertos

1954 [[BRIERLEY, Peter: [Discography] in Disc (Bristol) III/10 (Spring 1949): 4-5]]

Concertos, Piano

1955 [[BRIERLEY, Peter: [Discography] in Disc (Bristol) III/9 (Winter 1948): 17-18]]

1956 BRODER, Nathan: Mozart: the piano concertos in High Fidelity, VIII/10 (October 1958): 111-120 ((-))

1957 CUMING, G. J.: A discography of Mozart piano concertos in Gramophone, No. 210 (November 1940): 130 ((-))

1958 List of gramophone records in GIRDLE-STONE, Cuthbert Morton: Mozart's piano concertos. London: Cassell, 1948: [505]-506 ((-))

1959 List of gramophone records in GIRDLE-STONE, Cuthbert Morton: Mozart and his piano concertos. [1st American ed.] Norman: University of Oklahoma Press, [1952]: [505]-506 ((-))

Concerto, Piano, K.466, D Minor

1960 REHM, Wolfgang: Mozarts Klavierkonzert in d-Moll; eine vergleichende Discographie in Phono, VIII/5 (May-June 1962): 101-105 ((-)); [[VIII/6 (July-August 1962)]]

Concerto, Piano, K.467, C Major

1961 BOLLERT, Werner: [Diskografie] in fono forum 1964 (No. 9, September): 365 ((-))

Concertos, Violin

1962 LEWINSKI, Wolf-Eberhard von: Die Aufnahmen in fono forum 1970 (No. 11, November): 824 ((-))

Cosi fan tutte

1963 JEFFERSON, Alan: Così fan tutte in Opera, XIX/5 (June 1968): 451-460 (Opera on the gramophone, 19) ((5)); Addenda: Opera, XIX/8 (September 1968): 772-773 ((-))

Don Giovanni

1964 Discographie comparée in Harmonie, No. 25 (March 1967): 68-72 ((-))

1965 Diskografie "Don Giovanni"; eine vergleichende Diskografie in fono forum 1961 (No. 4, April): 13 ((-))

1966 KRAUS, Gottfried: [Diskografie] in fono forum 1967 (No. 2, February): 60 ((-))

1967 PAULI, Friedrich Wilhelm: Diskografie in fono forum 1964 (No. 1, January): 11 ((-))

1968 WERBA, Robert: Mozarts "Don Giovanni" in der Prä-LP-Ära in Österreichische Musikzeitschrift, XXIII/9 (August 1968): 448-453 ((-))

Die Entführung aus dem Serail

1969 BOLLERT, Werner: [Diskografie] in fono forum 1966 (No. 3, March): 105 ((-))

1970 [[REHM, Wolfgang: Eine vergleichende Discographie in Phono, V/1]]

Le Nozze di Figaro

1971 [Diskografie] in fono forum 1968 (No. 10, October): 604 ((-))

1972 Mozart Le Nozze di Figaro; eine discographie in Phono, X/1 (September-October 1963): 18-19 ((-))

Operas

1973 BRODER, Nathan: The Mozart operas on record in High Fidelity, X/11 (November 1960): 56-57, 125-131 ((-))

1974 KRAUS, Gottfried: Diskografie hinweise in fono forum 1966 (No. 7, July): 339 ((-))

1975 OSBORNE, Conrad L.: The operas of Mozart on microgroove; a discography-in-depth in High Fidelity, XV/11 (November 1965): 65-73, 128-141 ((-))

Requiem

1976 NYS, Carl de: Discographie in Diapason, No. 169 (September 1972): 36 ((-))

1977 WIENKE, Gerhard: Diskografie in fono forum 1965 (No. 4, April): 146 ((-))

Serenade, K. 370a (361), Bb Major

1978 KRAUS, Gottfried: Diskografie in fono forum 1972 (No. 11, November): 936 ((-))

Symphonies

1979 [[BRIERLEY, Peter: [Discography] in Disc (Bristol) II/8 (Autumn 1948): 159-160]]

1980 KRAUS, Gottfried: Diskografische Angaben in fono forum 1969 (No. 6, June): 365 ((-))

Symphony, K. 550, G Minor

1981 LEWINSKI, Wolf-Eberhard von: Diskografie in fono forum 1964 (No. 2,
February): 75 ((-))

Symphony, K. 551, C Major

1982 [[FÜSSL, K. H.: Eine vergleichende
Discographie in Phono, VII/6]]

Die Zauberflöte

1983 [[[Discography] in CORNELISSEN,
Thilo: Die Zauberflöte von W. A.
Mozart. Berlin: R. Lineau, 1963:
107 pp.]]

1984 Discographie in Diapason, No. 158
(June-July 1971): 28 ((-))

MÜNCHINGER, KARL, 1915-

1985 Discographie in GAVOTY, Bernard:
Karl Münchinger. Genève: R. Kister,
c1959: [32] (Les Grands interprètes)
((-))

MULLINGS, FRANK

1986 FRYER, J. J., and J. B. RICHARDS:
Recordings in Record Collector, VII/1
(January 1952): 16-19 ((3, 5, 7))

MUNCH, CHARLES, 1891-1968

1987 Diskografie in BURIAN, Karel Vladimír:
Charles Munch. 1.vyd. Praha: Supra-
phon, t. ST 2, 1971: 47-[50] (Edice
Lyra) ((-))

1988 CLOUGH, F. F., and G. J. CUMING:
Discography in Audio and Record Review, II/9 (September 1963): 18, 83-86
((-))

1989 Discographie in Diapason, No. 101
(November 1965): 11 ((-))

1990 HAMON, Jean: Discographie in Diapason, No. 131 (December 1968): 6-7
((-))

MURO, BERNARDO DE
See DE MURO, BERNARDO

MURO LOMANTO, ENZO DE
See DE MURO LOMANTO, ENZO

MUSIC
See also such specific headings as
COMPOSERS, SYMPHONIES, other
form entries, and proper names of
composers and performers

1991 Åarhus, Denmark. Statsbibliothek:
Fortegnelse over musikplander:
klassik musik og folkemusik. Århus,
1968: 127 pp. ((-))

1992 [[[Discography] in ARNTSEN, Ella:
Musikkbiblioteket: hjelpebok for
bibliotekarer. Oslo: Statens
biblioteket, 1963: 179-200]]

1993 Discography in BALL, Charles H.:
Musical structure and style: an intro-
duction. Morristown, NJ: General
Learning Press, [1975]: [241]-249
((-))

1994 [Discographies included] in BARBOUR,
Harriot Buxton: A story of music.
Rev. ed. Evanston, IL: Summy-
Birchard Pub. Co., [1958]: 301 ((-))

1995 BAUER, Robert: Historical records.
Milano: G. Martucci, 1937: 293 pp. ((7))

1996 BAUER, Robert: The new catalogue of
historical records, 1898-1908/09.
2d ed. London: Sidgwick and Jackson,
1947: 494 pp. ((7))

1997 Diskoteek in BECKER, G. de: Wezen &
gestalte van de muziek. Tielt: Lannoo,
[1946?]: [121]-123 ((-))

1998 BELINFANTE, Sam: Kies uw plaat: een
beknopte wegwijzer voor de muziek-
liefhebber-gramofoonbezitter. Blari-
cum: Bigot & Van Rossum, [1956]: 143
pp. ((-))

1999 Discography in BENJAMIN, Edward B.:
The restful in music. [1st ed.]. New
Orleans: Restful Music, [1970]: 131
((-))

2000 Nahrávy na čs. gramofonových deskách
in BERNSTEIN, Leonard: Hudbouk
Radosti. Praha, Bratislava: Edition
Supraphon, 1969: 121-[122] ((-))

2001 BLAUKOPF, Kurt: Langspielplatten-
buch: Konzert und Oper. Wien: Verlag
für Jugend und Volk, [1956-57]: 2 v.
((-))

2002 Discographie in BOEREBOOM, Marcel:
Handboek van de muziek. Amsterdam:
Wereldbibliotheek, 1947: 552-566 ((-))

2003 BREMMICKE, Helmut: Der Weg zur
Diskothek. Schallplattenbuch für den
Musikfreund. Zürich: W. Classen,
[1959]: 183 pp. ((-))

2004 BRUUN, Carl L.: Att samla grammofonskivor. Stockholm: Wahlström &
Widstrand, [1950]: 265 pp. ((-))

2005 Discographie in CANDÉ, Roland de: La
musique: histoire, dictionnaire, discographie. [Paris]: Éditions du Seuil,
[1969]: [672]-674 ((-))

2006 [[Discography in CANDÉ, Roland de:
La musique: histoire, dictionnaire,

discographie. Paris: Éditions du Seuil, 1969: 623-661]]

2007 Discographie in CANDÉ, Roland de: Ouverture pour une discothèque. [Bourge]: Éditions du Seuil, [1956]: 287 pp. (Solfèges) ((-))

2008 CARLID, Göte: Musik på skiva: en orientering i svensk skivmarknad, [av] Göte Carlid och Bengt PLEIJEL. Stockholm: Wahlström & Widstrand, [1951]: 226 pp. ((-))

2009 Discography in CHRIST, William: Involvement with music, by William Christ, Richard DeLONE, Allen WINOLD. New York: Harper's College Press, [1975]: 455-457 ((-))

2010 Discografie in COLLAER, Paul: Beteekenis van de muziek: vorm en uitdrukking in de muziek. 2. bijgewerkte druk. Brussel: Uitgeversmij A. Manteau, [1943]: 74-77 ((-))

2011 Suggested recordings in DARNTON, Christian: You and music. New York: Penguin Books, Inc., [1945]: 171-174 (Pelican books) ((-))

2012 DOUGLAS, John R.: Classical recordings for a song; a discography of historic reissues in Library Journal (February 15, 1971): 597-607 ((-))

2013 FINNEY, Theodore Mitchell: Lists of recordings. New York: Harcourt, Brace, 1949. 46 pp. (Accompanies the author's A History of music. New York: Harcourt, Brace, 1947)

2014 GRONOW, Pekka: Äänilevytieto [kirj.], Pekka Gronow, Ilpo SAUNIO. Porvoo: W. Söderström, [1970]: 360 pp. ((-))

2015 [Discographies included] in HUNT, Reginald; The musical touchstone: a course in musical appreciation. London; New York: Boosey & Hawkes, [1946-8]: 2 v. ((-))

2016 Discography in KAMIEN, Roger: Music: an appreciation. New York: McGraw-Hill, [1975]: 552-554 ((-))

2017 Recommended recordings in KAUFMANN, Helen L.: You can enjoy music. New York: Reynal & Hitchcock, 1940: 310-317 ((-))

2018 Recommended recordings in KAUFMANN, Helen Loeb: You can enjoy music. Plainview, NY: Books for Libraries Press, 1975, c1940: 310-317 (Essay index series) ((-))

2019 Records in MILLER, William Hugh: Introduction to music appreciation: an objective approach to listening. [1st. ed.] Philadelphia: Chilton Co., [1961]: 265-313 ((-))

2020 Discography in MILLER, William Hugh: Introduction to music appreciations: an objective approach to listening. Rev. ed. Philadelphia: Chilton Book Co., [1970]: [277]-330 ((-))

2021 [Discographies included] in NAUR, Robert: Veje til den klassiske musik. 2. udg. København: Gyldendal, 1973: 235 pp. ((-))

2022 [Discographies included] in POLITOSKE, Daniel T.: Music. Englewood Cliffs, NJ: Prentice-Hall, [1974]: xi, 497 pp. ((-))

2023 Discography in ROSSI, Nick: The realm of music. Boston: Crescendo Pub. Co., [1974]: 155-158 ((-))

2024 Recommended records in YOUNG, Percy M.: Great ideas in music. London: Maxwell, 1967: 203-205 ((-))

2025 Recommended records in YOUNG, Percy M.: Great ideas in music. New York: D. White Co., 1968: 203-205 ((-))

Ancient

2026 Discography in GOLDRON, Romain: Ancient and Oriental music. [n.p.]: H. S. Stuttman Co., [1968]: [4] p. at end of book ((-))

Medieval (400-1500)

2027 [[JAHIEL, Edwin: French and Provençal poet musicians of the Middle Ages: a bibliodiscography in Romance Philology, XIV (1961): 200-207]]

2028 Record list in REESE, Gustave: Music in the Middle Ages. New York: Norton, 1940: 465-479 ((-))

2029 Record list in REESE, Gustave: Music in the Middle Ages. New York: Norton, 1948: 465-480 ((-))

2030 Discography in STERNFIELD, F. W.: Music from the Middle Ages to the Renaissance. New York: Praeger, [1973]: [431]-437 (A History of Western music, 1) ((-))

2031 [[ZOBELEY, Fritz: Altere Musik auf Schallplatten in Zeitschrift für Musikwissenschaft, XIV/2 (1931-1932): 117-128]]

16th Century

See also listing MUSIC, Medieval. Discography in Sternfield, F. W.:

Music from the Middle Ages to the
Renaissance

2032 Discography in GOLDRON, Romain:
Music of the Renaissance. [n.p.]:
H. S. Stuttman Co., [1968]: 122-125
((-))

2033 Discography in THOMSON, James C.:
Music through the Renaissance.
Dubuque, Iowa: W. C. Brown Co.,
[1968]: 145-151 (The Brown music
horizons series) ((-))

To 1800

2034 COOVER, James B.: Medieval and
Renaissance music on long-playing
records, by James Coover [and]
Richard COLVIG. [Detroit: Information
Service], 1964: xii, 122 pp. (Detroit
studies in music bibliography, 6) ((4))

2035 COOVER, James B.: Medieval and
Renaissance music on long-playing
records: supplement, 1962-1971, by
James Coover and Richard COLVIG.
Detroit: Information Coordinators,
1973: 258 pp. (Detroit studies in
music bibliography, 26) ((4))

20th Century

See also listings for ELECTRONIC
MUSIC and IMPRESSIONISM

2036 [[Discography in BRAY, Trevor:
Twentieth century music, 1900-1945.
Milton Keynes [U.K.]: Open Univer-
sity Press, 1974: 113-114]]

2037 Schallplattenverzeichnis in DIBELIUS,
Ulrich: Moderne Musik 1945 bis
1965. Stuttgart: Deutscher Bücherbund,
1968: [359]-368 ((-))

2038 [Discographies included] in GOLÉA,
Antoine: Vingt ans de musique contemporaine. [n.p.]: Éditions Seghers,
[c1962]: 2 v. in 1 ((-))

2039 A selective discography in HODIER,
André: Since Debussy: a view of con-
temporary music. New York: Da Capo
Press, 1975, c1961: 243-250 ((-))

2040 Discography in HOWARD, John Tasker:
This modern music: a guide for the be-
wildered listener. Freeport, NY: Books
for Libraries Press, [1969, c1957]:
217-224 (Essay index reprint series)
((-))

2041 Schallplattenverzeichnis in MEYER-
DENKMANN, Gertrud: Struktur und
Praxis neuer Musik im Unterricht:
Experiment und Methode. [Wien]:
Universal Edition, [1972]: 273-282
((-))

2042 [Discographies included] in Musique de
notre temps. [Paris]: Casterman,
[1973]: 1 v. ((-))

2043 New Recordings in Contemporary
Music Newsletter, VIII/4-5 (November-
December 1974): 5-8 ((-))

2044 [[SIMPSON, Robert, and Oliver PRENN:
Guide to modern music on records.
London: Blond, 1958. 206 pp.]]

2045 Discography in STERNFIELD, F. W.:
Music in the modern age. New York:
Praeger, [1973]: [443]-461 (A History
of Western music, 5) ((-))

MUSIC, AMERICAN

2046 Discography in EDWARDS, Arthur C.:
Music in the United States, by Arthur
C. Edwards, W. Thomas MARROCCO.
Dubuque, Iowa: W. C. Brown Co.,
[1968]: 143-158 (The Brown music
horizons series) ((-))

2047 ELLSWORTH, Ray: Americans on
microgroove; a discography in High
Fidelity, VI/7 (July 1956): 63-69 ((-));
VI/8 (August 1956): 60-66 ((-))

2048 [[FRANKENSTEIN, Alfred: American
music on the gramophone in Music and
letters, XLI (1960): 360-365]]

2049 Recordings of American music in
HOWARD, John Tasker: A short history
of music in America, by John Tasker
Howard and George Kent BELLOWS.
New York: Thomas Y. Crowell Co.,
[1967]: 429-456 (Apollo editions,
A-162) ((-))

2050 INGLIS, Franklin F.: A discography of
American music in American Music
Lover, V/10 (February 1940): 366-371
((-))

2051 KEATS, Sheila: American music on LP
records—an index in Juilliard Review,
II/1 (Winter 1955): 24-33 ((-)); II/2
(Spring 1955): 31-43 ((-)); II/3 (Fall
1955): 48-51 ((-)); Supplement in Juilliard Review, III/3 (Fall 1956): 17-20
((-))

2052 KEATS, Sheila: American music on LP
records in Juilliard Review, IV/1
(Winter 1956-1957): 33-39 ((-)); IV/3
(Fall 1957): 36-40 ((-))

2053 Discography in MELLERS, Wilfrid:
Music in a new found land: themes and
developments in the history of American music. [1st American ed.] New
York: A. A. Knopf, 1965 [c1964]:
[425]-519 ((-))

2054 Recordings in SABLOSKY, Irving:
American music. Chicago: University
of Chicago Press, [1969]: 206-213 ((-))

2055 Discographic notes in TURPIE, Mary C.: American music for the study of American civilization. Minneapolis: Program in American Studies, University of Minnesota, 1964: 1 v. ((-))

20th Century

2056 Discography in COHN, Arthur: The collector's twentieth-century music in the Western Hemisphere. Philadelphia: Lippincott, [1961]: 256 pp. ((-))

2057 Discography in COHN, Arthur: The collector's twentieth-century music in the Western Hemisphere. New York: Da Capo Press, 1972 [c1961]: 256 pp. ((-))

MUSIC, AUSTRALIAN

2058 [[BRUMBY, Colin: Discography of Australian music in Australian Journal of Music Education, I (October 1967): 51-52]]

2059 Selective discography in COVELL, Roger: Australia's music: themes for a new society. Melbourne: Sun Books, 1967: [307]-313 ((-))

2060 Discography in Musical composition in Australia. Canberra: Published by the Australian Government through the Advisory Board, Commonwealth Assistance to Australian Composers, 1969: 29-31 (Music by Australian composers, 1) ((-))

MUSIC, AUSTRIAN

2061 [[BLAUKOPF, Kurt: Musik aus Österrich. Ein diskographisches Verzeichnis, das einen Überblick über die wichtigsten Werke in möglichst repräsentativen Aufnahmen bietet. Wien: Österrichische Gesellschaft für Musik, 1968: 32 pp.]]

MUSIC, BELGIAN

20th Century

2062 Discographie in WANGERMÉE, Robert: La musique belge contemporaine. Bruxelles: La renaissance du livre, [1959]: 145-147 (Collection "Notre passé") ((-))

MUSIC, BRITISH

2063 DODGSON, Stephen: Recordings of British music, December 1965-June 1966 in Composer, No. 20 (August 1966): 25, 27-28 ((-))

2064 DODGSON, Stephen: Recordings of British music, July to November 1966 in Composer, No. 22 (Winter 1966-1967): 22-23 ((-))

2065 DODGSON, Stephen: Recordings of British Music, new issues December 1966—August 1967 in Composer, No. 25 (Autumn 1967): 19-21 ((-))

2066 DODGSON, Stephen: Recordings of British music, new issues September 1967—March 1968 in Composer, No. 27 (Spring 1968): 23-26 ((-))

2067 STANDFORD, Patric: Living British composers on record in Composer, No. 56 (Winter 1975-1976): 19-23 ((-))

MUSIC, BYZANTINE

2068 Discography in GOLDRON, Romain: Byzantine and medieval music. [n.p.]: H. S. Stuttman Co., distributed by Doubleday, [1968]: 121-125 (History of music, 2) ((-))

MUSIC, CANADIAN

2069 Canadian Music Centre, Toronto: Recordings of works by Canadian composers included in the library of the Canadian Music Centre. [Toronto: 1967?]: 11 pp. ((-))

MUSIC, CZECH

2070 Gramofonové závody, Prague: Československá hudba na gramofonových deskách: Ultraphon, Esta, Supraphon. [Vyd. 1.] V Praze, [1947]: 61 pp. ((-))

2071 [Discographie included] in KOZÁK, Jan: Českoslovenští koncertní umělci a komorní soubory. [1. vyd.] Praha: Státní hudební vydavatelství, 1964: 482 pp. ((-))

MUSIC, DANISH

2072 DIREKINCK-HOLMFELD, Gregers: Ny dansk musik på Lp-inspilninger in Nutida Musik, VI/5 (1962-1963): 44-46 ((-))

2073 [[ROSENBERG, Herbert: Discography; from the archives of Skandinavisk Grammophon Aktieselskab. in Edition Balzer: a Danish history of music in sound. Copenhagen: Nationaldiskoteket, 1966: 12 pp. (Nationaldiskoteket. Discographies, 204)]]

MUSIC, EAST GERMAN

2074 PANEK, Wacław: Dyskografia i piśmiennictwo muzyczne na Łuzycach po 1945 roku in Muzyka, XV/2 (1970): 117-122 ((-))

MUSIC, ENGLISH

17th Century

2075 Discography in JOHNSON, Paula: Form and transformation in music and poetry of the English Renaissance. New Haven: Yale University Press, 1972: [163]-165 (Yale studies in English, 179) ((-))

MUSIC, EUROPEAN

2076 Soupis vybraných dlouhoh rajících desek . . . in ČERNUŠÁK, Gracian: Dějiny evropské hudby. Praha: Panton, 1964: 447-464 ((-))

2077 Soupis dlouhohrajících desek in ČERNUŠÁK, Gracian: Dějiny evropské hudby. Praha: Panton, 1972: 469-491 ((-))

2078 [Discography] in DUFOURCQ, Norbert: Petite histoire de la musique en Europe. Nouv. éd. rev. et mise à jour. Paris: Larousse, [1954, c1942]: 174 pp. ((-))

2079 Discothèque in DUFOURCQ, Norbert: Petite historie de la musique européenne. Nouvelle édition revue et mise à jour. Paris: Larousse, 1969: [121]-126 ((-))

2080 Discographie in GOLÉA, Antoine: La musique dans la société européenne depuis le moyen age jusqu'à nos jours. Paris: Bibliotheque de l'homme d'action, [1960]: [109]-141 ((-))

2081 Discography in HURD, Michael: An outline history of European music. London: Novello, [1968]: 119-123 ((-))

20th Century

2082 COHN, Arthur: Twentieth-century music in western Europe: the compositions and the recordings. New York: Da Capo Press, 1972 [c1965]: xii, 510 pp. (Da Capo Press music reprint series) ((-))

MUSIC, EXPERIMENTAL

2083 Discographie in PRIEBERG, Fred K.: Musica ex machina. Berlin: Ullstein, 1960: 263-[281] ((-))

MUSIC, FLEMISH

Renaissance

2084 Discography in WANGERMÉE, Robert: Flemish music and society in the fifteenth and sixteenth centuries. Brussels: Editions Arcade, 1968: 329-341 ((-))

2085 Discography in WANGERMÉE, Robert: Flemish music and society in the fifteenth and sixteenth centuries. New York: F. A. Praeger, [1968]: 329-341 ((-))

MUSIC, FRENCH

2086 Discographie in BARRAUD, Henry: La France et la musique occidentale. [Paris]: Gallimard, [1956]: [187-197] (Pour la musique, 1) ((-))

2087 Discographie in STRICKER, Rémy: La Musique française du romantisme à nos jours. Paris: La Documentation française, 1966: 94-95 ((-))

20th Century

2088 Breve discografia da moderna musica francesca in Arte Musical, 3d Series, No. 1 (March 1958): [32]-35 ((-))

MUSIC, HISPANIC

2089 New Mexico. University. Fine Arts Library: A discography of Hispanic music in the Fine Arts Library of the University of New Mexico, compiled by Ned SUBLETTE. Albuquerque, 1973: 110 pp. (New Mexico. University. General Library Sources, 1) ((-))

MUSIC, ITALIAN

2090 [Works in RAI Archives] in Recorded Sound, No. 38 (April 1970): 615-620 ((1, 7))

MUSIC, JEWISH

2091 National Jewish Music Council. Committee on Recordings: Bibliography of Jewish recordings. New York: National Jewish Music Council, 1948: 19 pp. ((-))

2092 National Jewish Music Council. Committee on Recordings: List of instrumental and vocal recordings. New York: Jewish Music Council, 1946: 7 pp. ((-))

MUSIC, LITHUANIAN

2093 List of gramophone records in
TAURAGIS, Adeodatas: Lithuanian
music: past and present. Gintaras:
Vilnius, 1971: 215-[224] ((-))

MUSIC, MEXICAN

20th Century

2094 [[Discography in MALSTRÖM, Dan:
Introduction to twentieth-century
Mexican music. [Uppsala: Alrad.
auh. Uppsala univ.], 1974]]

MUSIC, NORWEGIAN

20th Century

2095 Recordings of Norwegian orchestral
music in KORTSEN, Bjarne: Contemporary Norwegian orchestral
music. Bergen: Forfatteren, Solbakken
17, 1969: 453-456 ((-))

MUSIC, POLISH

2096 [[DANUTA, Idaszak, and Maria
BURCHARDT: Discographie de la
musique polonaise 1 mai 1966-20
novembre 1971 in Musique Pologne,
VIII (1972): 61-104]]

2097 [Discography included] in ERHARDT,
Ludwik: Music in Poland. Warsaw:
Interpress Publishers, 1975: 164 pp.
((-))

20th Century

2098 Foreign recordings of contemporary
Polish music (selection) in ERHARDT,
Ludwik: Music in Poland. Warsaw:
Interpress Publishers, 1975: 161-164
((-))

2099 Recordings by "Polskie Nagrania—
Muza" of newest Polish music (selection) in ERHARDT, Ludwik: Music in
Poland. Warsaw: Interpress Publishers, 1975: 159-[160] ((-))

MUSIC, ROUMANIAN

2100 Schallplatten; discuri in Romania.
Comitetul de Stat pentru Cultura si
Artă: Musik in Rumänien. Köln;
Stuttgart; München, 1968: 52-[60] ((-))

MUSIC, SCANDINAVIAN

2101 Selective international discography in
YOELL, John H.: The Nordic sound:

explorations into the music of Denmark,
Norway, Sweden. Boston: Crescendo
Pub. Co., [1974]: [231]-259 ((-))

MUSIC, SPANISH

2102 [Discographies included] in Una Década
de música catalana. 1960-1970.
Barcelona, octunre 1970: Esposicio'
muntada per Joventuts Musicals.
Barcelona, [1970]: 114 pp. ((-))

2103 [[LAADE, Wolfgang: Sechs Jahrhunderte
spanischer Musik auf Schallplatten in
Musik und Bildung, III/2 (February
1971): 82-88]]

MUSIC, SWEDISH
See also ELECTRONIC MUSIC, SWED-
ISH

2104 ÅHLÉN, Carl-Gunnar: Svensk skivförteckning 1964-66 in Svensk
Tidskrift för Musikforskning, no. 50
(1968): 199-232 ((-))

2105 ÅHLÉN, Carl-Gunnar: Svensk skivförteckning 1967-68 in Svensk
Tidskrift för Musikforskning, No. 51
(1969): 225-250 ((-))

2106 [[A Basic library of Swedish music on
record; Swedish music, past and present in Musik revy (special edition),
1967: 101-105]]

2107 Skivförteckning in JACOBSSON, Stig:
Musiken i Sverige; skivlyssnarens
handbok i svensk musik från äldsta tid
till 1970-talet, med utförlig skivförteckning. Västeras: Icaförlaget, 1975: 223-
260 ((-))

MUSIC, SWISS

2108 FIERZ, Gerold: Schweizer Musik auf
Schallplatten in Schweizerische
Musikzeitung, C/2 (1960): 105-106
((-)); C/6 (1960): 372-374 ((-))

MUSIC THERAPY

2109 Discography in HARBERT, Wilhelmina
K.: Opening doors through music: a
practical guide for teachers, thera-
pists, students, parents. Springfield,
Ill.: C. C. Thomas, [1974]: 83-94 ((-))

MUSICAL INSTRUMENTS

2110 Nota discografica in RATTALINO,
Piero: Gli strumenti musicali. 2 ed.
riveduta. Milano: Ricordi, 1973: 162-
164 ((-))

I MUSICI

2111 SPINGEL, Hans Otto: Diskografie in
fono forum 1962 (No. 8, August): 14
((-))

MUSICIANS

2112 Discographies in BLAUKOPF, Kurt:
Grosse Virtuosen. Teufen: A. Niggli u.
W. Verkauf, [1954?]: 181-193 (Bücher
der Weltmusik, 6) ((4))

MUSIQUE CONCRÈTE

2113 Disques in Revue Musicale, No. 236:
141 ((-))

MUSORGSKIĬ, MODEST PETROVICH, 1839-
1881

2114 [[[Discography] in Discofilia, No. 39
(July-August 1959): 289]]

2115 Discografía in GARCÍA MORILLO,
Roberto: Musorgsky. Buenos Aires:
Ricordi americana, sociedad anónima
editorial y comercial, [1943]: 145-151
((-))

2116 Discographie in MARNAT, Marcel:
Moussorgsky. [Paris]: Éditions de
Seuil, [1962]: 182-[186] (Solfèges, 21)
((-))

2117 WALRAET, J.: Discografie in POLS,
André M.: Modest Petrovitsj
Moessorgski; een studie. Amsterdam: Wereld-Bibliotheek, [1957]: 121-
125 ((-))

Boris Godunov

2118 DUNLOP, Lionel: Boris Godunov in
Opera, IX/10 (October 1958): 636-649
(Opera on the gramophone, 6) ((-))

2119 KRAUS, Gottfried: Diskografie in fono
forum 1965 (No. 6, June): 270 ((-))

Pictures at an Exhibition

2120 [[REICH, H.: Eine vergleichende Discographie in Phono, IV/4]]

MUSZELY, MELITTA

2121 Diskographie (Auswahl) in Musica/
Phonoprisma, XXII/1 (January-February 1968): 65 ((-))

MUŽ, STANISLAV, 1896-1955

2122 Snímky Stanislava Muže na gramofonových deskach in MIKULA, Joža:
Stanislav Muž; pěvec Národního divadla,
z kroniky umělcova života, k nedožitým
umělcovým sedmdesátinám. [Vyd. 1.]
Plzeň: Západočeské nakl., [1967]: 69
((-))

MUZA RECORDS
See listings for MONIUSZKO, STAN-
ISLAW; MUSIC, POLISH. 20th Century.
Recordings by "Polskie Nagrania—
Muza"; SZYMANOWSKI, KAROL.
Works of Karel Szymanowski on Muza
records

MUZIO, CLAUDIA, 1889-1936

2123 BARNES, Harold M.: Discography in
BARNES, Harold M.: Claudia Muzio; a
biographical sketch and discography.
Revised. [Austin, Tex.], 1937: [15]-18
((-))

2124 Claudia Muzio—discography in
BARNES, Harold M.: Claudia Muzio; a
biographical sketch and discography.
Zürich; Princeton, 1941: [13]-[15]
((-))

2125 BARNES, Harold: Discography in Record Collector, XVII/9-10 (February
1968): 224-237 ((1, 3, 4, 6, 7)) [Includes
unpublished records] Corrections:
Record Collector, XVIII/1-2 (October
1968): 47 ((-))

2126 VEGETO, R.: Discografia in Musica e
Dischi, X (No. 97, October 1954): 31
((-)); Addenda: Musica e Dischi, XI
(No. 111, November 1955): 43 ((-))

2127 WILE, Raymond R.: Claudia Muzio's
Edison legacy—a discography in
American Record Guide, XXVII/8
(April 1961): 634-637 ((3, 7))

NBC SYMPHONY
See TOSCANINI, ARTURO. Marsh,
Robert Charles

NANI, ENRICO

2128 Discografia di E. Nani in Musica e
Dischi, XVII (No. 177, March 1961): 62
((-))

NASH, HEDDLE, 1896-1961

2129 Heddle Nash: a discography in 78 RPM,
No. 6 (June 1969): 3-10 ((3, 7)); No. 7
(September 1969): 7 ((3, 7))

2130 JARRETT, Jack: Heddle Nash in Record Advertiser, III/5 (July-August
1973): 6-12 ((3, 5)); III/6 (September-
October 1973): 22 ((3, 5))

NAT, YVES, 1890-1956

2131 ROSTAND, C.: Essai de discographie
complète d'Yves Nat in Disques, No. 81
(October 1956): 615 ((-))

NAVARINI, FRANCESCO

2132 CELLETTI, Rodolfo: The records in
Record News, IV/1 (September 1959):
10 ((3, 5)) [From Musica e Dischi,
September 1958]

2133 VEGETO, Raffaele: Discografia del
basso Francesco Navarrini [i.e. Nava-
rini] in Musica e Dischi, XIV (No. 147,
September 1958): 53 ((7))

NAVARRA, ANDRÉ

2134 Discographie in Courrier Musical de
France, No. 14 (1966): 117-118 ((-))

NAZARETH, ERNESTO, 1863-1934

2135 [[Discography] in Rio de Janeiro.
Biblioteca Nacional. Exposiçao comemorativa do centenário do nascimento de Ernesto Nazareth, 1863-1934.
Rio de Janeiro: Biblioteca Nacional,
1963: 60-66]]

NEDBAL, OSKAR, 1874-1930

2136 Seznam Nedbalových Tištěných děl a
zyukouých Záznamů [includes discographical references] in ŠULC, Miroslav:
Oskar Nedbal. [1. vyd.] Praha: Státní
nakl. krásné literatury, hudby a umění
1959: 327-333 ((-))

NEGRI, GIOVANNI BATTISTA DE
See DE NEGRI, GIOVANNI BATTISTA

NEGRO MUSIC

2137 [[DeLERMA, Dominique-René de: The
teacher's guide to recent recordings of
music by black composers in College
Music Symposium, XIII (Fall 1973):
114-119]]

NEÏGUAZ, GENRIKH GUSTAVOVICH, 1888-
1964

2138 [Discography] in DEL'SON, Viktor
IUl'evich: Genrikh Neïgauz. Moskva:
Muzkya, 1966: 183-[185] ((-))

NEVEU, GINETTE, 1919-1949

2139 Diskografie in fono forum 1961 (No. 12,
December): 29 ((-))

2140 HUGHES, E. A.: Ginette Neveu: discography in British Institute of Recorded
Sound Bulletin, No. 7 (Winter 1957):
23 ((-))

2141 Records by Ginette Neveu in Disc, I/3
(Summer 1947): 127 ((-))

2142 Works which have been recorded by
Ginette Neveu (for His Master's Voice)
in RONZE-NEVEY, Marie-Jeanne:
Ginette Neveu. London: Rockliff, 1957:
109-110 ((-))

NEW QUEEN'S HALL ORCHESTRA
See listing for WOOD, SIR HENRY J.

NEW YORK PHILHARMONIC

2143 Recorded works of the New York Philharmonic in Phonograph Monthly Review, II/4 (January 1928): 130-132 ((-))

NEY, ELLY, 1882-1968

2144 Verzeichnis der zuletzt eingespielten
Schallplatten in Worte des Dankes an
Elly Ney. Tutzing: H. Schneider, 1968:
81-[83] ((-))

NICOLET, AURELE

2145 Flute; Claude Debussy: Syrinx. Zürich:
Panton Verlag; distributed by C. F.
Peters, New York, 1968: 115-118 [Note:
Master class lesson with accompanying
sound recording] ((-))

2146 ROEMER, Friedrich: Diskografie in
fono forum 1961 (No. 9, September):
27 ((-))

NIELSEN, CARL, 1865-1931

2147 FABRICIUS-BJERRE, Claus: Carl Nielsen diskografi. Nationaldiskoteket,
1965: 22 leaves ((4, 7))

2148 FABRICIUS-BJERRE, Claus: Carl Nielsen: a discography. 2nd ed. Copenhagen: Nationaldiskoteket, 1968: 44 pp.
(Nationaldiskoteket. Discographies,
201) ((4, 5, 7))

2149 [FREED, Richard]: A Nielsen discography in Saturday Review (October 29,
1960): 56-57 ((-))

2150 [[SIMPSON, Robert: [Discography] in
Disc (Bristol) III/11 (Summer 1949):
106]]

2151 Recordings available in Great Britain
in SIMPSON, Robert: Carl Nielsen:
symphonist, 1865-1931. London: J. M.
Dent, [1952]: 227-230 ((-))

NIGG, SERGE, 1924-

2152   Discographie in Courrier Musical de
France, No. 13 (1966): 48 ((-))

NIKISCH, ARTHUR, 1855-1922

2153   ÅHLÉN, Carl-Gunnar: Arthur Nikisch—
diskografi in Musik Revy, XXIX/1
(1974): 45 (Grammofonens veteraner,
9) ((3, 5, 6, 7))

2154   FISCHER, Gert: Diskografie Arthur
Nikisch in fono forum 1972 (No. 1, January): 32 ((5, 7))

2155   HUGHES, Eric: Arthur Nikisch discography in Recorded Sound, I/4 (Autumn 1961): 114-115 ((3, 7))

2156   [[STONE, Ralph: Arthur Nikisch in Le
Grand Baton (May 1968): 17-21]]

NILSSON, BO, 1937-

2157   LAABAN, Ilmar: Inspelningar av Bo
Nilssons musik in Nutida Musik, VIII/1
(1964-1965): 6 ((-))

NONO, LUIGI, 1924-

2158   Luigi Nono—Diskographie in NONO,
Luigi: Luigi Nono: Texte, Studien zu
seine Musik. Zürich: Atlantis, c1975:
456-458 ((-))

2159   Works by Nono on records in Recorded
Sound, No. 24 (October 1966): 121 ((-))

NORDICA, LILLIAN, 1859-1914

2160   DENNIS, J.: Lillian Nordica: the records in Record Collector, VI/9 (September 1951): 197-206 ((-))

2161   Discography in GLACKENS, Ira: Yankee
diva: Lillian Nordica and the golden
days of opera. With Lillian Nordica's
Hints to singers. New York: Coleridge
Press, [1963]: 292-300 ((3, 4, 6, 7))

2162   GREGORY, Randolph: Nordica records
in Hobbies, LXIV (February 1960): 32-
33 ((7))

2163   WEHLING, Albert: Lillian Nordica in
Hobbies, XLI/5 (July 1936): 116, 122
((5)); SELTSAM, W. H.: Addendum;
Lillian Nordica discography in Gramophone, No. 168 (May 1937): 512 ((7))

NOSKOWSKI, ZYGMUNT, 1846-1909

2164   Nagrania in WROŃSKI, Witold: Zygmunt
Noskowski. Wyd. 1. Warszawa: Polskie Wydawn. Muzyczne, [1960]: 176-
181 (Studia i materiały do dziejów
muzyki polskiej, 6) ((1))

NOVAES, GUIOMAR, 1895-

2165   [[CHASINS, A.: The realm of Queen
Guiomar (Guiomar Novaës) in Saturday
Review (March 31, 1956): 40-41]]

NOVÁK, VÍTĚZSLAV, 1870-1949

2166   Dílo Vítězslava Nováka na gramo-
fonových deskách in BUDIŠ, Ratibor:
Vítězslav Novák: výběrová bibliografie.
[V Praze: Kniha, 1967]: 135-140 ((-))

2167   Vývěrový seznam skladeb [includes
discographic notes] in LÉBL, Vladimír:
Vítezslav Novak. [1. vyd.] Praha:
Supraphon, 1967: 56-66 ((-))

2168   Soupis skladeb Vítězslava Nováka na
čs. dlouhohrajících deskách Supraphon
in NOVÁK, Vitězslav: O sobě a o jiných.
1 vyd. Praha: Supraphon, t. ST 4, 1970:
406-408 (Hudba v zrcadle doby, 7)) ((-))

NOWOWIEJSKI, FELIKS, 1877-1946

2169   KONRAD, Michakowski: Dyskografia in
NOWOWIEJSKI, Feliks M.: Dookoła
kompozytora wspomnienia o ojcu. Wyd.
1. Poznań: Wydawn. Poznańskie, 1968:
287-288 ((7))

NYSTROEM, GÖSTA, 1890-1966

2170   [[MÖRNER, Carl-Gabriel Stellan:
Gösta Nystroem på skiva—en diskografi in Biblioteksbladet, LXII/3-4
(1967): 290-293]]

OBOE

2171   STOLPER, Daniel, and Virginia K.
LOWREY: Baroque music for oboe—a
discography in Journal of the International Double Reed Society, No. 2 (May
1974): 46-53 ((4))

OBRECHT, JACOB, d. 1505

2172   Verant woording discografie in HUI-
ZINGA, Josien C. E.: Jacob Obrecht:
bibliografie, lijst van composities,
discografie. [Werkstuk 2. cyclus
Bibliotheek-en Documentatieschool,
Amsterdam. [Amsterdam: Bibliotheek-
en Documentatieschool], 1969: 27-29
((-))

ODEON RECORDS
See listing for MCCORMACK, JOHN.
Roden, Philip F.: The McCormack
Odeons; Webster, Robert L.: Matrix
list of the McCormack Odeons

ODEON-NACIONAL RECORDS
See listing for LAURI-VOLPI,
GIACOMO. Moran, William

ODMANN, ARVID

2173 BRUUN, Carl L.: Discography in Record News, IV/6 (February 1960): 206-
208 ((5))

ÖSTBERG, CAROLINA

2174 BRUUN, Carl L.: [Carolina Östberg
discography] in Gramophone, No. 368
(January 1954): 278 ((3, 7))

2175 BRUUN, Carl L.: Collector's corner in
Gramophone, No. 184 (September 1938):
179 ((-))

OFFENBACH, JACQUES, 1819-1880

2176 Discographie in DECAUX, Alain: Offenbach: roi du Second Empire. [Paris]:
P. Amiot, [1958]: [277]-278 ((-))

2177 FOLSTEIN, Robert L., Ed. by Stephen
WILLIS: A bibliography of Jacques
Offenbach. VIII. Discography in Current Musicology, No. 11 (1971): 127-
128 ((-))

OHANA, MAURICE

2178 Discographie de Maurice Ohana in
Courrier Musical de France, No. 51
(1975): 123-124 ((-))

2179 ROY, Jean: Discographie in Diapason,
No. 186 (April 1974): 13 ((-))

OÏSTRAKH, DAVID FEDOROVICH, 1908-1974

2180 Discographie in Diapason, No. 192
(December 1974): 15-16 ((-))

2181 Discography in JAMPOL'SKIJ, Israil'
David: David Ojstrah. Moskva: Muzyka,
1968: 144 ((-))

2182 Diskographie in RICHTER, Evelyn:
David Oistrach: ein Arbeitsporträt.
Berlin: Henschelverlag Kunst und
Gesellschaft, 1973: 157-169 ((-))

2183 SPINGEL, Hans Otto: Diskografie David
Oistrach in fono forum 1963 (No. 12,
December): 500 ((-)); Additions and
corrections: fono forum 1964 (No. 2,
February): 88 ((-))

OLDHAM, DEREK

2184 [[Recollections of Derek Oldham in
Record Advertiser, III/6 (September-
October 1973): 19-22]]

OLIVERO, MAGDA

2185 CELLETTI, Rodolfo: Magda Olivero in
Discoteca, No. 87 (January-February
1969): 25 ((-))

OLSZEWSKA, MARIA, 1892-

2186 BARNES, H. M.: Maria Olszewska discography (born 1892) in British Institute
of Recorded Sound Bulletin, No. 6 (Autumn 1957): 17-20 ((3, 6, 7))

O'MARA, JOSEPH

2187 [[POTTERTON, R.: Joseph O'Mara in
Record Collector, XIX/1-2 (1970): 33-
42]]

ONDŘÍČEK, FRANTIŠEK, 1857-1922

2188 Diskografie in ŠICH, Bohuslav: František Ondříček. Praha; Bratislava:
Supraphon, 1970: 334 ((-))

ONEGIN, SIGRID

2189 DENNIS, J.: Sigrid Onegin in Record
Collector, V/10 (October 1950): 229-
231 ((-))

OPERA BUFFA

2190 BURKE, C. G.: Opera buffa on records
in High Fidelity, I/3 (Winter 1951): 33-
38 ((-))

OPERAS
See also MUSIC

2191 [[A basic discography: opera and
operetta in New York times, 106/2
(November 18, 1956): section 10]]

2192 BEAUJEAN, A.: Das neue Musiktheater und die Schallplatte in Hi Fi
Stereophonie, IV/6 (June 1965): 352-
355 ((-))

2193 [[DAILLY, Clément: Discographie de
l'opera. Supplement au no. 1 de Poly-
phonie 'Le théatre musical.' [Paris]:
[Richard-Masse Editeurs], 1947]]

2194 Discography in DRINKROW, John: The
vintage operetta book. Reading: Osprey
Publishing, 1972: 112-124 ((-))

2195 Discography in DRINKROW, John: The
operetta book. New York: Drake Publishers, [1973]: 112-124 ((-))

2196 HARRIS, Kenn: Opera recordings: a
critical guide. New York: Drake Publishers, [1973] : 328 pp. ((-))

2197 HEINITZ, Thomas: Opera on records in
STREATFIELD, Noel: The first book of

the opera. [1st American publication].
New York: F. Watts, [1966]: 61-62 ((–))

2198   Discography in JACOBS, Arthur: The
Pan book of opera, by Arthur Jacobs
and Stanley SADIE. London: Pan Books,
[1964]: [489]-495 (Pan piper TP55)
((–))

2199   LIMBACHER, James L.: Theatrical
events a selected list of music and dra-
matic performances on long-playing
records. 5th ed. [Dearborn, MI:
Dearborn Public Library, Audiovisual
Division], 1968: 95 leaves ((–))

2200   LUTEN, C. J.: Annotated list of recordings in PELTZ, Mary Ellis: Introduction to opera. 2d ed. New York:
Barnes & Noble, [1962]: 415 pp. ((–))

2201   Recordings of complete operas in
MOORE, Frank Ledlie: Crowell's hand-
book of world opera. New York:
Crowell, 1961: 654-662 ((–))

2202   Recordings of complete operas in
MOORE, Frank Ledlie: Crowell's
handbook of world opera. Westport,
Conn: Greenwood Press, [1974, c1961]:
654-662 ((–))

2203   Opern auf Schallplatten, 1900-1962: ein
historischer Katalog. [Vienna: Karls-
ruhe Universal; G. Braun, c1974]:
184 pp. (5, 7))

20th Century

2204   [[Deutsche Musik-Phonothek: Die Oper
in 20. Jahrhundert, Diskographie: Teil-
katalog herausgegeben des Kongresses
"Zeitgenoss. Musiktheater" in Hamburg Juni 1964. Berlin, 1964.]]

2205   Discografia in Rassegna Musicale,
XXXII/2-4 (1962): [344]-350 ((–))

Russian

2206   WEINSTOCK, Herbert: Russian opera
on microgroove in High Fidelity, VI/11
(November 1956): 105-118 ((-))

ORCHESTRE DE CHAMBRE DE ROUEN

2207   Discographies de L'Orchestre de
Chambre de Rouen (dir. A. Beauchamp)
et de Claire Bernard in Diapason, No.
104 (February 1966): 15 ((–))

ORCHESTRE DE LA SUISSE ROMANDE
See also ANSERMET, ERNEST
ALEXANDRE

2208   Discographie in Orchestre de la Suisse
romande, 1918-1968: un demi siècle

d'historie. Genève, 1968: 132-[135]
((–))

ORCHESTRE DU COLLEGIUM MUSICUM DE PARIS
See DOUATTE, ROLAND

ORCHESTRAL MUSIC
See also listings for SYMPHONIES

2209   List of records in BARNE, Kitty:
Listening to the orchestra. Indianapolis, New York: The Bobbs-Merrill Co.,
[1946]: 259-288 ((–))

2210   Selected recordings of orchestral music
in BROWN, Alice: Know your orchestra:
a guide to the appreciation of orchestral
music. Melbourne: F. W. Cheshire,
[1948]: [60]-74 ((–))

2211   KOLODIN, Irving: Orchestral music.
[1st ed.]   New York: Knopf, 1955:
258 pp. (The guide to long-playing records, 1) ((–))

2212   Beknopte discografie in METZ, Louis:
Over dirigeren, dirigenten en orkesten.
Lochen: De Tijdstroom, 1968: 289-333
((–))

2213   A list of modern Victor recordings of
symphonic music in O'CONNELL,
Charles: The Victor book of the symphony. Rev. ed. New York: Simon and
Schuster, [c1941]: 637-645 ((–))

2214   Columbia/Victor records of great orchestral music in SPAETH, Sigmund:
A guide to great orchestral music.
New York: The Modern Library,
[1943]: 469-506 ((–))

2215   STEVENSON, Edward Prime: A reper-
tory of one hundred symphonic pro-
grames for public auditions of the or-
thophonic phonograph-gramophone.
Florence: The Giutina Press, [1932?]:
205 ((–))

ORFF, CARL, 1895-

2216   BOYARS, Arthur: A discography in
LIESS, Andreas: Carl Orff. London:
Calder & Boyars, 1966: [180]-181
((–))

2217   [[DEGENS, Ralph N.: [Discography] in
Luister, No. 276 (September 1975): 29]]

2218   FREYSE, Renate: Discographie in Neue
Zeitschrift für Musikwissenschaft,
CXXVI (July-August 1965): 320 ((–))

Carmina Burana

2219   KRAEMER, Uwe: Orff, Carmina
Burana; die Gesamtaufnahmen in

chronologister Reihenfolge in fono
forum 1974 (No. 6, June): 516 ((5))

ORGAN MUSIC

See also listing for BACH, JOHANN
SEBASTIAN—WORKS, ORGAN. Dis-
cography in Hendrie, Gerald: The
Baroque organ

2220 CARLSSON, Curt: Diskografi över alla
svenska orglar som finns inspelade på
skiva. Stockholm: Proprius, 1973:
47 pp. ((7))

2221 Records in CONELY, James: A guide
to improvisation: an introductory handbook for church organists. Nashville:
Abingdon Press, [1975]: 63-64 ((-))

2222 Organ records in DE BRISAY, Aubrey
C.: Delacour. The organ and its music:
a guide for wireless and gramophone
listeners. London: K. Paul, Trench,
Trubener & Co., Ltd.; J. Curwen &
Sons, Ltd., 1934. 175-187 ((-))

2223 [[DONER, M. H.: A catalogue of international pipe organ recordings of classical organ literature; a list of over
450 records compiled from U. S. and
European sources with notes by M. H.
Doner and James CAMERON. [Winona,
Minn.?], 1948. 56 leaves. Collective
addenda to Catalogue. [Winona, Minn.?,
1949] 13 1.]]

2224 [[Discography in HENDRIE, Gerald: The
baroque organ. Milton Keynes, [U.K.]:
Open University Press, 1974: 84-86]]

2225 LAADE, Wolfgang: Klangdokumente
historischer Tasteninstrumente: Orgeln,
Kiel- und Hammerklaviere; diskographie. Zürich: Musikverlag zum Peli-
kan, [c1972]: ii, 133 pp. ((-))

2226 Discographie in LOUIS, Anne Marie:
L'orgue. Molenbeek-Bruxelles: Éditions du Trèfle à quatre feuilles, [n.d.]:
[109]-115 (Collection Syriax, 9) ((-))

2227 [Discographies included] in SCHÄFER,
Ernst: Laudatio organi: eine Orgelfahrt.
Leipzig: Deutscher Verlag für Musik,
1972: 21 pp. ((-))

ORGANISTS

2228 [[A catalogue of organists in Notes on
Records, I/3 (March-April 1958): 45-
52]] [Includes notes on organ locations]

ORGANISTS, SWEDISH

See listing for ORGAN MUSIC. Carlsson, Curt: Diskografi över alla svenska
orglar som finns inspelade på skiva

ORGANS, SWEDEN

See listing for ORGAN MUSIC. Carlsson, Curt: Diskografi över alla svenska
orglar som finns inspelade på skiva

ORGANS, UNITED STATES

See listing for TANNENBERG, DAVID

OSTRČIL, OTAKAR, 1879-1935

2229 Skladby Otkara Ostrčila na gramofonových deskách in ČERVINKOVÁ, Blanka:
Otakar Ostrčil, 25.2.1879-20.8.1935:
zákl. bibliografie. 1. vyd. Praha:
Měst. knihovna, rozmn., 1971: 93-94
(Ediční řada Hudebního a divadelního
odboru) ((-))

OTTEIN, ANGELES

2230 RICHARDS, John B.: The recordings in
Record Collector, XVII/7 (August
1967): 152-154 ((7))

PABLO, LUIS DE

2231 Discografía in MARCO, Tomás: Luis de
Pablo. [Madrid: Dirección General de
Bellas Artes, Ministerio de Educación
y Ciencia, 1971]: 69-70 (Artistas
españoles contemporáneos, 6. Serie
músicos) ((-))

PACHMANN, VLADIMIR DE, 1848-1933

2232 Essai discographique sur le pianiste
Vladimir de Pachmann in Bulletin de la
Phonotheque nationale, VIII/2 (Second
Quarter 1970): 15-17 ((-))

2233 HOWARD, Geoffrey: Vladimir de Pachmann, a discography in 78 RPM, No. 1:
7-8 ((3- 7))

PADEREWSKI, IGNACY JAN, 1860-1941

2234 [[ANDERSON, H. L.: Ignace Jan Paderewski—discography in British Institute of Recorded Sound Bulletin, No. 10
(Autumn 1958): 1-7]]

2235 FASSETT, Stephen: A Paderewski discography in American Music Lover,
VII/12 (August 1941): 429-431 ((5))

2236 KAŃSKI, Józef: Płytowe dokumenty
sztuki Ignacego Paderewskiego (w 30
rocznicę urodzin) in Ruch Muzyczny,
XV/14 (16-31 July 1971): 5-6 ((3, 6, 7))

2237 A list of Paderewski's recordings in
PHILLIPS, Charles: Paderewski: the
story of a modern immortal. New
York: Macmillan Co., 1933: 550-552
((-))

PAGLIUGHI, LINA

2238 DI CAVE, Luciano: Lina Pagliughi discography in Record Collector, XXI/5-6 (October 1973): 118-125 ((1, 3, 7))

2239 GAISBERG, F. W.: Lina Pagliughi records in Gramophone, No. 242 (July 1943): 23 ((-))

PAINI, LEONILDE

2240 CELLETTI, Rodolfo: Discografia in Musica e Dischi, XIII (No. 128, April 1957): 52 ((7))

PAKALNIS, JUOZAS, 1912-1948

2241 J. Pakalnio kúriniy magnetofoniniai įrašai in JUODPUSIS, Vaclovas: Juozas Pakalnis. Vilnius: Vaga, 1972: 70-71 ((-))

PALET, JOSÉ

2242 VEGETO, R.: Discografia in Discoteca, No. 74 (October 1967): 63-64; [Includes unpublished records] ((3, 5))

PANDOLFINI, ANGELICA

2243 CELLETTI, Rodolfo: I dischi di A. Pandolfini...in Musica e Dischi, XV (No. 160, October 1959): 28 ((5, 7))

2244 CELLETTI, Rodolfo: The records in Record News, IV/8 (April 1960): 282; [From Musica e Dischi, October 1959] ((5, 7))

2245 HENSTOCK, Michael: Discography in Recorded Sound, No. 38 (April 1970): 625; [Includes notes on playing speeds] ((3, 6, 7))

PANKIEWICZ, EUGENIUSZ, 1857-1898

2246 Spis ragraú in POŹNIAK, Włodzimierz: Eugeniusz Pankiewicz. Wyd. 1. Kraków: Polskie Wydawn. Muzyczne, [1958]: 157 (Studia i materiały do dziejów muzyki polskiej, 5) ((-))

PANZERA, CHARLES, 1896-1976

2247 Discographie in Courrier Musical de France, No. 9 (1965): 64 ((-))

PAOLI, ANTONIO

2248 DENNIS, J.: Antonio Paoli discography in Record Collector, XXII/1-2 (May 1974): 19-22 ((3, 6, 7))

PARAY, PAUL, 1886-

2249 Quelques disques selectionnes in LANDOWSKI, Wanda Alice L.: Paul Paray: musicien de France et du monde. Lyon: Éditions et imprimeries du sud-est, [1956]: 93-94 (Collection Nos amis les musiciens) ((-))

PARETO, GRAZIELLA

2250 FRASER, G.: Graziella Pareto in Record Collector, XVII/4 (April 1967): 84-89 ((3, 6, 7))

PARLOPHON RECORDS
See listing for ANSORGE, CONRAD

PARVIS, TAURINO

2251 [FAVIA-ARTSAY, Aida: Taurino Parvis discography] in Hobbies, LXI (August 1956): 25-26 ((5, 7))

PASSMORE, WALTER

2252 FREESTONE, John: Collectors' corner in Gramophone, No. 360 (May 1953): 316 ((-))

PATHÉ RECORDS
See listings for LASSALLE, JEAN-LOUIS. Freestone, John; VAN DYCK, ERNST MARIE HUBERT

PATTI, ADELINA, 1843-1919

2253 ÅHLÉN, Carl-Gunnar: Adelina Patti: diskografi in Musik Revy, XXIX/3 (1974): 168 (Grammofonens veteraner; 10) ((3, 7))

2254 HURST, P. G.: Records in Gramophone, No. 237 (February 1943): 124 ((5, 7))

2255 WILLIAMS, Clifford, and W. R. MORAN: Adelina Patti: discography in Record Collector, X/8-9 (July-August 1956): 184-185 ((3, 6, 7))

PATTIERA, TINO

2256 BREW, Dennis: Tino Pattiera, discography in Record Collector, XVII/12 (July 1968): 281-285 ((3, 6, 7)); Addenda: Record Collector, XVIII/11-12 (December 1969): 279 ((-))

2257 HÖSLINGER, Clemens: Diskografie in fono forum 1966 (No. 11, November): 575 ((1))

PATZAK, JULIUS, 1898-1974

2258 BREW, Dennis: Julius Patzak discography in Record Collector, XIX/9-10 (February 1971): 209-222 ((3, 4, 6, 7))

2259 PFLUGER, Rolf: Diskographie Julius
Patzak in Österreichische Musikzeitschrift, XXIX/3 (March 1974): 169 ((-))

PAUMGARTNER, BERNHARD, 1887-1971

2260 FISCHER, Gert: Paumgartner—eine
Diskografie in fono forum 1972 (No. 8,
August): 593 ((-))

PEARS, PETER, 1910-

2261 MCLACHLAN, Don: Peter Pears discography in Records and Recording,
XVI/9 (June 1973): 21-22; [Includes
unpublished records] ((5))

PENDERECKI, KRZYSZTOF, 1933-

2262 Dyskografia in ERHARDT, Ludwik:
Spotkania z Krzysztofem Pendereckim.
Wyd. 1. Kraków: Polskie Wydawn.
Muzyczne, 1975: 229-233 ((-))

2263 Dyskografia in LISICKI, Krzystof:
Szkice o Krzysztofie Pendereckim.
[Wyd. 1.] Warszawa: Pax, 1973: 206-
[210] ((-))

PERCUSSION MUSIC

2264 Discography in BARTLETT, Harry R.:
Guide to teaching percussion. Dubuque,
Iowa: W. C. Brown Co., [1964]: 162-163
(College instrumental technique series)
((-))

PERCUSSIONS DE STRAUSBOURG

2265 Discographie de Percussions de Strausbourg in Courrier Musical de France,
No. 39 (1972): 201 ((-))

PERGOLESI, GIOVANNI BATTISTA, 1710-
1736

2266 Discografia essenziale in MARGA-
DONNA, Michele: Pergolesi. [Milano]:
Nuova Accademia editrice, [1961]:
205-207 (Le Vite dei musicisti) ((-))

PEROSI, LORENZO, 1872-1956

2267 Catalogo in RINALDI, Mario: Lorenzo
Perosi. Roma: De Santis, 1967: 572-
585 ((1))

PERSICHETTI, VINCENT, 1915-

2268 EVETT, Robert: List of records in
Juilliard Review, II/2 (Spring 1955):
30 ((-))

PERTILE, AURELIANO, 1885-1952

2269 BARNES, H. M., and Victor GIRARD:
Aureliano Pertile records in Record
Collector, VII/11 (November 1952):
245-260, 267-274 ((3, 6, 7))

2270 Pertile's recordings from Boito's
"Nerone" and the premiere of the
Mascagni version in Record Collector,
VIII/2 (February 1953): 37-39 ((-))

2271 VEGETO, Raffaele: Discografia in
Musica e Dischi, XI (No. 109, September 1955): 35 ((7)); Addenda: Musica
e Dischi, XI (No. 111, November 1955):
43 ((-))

PETERS, ROBERTA, 1930-

2272 GRASSL, Friederike: Diskografie in
fono forum 1964 (No. 8, August): 306
((-))

PETERSON, MAY

2273 GARDNER, M. L.: May Peterson: a
discography in Recorded Sound, No. 32
(October 1968): 346 ((3, 7))

PETERSON-BERGER, WILHELM, 1867-1942

2274 Grammofonskivor med musik an
Peterson-Berger in BEITE, Sten: Wilhelm Peterson-Berger: en känd och
okänd tondiktare. [n.p., 1965]: 35-40
((-))

PETIT, PIERRE, 1893-

2275 Discographie in Courrier Musical de
France, No. 10 (1965): 126 ((-))

PETRASSI, GOFFREDO, 1904-

2276 Appendice discografica in ANNIBALDI,
Claudio: Goffredo Petrassi: catalogo
delle opere e bibliografia. Milano: Edizioni Suvini Zerboni, [1971]: [103]-108
((-))

2277 Discografia di Goffredo Petrassi in
Quaderni della Rassegna Musicale 1964
(No. 1): 143-144 ((-))

2278 Discography in WEISSMANN, John S.:
Goffredo Petrassi. Milano: Suvini
Zerboni, 1957: [80] ((-))

PETRI, EGON
See also listings for BUSONI,
FERRUCCIO. Åhlén, Carl-Gunnar:
Ferruccio Busoni (1866-1924); Dis-
cography in Busoni's pupils play
Busoni compositions

2279 MASON, D. H.: Egon Petri: a discography in 78 RPM, No. 7 (September 1969): 24-28 ((3, 6, 7))

PFISTER, HUGO

2280 Werkverzeichnis [includes discographical references] in TSCHUPP, Räto: Hugo Pfister: ein Schweizer Komponist der mittleren Generation. Zürich, Freiburg i. Br.: Atlantis, 1973: 142-179 ((-))

PFITZNER, HANS, 1869-1949

2281 BEAUJEAN, Alfred: Pfitzner—Diskographie in Hi Fi Stereophonie, X/11 (November 1971): 1012 ((-))

2282 HÖSLINGER, Clemens: Diskografische Notiz in fono forum 1969 (No. 1, January): 19 ((-))

2283 MOORE, Jerrold N.: Hans Pfitzner discography in Recorded Sound, No. 45-46 (January-April 1972): 54-57 ((1, 3, 6, 7))

2284 WEBER, J. F.: Pfitzner and Marx. Utica, NY: Weber, 1975: 18 pp. (Discography series, 15) ((3, 5, 6, 7))

PHILADELPHIA ORCHESTRA

2285 Discography in KUPFERBERG, Herbert: Those fabulous Philadelphians. New York: Scribners, 1969: 239-247 ((-))

2286 Discography in KUPFERBERG, Herbert: Those fabulous Philadelphians. London: Allan, 1970: 239-247 ((-))

PHILIPP, ISIDORE, 1863-1958

2287 Isidore Philipp discography in Recorded Sound, I/8 (Autumn 1962): 248 ((1, 7)) [Includes unpublished records]

PHILIPPOT, MICHEL

2288 Discographie in Courrier Musical de France, No. 25 (1969): 64 ((-))

PHILIPS RECORDS
See listings for BEETHOVEN, LUDWIG VAN. Ludwig van Beethoven 1770-1827; complete discography; GRUMIAUX, ARTHUR. From the discography of Arthur Grumiaux; GRUMIAUX TRIO; SZERYNG, HENRYK. Henryk Szeryng on Philips records

PIANISTS

2289 CAPES, S. J.: Early pianoforte records in British Institute of Recorded Sound Bulletin, No. 3 (Winter 1956): 13-19 ((4, 5))

2290 Discography in CHAPIN, Victor: Giants of the keyboard. [1st ed.] Philadelphia: Lippincott, [1967]: [181]-182 ((-))

2291 CLOUGH, F. F.: Discography in KAISER, Joachim: Great pianists of our time. London: Allen and Unwin, 1971: 199-224 ((-))

2292 CLOUGH, F. F.: Discography in KAISER, Joachim: Great pianists of our time. [New York]: Herder and Herder, [1971]: 199-224 ((-))

2293 Schallplattenverzeichnis in KAISER, Joachim: Grosse Pianisten in unserer Zeit. München: Rütten u. Loening, [1965]: 219-226 ((-))

2294 Schallplattenverzeichnis in KAISER, Joachim: Grosse Pianisten in unserer Zeit. Gütersloh: Bertelsmann[-Lesering]; Wien Buchgemeinschaft Donauland; Gütersloh Kelen, [1967]: 219-226 ((-))

2295 Schallplattenverzeichnis in KAISER, Joachim: Grosse Pianisten in unserer Zeit. Stark erw. und überarb. Neuausg. München: R. Piper, [c1972]: 241-[251] ((-))

PIANO

2296 Discography in WAINWRIGHT, David: The piano makers. London: Hutchinson, 1975: 183-184 ((-))

PIANO MUSIC
See also listings for COMPOSERS. [Discographies included] in Range, Hans Peter: Von Beethoven bis Brahms; ORGAN MUSIC. Laade, Wolfgang: Klangdokumente historischer Tasteninstrumente: Orgeln, Kiel- und Hammerklaviere; diskographie; PIANISTS

2297 Discography in BALLANTINE, Bill: The piano: an introduction to the instrument. New York: F. Watts, [1971]: [110]-123 (A Keynote book) ((-))

2298 Discografie in FLOTHIUS, Marius: Pianomuziek. Bilthoven: H. Nelissen, 1958: 62-63 ((-))

Norwegian (20th Century)

2299 Bibliography and discography in KORTSEN, Bjarne: Contemporary Norwegian piano: a catalogue. Bergen: Bjarne Kortsen, 5033 Fyllingsdalen, Ortustranden 45, 1973: 29-31 leaves ((-))

2 Pianos

2300   Recorded two-piano music in MOLDEN-
HAUER, Hans: Duo-pianism: a disserta-
tion. Chicago: Chicago Musical College Press, 1951, c1950: 363-373 ((-))

PIATIGORSKY, GREGOR, 1903-1976

2301   Piatigorsky-Discographie in PIATI-
GORSKY, Gregor: Mein Cello und ich:
und unsere Begegnungen mit Béla
Bartók, Sir Thomas Beecham, Pablo
Casals. Tübingen: Wunderlich, [1968]:
[255]-[256] ((-))

PICCAVER, ALFRED, 1884-1958

2302   DENNIS, J.: Alfred Piccaver discography in Record Collector, XXII/5-7
(November 1974): 128-155 ((3, 4, 6, 7))

2303   NATAN, Alex: Wichtige einzel-Aufnah-
men mit Alfred Piccaver in fono forum
1968 (No. 3, March): 130 ((-))

PILARCZYK, HELGA

2304   Diskografie in fono forum 1961 (No. 7,
July): 27 ((-))

PILK, JURIJ, 1858-1926

2305   Spis tačelowych nahračow Pilkowych
wobdźitleow ludoweje hudźby in
KOŚCIÓW, Zbigniew: Jurij Pilk; wobrys
žiwjenja a skutkowanja. Budyšin
[Bautzen]: ludowe nakładmistwo
Domowina-Verl., [1968]: 95 ((-))

PINI-CORSI, ANTONIO

2306   [[FAVIA-ARTSAY, Aida: Additions to
the Pini-Corsi discography in Hobbies,
LIX (February 1955): 25]]

PINZA, EZIO, 1892-1957

2307   ALLEN, Vic: The records in Record
News, I/11 (July 1957): 394-402 ((1));
Addenda: Record News, I/12 (August
1957): 444-445; II/1 (September 1957)

2308   PHILLIPS, Ronald: The Pinza records
in Record Collector, [III/1] (January
1948): 12-15 ((-))

2309   SOKOL, Martin L.: An Ezio Pinza discography in Hobbies, LXXX/6 (August
1975): 117-119, 124, 127 ((3, 6, 7))

2310   VERDUCCI, Pasquale: The first Pinza
discography. [New York], c1957: 16
leaves ((1, 3, 6, 7))

PISCHNER, HANS

2311   Diskographie in Medium Schallplatte,
No. 12 (No. 3, 1969): 12 ((-))

PISTON, WALTER, 1894-1976

2312   ROY, Klaus George: The music of Walter Piston on records in Stereo Review,
XXIV/4 (April 1970): 65 ((-))

PIZZETTI, ILDEBRANDO, 1880-1968

2313   Discografia in GATTI, Guido Maria:
Ildebrando Pizzetti. [Milano]: Ricordi,
[155, c1954]:124-125 ((-))

2314   Recordings in GATTI, Guido Maria:
Ildebrando Pizzetti. London: D. Dobson, [1951]: 122 (Contemporary composers) ((-))

PLAICHINGER, THILA

2315. HEGERMANN-LIDENCRONE, Knudde:
Thila Plaichinger; in memoriam in
Gramophone, No. 193 (June 1939): 40
((-))

PLAIN CHANTS
See CHANTS (PLAIN, GREGORIAN,
ETC.)

PLANÇON, PAUL HENRI, 1851-1914

2316   DENNIS, J.: Record tabling in Record
Collector, VIII/7-8 (July-August 1953):
190-191 ((3, 6, 7))

2317   HEVINGHAM-ROOT, L.: Pol Plancon:
a discographical survey in Record Collector, VIII/7-8 (July-August 1953):
153-191 ((3, 4, 6, 7))

2318   HIGGINS, Ralph E., and L. HEVING-
HAM-ROOT: Collector's corner in
Gramophone, No. 188 (January 1939):
356-357 ((-))

PLANTÉ, FRANCIS, 1839-1934

2319   SOALL, T. A.: Francis Planté discography in Recorded Sound, No. 35
(July 1969): 494; [Includes unpublished
records] ((3, 6, 7))

PODVALOVÁ, MARIE

2320   Snímky Marie Podvalové na deskách
Supraphon in POSPÍŠIL, Vilém: Marie
Podvalová. [1. vyd.] Praha: Panton,
1964: 40-41 (Umělci národního divadla,
2) ((-))

POLLINI, MAURIZIO, 1942-

2321 Diskografie Maurizio Pollini in fono
forum 1973 (No. 3, March): 204 ((-))

PONS, LILY, 1904-1976

2322 PARK, Bill: A Lily Pons discography in
Record Collector, XIII/11-12 (April
1961): 252-271, 283 ((3, 7)); Addenda:
Record Collector, XIV/9-10: 235 ((-))

PONSELLE, ROSA, 1897-

2323 THORPE, L. J.: Rosa Ponselle in
Gramophone, No. 72 (May 1929): 556
((-))

2324 [[SECRIST, John B.: Rosa Ponselle
biography and discography in Record
Collector V (May 1950): 104-116]] ;
Additions and corrections in Record
Collector, V/12 (December 1950): 288
((7))

2325 VILLELLA, Tom, and Bill PARK: Rosa
Ponselle—a discography in Le Grand
Baton, VII/1-2 (February-May 1970):
5-14 ((1, 3, 6, 7)); Addenda: Le Grand
Baton, XI/1 (March 1974): 31

POULENC, FRANCIS, 1899-1963

2326 Discografía de Francis Poulenc in Arte
Musical, 3d Series, No. 20-22 (July-
November 1963; March 1964): 471-472
[Note: Reprinted from Journal Musical
Français] ((-))

2327 Discographie in HELL, Henri: Francis
Poulenc musicien français. Paris:
Plon, [1958]: [245]-250 ((-))

2328 Discography in HELL, Henri: Francis
Poulenc. New York: Grove Press,
[c1959]: 107-115 ((-))

2329 L'oeuvre de Poulenc et le disque in
Musique et Radio, LIII (July 1963): 238
((-))

2330 Pour une discographie Francis Poulenc
in Diapason, No. 134 (March 1969): 50-
52 ((-))

2331 Discographie in ROY, Jean: Francis
Poulenc: l'homme et son oeuvre; liste
complète des oeuvres, discographie,
illustrations. [Paris]: Seghers, [1964]:
175-183 (Musiciens de tous les temps,
7) ((-))

PREOBAZENSKAJA, SOF'JA PETROUNA

2332 [[[Discography] in TRAJNIN, Vladimir:
Sof'ja Petrovna Preobraženskaja. Leningrad: Muzyka, 1972: 71 pp.]]

PREVIN, ANDRÉ, 1929-

2333 WALKER, Malcolm: Discography in
GREENFIELD, Edward: André Previn.
London: Allan, 1972: 93-96 ((7))

2334 WALKER, Malcolm: Discography in
GREENFIELD, Edward: André Previn.
New York: Drake Publishers, [1973]:
93-96 ((7))

PREY, HERMANN, 1929-

2335 Aus der Diskographie Hermann Preys
in Phonoprisma, VI/2 (March-April
1963): 51 ((-))

PRICE, LEONTYNE, 1927-

2336 GHEUSI, Jacques: Discographie in Diapason, No. 124 (March 1968): 15 ((-))

2337 Discography in LYON, Hugh Lee: Leontyne Price; highlights of a prima donna.
[1st ed.] New York: Vantage Press,
[c1973]: 215-216 ((-))

PŘIHODA, VÁŠA, 1900-1960

2338 DREWING, Arnold: Diskografie in fono
forum 1965 (No. 1, January): 37 ((-))

2339 Příhodorská diskografie in VRATI-
SLAVSKÝ, Jan: Váša Příhoda. 2. vyd.
Praha: Supraphon, 1974: 66-69 (Edice
Lyra) ((-))

PRINTEMPS, YVONNE

2340 LIFF, Vivian: Yvonne Printemps: a
discography in Recorded Sound, No. 31
(July 1968): 311-313 ((3, 6, 7))

PROJOFJEW, SERGEI
See PROKOF'EV, SERGEĬ SERGE-
EVICH

PROKOF'EV, SERGEĬ SERGEEVICH, 1891-
1953
See also listing for RAVEL, MAURICE.
Odriozola, Antonio: Las grabacionnes
en discos LP de seis grandes figuras
de la música contemporanea....

2341 Auswahlliste mit empfehlenswerten
Schallplatten von Prokofieffs Werke in
Hi Fi Stereophonie, III/9 (September
1964): 464-465 ((-))

2342 Schallplattenverzeichnis in BROCK-
HAUS, Heinz Alfred: Sergei Projofjew;
mit einer Auswahl von Aufsätzen des
Komponisten. Leipzig: P. Reclam,
[1964]: 226-[230] (Reclams Universal-
Bibliothek, 116) ((-))

2343 CLOUGH, F. F., and G. J. CUMING:
Prokofieff on records in Tempo, No. 11
(Spring 1949): 32-34 ((5))

2344 FRANKENSTEIN, Alfred: Prokofiev on
microgroove in High Fidelity, VI/3
March 1956): 95-104 ((-))

2345 Discographie in HOFMANN, Rostislav:
Serge Prokofiev: l'homme et son oeu-
vre. [Paris]: Seghers, 1964: 182-188
(Musiciens de tous les temps, 2) ((-))

2346 LEYDI, R.: Discografia in L'Approdo
Musicale, IV/13 (1961): 152-160 ((-))

2347 Prokofieff auf Schallplatten in Serge
Prokofieff: mit Beiträgen von Serge
Prokofieff [et al.] Bonn: Boosey &
Hawkes, [c1953]: 58 ((-))

2348 Schallplatten mit Werken Prokofjews
in STOMPER, Stephan: Sergej Prokof-
jew: das Leben, Schaffen u. Wirken d.
sowjet. Komponisten; Anlässlich d. 80.
Geburtstages Prokofjews im April 1971.
Berlin: Gesellschaft f. deutsch-
sowjetische Freundschaft, Abt. Kulturpolitik, 1971: [85]-87 ((-))

Works, Piano

2349 [Discography] in DEL'SON, Viktor
IÛl'evich: Fortepiannoe tvorchestvo i
pianism Prokof'eva. Moskva: Sov.
kompositor, 1973: 281-285 ((-))

Works, Violin

2350 [Discography] in SOROKER, ÎAkov
L'vovich: Skripichnoye tvorchestvo S.
Prokof'eva. Moskva: Muzyka, 1965:
117-[119] ((-))

Operas

2351 STRELLER, Friedbert: Prokofiews
opern auf Schallplatten in Musik und
Gesellschaft, XV (September 1965):
631-632 ((-))

Symphonies

2352 HARDEN, Ingo: Die besprochenen Aufnahmen in fono forum 1971 (No. 3,
March): 177 ((-))

PROKOFIEFF, SERGEI
See PROKOF'EV, SERGEI SERGEEVICH

PRUDEN, LARRY
See listing for FARQUHAR, DAVID

PUCCINI, GIACOMO, 1858-1924

2353 Discographie in AMY, Dominique: Giacomo Puccini: l'homme et son oeu-

vre . . . , catalogue des oeuvres, discographie. [Paris]: Seghers, [1970]:
[179]-182 (Musiciens de tous les temps,
44) ((-))

2354 BELLINGARDI, Luigi: Contributo alla
discografia della produzione lirica in
PINZAUTI, Leonardo: Giacomo Puccini.
Torino: ERI, 1975: [227]-277 ((5))

2355 Discografia in L'Approdo Musicale,
II/6 (April-June 1959): 110-116 ((-))

2356 Discografía de Puccini (1858-1924) in
Musica (Madrid), III (December 1954):
52-58 ((-))

2357 Discographie Puccini in Diapason, No.
193 (January 1975): 16 ((-))

2358 Operas de Puccini en la discografía
española in FERNÁNDEZ-CID, Antonio:
Puccini: el hombre, la obra, la estela.
Madrid: Guadarrama, [1974]: 141-146
(Punto omega, 183: Sección Biografías
autobiografías y memorias) ((-))

2359 Discographie in GAUTHIER, André:
Puccini. [Bourges]: Éditions du Seuil,
[1961]: 180-181 (Solfèges, 20) ((-))

2360 [Discographical notes included] in
MAGRI, Giorgio: Puccini e le sue rime.
Milano: G. Borletti, [1974]: 371 pp.
(Oggi nell'arte) ((-))

2361 Discografia (limitata alla incisioni di
opere intere) in SARTORI, Claudio:
Puccini. [Milano]: Nuova accademia,
[1958]: 381-387 (Le Vite del musicisti)
((-))

2362 VEGETO, Raffaele: Discografia in
PUCCINI, Giacomo: Carteggi puc-
ciniana. [Milano]: Ricordi, [1958]:
[609]-691 ((1, 5))

2363 VINCENTINI, Mario: Puccini in microsolco in Discoteca, No. 147 (January-
February 1975): 36-38 ((-))

Operas

2364 JOHNSON, David: The Puccini operas
on records in High Fidelity, VIII/12
(December 1958): 93-116 ((-))

La Boheme

2365 GREENFIELD, Edward: La Boheme in
Opera, IX/12 (December 1958): 758-
767 (Opera on the gramophone, 7) ((-))

Fanciulla del West

2366 ROSENTHAL, Harold: Puccini's Wild
West in Opera, XIII/12 (December
1962): 781-789 (Opera on the gramophone, 11) ((-))

Manon Lescaut

2367 GREENFIELD, Edward: Manon in
Opera, XIX/12 (December 1968): 958-
965 (Opera on the gramophone, 21) ((-))

Tosca

2368 GREENFIELD, Edward: Tosca in
Opera, XV/1 (January 1964): 6-15
(Opera on the gramophone, 13) ((-))

2369 SCHÖNEGGER, Hermann: Tosca;
Zusammenstellung der Gesamtaufnahmen in fono forum 1972 (No. 5, May):
356 ((-))

2370 Discography in A teacher's guide to
Tosca. New York: Education Dept., the
Metropolitan Opera Guild, [c1968]: 45
((-))

Trittico

2371 TRACEY, Edmund: Puccini's Trittico
in Opera, XVI/4 (April 1965): 247-253
(Opera on the gramophone, 15) ((-))

Turandot

2372 BOURGEOIS, Jacques: Giacomo
Puccini—Turandot in Harmonie, No.
22 (December 1966), 75-78 ((-))

2373 GREENFIELD, Edward: Turandot in
Opera, XXII/1 (January 1971): 9-19
(Opera on the gramophone, 29); [In-
cludes unpublished records] ((1))

PUGNO, RAOUL, 1852-1914

2374 BRY, Michel de: Stéphane Raoul Pugno;
une discographie in Disques, No. 3
(March 15, 1948): 108 ((7))

PURCELL, HENRY, 1658 (or 9)-1695

2375 Discographie in DEMARQUEZ, Suzanne:
Purcell. Paris: La Colombe, [1951]:
[179]-180 (Collection Euterpe) ((-))

2376 MAYER, George Louis: The vocal
works of Henry Purcell—a discography
in American Record Guide, XXV/8
(May 1959): 588-591, 670-686 ((-))

2377 A selected discography in MOORE,
Robert Ethridge: Henry Purcell & the
restoration theatre. London: Heinemann, [1961]: 215 ((-))

QUALITON RECORDS
See listing for KODÁLY, ZOLTÁN.
Barna, István

QUARTETTO ITALIANO

2378 Diskographie in Hi Fi Stereophonie,
XI/12 (December 1972): 1230 ((-))

2379 RATTALINO, Piero: Quartetto italiano
in Discoteca, No. 101 (June 1970): 20
((-))

QUATUOR TCHÉQUE
See CZECH QUARTET

RCA VICTOR RECORDS
See listings for BOSTON SYMPHONY
ORCHESTRA; CLIBURN, VAN; DE
LUCA, GIUSEPPE. Favia-Artsay,
Aida; FIEDLER, ARTHUR. Wilson,
Carol; LEINSDORF, ERICH; ORCHES-
TRAL MUSIC. O'Connell, Charles, and
Sigmund Spaeth

RABIN, MICHAEL, 1936-1972

2380 GRÄTER, Manfred: Diskografie in fono
forum 1961 (No. 5, May): 27 ((-))

RACHMANINOFF, SERGEI, 1873-1943

2381 Discographie in ANDRIESSEN, Johan:
Rachmaninow. Amsterdam: A. J. G.
Strengholt, [1950]: 251-256 (Meesters
der melodie) ((-))

2382 BENKO, Gregor: The performances of
Rachmaninoff: a discography in The
complete Rachmaninoff [Sound record-
ing] RCA ARM 3-0260, ARM 3-0261,
ARM 3-0294, ARM 3-0295, ARM 3-
0296, 1973: [18-19] of the notes ((3, 6,
7))

2383 Discography in CULSHAW, John: Sergei
Rachmaninow. London: D. Dobson,
1949: 168-171 (Contemporary composers) ((-))

2384 Discographie in Diapason, No. 177
(May 1973): 20-21 ((-))

2385 ERICSON, Raymond: Rachmaninoff: a
discography in High Fidelity, V/3 (May
1955): 76-84 ((-))

2386 [[LANG, C.: Der Pianist Sergej Wassi-
lijewitsch Rachmaninoff in Österreichische Musikzeitschrift, XXVIII (September 1973): 425-432]]

2387 MILLER, Philip L.: Work on records in
BERTENSSON, Sergei: Sergei Rachmaninoff: A lifetime in music. New
York: New York University Press,
1956: [420]-438 ((1, 3, 6, 7))

2388 SMOLIAN, Steven: Rachmaninoff discography in American Record Guide,
XXXIII/2 (October 1966): 159-165
((3, 6, 7))

Concertos, Piano

2389 Rachmaninoff piano concerti in Saturday Review (November 26, 1955): 46
((-))

Concerto, Piano, No. 2

2390 MEYER-JOSTEN, Jürgen: Aufnahmen
in fono forum 1969 (No. 2, February):
71 ((-))

RADFORD, ROBERT

2391 KENYON, J. P.: The records of Robert
Radford in Record Collector, XIV/9-10
(n.d.): 212-230 ((3))

2392 The Radford records in Record News,
I/10 (June 1957): 376-378; Addenda:
Record News, I/11 (July 1957): 413-
414; I/12 (August 1957): 450-453; II/3
(November 1957): 113 ((-))

RAFF, JOACHIM, 1822-1882

2393 Diskografie in KÄLIN, Josef: Leben und
Werk des vor 150 Jahren geborenen
Komponisten Joachim Raff. Zürich:
[Froschaugasse 5, Joseph-Joachim-
Raff-Gesellschaft], 1972: 62 ((-))

RAMEAU, JEAN PHILIPPE, 1683-1764

2394 BENOIT, Marcelle: Discographie in
GARDIEN, Jacques: Jean-Philippe
Rameau: le cadre et le milieu, les
oeuvres, appréciation sur l'oeuvre.
Paris: Colombe, 1949: 125-126 ((-))

2395 Discographie in MALIGNON, Jean:
Rameau. [n.p.]: Éditions du Seuil,
[1960]: 182-[185] ((-))

RÁNKI, GYÖRGY, 1907-

2396 Diszkográfia in BARNA, István: Ránki
György. Budapest: Zenemükiadó, 1966:
[32] (Mai magyar zeneszerzök) ((5))

RAPPOLD, MARIE, 1873-1957

2397 TRAYNOR, Francis: The Edison recordings of Marie Rappold in Hill and
Dale News, No. 26 (August 1965): 45
((-))

RAVEL, MAURICE, 1875-1937

2398 BARBIER, Pierre-E.: Discographie
Ravel; discographie selective in Diapason, No. 195 (March 1975): 15 ((-))

2399 CALVÉ, Jacques de: Discographie critique in JANKÉLÉVITCH, Vladimir:
Ravel. Bourges: Éditions du Seuil,
1956: 188-191 ((-))

2400 Discografía in Arte Musical, 3d Series,
No. 1 (March 1958): [6] ((-))

2401 Discografia in L'Approdo Musicale, I/2
(April-June 1958): 74-84 ((-))

2402 Discographie générale de Maurice
Ravel in Disques, No. 3 (March 15,
1948): 91-92; No. 4 (April 1948): 118
((5))

2403 Une discographie sélective de Maurice
Ravel in Diapason, No. 104 (February
1966): 43 ((-))

2404 [[[Discography] in Discofilia, No. 3
(May 1956): 119]]

2405 Discografie in GERAEDTS, Jaap: Ravel.
Haarlem: Gottmer, [1957]: 204-209
(Componisten-serie, 34.) ((-))

2406 Discografie in GERAEDTS, Jaap: Ravel.
Haarlem: J. H. Gottmer, [c1960]: 151-
192 (Gottmer-muziek-pockets, 13) ((-))

2407 Recordings of Ravel's works in GOSS,
Madeleine: Bolero: the life of Maurice
Ravel. New York: H. Holt and Co.,
[c1940]: 275-281 ((-))

2408 Skladby Maurice Ravela na čs. dlouhoh-
rajících deskách in HOLZKNECHT,
Václav: Maurice Ravel. [1. vyd.]
Praha: Supraphon, 1967: 199-201
(Hudební profily, 15) ((-))

2409 A selected discography from Great
Britain and America in JANKÉLÉ-
VITCH, Vladimir: Ravel. New York:
Grove Press, [c1959]: 190-191 (Ever-
green profile book; 3) ((-))

2410 A selected discography from Great
Britain and America in JANKÉLÉ-
VITCH, Vladimir: Ravel. Westport,
Conn: Greenwood Press, 1976, c1959:
190-191 ((-))

2411 LANDORMY, P.: La musique enregistrée de Maurice Ravel in Revue Musicale (December 1938): [135]-142 ((-))

2412 Disques sélectionnées in LANDOWSKI,
Wanda Alice L.: Maurice Ravel: sa vie,
son oeuvre. Paris: Les Éditions
ouvrières, [1950]: [129-133] ((-))

2413 Discographie in LÉON, Georges: Mau-
rice Ravel: l'homme et son oeuvre.
[Paris]: Seghers, [1964]: 183-188
(Musiciens de tous les temps, 11) ((-))

2414 Luybrana dyskografia utworow Ravela
in Ruch Muzyczny, VI/24 (1962): 7 ((-))

2415 Discographie in MACHABEY, Armand:
Maurice Ravel. Paris: Richard-Masse,

1947: [121]-122 (Collection Triptyque. Musique, 1) ((-))

2416 Discografia in MACHABEY, Armand: Maurice Ravel. [Modena]: Guanda, [1951]: 113-114 (Biblioteca di cultura musicale, 3) ((-))

2417 Discography in MANUEL, Roland: Maurice Ravel. London: D. Dobson, 1947: 142-144 (Contemporary composers) ((-))

2418 Discographie in Maurice Ravel; sa vie—son oeuvre. Paris: B. Grasset, [1938]: [92-95] (Le vie et les oeuvres des grands musiciens) ((-))

2419 Selected discography in MYERS, Rollo H.: Ravel: life and works. London: G. Duckworth, [1960]: 231-232 ((-))

2420 Selected discography in MYERS, Rollo H.: Ravel: life & works. Westport, Conn: Greenwood Press, [1973, c1960] 231-232 ((-))

2421 ODRIOZOLA, Antonio: Las grabacion-nes en discos LP de seis grandes figuras de la música contemporánea: Ravel, Falla, Bartok, Strawinsky, Prokofiev [y] Hindemith. Madrid, 1953: 61 pp. ((-))

2422 Ravel's complete works with indications of most important gramophone record-ings in ONNEN, Frank: Maurice Ravel. Stockholm: Continental Book Co., [1947]: 59-63 ((-))

2423 Het complete oeuvre van Maurice Ravel, met opgave der belangrijkste gramofoonplaten in ONNEN, Frank: Maurice Ravel. Amsterdam: H. J. W. Becht, [1948?]: 56-59 ((-))

2424 Discography in PETIT, Pierre: Ravel. Paris: Hachette, 1970: [94]-95 (Classiques Hachette de la musique) ((-))

2425 List of long-playing (33 1/3) record-ings of music by Maurice Ravel in SEROFF, Victor: Maurice Ravel. [1st. ed.] New York: Holt, [1953]: 292-296 ((-))

2426 List of long-playing (33 1/3) record-ings of music by Maurice Ravel in SEROFF, Victor: Maurice Ravel. Free-port, NY: Books for Libraries Press, [1970, c1953]: 292-296 ((-))

2427 [[SORDET, Dominique: Ravel et l'édition phonographique in Maurice Ravel par quelques-uns de des familiers. Paris: Éditions du Tambourinaire, 1939: 177-186]]

2428 TOUZELET, Jean: Historical record-ings, 1912-1939 in ORENSTEIN, Arbie: Ravel: man and musician. New York: Columbia University Press, 1975: 247-[270]; Note: Includes piano rolls ((5))

Vocal Music

See listing for DEBUSSY, CLAUDE—WORKS, VOCAL. Morse, Peter: Debussy and Ravel vocal music

Works, Piano

2429 [[Discographie sommaire in PERLE-MUTER, Vlado, and Hélène JOURDAN-MORHANGE: Ravel d'apres Ravel: les oeuvres pour piano, les deux concertos. Lausanne: Editions du Cervin, 1970: 90]]

Concertos, Piano

2430 HARDEN, Ingo: Diskografie in fono forum 1971 (No. 6, June): 421 ((-))

RAWSTHORNE, ALAN, 1905-1971

2431 [[Complete list of gramophone record-ings in Oxford University Press: Alan Rawsthorne—a catalogue of music. London: OUP, [1970]: 11-12]]

2432 [[[Discography] in Disc (Bristol) I/3 (Summer 1947): 100]]

REGER, MAX, 1873-1916

2433 [[Bibliographie Max Reger in Musik und Bildung, V (December 1973): 677-681]]

2434 [[Deutsches Rundfunkarchiv: Sonder-Hinweisdienst Musik. Max Reger 1873-1916. 100 Geburstag. Frankfurt am Main: Deutsches Rundfunkarchiv, 1973]]

2435 [[PFLUGER, Rolf: Diskographie der Werke von Max Reger in Österreichische Musikzeitschrift, XXVIII (March 1973): 153-156]]

2436 ROCKWELL, John: Max Reger: windbag or prophet? in High Fidelity, XXIV/5 (May 1974): 53-59 ((-))

2437 ROSENTHAL, Christian: Sélection d'oeuvres enregistrées de Max Reger in Diapason, No. 113 (January 1967): 40 ((-))

2438 [[Schallplattenverzeichnis Reger in Mitteilungen des Max-Reger-Instituts (Sonderheft 1973): 90-100]]

2439 [[SCHERMALL, Herbert: Max Reger: eine Diskographie. Berlin: Deutsche Musikphonothek, 1966]]

2440 SCHREIBER, Max: Verzeichnis der Schallplatten mit Werken von Max Reger in Mittelungen des Max Reger-Instituts, No. 2 (1954): 18-20; No. 3 (1955): 28 ((-))

2441 WIENKE, Gerhard: Hinweise zur
Reger-Diskographie (Auswahl) in
Phonoprisma (March-April 1966): 37
((-))

2442 WIRTH, Helmuth: Max Reger; Ein
Diskographie zu seinem 50. Todestag
in fono forum 1966 (No. 5, May): 228-
229 ((-))

2443 Musik von Reger auf Schallplatten in
WIRTH, Helmuth: Max Reger in Selbstzeugnissen und Bilddokumenten.
Reinbek (bei Hamburg): Rowohlt, 1973:
168-[174] (Rowohlts Monographien, 166)
((-))

Works, Chamber Music

2444 KONOLD, Wulf: Regers Kammermusik;
Chronologie und Interpretation in fono
forum 1974 (No. 3, March): 216 ((-))

Works, Organ

2445 HERAND, Frank: A Reger organ discography in Diapason, LXII (June 1971):
27 ((-))

REHKEMPER, HEINRICH

2446 HÖSLINGER, Clemens: Heinrich
Rehkemper—Diskographie in Program
notes for Preiser LV 127 [Sound re-
cording] [196-?] ((5))

2447 JONES, Robert, and Dennis BREW:
Rehkemper discography in Record Collector, XXII/12 (August 1975): 280-286
((1, 3, 7))

2448 SMOLIAN, Steven: Heinrich Rehkemper—a discography in American Record Guide, XXVIII/11 (July 1962): 899-
901 ((3, 5))

REINER, FRITZ, 1888-1963

2449 CLOUGH, F. F., and CUMING, G. J.:
Discography in Audio and Record Review, III/7 (March 1964): 27-30 ((1))

2450 HART, Philip: Reiner on records in
High Fidelity, XIV/4 (April 1964): 45,
126-127 ((-))

2451 SCHREIBER, Ulrich: Diskographie der
mit Fritz Reiner erhältlichen Schallplatten in Hi Fi Stereophonie, III/7
(July 1964): 360 ((-))

2452 SCHUMANN, Karl: Diskografie in fono
forum 1962 (No. 9, September): 18 ((-))

REINER, KAREL, 1910-

2453 [Discographical references included]
in ANTONOVÁ, Jana: Zasloužilý

umělec Karel Reiner: uplná bibliogr.
1. vyd. Praha: Měst. knihovna, rozma.,
1972: 128 pp. ((-))

RENARDY, OSSY

2454 FORD, Peter: Discography in Gramophone, No. 370 (March 1954): 375 ((-))

RENAUD, MAURICE, 1861-1933

2455 HEVINGHAM-ROOT, L.: Maurice
Renaud: a discographical survey in
Record Collector, XI/4-5 (April-May
1957): 81-119, and inside front cover
((3, 6, 7)); Addenda: Record Collector,
XI/7 (July 1957): 166-167 ((3, 6));
XII/1-2 (January-February 1958): 37
((3, 6))

RESNIK, REGINA, 1922-

2456 Resnik recordings in Resnik Rondo
[Magazine of the Regina Resnik Music
Club] (Winter 1967): 21-22 ((-))

RESPIGHI, OTTORINO, 1879-1936

2457 Discografie in MUŞAT-POPOVICI,
Alina: Respighi. Bucureşti: Editura
muzicală, 1975: 133-134 ((-))

2458 Discographie in RENSIS, Raffaello de:
Ottorino Respighi. Sion: Gessler, 1957:
97 ((-))

RESZKE, EDOUARD DE, 1853-1917

2459 DENNIS, J.: Edouard De Reszke in
Record Collector, VI/5 (May 1951):
101-106 ((-))

2460 HARVEY, H. Hugh: Edouard de Reszke;
a centenary tribute in Gramophone, No.
367 (December 1953): 230 ((-))

RESZKE, JAN DE, 1850-1925

2461 CELLETTI, Rodolfo: Jean de Reszke in
Musica e Dischi, IX (No. 76, January
1953): 18 ((5))

2462 READ, James: The recordings of Jean
de Reszke in Record Collector, XI/7
(July 1957): 165 ((-))

2463 STRATTON, John: The recordings of
Jean de Reszke in Recorded Sound, No.
27 (July 1967): 209 ((1, 7))

2464 VEGETO, Raffaele: Discografie di Jean
de Retszke [i.e., Reszke] in Musica e
Dischi, XVI (No. 172, October 1960):
50 ter. ((7))

2465 VEGETO, Raffaele: Discografie di Jan
De Retszke [i.e., Reszke] in Musica e
Dischi, XVI (No. 173, November 1960):
72 ((7))

2466 VEGETO, Raffaele: Discografia di Jan
de Retszke [i.e., Reszke] in Musica e
Dischi, XVII (No. 175, January 1961):
64 ((7))

RETHBERG, ELISABETH, 1894-1976

2467 RICHARDS, J. B.: Rethberg discography: additions and amendments in Rec-
cord Collector, V/1 (January 1950):
12-13 ((-))

2468 RICHARDS, J. B.: Rethberg's recordings in Record Collector, VIII/1 (January 1953): 5-10 ((3, 7))

RICHTER, SVJATOSLAV
See RIKHTER, SVIATOSLAV

RIDKÝ, JAROSLAV, 1897-1956

2469 Skladby a nahrávky J. Řídkého na
deskách in VÁLEK, Jiří: Jaroslav
Řídký: život a odkaz českého skladatele
a učitele. [1. vyd.] Praha: Panton,
1966: 208-213 (Edice Hudební vědy, 3)
((-))

RIEGGER, WALLINGFORD, 1885-1961

2470 GOODFRIEND, James: Riegger recorded in Hi Fi Stereo Review, XX/4
(April 1968): 66 ((-))

2471 Riegger discography in Bulletin of the
American Composers Alliance, IX/3
(1960): 19 ((-))

RIISAGER, KNUDÅGE, 1897-1974

2472 List of records in BERG, Sigurd:
Knudåge Riisager. København, 1950:
17 ((-))

RIKHTER, SVIATOSLAV, 1914-

2473 CLOUGH, F. F., and G. J. CUMING: A
Richter discography in Audio and Record Review, II/7 (March 1963): 16-18
((-))

2474 Diskographie in Phonoprisma, VI/4
(July-August 1963): 85 ((-))

2475 Diskografie in JURÍK, Marián: Svjatoslav Richter. 1. vyd. Praha: Supraphon, 1974: 54-58 (Edice Lyra) ((-))

2476 KRAUS, Gottfried: Diskografie in fono
forum 1963 (No. 5, May): 169 ((-))

2477 Richter discography in Saturday Review
(October 15, 1960): 66 ((-))

RILLING, HELMUTH

2478 Diskographie Helmuth Rilling in Phonoprisma, VII/5 (September-October
1964): 151 ((-))

2479 Helmuth Rilling auf Schallplatten in
Festschrift Helmuth Rilling. Stuttgart:
Stuttgarter Musikfreunde, 1973: 127-
134 ((-))

RIMSKIĬ-KORSAKOV, NIKOLAĬ ANDRE-
EVICH, 1844-1908

2480 Discografía in GARCÍA MORILLO, Roberto: Rimsky-Korsakov. Buenos
Aires: Ricordi Americana, [1945]: 202-
206 (Músicos célebres) ((-))

2481 Discographie critique in HOFMANN,
Rostislav: Rimski Korsakov; sa vie,
son oeuvre. Paris: Flammarion, 1958:
[232]-233 ((-))

2482 Pour une discographie Rimsky-
Korsakov Roussel in Diapason, No. 137
(June 1969): 8-9 ((-))

RIVIER, JEAN, 1896-

2483 Discographie in Courrier Musical de
France, No. 6 (1964): 124 ((-))

ROBESON, PAUL, 1898-1976

2484 Gramofonové závody, Prague: Robeso-
nova píseň zní: k serii snímků nazpí-
vaných v roce 1955 v New Yorku
Paulem Robesonem pro československé
Gramofonové zavody. Praha: [Osveta]
1957: 33 pp. ((-))

ROBIN, MADO

2485 PARYLAK, Robert: Mado (Madeleine)
discography in Record Collector,
XIX/9-10 (February 1971): 231-235
((3, 5, 7))

RODRIGO, JOAQUÍN, 1902-

2486 [[MOLES, E.: [Discography] in Discofilia, No. 11 (March 1957): 60]]

2487 Discografía in SOPEÑA, Federico:
Joaquín Rodrigo. [Madrid]: Dirección
General de Bellas Artes, Ministerio de
Educación y Ciencia, [1970]: 57-61
(Colección Artistas espanoles contem-
poráneos. Serie músicos, 1) ((-))

ROLF, ERNST

2488 LILIEDAHL, Karleric: Ernst Rolf.
[Stockholm?]: Kungliga biblioteket,

1970: 71 pp. (Nationalfonotekets diskografier, 501) ((3, 4, 6, 7))

ROPARTZ, JOSEPH-GUY, 1864-1955

2489 Discographie in Courrier Musical de France, No. 7 (1964): 190 ((-))

ROSAS, JUVENTINO, 1868-1894

2490 Diskografía in ALVAREZ CORAL, Juan: Juventino Rosas. 2. ed. México: B. Costa-Amic, [1972]: 62 ((-))

ROSBAUD, HANS, 1895-1962

2491 Diskografie Rosbaud in fono forum 1960 (No. 6, June): 6 ((-))

2492 GERBER, Leslie: Hans Rosbaud: a discography in Association for Recorded Sound Collections Journal, IV/1-3 (1972): 47-53 ((5))

2493 LINDLAR, Heinrich: Diskografie in fono forum 1963 (No. 2, February): 54 ((-))

ROSENBLATT, JOSEF, 1882-1937

2494 GREENBERGER, Joseph: Cantor Josef Rosenblatt—discography in Record Collector, XX/6-7 (May 1972): 129-146 [Includes notes on playing speeds] ((3, 4, 6, 7))

2495 Discography in ROSENBLATT, Samuel: Yossele Rosenblatt: the story of his life. New York: Farrar, Strauss and Young, [1954]: 369-371 ((-))

ROSENTHAL, MORIZ, 1862-1946

2496 ANDERSON, H. L., and Patrick SAUL: Moriz Rosenthal discography in Recorded Sound, I/7 (Summer 1962): 217-220 ((3, 4, 6, 7))

ROSSINI, GIOACCHINO ANTONIO, 1792-1868

2497 Discografia in CAUSSOU, Jean Louis: Gioachino Rossini: l'homme et son oeuvre. Paris: Seghers, 1967: 185-189 (Musiciens de tous les temps, 35) ((-))

2498 Discographie in CAUSSOU, Jean Louis: Gioacchino Rossini. [Lausanne]: La Guilde du livre, [1971]: 185-189 (Musiciens de tous les temps) ((-))

2499 Discografía de las obras de Rossini in GIACOBBE, Juan Francisco: Rossini. Buenos Aires: Ricordi Americana, 1942: 145-151 (Músicos célebres) ((-))

2500 MARINELLI, Carlo: Discografia rossiniana in Rassegna Musicale, XXIV/3 (1954): 273-289 ((-))

2501 Discografie in POLS, André M.: Het leven van G. Rossini. Brussel-Roosendaal: Reinaert Uitgaven, [1970]: 44-48 (Meesters der toonkunst, 14) ((-))

2502 Discografia in ROGNONI, Luigi: Gioacchino Rossini. Torino: ERI, 1968: 481-492 ((-))

2503 VEGETO, Raffaele: Nota discografica Rossiniana in Discoteca, No. 82 (July-August 1968): 26-29 ((-))

Il Barbiere di Siviglia

2504 FIERZ, Gerold: Diskografie in fono forum 1962 (No. 3, March): 31 ((-))

2505 [[NEMETH, C.: Eine vergleichende Discographie in Phono, VIII/2]]

ROSTROPOVITCH, MSTISLAV, 1927-

2506 BROWN, Nathan E.: The "unauthorized" Rostropovitch in Le Grand Baton, VII/3 (August 1970): 3-8 ((1, 7))

2507 MARKLE, David: A selective Rostropovitch discography in Le Grand Baton, VII/3 (August 1970): 12 ((-))

ROSVAENGE, HELGE

2508 Schallplatten in TASSIÉ, Franz: Helge Rosvaenge. Augsburg: Schroff-Verlag, 1975: [211]-215 ((-))

ROTHENBERGER, ANNELIESE

2509 LEWINSKI, Wolf-Eberhard von: Diskografie in fono forum 1964 (No. 7, July): 266 ((-))

2510 Diskografie Anneliese Rothenberger in LEWINSKI, Wolf-Eberhard von: Anneliese Rothenberger. [1. Aufl.] Velber bei Hannover: Friedrich, [1968]: 89-98 ((-))

2511 Diskographie in ROTHENBERGER, Anneliese: Melodie meines Lebens: Selbsterlebtes, Selbsterzähltes; mit eine Diskographie, einem Repertoire-Verzeichnis und einer Biographie in Datenform. 2. Aufl. München: Lichtenberg, [c1972]: [175]-180 ((-))

ROUSSEL, ALBERT CHARLES PAUL, 1869-1937

2512 Discographie in Courrier Musical de France, No. 22 (1968): 144 ((-))

2513 Discographie in HOÉREE, Arthur: Albert Roussel. Paris: Rieder, 1938: 129 (Maîtres de la musique ancienne et moderne, 17) ((-))

2514 HUGHES, Eric: A selected discography
of Albert Roussel in DEANE, Basil:
Albert Roussel. London: Barrie and
Rockliff, [1961]: 173-176 ((-))

2515 MANAL, Georges: Albert Roussel
1869-1937 in Recorded Sound, No. 38
(April 1970): 621 ((1, 7))

2516 [[NEILL, Edward D. R.: Albert Roussel
in Musicalia, I/1 (February 1970):
5-10]]

2517 Pour une discographie Rimsky-
Korsakov Roussel in Diapason, No. 137
(June 1969): 8-9 ((-))

2518 Discographie in SURCHAMP, Angelico:
Albert Roussel: l'homme et son oeuvre.
Catalogue des oeuvres, discographie.
Paris: Seghers, 1967: [186]-189 (Musi-
ciens de tous les temps, 32) ((-))

ROWICKI, WITOLD

2519 SPINGEL, Hans Otto: Diskografie in
fono forum 1962 (No. 11, November):
29 ((-))

RUBINSTEIN, ARTUR, 1887-

2520 ASHMAN, Mike: Rubinstein discography
in Records and Recording, XVII/1
(October 1975): 27-28; [Based on discography issued by fono forum, 1972]
((5))

2521 CLOUGH, F. F., and G. J. CUMING:
Artur Rubinstein; a microgroove disko-
graphy in Gramophone Record Review,
No. 41 (March 1957): 346-347 ((-))

2522 Discographie Arthur Rubinstein in
Diapason, No. 192 (December 1974):
11-12 ((-))

2523 Diskografie in fono forum 1963 (No. 4,
April): 151 ((-))

2524 Diskographie in Collegium Musicum
1971 (No. 12): 14 ((-))

2525 Discographie d'Artur Rubinstein in
GAVOTY, Bernard: Arthur Rubinstein.
Genève: R. Kister, c1955: [32] (Les
Grands interprètes) ((-))

2526 Recordings realized by Arthur Rubinstein in GAVOTY, Bernard: Arthur
Rubinstein. Geneva: R. Kister, c1956:
[32] (Great concert artists) ((-))

RUFFO, TITTA, 1877-1953

2527 DE LUIGI, Mario: Discografia completa
di Titta Ruffo in Musica e Dischi, IX
(No. 83, August, 1953): 10 ter. ((7))

2528 [[DENNIS, J.: Titta Ruffo in Record
Collector, VI/ (June 1951): 125-143]]

RUSNAK, OREST, 1895-1960

2529 [Discography] in Orest Rusnak: Zhit-
tevii schlyakh; zbirnik dlya vshanu-
vannya pam'yati vidatnogo spivaka
nezabutnogo zemliyaka. Niu York
Tsentr obedannya bukovinskikh ukraint-
siv u ZSA 1971: 132-133 ((-))

RUSSO, DOMENICO

2530 [KNIGHT, Arthur E.]: The Domenico
Russo heritage in Record Collector,
X/1 (June 1955): 13-14 ((3, 6, 7))

RŮŽÍČKOVÁ-KALABISOVÁ, ZUZANA

2531 [Discographical references included]
in BERKOVEC, Jiří: Zuzana Růžíčková.
[1. yvd.] Praha: Supraphon, t.ST2,
1972: 73 pp. ((-))

RYBA, JAKUB JAN, 1756-1815

2532 Gramofonové desky in NĚMEČEK, Jan:
Jakub Jab Ryba: život a dílo. [1. vyd.]
Praha: Státní hudební vydavatelství,
1963: 356 ((-))

RZEWUSKA, COUNTESS
See BORONAT, OLIMPIA

SABATA, VICTOR DE
See DE SABATA, VICTOR

SACRED MUSIC

2533 KIRBY, Lewis M.: A catalog of sacred
music. Alexandria, Va.: Seminary
Books Service, Record Dept., 196-?:
79 pp. ((-))

2534 NYS, Carl de: Les enregistrements de
musique sacrée in Revue Musicale, No.
239-240: 315-326 ((-))

SAINT-SAËNS, CAMILLE, 1835-1921

2535 BARBIER, Pierre E.: Discographie in
Diapason, No. 161 (November 1971):
28-29 ((-))

2536 Discographie in CHANTAVOINE, Jean:
Camille Saint-Saëns. Paris: Richard-
Masse, 1947: [124-126] (Collection
Triptyque Musique, 3) ((-))

SALMOND, FELIX, 1888-1952

2537 HALL, David: A Felix Salmond discography in Violoncello Society

Newsletter (Winter 1972): inserted
in issue ((–))

SAMMARCO, MARIO, 1873-1930

2538 FREESTONE, John: Records in Gramophone, No. 341 (October 1951): 96 ((7))

2539 [[SOKOL, M. L.: A Mario Sammarco
discography in Hobbies, LXXVIII (December 1973): 35-36]]

SAMUEL, HAROLD, 1879-1937

2540 ANDERSON, H. L.: Harold Samuel discography in Recorded Sound, I/6
(Spring 1962): 191-192 ((3, 5, 6, 7))

SANTLEY, SIR CHARLES, 1834-1922

2541 FREESTONE, John: Collectors' corner
in Gramophone, No. 356 (January 1953):
192-193 ((–))

2542 JARRETT, Jack: Sir Charles Santley—
the records in Record Advertiser, No.
3 (March-April 1971): 4 ((–))

SARASATE, PABLO DE, 1844-1908

2543 ÅHLÉN, Carl-Gunnar: Pablo de
Sarasate (1844-1908) in Musik Revy
XXVI/6 (1971): 365 (Grammofonens
veteraner, 3) ((3, 7))

SATIE, ERIK, 1866-1925

2544 HELM, Everett: Diskografie Erik
Satie in fono forum 1960 (No. 7, July):
11 ((–))

2545 MARNAT, Marcel: Discographie in
REY, Anne: Erik Satie. Paris: Seuil,
[1974]: 186-[191] (Collections Microcosme: Solfèges, 35) ((–))

2546 Recordings in MYERS, Rolo H.: Erik
Satie. London: D. Dobson, 1948: 144
(Contemporary composers) ((–))

2547 Discographié in MYERS, Rolo H.: Erik
Satie. [Paris]: Gallimard, [1959]:
[196] (Leurs figures) ((–))

2548 Recordings in MYERS, Rollo H.: Erik
Satie. St. Clair Shores, Mich.:
Scholarly Press, 1974: 144 ((–))

2549 ROY, Jean: Discographie selective in
Diapason, No. 198 (June-July 1975):
15 ((–))

2550 SAUGUET, Henri: Discographie in
Diapason, No. 108 (June-July 1966): 12
((–))

2551 Erik Satie: a discography in TEMP-
LIER, Pierre Daniel: Erik Satie.

Cambridge: MIT Press, [1969]: [113]-
127 ((1))

SÄTTLER, ELISABETH
See RETHBERG, ELISABETH

SAUGUET, HENRI, 1901-

2552 Discographie in BRIL, France Yvonne:
Henri Sauget: l'homme et son
oeuvre, . . . avec des écrits d'Henri
Sauguet. Paris: Seghers, 1967: [187]-
188 (Musiciens de tous les temps, 33)
((–))

2553 Discographie in SCHNEIDER, Marcel:
Henri Sauguet. Paris: Ventadour,
[1959]: [46] (Collection "Musiciens
d'aujourd'hui") ((–))

SAWALLISCH, WOLFGANG, 1923-

2554 CLOUGH, F. F., and G. J. CUMING:
Discography in Audio and Record Review, II/12 (August 1963): 13-14 ((–))

2555 Diskografie in fono forum 1960 (No. 9,
September): 12 ((–))

2556 Schallplatten mit Wolfgang Sawallisch
in Phonoprisma, V/5 (September-
October 1962): 134 ((–))

SAYAO, BIDÚ, 1902-

2557 LEÓN, Jacques Alain, and Alvisio
GUIMARES: Discography in Record
Collector, XIII/6 (August 1960): 125-
133 ((7))

2558 UBRIACO, Rita: Bidú Sayao—the records in Record News, II/11 (July 1958):
392-395 ((3, 6, 7))

SAYYID DARWISH, 1892-1923

2559 [Discography] in AL-HIFNI, Muhmūd
Ahmad: Sayyid Darwish: Hayatuhu wa
athaar abqariyyatihi. At-tab'ah al-
Thaniyah; Tab'ah khaassah- al-Qahira:
al-Hay'ah al-Misriyyah al-'Aamma
Lilkitab, 1974: [239]-[240] ((–))

SCARLATTI, ALESSANDRO, 1660-1725

2560 Discografia in PAGANO, Roberto:
Alessandro Scarlatti. Torino: ERI,
1972: 569-575 (Collana di monografie
per servire alla storia della musica
italiana) ((–))

SCHAEFFER, PIERRE, 1910-

2561 Discographie in Courrier Musical de
France, No. 34 (1971): 101 ((–))

SCHALK, FRANZ, 1863-1931

2562 HUGHES, Eric: Franz Schalk discography in Recorded Sound, No. 38 (April 1970): 605 ((3, 6, 7))

SCHERCHEN, HERMANN, 1891-1966

2563 CLOUGH, F. F., and G. J. CUMING: Hermann Scherchen; a microgroove diskography in Gramophone Record Review, No. 44 (June 1957): 619-620, 623 ((-))

SCHIAVAZZI, PIERO

2564 CELLETTI, Rodolfo: Discografia in Musica e Dischi, X (No. 96, September 1954): 37 ((5, 7))

2565 CELLETTI, Rodolfo: The records in Record News, V/1 (September 1960): 6-7 [From Musica e Dischi] ((5, 7))

SCHIØTZ, AKSEL, 1906-1975

2566 Aksel Schiøtz plader. [Copenhagen]: National museet, 1961: 21 pp. (Det National Diskotek Katalog, 1) ((3, 4, 6, 7))

2567 [[Nationaldiskoteket: Aksel Schiøtz: a discographie. Copenhagen, 1966: 48 pp. (Nationaldiskoteket. Discographies, 206)]]

SCHIPA, TITO, 1889-1965

2568 VEGETO, Raffaele: La discografia di Tito Schipa in Musica e Dischi, XIII (No. 125, January 1957): 48 ((5, 7))

2569 VEGETO, Raffaele: Discografia di Tito Schipa in Musica e Dischi, XVI (No. 168, June 1960): 12 ((7))

2570 WINSTANLEY, Sydney, and Tom HUTSCHINSON: Schipa discography in Record Collector, XIII/4-5 (June-July 1960): 77-109 ((3))

SCHIPPER, EMIL

2571 Dr. Emil Schipper—records in Record News, II/1 (September 1957): 33-35 ((-)); Addenda: Record News, II/2 (October 1957): 56 ((-))

2572 Records in Record Collector, II/1 (September 1957): 33-36 ((-))

SCHLUSNUS, HEINRICH, 1888-1952

2573 CSAN, E., and A. G. ROSS: A Schlusnus discography in Record News, III/6 (February 1959): 164-181 ((1, 3, 5, 6));

III/7 (March 1959): 196-206 ((1, 3, 5, 6)); Addenda: Record News, III/9 (May 1959): 319-324; III/11 (July 1959): 402-403; IV/4 (December 1959): 136-140

2574 MANN, Carl-Heinz: Diskografie (Auswahl) in fono forum 1961 (No. 5, May): 13 ((-))

2575 Die Erinnerung an die Stimme von Heinrich Schlusnus wird von der Deutsche Grammophon Gesellschaft bewahrt in NASO, Eckart von: Schlusnus: Mensch und Sanger. Hamburg: W. Krüger, [1962, c1957]: 255-256 ((-))

2576 POTTER, Robert W. F.: Heinrich Schlusnus in Gramophone, No. 197 (October 1939): 187-191 ((-))

2577 [[SMOLIAN, S.: Heinrich Schlusnus, a discography in British Institute of Recorded Sound Bulletin, No. 14 (Autumn 1959): 5-24; No. 15-16 (Spring 1960): 16-26 ((4, ...))]]

SCHMIDT, FRANZ, 1874-1939

2578 Discographie in Revue Musicale, No. 298-299 (1975): 163 ((-))

2579 Discographie in NEMETH, Carl: Franz Schmidt: ein Meister nach Brahms und Bruckner. Zürich: Amalthea-Verlag, [1957]: 279 ((-))

2580 PFLUGER, Rolf: Diskographie Franz Schmidt (1874-1939) in Österreichische Musikzeitschrift, XXIX/11 (November 1974): 586-587 ((-))

Chamber Music

2581 WIRTH, Helmuth: Diskografie in fono forum 1965 (No. 11, November): 506 ((-))

SCHMIDT, JOSEPH, 1904-1942

2582 FROST, H.: Joseph Schmidt—the records in Record News, II/4 (December 1957): 120-130 ((3, 4)); Addenda: Record News, II/12 (August, 1958): 439-440

SCHMIDT-ISSERSTEDT, HANS, 1900-1973

2583 Diskografie Schmidt-Isserstedt in fono forum 1960 (No. 6, June): 7 ((-))

2584 In mémoriam K. Ančerl et H. Schmidt-Isserstedt—discographie selection in Diapason, No. 179 (September 1973): 9 ((-))

SCHMITT, FLORENT, 1870-1959

2585 Discographie in Courrier Musical de France, No. 17 (1967): 63 ((-))

2586 Discographie des oeuvres de Florent
Schmitt in HUCHER, Yves: Florent
Schmitt: l'homme et l'artiste, son
époque et son oeuvre. Paris: Éditions
Le Bon Plaisir, [1953]: [268]-269
(Amour de la musique) ((-))

2587 Discographie in MARCERON, Made-
leine: Florent Schmitt. Paris:
Ventadour, [1959]: [46]-47 (Collection
"Musiciens d'aujourd'hui") ((-))

SCHNABEL, ARTUR, 1882-1951

2588 CLOUGH, F. F., and G. J. CUMING:
Artur Schnabel; diskography in Gramophone Record Review, No. 57 (July
1958): 737-738 ((-))

2589 COHN, Bernardo: Artur Schnabel dis-
cography in SAERCHINGER, César:
Artur Schnabel: a biography. London:
Cassell, [1957]: 333-343 ((-))

2590 COHN, Bernardo: Artur Schnabel discography in SAERCHINGER, César:
Artur Schnabel: a biography. New
York: Dodd, Mead, [1958, c1957]: 333-
343 ((-))

2591 COHN, Bernardo: Artur Schnabel discography in SAERCHINGER, César:
Artur Schnabel: a biography. Westport,
CN: Greenwood Press, [1973, c1957]:
333-343 ((-))

2592 Diskographie in Collegium Musicum
1971 (No. 8): 38 ((-))

2593 GERBER, Leslie: Artur Schnabel: a
discography in Piano Quarterly, No. 84
(Winter 1973-1974): 54-62 ((1, 6, 7))

2594 GLUTH, Walter: Diskografie Artur
Schnabel in fono forum 1961 (No. 9,
September): 29 ((-))

2595 STONE, Ralph: An Artur Schnabel
discography in Le Grand Baton, IX/3
(August 1972): 22-27 ((1, 7)); Addenda:
Le Grand Baton, XI/1 (March 1974): 31
((-))

SCHNEIDERHAN, WOLFGANG, 1915-

2596 Diskographie (sämtliche Aufnahmen
Deutsche Grammophon Gesellschaft)
in Phonoprisma (March-April 1967):
59 ((-))

2597 Discographie in FASSBIND, Franz:
Wolfgang Schneiderhan [und] Irmgard
Seefried: eine Künstler- und Lebensgemeinschaft. Bern: A. Scherz, [1960]:
293-[308]; Note: Schneiderhan discography: 293-298; Schneiderhan and Seefried
discography: 298-299; and Seefried discography: 299-[308] ((-))

SCHOECK, OTHMAR, 1886-1957

2598 Schallplatten in VOGEL, Werner:
Thematisches Verzeichnis der Werke
von Othmar Schoeck. Zürich: Atlantis
Verlag, [1956]: 285 ((-))

SCHÖFFLER, PAUL, 1897-

2599 Diskographie in CHRISTIAN, Hans: Paul
Schöffler: versuch einer Würdigung.
Wien, München: Österreichischer
Bundesverlag, 1967: 37-40 ((-))

SCHÖNBERG, ARNOLD, 1874-1951
See also BERG, ALBAN. Nijman,
Julius

2600 BARBIER, Pierre-E.: Schoenberg discographie in Diapason, No. 189 (September 1974): 14-15 ((-)); No. 191
(November 1974): 21-23 ((-))

2601 Discographie in Musique en Jeu, No. 16
(November 1974): [74]-76 ((-))

2602 Discographie in Revue Musicale, No.
298-299 (1975): 163 ((-))

2603 HAMILTON, David: Schoenberg on
records in High Fidelity, XXIV/9
(September 1974): 66-70 ((-))

2604 MARINELLI, Carlo: Discografia in
Guerre-Lieder. [Venezia]: Stamperia
di Venezia, [1972?]: 59-61 (Quaderni
del Teatro La Fenice) ((5))

2605 MARNAT, Marcel: Discographie in
LEIBOWITZ, René: Schoenberg.
Paris: Éditions du Seuil, 1969: 182-
187 (Solfèges, 30) ((-))

2606 Discografía in PAZ, Juan Carlos:
Arnold Schönberg: o, El fin de la era
tonal. Buenos Aires: Editorial Nueva
Visión, 1958: [276]-278 (Nueva visión;
música, 5); Note: No record numbers
in discography ((-))

2607 Discography in Perspectives on
Schoenberg and Stravinsky. Princeton: Princeton University Press, 1968:
255-267 ((-))

2608 PFLUGER, Rolf: Arnold-Schönberg-
Diskographie in Österreichische
Musikzeitschrift, XXIX/6 (June 1974):
321-324 ((-))

2609 Discografia in ROMANO, Jacob: El
otro Schoenberg. [Buenos Aires?]:
Editores Dos, [1969]: 173-178 (Serie
plural) ((-))

2610 Schallplatten in RUFER, Josef: Das
Werk Arnold Schönbergs. Kassel, New
York: Bärenreiter, 1959: [181]-182 ((1))

2611 Recordings in RUFER, Josef: The
works of Arnold Schoenberg: a cata-

logue of his compositions, writings,
and paintings. London: Faber and
Faber, [1962]: 189-190 ((1))

2612 Recordings in RUFER, Josef: The
works of Arnold Schoenberg: a catalogue of his compositions, writings, and
paintings. [New York]: Free Press of
Glencoe, [1963, c1962]: 189-190 ((1))

2613 Schallplatten in RUFER, Josef: Das
Werk Arnold Schönbergs. [Neuaufl.]
Kassel, Basel, London, New York:
Bärenreiter, [1974, c1958]: [181]-182
((1))

2614 Skladby Arnolda Schönberga na
dlouhohrajících deskách Supraphon
in STUCKENSCHMIDT, H. H.: Arnold
Schoenberg. Praha: Editio Supraphon,
1971: 146 ((-))

2615 Noten und Schallplatten in Stuttgart.
Stadtbücherei. Musikabteilung: Arnold
Schönberg, 1874-1951: Noten, Schall-
platten, Schrifttum aus d. Beständen d.
Musikabt. zusammengestellt z. 100.
Geburtstag 1974. Stuttgart: Stadt-
bücherei, 1974: [5]-21 ((-))

SCHØNBERG, IB

2616 ANDREASEN, Axel: Ib Schønberg og
grammonfonen en discografi.
København: Axel Andreasen (Ekäp.:
Hothers Plads 23/1, 2200 København),
1974: 57 leaves ((3, 4, 6, 7))

SCHÖNE, LOTTE

2617 STRATTON, John: Lotte Schone, discography in Record News, V/9 (May
1961): 301 ((3, 6))

2618 TUBEUF, Andre: Lotte Schoene discography in Record Collector, XX/4
(December 1971): 84-89 ((3, 5, 6, 7))

SCHORR, FRIEDRICH, 1888-1953

2619 DENNIS, J.: Friedrich Schorr discog-
raphy in Record Collector, XIX/11-12
(April 1971): 262-274 ((1, 3, 4, 5, 6, 7));
Addenda: Record Collector, XX/3
(October 1971): 71 ((-))

2620 HARVEY, H. Hugh: Friedrich Schorr—
records in Gramophone, No. 365 (October 1953): 130 ((-))

2621 [[SMOLIAN, S.: Friedrich Schorr: the
records in British Institute of Recorded Sound Bulletin, No. 8 (Spring
1958): 6-10]]

SCHOSTAKOWITSCH, DMITRI
See SHOSTAKOVICH, DMITRII
DMITRIEVICH

SCHREIER, PETER

2622 Diskographie in Medium Schallplatte,
No. 12 (No. 3, 1969): 13 ((-))

2623 Diskographie in Musica/Phonoprisma,
XXII/5 (September-October 1968): 409
((-))

2624 SPIELER, Heinrich: Diskographie in
Medium Schallplatte, No. 3 (No. 2,
1967): 11 ((5))

SCHROEDER, HERMANN, 1904-

2625 Schallplattenverzeichnis in KEUSEN,
Raimund: Die Orgel- und Vokalwerke
von Hermann Schroeder. Köln: Volk,
1974: 183 (Beiträge zur sheinischen
Musikgeschichte, 102) ((-))

SCHUBERT, FRANZ PETER, 1797-1828

2626 Discographie des oeuvres de Schubert
in BRUYR, José: Franz Schubert:
l'homme et son oeuvre. [Paris]:
Éditions Seghers, [1965]: 184-188
(Musiciens de tous les temps, 17) ((-))

2627 Discographie Schubertienne in
BUENZOD, Emmanuel: Franz Schubert. [Paris]: Corrêa, [1937]: [221]-
226 ((-))

2628 BURKE, C. G.: Schubert on records in
High Fidelity, I/2 (Fall 1951): 36-39,
66, 81 ((-))

2629 Schallplattenverzeichnis in MARGGRAF,
Wolfgang: Franz Schubert. Leipzig:
Reclam, 1967: 236-[239] (Reclams Uni-
versal-Bibliothek, 87) ((-))

2630 The recorded works of Franz Schubert
in Phonograph Monthly Review, III/2
(November 1928): 52-54 ((-))

2631 Recorded works of Schubert in
SCHAUFFLER, Robert Haven: Franz
Schubert: the Ariel of music. New
York: G. P. Putnam's Sons, [1949]:
413-418 ((-))

2632 A selected discography from America
in SCHNEIDER, Marcel: Schubert.
Westport, Conn.: Greenwood Press,
1975, c1959: 188-190 ((-))

2633 SVOBODA, V.: Skladby Franze
Schuberta na dlouhoh rajících deskách
Supraphon in HOLZKNECHT, Václav:
Franz Schubert. 1. vyd. Praha:
Supraphon, t. ST 2, 1972: 233-[237]
(Hudební profily, 22) ((-))

2634 Quelques disques de Schubert in
TRAMOND, Renée: Franz Schubert.
Lyon: Éditions et imprimeries du
Sud-Est, [1955]: 81-82 (Collection
Nos amis les musiciens) ((-))

Works, Chorus

2635 MORSE, Peter: Schubert/Schumann/ Brahms choral music. Utica, NY: J. F. Weber, 1970: 12 pp. (Discography series, 5) ((3, 4, 6, 7))

Works, Chamber Music

2636 BURKE, C. G.: Schubert on micro- groove—1954. Part II: Chamber music in High Fidelity, IV/5 (July 1954): 66-72 ((-))

Works, Instrumental

2637 BURKE, C. G.: Schubert on micro- groove—1954. Part I: Orchestral, instrumental in High Fidelity, IV/4 (June 1954): 60-74 ((-))

Works, Vocal

2638 BURKE, C. G.: Schubert on micro- groove—1954. Part III: Vocal music in High Fidelity, IV/6 (August 1954): 62-68 ((-))

Quintet, Strings, C Major, D. 956

2639 HALBREICH, Harry: Discographie comparée in Harmonie, No. 14 (Febru- ary 1966): 80-85 ((-))

2640 KRAUS, Gottfried: Eine vergleichende Diskografie in fono forum 1971 (No. 4, April): 257 ((-))

Quintet, Piano and Strings, A Major, D. 667

2641 Le truite de Schubert; les enregistre- ments in Diapason, No. 147 (May 1970): 8-11 ((-))

2642 LEWINSKI, Wolf-Eberhard: Diskografie in fono forum 1963 (No. 9, September): 350 ((-))

Die schöne Müllerin, D. 795

2643 HÖSLINGER, Clemens: Die schöne Müllerin—Diskografie in fono forum 1972 (No. 3, March): 183 ((-))

Sonata, Piano, B-Flat Major, D. 960

2644 Les enregistrements in Diapason, No. 142 (December 1969): 9 ((-))

Songs

2645 WEBER, J. F.: Schubert lieder dis- cography: a list of every Schubert song ever recorded, with a selected list of artists for each. Utica, NY: Weber, [1969]: 20 leaves ((4, 5))

2646 WEBER, J. F.: Schubert Lieder. Rev. ed. Utica, NY: Weber, [1970]: 49 pp. (Discography series, 1) ((4, 5))

Symphonies

2647 LEGIN, P.: Discographie des sym- phonies de Schubert in Disques, No. 7 (August-September 1948): 193 ((-))

Symphony, D. 759, B Minor

2648 GRIMMINGER, Karl: Diskografie in fono forum 1962 (No. 9, September): 29 ((-))

Die Winterreise, D. 911

2649 KRAUS, Gottfried: [Diskografie] in fono forum 1968 (No. 6, June): 325 ((-))

SCHÜTZ, HEINRICH, 1585-1672

2650 BLUM, Klaus: International Heinrich Schütz Diskographie, 1928-1972, [von] Klaus Blum [und] Martin ELSTE. Bremen: Blum, (Holzmeier-str. 1), 1972: 232 pp. ((3, 4, 5, 6, 7))

2651 DELALANDE, Jacques: Heinrich Schütz Diskographie in Hi Fi Stereo- phonie, XI/11 (November 1972): 1082- 1084 ((-))

2652 Frankfurt am Main. Deutsches Rund- funkarchiv. Sonder-Hinweisdienst Musik: Heinrich Schütz, 1585-1672: 300. Todestag. Frankfurt am Main: Deutsches Rundfunkarchiv, 1972: 175 leaves ((1, 5, 7))

2653 Schallplatten in KÖHLER, Siegfried: Heinrich Schütz, 1585-1672. Berlin: Deutscher Kulturbund, 1972: 69-70 ((-))

2654 Discography in MOSER, Hans Joachim: Heinrich Schütz: a short account of his life and works. London: Faber, 1967: 111-116 ((-))

2655 Discography in MOSER, Hans Joachim: Heinrich Schütz: a short account of his life and works. New York: St. Martins, [1967]: 111-116 ((-))

2656 SCHOOR, Hans: Schütz-Discographie in Phono, IX/5 (May-June 1963): 103 ((-)); Zur Heinrich-Schütz-Discographie in Phono, IX/6 (July-August 1963): 137- 138 ((-)); X/1 (September-October 1963): 21 ((-)); Geistliche Chormusik in Phono X/2 (November-December 1963): 47

2657 Discographie in TELLART, Roger: Heinrich Schütz: l'homme et son oeuvre. Paris: Seghers, 1968: [183]-

188 (Musiciens de tous les temps, 38)
((-))

2658 WIENKE, Gerhard: ... Schallplatten in
Phonoprisma (March-April 1965): 37
((-))

SCHUETZENDORF, GUSTAV

2659 DENNIS, J.: Gustav Schuetzendorf in
Record Collector, XVIII/11-12 (December 1969): 282-283 ((-)); Addenda:
Record Collector, XIX/7-8 (November
1970): 91-92 ((-))

SCHUMAN, WILLIAM HOWARD, 1910-

2660 List of records in SCHREIBER, Flora
Rheta: William Schuman, by Flora
Rheta Schreiber and Vincent PERSI-
CHETTI. New York: G. Schirmer,
[1954]: 131-132 ((-))

SCHUMANN, ELISABETH, 1885-1952

2661 CONE, John: The records in Record
Collector, VII/10 (October 1952):
233-239 ((3, 6)); Addenda: Record Collector, VIII/2 (February 1953): 44-45
((-)); VIII/5 (May 1953): 119 ((-))

SCHUMANN, ROBERT ALEXANDER, 1810-
1856

2662 Les disques in BOUCOURECHLIEV,
André: Schumann. [Paris]: Éditions du
Seuil, [1956]: 188-189 (Solfèges, 2) ((-))

2663 A selected discography from Great
Britain and America in BOUCOURECH-
LIEV, André: Schumann. New York:
Grove Press, [c1959]: 190-192 (Ever-
green profile book, 2) ((-))

2664 Discographie in BRION, Marcel:
Schumann et l'âme romantique. Paris:
A. Michel, [1954]: [411]-412 (Génie et
destinée) ((-))

2665 List of recommended recordings in
BRION, Marcel: Schumann & the
romantic age. London: Collins, 1956:
363-367 ((-))

2666 Discographie in BUENZOD, Emmanuel: Robert Schumann: l'homme et
son oeuvre. [Paris]: Éditions Seghers,
[1965]: 187-190 (Musiciens de tous les
temps, 16) ((-))

2667 Discographie in COEUROY, André:
Robert Schumann. Paris: La Colombe,
[1950]: [182]-190 (Collection Euterpe,
[no. 9]) ((-))

2668 Schallplattenverzeichnis in LAUX,
Karl: Robert Schumann. [1. Aufl.]

Leipzig: P. Reclam, 1972: 309-317
(Reclams Universal-Bibliothek, 119)
((-))

2669 LAWRENCE, Harold: Schumann on LP
in Saturday Review (July 28, 1956):
36-37, 41 ((-))

2670 NYS, Carl de: Catalogue commenté et
discographie critique in Schumann.
Paris: Réalités/Hachette 1970: [249]-
[273] ((-))

2671 PIRIE, Peter J.: A bibliography of
Schumann records in Music Review,
XVII/3 (August 1956): 238-242 ((5))

2672 [[PLE, Roberto: [Discography] in
Discofilia (July-August 1956): 180]]

2673 Recorded works of Schumann in
SCHAUFFLER, Robert Haven:
Florestan: the life and work of
Robert Schumann. New York: Holt,
[1945]: 533-538 ((-))

2674 Recorded works of Schumann in
SCHAUFFLER, Robert Haven:
Florestan: the life and work of
Robert Schumann. New York: Dover
Publications, [1963, c1945]: 533-538
((-))

2675 SCHONBERG, Harold C.: The collector's Chopin and Schumann. Philadelphia: Lippincott, [1959]: 256 pp.
(Keystone books, KB-8) ((-))

2676 Recorded works of Schumann in
SPAETH, Sigmund: Dedication: the
love story of Clara and Robert Schumann. New York: Holt, [1950]: 167-171
((-))

2677 Skladby Roberta Schumanna na čs.
dlouhohrajících deskách in SÝKORA,
Václav Jan: Robert Schumann [1. vyd.]
Praha: Supraphon, 1967: 206-209
(Hudební profily, 16) ((-))

2678 Discography in YOUNG, Percy M.:
Tragic muse: the life and works of
Robert Schumann. London: Hutchinson,
[1957]: 241-243 ((-))

2679 Discography in YOUNG, Percy M.:
Tragic music: the life and works of
Robert Schumann. [Enl. ed.] London:
D. Dobson, [1961]: 241-243 ((-))

Works, Chorus

2680 MORSE, Peter: Schubert/Schumann/
Brahms choral music. Utica, NY: J. F.
Weber, 1970. 12 pp. (Discography
series, 5) ((3, 4, 6, 7))

Works, Instrumental

2681 SCHONBERG, Harold C.: Schumann:
orchestral and chamber music in High

Fidelity, VII/12 (December 1957): 103-112 ((–))

Works, Piano

2682 SCHONBERG, Harold C.: The piano music of Robert Schumann in High Fidelity, VI/9 (September 1956): 85-93 ((–))

Concerto, Piano

2683 Discographie 1971 in Diapason, No. 155 (March 1971): 31 ((–))

Dichterliebe

2684 ROSTAND, Claude: Discographie comparée in Harmonie, No. 18 (June 1966): 81-83 ((–))

2685 WORBS, Hans-Christoph: Schumann Dichterliebe—eine vergleichende Dis-kografie in fono forum 1961 (No. 11, November): 30 ((–))

Frauenliebe und Leben

2686 Schumann: Frauenliebe und Leben; eine vergleichende Discographie zum Leiderzyklus op. 42 in Phono, X/1 (September-October 1963): 20-21 ((–))

Songs

2687 WEBER, J. F.: Schuman Lieder. Utica, NY: Weber, 1971: 20 pp. (Discography series, 3) ((–))

Symphonies

2688 VOKURKA, Klaus Alexander: Die vier Symphonien Robert Schumanns auf Schallplatten. Eine vergleichende Discographie in Phono, XII/4 (March-April 1966): 99-102 ((–))

SCHUMANN-HEINK, ERNESTINE, 1861-1936

2689 FREESTONE, J.: The records—Ernestine Schumann-Heink in Record News, II/8 (April 1958): 272-277 ((–)); Addenda: Record News, II/9 (May 1958): 333 ((–)); III/9 (May 1959): 333 ((–))

2690 MORAN, W. R.: Recordings of Ernestine Schumann-Heink in Record Collector, XVII/5-6 (June 1967): 118-144 ((1, 3, 4, 5, 6, 7)) [Includes notes on playing speeds] Corrections: Record Collector, XX/6-7 (May 1972): 163-166 ((–))

2691 NATAN, Alex: [Diskografie] in fono forum 1969 (No. 1, January): 16 ((–))

SCHURICHT, KARL, 1880-1967

2692 Enregistrements réalises sous la direction de Carl Schuricht in GAVOTY, Bernard: Carl Schuricht. Genève: R. Kister, 1954: [32] (Les Grands interprètes) ((–))

2693 Recordings by Carl Schuricht in GAVOTY, Bernard: Carl Schuricht. Geneva: R. Kister, c1956: [32] (Great concert artists) ((–))

2694 SCHREIBER, Ulrich: Diskografie in Hi Fi Stereophonie (January 1971): 9 ((–))

2695 SCHREIBER, Ulrich: Erhältiche Schallplatten mit Carl Schuricht in Hi Fi Stereophonie, III/4 (April 1964): 207-208 ((–))

SCHUTZENDORF, LEO, 1886-1931

2696 DENNIS, J.: The records in Record Collector, XVI/9-10 (January 1966): 235-236 ((–))

SCHWARZKOPF, ELISABETH, 1915-

2697 CLOUGH, F. F., and G. J. CUMING: A Schwarzkopf diskography in Gramophone Record Review, No. 56 (June 1958): 660, 706 ((–))

2698 Diskographie in Collegium Musicum 1970 (No. 1): 14-17 ((–)); 1971 (No. 8): 13-14 ((–))

2699 FRANCESCO, A. di: The records of Elisabeth Schwarzkopf in Record News, I/9 (May 1957): 322-332 ((–))

2700 Records made by Elisabeth Schwarzkopf in GAVOTY, Bernard: Elisabeth Schwarzkopf. Geneva: R. Kister, [195-]: 25-30 (Great concert artists) ((–))

2701 KESTING, J.: Diskographie Elisabeth Schwarzkopf in Opern Welt (February 1972): 28 ((5))

SCHWEITZER, ALBERT, 1875-1965

2702 IONIO, Daniele: Discografia italiana di Albert Schweitzer in Discoteca, No. 54 (October 1965): 16 ((–))

SCOTT, CYRIL, 1879-1970

2703 MASON, D. H.: Cyril Scott: a discography [as performer] in 78 RPM, No. 8 (November 1969): 56 ((3, 6, 7))

SCOTTI, ANTONIO, 1866-1936

2704 HARVEY, H. Hugh: List of records in Gramophone, No. 193 (June 1939): 37-38 ((7))

2705 REUTLINGER, Dale: Antonio Scotti: a
discography in Maestro, I/1-2 (Janu-
ary-July 1969): 36-38 ((7)); I/3-4
(August-December 1969): 31 ((7))

SCOTTO, RENATA

2706 VEGETO, Raffaele: Discografia del
soprano Renata Scotto in Discoteca,
No. 73 (November 1967): 26-27 ((5))

SCRIABIN, ALEXANDER
See SKRIABIN, ALEKSANDR
NIKOLAEVICH

SEEFRIED, IRMGARD, 1919-
See also listing for SCHNEIDERHAN,
WOLFGANG. Discographie in Fass-
bind, Franz: Wolfgang Schneiderhan,
Irmgard Seefried: eine Künstler [und]
Lebensgemeinschaft

2707 KRAUS, Gottfried: Schallplattenverzeichnis in fono forum 1974 (No. 9,
September): 812-813 ((7)); Addenda:
fono forum 1974 (No. 12, December):
1227 ((-))

SEINEMEYER, META

2708 HESSER, J. W. C.: Meta Seinemeyer in
Record Collector, XIV/7-8 (n.d.): 163-
168 ((3)); Addenda: Record Collector,
XIV/11-12: 278 ((3))

SEMBRICH, MARCELLA, 1858-1935

2709 MORAN, W. R.: The recordings of
Marcella Sembrich in Record Collector, XVIII/5-6 (May 1969): 110-138
((1, 3, 4, 5, 6, 7)); Addenda: Record
Collector, XVIII/7 (July 1969): 164;
XX/6-7 (May 1972): 165-166 [In-
cludes notes on playing speeds]

2710 STEINBERG, B. E.: Marcella
Sembrich: the records in Record
Collector, IV/7 (July 1949): 106-108
((-))

SENIUS, FELIX

2711 [[WILHELM, P.: [Discography] in
Record News, III/2 (July 1959)]]

SERKIN, RUDOLF, 1903-

2712 HAMON, Jean: Discographie de Rudolf
Serkin in Diapason, No. 106 (April
1966): 19 ((-))

SHAFRAN, DANIIL BORISOVICH, 1923-

2713 [Discography] in IAMPOL'SKIĬ, Izrail'
Markovich: Daniil Shafran: Nar. artist
RSFR. Moskva: Sov. kompositor, 1974:
52-[56] ((-))

SHALIÂPIN, FEDOR IVANOVICH, 1873-1938

2714 DECHAMPS, Eric: Discographie in
Diapason, No. 176 (April 1973): 15
((-))

2715 EDNEY, Eric: List of Chaliapin recordings available in the U.S.S.R. in
Record Collector, X/12 (November
1956): 275-276 ((-)); Addenda: Record
Collector, XII/3 (March 1958): 68
((3, 6))

2716 [Discography] in Fedor Ivanovich
Shaliapin. Moskva: Iskusstvo,
1959-1960: 509-519 ((7))

2717 Discographie de Chaliapine in
FESCHOTTE, Jacques: Ce géant:
Féodor Chaliapine. Paris: la Table
ronde, 1968: 223-[226] ((-))

2718 Discographie in GOURY, Jean: Fedor
Chaliapine: iconographie, biographie,
discographie. Paris: Société de dif-
fusion d'art lyrique, (19, rue du
Départ), [1969]: [64]-74 (Monstres
sacrés) ((7))

2719 KELLY, Alan: Fedor Ivanovich
Chaliapin—a discography in Record
Collector, XX/8-10 (August 1972):
184-230 ((3, 4, 6, 7))

2720 [[SEMEONOFF, Boris: Fedor
Chaliapine in Record Collector, V/6
(June 1950): 125-141]]; Addenda: Record Collector, VI/8 (August 1951):
189-190 ((-)); XI/7 (July 1957): 162-
163 ((3))

SHANKAR, RAVI, 1920-

2721 IONIO, Daniele: Discografia in Discoteca, No. 61 (June 1966): 20 ((-))

SHOSTAKOVICH, DMITRIĬ DMITRIEVICH,
1906-1975

2722 Schallplattenverzeichnis in BROCK-
HAUS, Heinz Alfred: Dmitri
Schostakowitsch. Leipzig: Philipp
Reclam Jun., [1962]: [190]-195 ((-))

2723 [Discography] in DANILEVICH, Lev
Vasil'evich: Nash Sovremennik;
tvorcestvo Shostakovicha. Moskva:
Muzyka, 1965: 327-[329] ((-))

2724 Discographie in HOFMANN, Rostislav:
Dimitri Chostakovich: l'homme et son
oeuvre. [Paris]: Seghers, [1963]: 183-

187 (Musiciens de tous les temps, 1)
((-))

2725 Schallplattenverzeichnis in LAUX,
Karl: Dmitri Schostakowitsch:
Chronist seines Volkes. Berlin:
Deutscher Kulturbund, 1966: 47-49
(Beiträge sur Kulturpolitik) ((-))

2726 [Discography] in SADOVNIKOV, E. L.:
D.D. Shostakovitch; Notografichiskii i
bibliograficheskii spravochnik.
Moskva: "Muzyka," 1965: 143-150
((-))

2727 SANTOMARTINO, Pasquale: Dimitri
Shostakovitch; discografia in Musica e
Dischi, XIX (No. 203, May 1963): 48
((-))

2728 WEBER, Jan: Dyskografia in MEYER,
Krzysztof: Szostakowicz. Wyd. 1.
Kraków: Polskie Wydawn. Muzyczne,
[1973]: 184-227 ((1, 5))

Works, Piano

2729 [Discography] in DEL'SON, Viktor
IUl'evich: Fortepiannoe tvorchestvo
D.D. Shostakovicha. Moskva: Sov.
Kompozitor, 1971: 243-[244] ((-))

Symphonies

2730 BROWN, Royal S.: Shostakovitch's
symphonies; an appraisal of the music
and the recordings in High Fidelity,
XIX/4 (April 1969): 43-47, 94 ((-))

2731 HARDEN, Ingo: Die besprochenen
Aufnahmen in fono forum 1971
(No. 9, September): 649 ((-))

SIBELIUS, JEAN, 1865-1957

2732 AFFELDER, Paul: A Sibelius discography in High Fidelity, V/9
(November 1955): 79-86 ((-))

2733 Records of Sibelius' works in
ARNOLD, Elliott: Finlandia: the
story of Sibelius. New York: H.
Holt and Co., [c1941]: 232-236 ((-))

2734 Recordings of Sibelius' works in
ARNOLD, Elliott: Finlandia: the
story of Sibelius. [1st rev. print-
ing]. New York: Holt, [1950]: 238-
242 ((-))

2735 BAUMAN, J. C.: Sibelius on record—
a selective review and discography
in Le Grand Baton, II/4 (October-
December 1965): 1-25 ((-))

2736 CLOUGH, F. F., and G. J. CUMING:
Sibelius on microgroove in Gramophone Record Review (Christmas
1955): vi-vii ((-))

2737 Diskographie (Auswahl) in Phonoprisma (November-December 1965):
159 ((-))

2738 HAMON, Jean: Discographie in Diapason, No. 103 (January 1966): 39 ((-))

2739 HEININEN, Paavo J.: Fennica
leveysarja skivserie—record series;
33 1/3 long playing in Music Journal,
XX/7 (October 1962): 44 ((-))

2740 JOHNSON, Harold Edgar: Jean
Sibelius: the recorded music—
Musiikkia äänilevyillä—Grammo-
foninspelningar. Helsinki: R. E.
Westerlund, [1957]: 31 pp. ((-))

2741 KRELLMANN, Hanspeter: Diskographie in Musica, XXIV/5 (September-
October 1970): 444 ((-))

2742 A selected discography in LEVAS,
Santeri: Sibelius: a personal portrait.
[1st American ed.] Lewisburg, [Pa.]:
Bucknell University Press, [1973,
c1972]: 154-157 ((5))

2743 [[MOLES, E.: [Discography] in
Discofilia, No. 17 (October 1957):
387]]

2744 Music on record: Jean Sibelius in
Audio and Record Review (April 1969):
254 ((-))

2745 TROTTER, William R.: Sibelius on
microgroove; a selective discography
in High Fidelity, XV/12 (December
1965): 52-53, 145 ((-))

2746 Discographie in VIGNAL, Marc: Jean
Sibelius l'homme et son oeuvre.
[Paris]: P. Seghers, 1965: [185]-188
(Musiciens de tous les temps, 22)
((-))

2747 Werke von Jean Sibelius auf Schallplatten in Sibelius Mitteilung, No. 1
(March 1958): 13-15 ((-))

Symphonies

2748 GOLDSMITH, Harris: Sibelius' seven
symphonies; a critic's view of the
recordings in High Fidelity, XIX/5
(May 1969): 56-60 ((-))

SIEMS, MARGARETHE

2749 WILHELM, P.: Discography in Record
News, II/12 (August 1958): 425-426 ((-))

SIGNORIANI, FRANCESCO

2750 CELLETTI, Rodolfo: Discografia
secondo del Bauer in Musica e Dischi,
IX (No. 81, June 1953): 8 ((7))

2751 [[[Discography] in Record News, II/10
(June 1958)]]

SILJA, ANJA

2752 Diskographie in Phonoprisma, V/6
(November-December 1962): 162
((-))

2753 SCHNEIDER, Günter: Diskografie in
fono forum 1962 (No. 8, August): 27
((-))

SILVESTRI, ALESSANDRO

2754 FREESTONE, John: Collectors' corner
in Gramophone, No. 356 (January
1953): 193 ((-))

SILVESTRI, CONSTANTIN, 1913-1969

2755 CLOUGH, F. F., and G. J. CUMING:
Constantin Silvestri; a diskography in
Gramophone Record Review, No. 87
(January 1961): 138-139 ((-))

2756 CLOUGH, F. F., and G. J. CUMING:
Discography in Audio and Record Review, III/2 (October 1963): 20-21 ((-))

SIMON-GIRAD, JULIETTE

2757 BRY, Michel de: Discographie in
Disques, No. 7 (August-September
1948): 209 ((5))

SIMPSON, ROBERT WILFRED LEVICK, 1921-

2758 [[List of works and discography in
Robert Simpson: fiftieth birthday es-
says. Edited by Edward JOHNSON.
London: Triad Press, 1971: 27-28]]

2759 Recordings of music by Robert Simpson in Recorded Sound, No. 47 (July
1972): 84 ((1, 7))

SINGERS

2760 Appendix in HURST, P. G.: The golden
age recorded. Henfield, Sussex, 1946:
133-175 ((7))

2761 [[Appendix in HURST, P. G.: The golden
age recorded. New and rev. ed. Ling-
field, Surrey: Oakwood Press, 1963]]

2762 [[Discography in NATAN, Alex: Prima
donna; Lob der Stimmen. Basel:
Basilius Presse, [1962]: 116-135]]

SKRÍABIN, ALEKSANDR NIKOLAEVICH,
1872-1915

2763 Selected discography in BOWERS,
Faubion: Scriabin: a biography of the
Russian composer, 1871-1915. Tokyo;
Palo Alto, CA: Kodansha Interna-
tional, [1969]: 283-292 ((-))

2764 LEMAIRE, Frans: Scriabin in Revue
des Disques, No. 203 (March 1972):
200-201 ((-))

2765 PRIEBERG, Fred K.: Skriabin Diskographie in Hi Fi Stereophonie, XI/1
(January 1972): 16-20 ((-))

2766 Schallplattenverzeichnis in SKRJABIN,
Alexander: Prometheische Phantasien.
München-Gräfelfing: W. Wollenweber,
1968: v-vii (Original edition published
Stuttgart, 1924, has no discography)
((-))

2767 SPINGEL, Hans Otto: Diskografie in
fono forum 1962 (No. 10, October): 14
((-))

SLEZAK, LEO, 1873-1946

2768 KAUFMAN, Thomas G.: Leo Slezak;
discography in Record Collector, XV/
9-10: 208-235 ((3, 4, 5, 6, 7))

SLOBODSKAYA, ODA, 1889-1970

2769 BARNES, Harold, and Sylvia JUNGE:
Oda Slobodskaya discography in Recorded Sound, No. 35 (July 1969):
502-511 ((1, 3, 4, 6, 7))

SLOVENSKÁ FILHARMÓNIA

2770 Dicla nahrané Slovenskou filharmónia
na gramofónové platne in KOVÁŘOVÁ,
Anna: Slovenská filharmónia. Praha:
Panton, 1966: 218-219 ((-))

SMETANA, BEDŘICH, 1824-1884

2771 [[BARTOŠ, Jaroslav: Smetanova
hudba na gramofonových deskách.
Praha: Universum, 1947: 209 pp.]]

2772 BENNETT, John Reginald: Smetana on
3000 records. [Blandford]: Oakwood
Press, 1974: 466 pp. ((4, 7))

2773 Discothek in BOESE, Helmut: Zwei
Urmusikanten: Smetana, Dvořák.
Zürich: Amalthea Verlag, [1955]:
426-429 ((-))

2774 Gramodesky in ČEJKOVÁ, Stanislava:
Bedřich Smetana, 1824-1884: výběrová
bibliogr. k 150. výročí narození.
Hradec Králové: Kraj. knihovna; Státní
vědecká knihovna, 1974: 44-84 ((-))

2775 ECKSTEIN, Pavel: Diskografie auf
Supraphon; auf Deutsche Grammophon
in fono forum 1960 (No. 10, October):
9 ((-))

2776 Výběrový seznam skladeb a diskografie
in KARÁSEK, Bohumil: Bedřich
Smetana. [1. vyd.]. Praha: Státní

hudební vydavatelství, 1966: 104-120
(Editio Supraphon) ((-))

2777   Bedřich Smetana's music on gramophone records in NOLAN, Liam: The
life of Smetana: the pain and the glory.
London; Toronto: Harrap, 1968:
[324]-328 ((-))

2778   [[OČADLÍK, Mirko: Smetanovská
diskografie kritický soupis gram.
snímků Smet. hudby. Praha: Orbis,
1939: 162 pp.]]

2779   Skladby Bedřicha Smetany nahrané na
gramofonových deskách in OČADLÍK,
Mirko: Vyprávění o Bedřichu
Smetanovi. [Praha]: Panton, 1960:
151-160 (Čtení o hudbě, 8) ((-))

2780   VOJAN, Jar. E. S.: Smetana's works
obtainable on records in Phonograph
Monthly Review, I/5 (February
1927): 239 ((-))

2781   VOJAN, J. E. S.: A Smetana discography in Phonograph Monthly Review,
IV/11 (August 1930): 372 ((-))

Piano Music

2782   [[OČADLÍK, Mirko: Klavirní dílo
Bedřicha Smetany: vydáno ke kompletu
gramofonových desek klavirního dla
Bedřicha Smetany. Praha: SHV, 1961]]

SMETANOVO KVARTETO

2783   ECKSTEIN, Pavel: Diskografie
Smetana-Quartett in fono forum 1964
(No. 4, April): 154 ((-))

2784   Diskografie Smetanova kvarteta in
ŠEFL, Vladimír: Smetanovo kvarteto.
1. vyd. Praha: Supraphon, 1974: 72-74
(Edice Lyra) ((7))

SMETERLIN, JAN, 1892-1967

2785   Appendix; Jan Smeterlin's recordings
in Karol Szymanowski, Jan Smeterlin
in correspondence and essays. London: Allegro Press, 196-?: 135-137
((1))

SMIRNOFF, DMITRI

2786   STRATTON, John: Smirnoff discography in Record Collector, XIV/11-12
(n.d.): 245-277 ((3))

SOBINOV, LEONID VITAL'EVICH, 1872-1934

2787   [Discography] in Leonid Vitalyevich
Sobinov. Vstupit ctat'ya V. M.
Boganova-Bepevovskogo, s 5-48.

Moskva: Iskusstvo, 1970: 427-[430]
((7))

2788   NADEJIN, Nicolai: Leonid Sobinoff in
Gramophone, IV/5 (October 1926): 188
((-))

SOFRONITSKIĬ, VLADIMIR LVADIMIROVICH,
1901-1961

2789   Diskografiya in Vospominaniya o
Siforonitskom. Sbornik. Moskva: Sov.
Kompozitor, 1970: 661-[672] ((-))

SOLER, ANTONIO, 1729-1783

2790   HUGHES, Eric, and Diana HULL: Soler
discography in Recorded Sound, No.
55-56 (July-October 1974): 353-356
((1)); Errata in Recorded Sound, No.
59 (July 1975), 464 ((-))

SOLTI, SIR GEORG, 1912-

2791   ASHMAN, Mike: Solti discography in
Records and Recording, XVIII/9
(June 1975): 16-17 ((5))

2792   CLOUGH, F. F., and G. J. CUMING: A
Solti discography in Audio and Record
Review, I/1 (September 1961): 29 ((-))

2793   Georg Solti on disc in High Fidelity,
XIX/10 (October 1969): 71 ((-))

2794   Georg Solti: 25 ans de disques; discographie complete in Diapason, No.
170 (October 1972): 6-7 ((-))

2795   HIRSCH, Nicole: Discographie Georg
Solti in Diapason, No. 114 (February
1967): 41 ((-))

2796   SPINGEL, Hans Otto: Aus der Diskografie in fono forum 1961 (No. 11,
November): 27 ((-))

SOMERS, HARRY STUART, 1925-

2797   Discography in CHERNEY, Brian:
Harry Somers. Toronto; Buffalo:
University of Toronto Press, [1975]:
[165]-166 ((-))

SONATAS, PIANO

2798   DARRELL, R. D.: Recorded piano
sonatas in Music Lover's Guide, I/10
(June 1933): 299-300, 304 ((-))

SONGS

2799   [Discography for each song] in
MOORE, Gerald: Singer and accom-
panist: the performance of fifty songs.
London: Methuen, 1953: 232 pp. ((-))

2800 [Discography for each song] in
MOORE, Gerald: Singer and accompanist: the performance of fifty songs.
Westport, Conn.: Greenwood Press,
1973: 232 pp. ((-))

2801 STAHL, Dorothy: A selected discography of solo song. Detroit: Information Coordinators, 1968: xi, 90 pp.
(Detroit studies in music bibliography,
13) ((-))

2802 STAHL, Dorothy: A selected discography of solo song: a cumulation through
1971. Detroit: Information Coordinators, 1972: 137 pp. (Detroit studies in
music bibliography, 24) ((-))

SONGS, CHILEAN

2803 Discographie in CLOUZET, Jean: La
nouvelle chanson chilienne. Paris:
Seghers, c1975: 253-256 ((-))

SOUZAY, GÉRARD, 1918-

2804 Auswahl Diskografie in fono forum
1967 (No. 7, July): 439 ((-))

2805 Discographie in Diapason, No. 163
(January 1972): 11 ((-))

2806 WEIHER-WAEGE, Hortensia: Folgende
Schallplatten... in fono forum 1961
(No. 3, March): 14 ((-))

SPANI, HINA

2807 The recordings of Hina Spani in Record
Collector, IX/4 (September 1954): 98-
99 ((3, 7))

SPOHR, LUDWIG, 1784-1859

2808 [[POWELL, M.: New appraisement of
Spohr in Music (SMA), IV/1 (1970):
6-8]]

SPRONGL, NORBERT

2809 Schallplattenverzeichnis in STOCK-
HAMMER, Robert: Norbert Sprongl:
eine Monographie. Wien: Lafite, 1973:
53 ((-))

STADER, MARIA, 1918-

2810 Discography in Soprano; Joh. Seb.
Bach: St. Matthew's Passion; Aria:
Aus Liebe will mein Heiland sterben.
Zürich: Panton Publishers; distributed
by C. F. Peters, 1968: 101-104 [Note:
Master class lesson with accompanying
sound recording] ((-))

STÁTNÍ FILHARMONIE BRNO

2811 Seznam gramofonových desek nahraných
Státní filharmonii Brno in MAJER, Jírí:
Státní filharmonie Brno: 1956-1966;
jubilejní sborník Státní filharmonie v
Brně, laureáta Státní ceny Klementa
Gottwalda. [Vyd. 1.] V Brně: Nakl.
Blok, 1965: 99 ((-))

STEEL, ROBERT

2812 ZITZMAN, Manfred S.: Early recordings by Robert Steel in Record Collector, XXII/1-2 (May 1974): 43 ((1, 7))

STEFANO, GIUSEPPE DI, 1921-

2813 Zehn Ausgewählte Schallplatten in
EGGERS, Heino: Giuseppe di Stefano.
Berlin: Rembrandt-Verlag, 1967: [30]-
[32] (Rembrandt-Reihe, 56) ((-))

2814 ROSENTHAL, Harold: Di Stefano recordings in Gramophone, No. 373
(June 1954): 4 ((-))

STEPP, CHRISTOPH

2815 LEWINSKI, Wolf-Eberhard von: Diskografie in fono forum 1962 (No. 9,
September): 27 ((-))

STERN, ISAAC, 1920-

2816 CLOUGH, F. F., and G. J. CUMING:
Discography in Audio and Record Review, II/11 (July 1963): 17, 61-62 ((-))

STEUERMANN, EDWARD
See listing for BUSONI, FERRUC-
CIO. Åhlén, Carl-Gunnar: Ferruccio
Busoni (1866-1924)

STEVENS, BERNARD, 1916-

2817 Recordings by Bernard Stevens in Recorded Sound, No. 60 (October 1975):
484-485 ((1, 7))

STEVENSON, RONALD, 1928-

2818 Ronald Stevenson recordings in Recorded Sound, No. 42-43 (April-July
1971): 755 ((1, 7))

STILL, WILLIAM GRANT, 1895-

2819 The discography in HAAS, Robert
Bartlett: William Grant Still and the
fusion of cultures in American music.

Los Angeles: Black Sparrow Press,
1972: [167]-170 ((5))

STOCK, FREDERICK, 1872-1942

2820 HURKA, Joseph H.: The Frederick
Stock recordings in Le Grand Baton,
VI/2 (May 1969): 7-13 ((-))

STOCKHAUSEN, KARLHEINZ, 1928-

2821 Discography in COTT, Jonathan:
Stockhausen; conversations with the
composer. New York: Simon and
Schuster, [1973]: 249-262 ((-))

2822 Discography in COTT, Jonathan:
Stockhausen; conversations with the
composer. London: Robson Books,
1974: 249-252 ((-))

2823 Discography in HARVEY, Jonathan:
The music of Stockhausen: an introduction. London: Faber, 1975: 136-139
((-))

2824 Discography in HARVEY, Jonathan:
The music of Stockhausen: an introduction. Berkeley: University of California Press, 1975: 136-139 ((-))

2825 Karlheinz Stockhausen diskografi in
Dansk Musiktidsskrift, XLVII/4 (December 1972): 120 ((-))

2826 SZERSNOVICZ, Patrick: Catalogue des
oeuvres; discographie in Musique en
Jeu, No. 15 (September 1974): [35]-40
((-))

2827 Catalogue of Stockhausen's works,
comprising discography in WÖRNER,
Karl H.: Stockhausen: life and work.
Berkeley: University of California
Press, 1973: [21]-29 ((-))

2828 Catalogue of Stockhausen's works,
comprising discography in WÖRNER,
Karl H.: Stockhausen: life and work.
London: Faber, 1973: [21]-29 ((-))

2829 Catalogue of Stockhausen's works,
comprising discography in WÖRNER,
Karl H.: Stockhausen: life and work.
London: Pan Books, 1974: [21]-29 ((-))

STOKOWSKI, LEOPOLD, 1882-1977

2830 Diskographie in Collegium Musicum
1970 (No. 3): 11 ((-))

2831 LUND, Ivan: The Leopold Stokowski
discography, [by] Ivan Lund and
Edward JOHNSON in JOHNSON, Edward:
Stokowski: essays in analysis of his
art. London: Triad Press, 1973: 85-
114 ((1, 4, 5, 7))

STOLZ, ROBERT, 1882-1975

2832 Discographie in BRÜMMEL, Wolf-
Dietrich: Robert Stolz: Melodie eines
Lebens; ein Komponist erobert die
Welt, von Wolf-Dietrich Brümmel und
Friedrich van BOOTH. Gütersloh:
Bertelsmann-Lesering; Stuttgart:
Europäischer Buch- und Phonoklub;
Wien: Buchgemeinschaft Donauland,
[1967]: 191-198 ((-))

STORCHIO, ROSINA, 1876-1945

2833 CELLETTI, Rodolfo: The records in
Record News, IV/12 (August 1960): 434-
436; [From Musica e Dischi, April
1954] ((-))

2834 GARA, Eugenio, and Rodolfo CEL-
LETTI: Edizione discografiche in
Musica e Dischi, X (No. 91, April
1954): 4 ((7))

2835 [HUTCHINSON, Tom]: Discography in
Record Collector, XII/3 (March 1958):
58-60 ((1, 3, 7))

STRACCIARI, RICCARDO

2836 ARMSTRONG, F.: The records in Record News, III/3 (November 1958): 84-
92 ((3, 5))

2837 CAPUTO, Pietro: Discografia di
Stracciari in Musica e Dischi, XVIII
(No. 188, February 1962): 72 ((7))

2838 CASKETT, James: Stracciari in
Gramophone I/7 (December 1923):
125 ((-))

2839 VEGETO, Raffaele: Discografia in
Musica e Dischi, XI (No. 106, June
1955): 18 ((7))

STRAUBE, KARL, 1873-1950

2840 ÅHLÉN, Carl-Gunnar: Karl Straube
(1873-1950) in Musik Revy, XXVII/2
(1972): 101-103 (Grammofonens
veteraner, 5) ((1, 3, 5))

STRAUSS, EDVARD

2841 [[POVEY, Philip G.: Recordings of the
music of the Strauss family conducted
by the late Edward Strauss. Wembley,
Eng.: Johann Strauss Society of Great
Britain, 1972]]

STRAUSS, JOHANN, 1825-1899
See also listing for WIENER PHIL-
HARMONIKER. Grasberger, Franz:
Die Wiener Philharmoniker bei Johann
Strauss

2842 Anhang: Waltzes by J. Strauss and others in ENDLER, Franz: Das Walzer-Buch: Johann Strauss: die Wiener Aufforderung zum Tanz. Wien: Kremayr & Scheriau, 1975: 233-235 ((-))

2843 Discografie in POLS, André M.: Het leven van J. Strauss. Brussel: Reinaert Uitgaven, [1969]: 44-48 (Meesters der toonkunst, 13) ((-))

2844 Walzer von Strauss in fono forum 1960 (No. 2, February): 33 ((-))

Die Fledermaus

2845 BOLLERT, Werner: [Diskografie] in fono forum 1966 (No. 10, October): 530 ((-))

2846 HÖSLINGER, Clemens: [Diskografie] in fono forum 1967 (No. 2, February): 62 ((-))

2847 TEMUSSINO, Ursula: Holdes Winder Fledermaus—Joh. Strauss in Phono, XII/6 (July-August 1966): 151-154 ((-))

STRAUSS, RICHARD, 1864-1949

2848 ÅHLÉN, Carl-Gunnar: Richard Strauss (1864-1949) in Musik Revy, XXVI/4 (1971): 218-219 (Grammofonens veteraner, 1) ((5, 7))

2849 Discographie in BÖHM, Karl: Begegnung mit Richard Strauss, hrsg. und eingeleitet von Franz Eugen DOSTAL. Wien: Doblinger, [c1964]: 66-71 ((5))

2850 BRITZIUS and FISHER: List of recorded music of Richard Strauss in Gramophone, III/4 (September 1925): 103; III/9 (February 1926): 421 ((-))

2851 BURKE, C. G.: Richard Strauss on microgroove in High Fidelity, IV/2 (April 1954): 59-76 ((-))

2852 COHN, Bernardo: Discografía in ERHARDT, Otto: Richard Strauss: su vida y su obra. Buenos Aires: Ricordi Americana, [1950]: 361-367 ((-))

2853 COHN, Bernardo: Discographie in ERHARDT, Otto: Richard Strauss: Leben, Wirken, Schaffen. Olten: O. Walter, [1953]: 370-384 (Musikerreihe, 13) ((-))

2854 Discography of Strauss as a performer in DEL MAR, Norman: Richard Strauss: a critical commentary on his life and works. Philadelphia: Chilton Book Co., [1969-]: v. 3, [505]-509 ((1))

2855 Richard Strauss: select discography in DEL MAR, Norman: Richard Strauss: a critical commentary on his life and works. London: Barrie and Jenkins, 1972: v. 3, 507-509 ((1))

2856 Discographie in DEPPISCH, Walter: Richard Strauss in Selbstzeugnissen und Bilddokumenten. [Reinbek b. Hamburg]: Rowohlt, [1968]: 174-[180] (Rowohlts Monographien, 146) ((-))

2857 Discografia in L'Approdo Musicale, II/5 (January-March 1959): 112-120 ((-))

2858 Empfehlenswerte Schallplatten mit Werken von Richard Strauss in Hi Fi Stereophonie, III/6 (June 1964): 309-310 ((-))

2859 [[Discography in ERHARDT, Otto: Richard Strauss: la vita e l'opera. Milan: Ricordi, 1957]]

2860 GLASS, Herbert: Richard Strauss on microgroove in High Fidelity, XII/3 (March 1962): 50-52, 115-[122] ((-))

2861 Choix de disques in GOLÉA, Antoine: Richard Strauss. Paris: Flammarion, [1965]: [273] ((-))

2862 Discographie in JAMEUX, Dominique: Richard Strauss. [Paris]: Éditions du Seuil, [1971]: 184-185 (Solfèges, 31) ((-))

2863 [[[Discography] in KRAUSE, Ernst: Richard Strauss: Gestalt und Werk. 3 veränd Aufl. Leipzig; Wiesbaden: Breitkopf & Härtel, 1963: 603 pp.]]

2864 [[[Discography] in KRAUSE, Ernst: Richard Strauss: Gestalt und Werk. 4 veränd Aufl. Leipzig: Breitkopf & Härtel, 1970: 619 pp.]]

2865 [[[Discography] in KRAUSE, Ernst: Richard Strauss Personalitatea şi opera. Bucuresti: Ed. muzicală a Uniunii compozitorilor din Republică Socialistă România, 1965: 574 pp.]]

2866 Records in KRAUSE, Ernst: Richard Strauss: the man and his work. [1st English ed.] London: Collett's, [1964]: 533-[556] ((5))

2867 Records in KRAUSE, Ernst: Richard Strauss: the man and his work. Boston: Crescendo Pub. Co., [1969]: 533-[556] ((5))

2868 [Discographical references] in MÜLLER von Asow, Erich Hermann: Richard Strauss: thematisches Verzeichnis. Wien: L. Doblinger, 1959 [i.e. 1955-1971] 2 v. ((-))

2869 [[MÜLLER VON ASOW, Erich Hermann: Richard Strauss als Interpret auf Schallplatten in Richard-Strauss Gesellschaft Mitteilung, No. 14 (August 1957): 13+]]

2870 Music on record: Richard Strauss in Audio and Record Review (May 1969): 330; Additions and corrections: Audio and Record Review (June 1969): 394 ((-))

2871 [[PENDERGAST, Herbert C.: Strauss and the phonograph in Richard-Strauss Gesellschaft Mitteilung, No. 25 (June 1960): 7]]

2872 PLEIJEL, Bengt: Richard Strauss och. grammofonen in Musik Revy, XIX/3 (1964): 103-106 ((-))

2873 [[Discographie in Richard Strauss, 1864-1949. Remscheid: Musikbiblio-thek d. Stadtbücheri, 1964: 10 leaves]]

2874 Discographie in ROSTAND, Claude: Richard Strauss. Paris: Colombe, 1949: [119]-121 ((-))

2875 Discographie selectionner in ROSTAND, Claude: Richard Strauss: l'homme et son oeuvre. [Paris]: Seghers, [1964]: [188]-189 (Musiciens de tous les temps, 12) ((-))

2876 Diskographie in Vienna. National-bibliothek: Richard-Strauss-Ausstell-ung zum 100. Geburtstag. Wien: Osterreichische Nationalbibliothek, 1964: 324-332 ((-))

Operas

2877 JEFFERSON, Alan: Richard Strauss's other operas in Opera, XX/10 (October 1969): 844-855 (Opera on the gramophone, 25) ((-))

2878 [[Discography] in NATAN, Alex: Die Opern. Basel; Stuttgart; Basilius Presse, 1963: 122 pp.]

2879 [[REULING, Karl F.: Opera on records in Opera News, XXI/13 (1956-1957): 22+]]

Songs

2880 HERZFELD, Friedrich: Diskografie in fono forum 1964 (No. 6, June): 247 ((-))

2881 MORSE, Peter: Richard Strauss Lieder. Preliminary edition. Utica, NY: Weber, 1970: 13 pp. ((3, 5, 6, 7))

2882 MORSE, Peter: Richard Strauss Lieder. Utica, NY: Weber, 1973: 46 pp. (Discography series, 7) ((3, 5, 6, 7))

Works, Orchestra

2883 SCHUMANN, Karl: Scheintod und Verklärung. Eine Diskografie der Orchesterwerke von Richard Strauss in fono forum 1964 (No. 6, June): 242-244 ((-))

Arabella

2884 JEFFERSON, Alan: Arabella in Opera, XVIII/1 (January 1967): 25-31 (Opera on the gramophone, 18) ((-))

Ariadne auf Naxos

2885 JEFFERSON, Alan: Ariadne auf Naxos in Opera, XIX/9 (September 1968): 203-213 (Opera on the gramophone, 20) ((-))

Don Juan

2886 [[SCHNOOR, Hans: Don Juan—sechsfach beleuchtet Richard Strauss und seine Dirigenten/versuch eines Querschnitts in Phono, II/4 (1955-1956): 6-9]]

Elektra

2887 JEFFERSON, Alan: Elektra in Opera, XVI/3 (March 1965): 164-168 (Opera on the gramophone, 14) ((-))

Die Frau ohne Schatten

2888 [[NORTON-WELSH, Christopher: Die Frau ohne Schatten—a discography in Richard Strauss Blätter, No. 2]]

Der Rosenkavalier

2889 Principaux enregistrements in Diapason, No. 144 (February 1970): 30-34 ((-))

2890 JEFFERSON, Alan: Der Rosenkavalier in Opera, XIV/3 (March 1963): 162-170 (Opera on the gramophone, 12) ((-))

2891 PIPER-ZIETHEN, Herta: Ein verg-leichende Diskografie in fono forum 1969 (No. 11, November): 736 ((-))

2892 Platten in PORNBACHER, Karl: Hugo von Hofmannsthal, Richard Strauss: Der Rosenkavalier; Interpretation. München: R. Oldenbourg, 1964: 109-110 (Interpretationen zum Deutschunterricht an den höhren Schulen) ((-))

Salome

2893 GEITEL, Klaus: Diskografie in fono forum 1962 (No. 6, June): 13 ((-))

2894 MANN, William: Salome in Opera, VIII/7 (July 1957): 420-425 (Opera on the gramophone, 3) ((-))

2895 SCHAUMKELL, Claus-Dieter: Salome ... ein vergleichende Dis-kografie in fono forum 1970 (No. 2, February): 72 ((1))

Till Eulenspigels lustige Streiche

2896 SCHUMANN, Karl: Diskografie in fono
forum 1963 (No. 5, May): 171 ((-))

STRAUSS FAMILY
See also listing for STRAUSS, EDVARD

2897 Recordings in PASTENE, Jerome:
Three-quarter time: the life and music
of the Strauss family of Vienna. Westport, Conn.: Greenwood Press, [1971,
c1951]: 262-279 ((-))

STRAVINSKIĬ, IGOR' FEDOROVICH, 1882-
1971
See also listings for: RAVEL, MAU-
RICE. Odriozola, Antonio: Las
grabacionnes en discos LP de seis
grandes figuras de la música contemporanea...and SCHÖNBERG,
ARNOLD. Discography in Perspectives on Schoenberg and Stravinsky.

2898 BOONIN, Joseph M.: Stravinsky records
Stravinsky; Stravinsky in print in Musical America, LXXXII/6 (June 1962):
12-13 ((-))

2899 BOYARS, Arthur: A selected discography in SIOHAN, Robert: Stravinsky.
London: Calder & Boyars, 1965 [i.e.
1966]: 177-188 ((-))

2900 BURNETT, James: Music on record:
Igor Stravinsky in Audio and Record
Review (September 1969): 606 ((-))

2901 CLOUGH, F. F., and G. J. CUMING:
Igor Stravinsky on records in Tempo,
No. 8 (Summer 1948): 29-30 ((5))

2902 Frankfurt am Main. Deutsches Rundfunkarchiv: Igor Strawinsky (1882-
1971) Phonographie. Seine Eigeninter-
pretation auf Schallplatten und in den
europäischen Rundfunkanstalten,
zusammen mit einem Verzeichnis der
in den deutschen Rundfunkanstalten
vorhandenen Rundfunkproduktionen und
historischen Schallplattenaufnahmen
von Strawinsky-Werken. Frankfurt am
Main: Deutsches Rundfunkarchiv,
[1972]: 216 pp. ((1, 3, 4, 5, 7))

2903 Discographie critique Stravinski in
Diapason, No. 157 (May 1971): 10-13
((-)); No. 158 (June-July 1971): 20-24
((-))

2904 [[[Discography] in Discofilia (May
1957): 163]]

2905 FRANKENSTEIN, Alfred: Stravinsky on
microgroove in High Fidelity, IV/9
(November 1954): 73-85 ((-))

2906 HALBREICH, Harry: Catalogue commenté et discographie critique in

Stravinsky. Paris: Hachette, 1968:
[241]-[274] ((-))

2907 HALBREICH, Harry: Strawinsky discographie critique in Harmonie, No. 24
(February 1967): 36-51 ((-))

2908 HALL, David: Discography in CORLE,
Edwin: Igor Stravinsky. [New York:
Duell, Sloan and Pearce, 1949]: 219-
230 ((-))

2909 HAMILTON, David: Igor Stravinsky: a
discography of the composer's performances in Perspectives of New
Music, IX/2 (Spring-Summer 1971)
X/1 (Fall-Winter 1971): 163-179 [Pre-
viously published in Perspectives on
Schönberg and Stravinsky (Princeton,
1969) and in Columbia D5S 775] ((7))

2910 HART, Philip: Stravinsky—just for the
record in Music Magazine, CLXIV
(June 1962): 42-47 ((-))

2911 Diskographie in ÎARUSTOVSKII, Boris
Mikhailovich: Igor Strawinsky. Berlin:
Henschelverlag, 1966: 206-[209] ((-))

2912 Columbia records of the music of Igor
Stravinsky with the composer partici-
pating as either pianist or conductor in
Igor Stravinsky. Edited by Merle
ARMITAGE. New York: Schirmer,
1936: 149-150 ((-))

2913 RCA-Victor records of the music of
Igor Stravinsky in Igor Stravinsky.
Edited by Merle ARMITAGE. New
York: Schirmer, 1936: 151 ((-))

2914 Strawinsky auf Schallplatten in Igor
Strawinsky [zum siebzigsten Geburt-
stag] Bonn: Boosey & Hawkes, [c1952]:
78-[79] (Musik der Zeit; eine Schriftenreihe zur Zeitgenössischen Musik) ((-))

2915 Igor Stravinsky. København: [National-
diskotek], 1962: 16 pp. (Det National
Diskotek Katalog, 13) ((4, 5))

2916 Werkverzeichnis [includes discograpi-
cal references] in KIRCHMEYER,
Helmut: Igor Strawinsky Zeitgeschichte
im Persönlichkeitsbild; Grundlagen und
Voraussetzungen zur modernen
Konstruktionstechnik. Regensburg: G.
Bosse, [1958]: 715-764 (Kölner Beiträge
zur Musikforschung, 10) ((-))

2917 [[KOLODIN, Irving: A Stravinsky discography; performances with, or by,
the composer in Saturday Review (May
12, 1962)]]

2918 Recordings of music by Igor Stravinsky
in LEDERMAN, Minna: Stravinsky in
the theatre. New York: Da Capo Press,
1975, c1949: 185-189 (A Da Capo paperback) ((-))

2919 Recordings of music by Igor Stravinsky
in LEDERMAN, Minna: Stravinsky in

the theatre. New York: Pellegrini & Cudahy, [1949]: 185-189 ((-))

2920 LINDLAR, Heinrich: Strawinskys Geistliche Musik auf Schallplatten in fono forum 1962 (No. 6, June): 11 ((-))

2921 MARINELLI, Carlo: Discografia Strawinskiana in Rassegna Musicale, XXII/3 (1952): 232-246 ((-))

2922 Discographie in MONNIKENDAM, Marius: Igor Strawinsky. Haarlem: Gottmer, [1951]: 203-206 (Componisten-serie, 17) ((5))

2923 Discographie in MONNIKENDAM, Marius: Strawinsky. Haarlem: J. H. Gottmer, [1958]: 187-194 (Gottmer muziek-pockets, 8) ((-))

2924 Discografie in MONNIKENDAM, Marius: Igor Strawinsky. Haarlem: J. H. Gottmer, [1966]: 264-278 (Componistenserie, 3) ((-))

2925 Suggested gramophone recordings in MYERS, Rollo H.: Introduction to the music of Stravinsky. London: D. Dobson, [1950]: [60-64] (Contemporary composers) ((-))

2926 [[ODRIOZOLA, A.: La discografía LP de Igor Stravinsky in Musica (Madrid), IV/14 (1955): 139-154]]

2927 Complete works... chronologically ar-ranged according to material supplied by the composer, with the most im-portant gramophone recordings in ONNEN, Frank: Stravinsky. Stockholm: Continental Book Co., [1949]: 54-57 (Symphonia books) ((-))

2928 Discographie in PHILIPPOT, Michel: Igor Stravinsky: l'homme et son oeuvre. [Paris]: Éditions Seghers, [1965]: [177]-188 (Musiciens de tous les temps, 18) ((-))

2929 Discografie in RAEDT, Paul de: Het leven en werk van I. Stravinski. Brus-sel: Reinaert, [1973]: 41-44 (Meesters der toonkunst, 21) ((-))

2930 Enregistrements gramophoniques in SCHAEFFNER, André: Strawinsky. Paris: Rieder, [c1931]: 122 ((-))

2931 Indice discográfico in SOPEÑA IBÁÑEZ, Federico: Strawinsky: vida, obra y estilo. Madrid: Sociedad de Estudios y Publicaciones, 1956: [265]-270 ((-))

2932 Discographie principale in TINTORI, Giampiero: Igor Stravinski. Paris: Éditions du Sud et A. Michel, 1966: 219-225 ((-))

2933 Werkverzeichnis Igor Strawinsky in fono forum 1962 (No. 6, June): 34 ((-))

2934 List of gramophone records and pianola rolls in WHITE, Eric Walter: Stravinsky's sacrifice to Apollo. London: L. and Virginia Woolf at the Hogarth Press, 1930: 142-143 ((-))

2935 List of recordings in WHITE, Eric Walter: Stravinsky: a critical survey. London: J. Lehmann, 1947: 182-186 ((-))

2936 List of recordings in WHITE, Eric Walter: Stravinsky: a critical survey. New York: Philosophical Library, [1948]: 182-186 ((-))

2937 Verzeichnis der Schallplatten in WHITE, Eric Walter: Strawinsky. Hamburg: Claassen, [Vorwort 1949]: 235-240 ((-))

Petrouska

2938 Diskografie in fono forum 1971 (No. 4, April): 254 ((-))

Le Sacre du printemps

2939 GEITEL, Klaus: Diskografie in fono forum 1961 (No. 1, January): 13 ((-))

STRAWINSKY, IGOR
   See STRAVINSKIĬ, IGOR' FEDOROVICH

STRAWINSKY, IGOR
   See STRAVINSKIĬ, IGOR' FEDOROVICH

STREICH, RITA

2940 Die wichtigsten Schallplatten Aufnahmen Rita Streichs in Phonoprisma, V/2 (March-April 1962): 42 ((-))

STRICKLAND, LILY, 1887-1958

2941 Artists performing music by Lily Strickland on recordings in HOWE, Ann Whitworth: Lily Strickland: South Carolina's gift to American music. [n.p.]: Published for the South Caro-lina Tricentennial Commission by R. L. Bryan Co., [1970]: 65 ((-))

STUPKA, FRANTIŠEK, 1879-1965

2942 Záznamy v čs. roshlase in ŠEFL, Vladimír: O věčné touze: příběh dirigenta národního umělce profesora Františka Stupky. 1. vyd. Praha: Panton, 1975: 237-238 ((1))

SÜSS, REINER, 1930-

2943 Schallplattenverzeichnis in STENGEL, Hansgeorg: Reiner Süss. 1. Aufl.

Leipzig: Deutscher Verlag für Musik,
1974: 26 ((-))

SUITNER, OTMAR

2944 KRAUSE, Ernst: Diskographie in
Medium Schallplatte, No. 2 (No. 1,
1967): 5 ((-))

SUK, JOSEF, 1874-1935

2945 [[BARTOŠ, Jaroslav: Diskografie
Josefa Suka in Tempo, no. 20, 1947:
3-4]]

2946 Historické gramofonové snímky
Českého kvarteta in BERKOVEC,
Jiří: Josef Suk. Praha: Supraphon,
1968: 73-[74] ((-))

2947 Historic gramophone recordings made
by the Czech Quartet in BERKOVEC,
Jiří: Josef Suk. Praha: Supraphon,
1969: 93 ((-))

2948 Enregistrements historiques réalises
par le Quatuor Tchéque in BERKOVEC,
Jiří: Josef Suk. Praha: Supraphon,
t. PG 3, 1970: 98 ((-))

2949 Skladby Josefa Suka na gramofonových
in Kńiha, Prague: Josef Suk; výběrová
bibliografie. Praha: Kńiha, 1965: 77-81
((-))

SULLIVAN, ARTHUR SEYMOUR, SIR
See listing for GILBERT, WILLIAM
SCHWENCK, SIR

SUPERVIA, CONCHITA, 1895-1936

2950 [[BARNES, H. M., and V. GIRARD:
Conchita Supervia in Record Collector,
VI/ (March 1951): 54-71]]; Addenda:
Record Collector, VIII/2 (February
1953): 41-44 ((1, 3, 5))

2951 BARNES, H. M.: Conchita Supervia
(1895?-1936); discography in British
Institute of Recorded Sound Bulletin,
No. 4 (Spring 1957): 19-26 ((3, 6))

2952 CATTANACH, David: Conchita Supervia
(1895-1936); discography in Recorded
Sound, No. 52 (October 1973): 212-229
((3, 4, 6, 7)); Corrections in Recorded
Sound, No. 57-58 (January-April 1975):
437 ((3, 6, 7))

SUPRAPHON
See listings for DVOŘÁK, ANTONIN.
Dvořáks Werke auf Supraphon Lang-
spielplatten 33 1/3; KRASVOÁ, MARTA;
MILHAUD, DARIUS. Skladby Daria
Milhauda na deskách Supraphon; NOVÁK,
VITĚZSLAV. Soupis skladeb Vitezslava

Nováka na čs...; PODVALOVÁ, MA-
RIE; SCHÖNBERG, ARNOLD. Skladby
Arnolda Schönberga na dlouhohrajících
deskách Supraphon; TALICH, VÁCLAV.
Seznam snímků národního umélce
Václava Talicha na deskách Supraphon;
VERDI, GIUSEPPE. Dílo G. Verdiho na
deskách Supraphon; VYCPALEK, LA-
DISLAV; WEBER, KARL MARIA
FRIEDRICH ERNST, FREIHERR VON;
WERICH, JAN

SUSKE, KARL

2953 Diskographie in Medium Schallplatte,
No. 12 (No. 3, 1969): 15 ((-))

SUTER, ROBERT, 1919-

2954 Auf Schallplatten erschienene Werke in
LARESE, Dino: Robert Suter, [von]
Dino Larese [und] Jacques WILDBER-
GER. [Amriswil]: Amriswiler
Bücherei, 1967: 36 ((-))

SUTERMEISTER, HEINRICH, 1910-

2955 Plattenaufnahmen in LARESE, Dino:
Heinrich Sutermeister. [Amriswil]:
Amriswiler Bücherei, 1972: 41 ((-))

SUTHERLAND, JOAN, 1926-

2956 Discography (U.S.A.) in BRADDON,
Russell: Joan Sutherland. New York:
St. Martin's Press, [1962]: 247-248
((-))

2957 [Diskographie] in Phonoprisma (July-
August 1966): 123 ((-))

2958 KOEGLER, Horst: Diskografie in fono
forum 1961 (No. 7, July): 14 ((-))

2959 WALKER, Malcolm: Joan Sutherland: a
discography in GREENFIELD, Edward:
Joan Sutherland. London: Allan, 1972:
59-64 ((7))

2960 [WALKER, Malcolm]: Joan Sutherland:
a discography in GREENFIELD, Edward: Joan Sutherland. New York:
Drake Publishers, [1973]: 59-64 ((7))

SVETLANOV, EVGENY FEDOROVITCH,
1928-

2961 Diskographie (sämtliche Aufnahmen bei
Eurodisc) in Phonoprisma (November-
December 1967): 199 ((-))

SYDEMAN, WILLIAM, 1928-

2962 [Discographical notes included] in
REICH, Nancy: Catalog of the works of

William Sydeman: a machine readable pilot project in information retrieval. 2d ed. [n.p.]: Division of Music Education, New York University, 1968: 9 leaves ((–))

SYMPHONIES
See also listings for ORCHESTRAL MUSIC

2963 Discography in NADEAU, Roland: The symphony: structure and style. Shorter ed., rev. Boston: Crescendo Publishing Co., [1974]: 233-238 ((–))

2964 Discography in O'CONNELL, Charles: The Victor book of symphonies. Completely rev. and enl. to include 138 symphonies. New York: Simon and Schuster, 1948: 549-556 ((–))

2965 [Discography] in PAAP, Wouter: De symfonie. Bilthoven: H. Nelissen, [1957]: 61-63 ((–))

2966 [Discography] in RAUCHHAUPT, Ursula von: Die Welt der Symphonie. [Hamburg]: Polydor International GmbH, [c1972]: 318-320 ((–))

2967 Discography in RAUCHHAUPT, Ursula von: The symphony. London: Thames and Hudson, [1973, c1972]: 318-320 ((–))

2968 List of phonograph records of symphonies in SPAETH, Sigmund: Great symphonies: how to recognize and remember them. New York: Perma Giants, [1949, c1936]: 319-356 ((–))

2969 Förteckning över grammofonskivor in WALLIN, Nils Lennart: Romantiska symfonier. Stockholm: H. Geber, [1947]: 261-[263] (Gebers musikböcker) ((–))

2970 Index of works and recordings in YOUNG, Percy M.: Symphony. Boston: Crescendo, [1968]: 143-149 (Phoenix music guides, 2) ((–))

SZÉKELY, ENDRE, 1912-

2971 Diszkográfia in VÁRNAI, Péter: Székely Endre. Budapest: Zenemükiadó, 1967: [24] (Mai magyar zeneszersök) ((–))

SZELL, GEORG ANDREAS, 1897-1970

2972 Diskographie in Collegium Musicum 1970 (No. 1): 43-44; 1970 (No. 2): 8; 1971 (No. 2): 21 ((–))

2973 HELM, Everett: Aus der Diskografie George Szell in fono forum 1961 (No. 11, November): 9 ((–))

2974 HIRSCH, Howard J., and Jack SAUL: George Szell discography in Le Grand Baton, IX/1-2 (February-May 1972): 88-120 ((3, 7)); Addenda: Le Grand Baton, XII/1 (March 1974): 32 ((–))

2975 A selective list of Szell recordings with groups other than the Cleveland Orchestra in MARSH, Robert C.: The Cleveland Orchestra. New York: World, 1967: 201-202 ((–))

2976 Szell—Discographie in Phono (Summer 1955): 5 ((–))

SZERYNG, HENRYK, 1918-

2977 Discographie Henryk Szeryng in Diapason, No. 137 (June 1969): 6 ((–))

2978 Diskographie in Collegium Musicum 1971 (No. 10): 11 ((–))

2979 Henryk Szeryng on Philips records in Philips Music Herald (Summer-Autumn 1967): 14 ((–))

2980 SCHRÖDER, U. Karin: Diskographie (Auswahl) in Musica, XXIV/5 (September-October 1970): 505 ((–))

2981 SPINGEL, Hans Otto: Diskografie in fono forum 1962 (No. 2, February): 28 ((–))

2982 Wichtige Schallplatten-Aufnahmen mit Henryk Szeryng in Phonoprisma, V/4 (July-August 1962): 102 ((–))

SZIGETI, JOSEPH, 1892-1973

2983 KRAUS, Gottfried: Auswahl-Diskografie in fono forum 1971 (No. 12, December): 997 ((–))

2984 MacDONALD, Ronald C.: The recorded legacy of Joseph Szigeti in Le Grand Baton, II/3 (July-September 1965): 1-22 ((–))

2985 [Discography] in SOROKER, ÍAkov L'vovich: Iozhev Sigeti. Moskva: Muzyka, 1968: 116-124 ((–))

2986 A list of recordings by Joseph Szigeti in SZIGETI, Joseph: With strings attached: reminiscences and reflections. New York: A. A. Knopf, 1947: 335-341 ((–))

2987 The recordings of Joseph Szigeti in SZIGETI, Joseph: With strings attached: reminiscences and reflections. 2d ed. rev. and enlarged. New York: A. A. Knopf, 1967: 365-376 ((–))

2988 [[Verzeichnis der Grammophon-platten von Joseph Szigeti in SZIGETI, Joseph: Zwischen der Saiten. Rüschlikon/Zürich: Müller, 1962]]

SZOSTAKOWICZ, DMITRI
See SHOSTAKOVICH, DMITRIĬ
DMITRIEVICH

SZYMANOWSKI, KAROL, 1882-1937

2989   Dyskografia in CHYLIŃSKA, Teresa:
Karol Szymanowski. [Wyd. 1.] Kraków: Polskie Wydawn. Muzyczne, 1961
[i.e. 1962]: 213-[217] ((-))

2990   Dyskografia in CHYLIŃSKA, Teresa:
Szymanowski i jego muzyka. [Wyd. 1.]
Warszawa: Państwowe Zakłady Wy-
dawnictw Szkolnych, 1971: 215-220 ((5))

2991   [[[Discography] in CHYLIŃSKA, Teresa: Szymanowski. New York:
Kościuszko Foundation, 1973]]]

2992   Discography in MACIEJEWSKI, B. M.:
Karol Szymanowski: his life and music;
with a foreword by Felix APRAHAMIAN.
London: Poets & Painters' Press, 1967:
135-140 ((-))

2993   Bibliography [includes discographical
notes] in MICHAŁOWSKI, Korneĺ:
Karol Szymanowski, 1882-1937: katalog
tematyczny dzieĺ i bibliografia—
Thematic catalogue of works and bibliography—Thematisches Werkverzeichnis und Bibliographie. Wyd. 1.
Kraków: Polskie Wydawn. Muzyczne,
[1967]: 285-326 ((-))

2994   Works of Karel Szymanowski on Muza
Records in Polish Music, VII/3 (1972):
14-[17] ((-))

TAILLEFERRE, GERMAINE, 1892-

2995   Discographie in Courrier Musical de
France, No. 9 (1965): 66 ((-))

TALICH, VÁCLAV, 1883-1961

2996   Gramofonové závody, Prague: Václav
Talich a gramofonová deska. Praha:
Gramofonové závody, [1960]: 29 pp.
((7))

2997   Seznam snímků národního umělce
Václava Talicha na deskách Supraphon
in Václav Talich: dokument života a
díla. [1. vyd.] Praha: Státní hudební
vydavatelství, 1967: 300-308 ((7))

2998   Soupis snímků, nahraných zahraničními
filmami in Václav Talich: dokument
života a díla. [1. vyd.] Praha: Státní
hudební vydavatelství, 1967: 309-316
((7))

TAMAGNO, FRANCESCO, 1850-1905

2999   FREESTONE, John: Collectors' corner
in Gramophone, No. 356 (January 1953):
193 ((7))

3000   FREESTONE, John: The published records of Francesco Tamagno in Record
Collector, VII/2 (February 1952): 37-
39 ((-))

3001   WADE, Philip H.: The records of Francesco Tamagno in Record Collector,
VII/2 (February 1952): 35-36 ((3))

TANNENBERG, DAVID, 1728-1804

3002   [[Discography in ARMSTRONG, William
H.: Organs for America: the life and
work of David Tannenberg. Philadelphia: University of Pennsylvania Press,
1967: 145]]

TANSMAN, ALEXANDRE, 1897-

3003   Discographie in Courrier Musical de
France, No. 17 (1967): 49 ((-))

TATE, MAGGIE
See TEYTE, MAGGIE

TATE, PHYLLIS, 1911-

3004   [[Discography in Oxford University
Press: Phyllis Tate. London: Oxford
University Press, 1972: 12]]

TAUBER, RICHARD, 1891-1948

3005   DENNIS, R.: Richard Tauber discogra-
phy in Record Collector, XVIII/8-10
(October 1969): 171-239 ((1, 3, 4, 5, 6,
7)); Addenda: Record Collector,
XVIII/11-12 (December 1969): 265
((-)); XIX/3-4 (June 1970): 81-85 ((-))

3006   Schallplattenverzeichnis in KORB,
Willi: Richard Tauber: Biographie eines
unvergessenen Sängers. Wien: Europäischer Verlag, 1966: 144-181 ((-))

3007   SHELDON, Scott: Richard Tauber—
discography in Record News, I/3
(November 1956): 81-111 ((-)); I/4
(December 1956): 142-153 ((-)); Addenda: Record News, I/5 (January
1957): 167-171 ((-)); I/7 (March 1957):
255-260 ((-))

TCHAĬKOVSKI, PIOTR ILLITCH
See CHAĬKOVSKIĬ, PETR IL'ICH

TCHAĬKOVSKY, PETER ILLICH
See CHAĬKOVSKIĬ, PETR IL'ICH

TEBALDI, RENATA, 1922-

3008   Diskografie in BURIAN, Karol Vladimír: Renata Tebaldi. Praha: Editio
Supraphon, 1973: 49-53 ((-))

3009 CLOUGH, F. F., and G. J. CUMING:
Renata Tebaldi; a microgroove diskography in Gramophone Record Review, No. 46 (August 1957): 789-790
((-))

3010 Discography in HARRIS, Kenn: Renata
Tebaldi: an authorized biography. New
York: Drake Publishers, [1974]: 155-
161 ((1))

3011 JELLINEK, George: Discography of
Renata Tebaldi recordings issued in the
United States in SEROFF, Victor:
Renata Tebaldi: the woman and the diva.
New York: Appleton-Century-Crofts,
[1961]: [203]-210 ((-))

3012 JELLINEK, George: Discography of
Renata Tebaldi recordings issued in the
United States in SEROFF, Victor: Re-
nata Tebaldi: the woman and the diva.
Freeport, NY: Books for Libraries
Press, [1970, c1961]: [203]-210 ((-))

3013 ROSENTHAL, Harold: Tebaldi recordings in Gramophone, No. 371 (April
1954): 422 ((-))

TE KANAWA, KIRI

3014 Discography in HARRIS, Norman: Kiri:
music and a Maori girl. Wellington:
A. H. & A. W. Reed, [1966]: [61]-62
((7))

TELEFUNKEN RECORDS
See listing for CARUSO, ENRICO.
Teuchtler, Roland: Diskografie

TELEMANN, GEORG PHILIPP, 1681-1767

3015 Schallplatten-Aufnahmen in Georg
Philipp Telemann: Ausgaben seiner
Werke, Literatur, Schallplatten.
[Kassel; Basel; London; u.a.]: Bären-
reiter-Verlag, [1967]: 26-28 ((-))

3016 Telemann und die Schallplatte in
GREBE, Karl: Georg Philipp Telemann
in Selbstzeugnissen und Bilddokumenten. Reinbek b. Hamburg: Rowohlt,
1970: 139-144 (Rowohlts Monographien,
170) ((-))

3017 Verzeichnis von Schallplatten mit
Werken Georg Philipp Telemanns in
VALENTIN, Erich: Telemann in seiner
Zeit: Versuch eines geistesgeschicht-
lichen Porträts. Hamburg: H. Sikorski,
[1960]: 51 (Veröffentlichungen der
Hamburger Telemann-Gesellschaft, 1)
((-))

TENORS

3018 MILLER, Philip L.: Tenors of the past
in High Fidelity, IX/3 (March 1959):

105-114 ((-)); IX/5 (May 1959): 85-94
((-))

TERTIS, LIONEL, 1876-1975

3019 WALKER, Malcolm: Recordings by
Lionel Tertis in TERTIS, Lionel: My
viola and I: a complete autobiography;
with Beauty of tone in string playing,
and other essays. London: Elek, 1974:
175-180 ((7))

3020 WALKER, Malcolm: Recordings by
Lionel Tertis in TERTIS, Lionel: My
viola and I: a complete autobiography.
1st U.S. ed. Boston: Crescendo Pub.
Co., 1975, c1974: 175-180 ((7))

TETRAZZINI, LUISA, 1871-1940

3021 WADE, Philip H.: List of Tetrazzini
records in Gramophone, No. 155 (April
1936): 489 ((-))

3022 Corrections to Tetrazzini article [in
correspondence] in Gramophone, No.
156 (May 1936): 540 ((-))

TEYTE, MAGGIE, 1888-1976

3023 DENNIS, J.: Maggie Teyte: recordings
in Record Collector, IX/6 (November
1954): 134-138 ((1, 3, 6, 7))

3024 TRON, David: Recordings of Maggie
Teyte in TEYTE, Maggie: Star on the
door. London: Putnam, 1958: 188-192
((1, 3, 7))

THEATRE MUSIC

3025 [[Bibliographie und Diskographie: Zeit-
genoessisches Musiktheater in Musik
und Bildung, III (November 1971): 556-
563]]

THEODORAKIS, MIKIS, 1925-

3026 [[Discography in GIANNARIS, George:
Mikis Theodorakis: music and social
change. New York: Praeger, 1972:
309-311]]

3027 GRÜNEWALD, Helge: Diskografie Mikis
Theodorakis in fono forum 1973 (No. 9,
September): 812 ((-))

THEODORINI, HELENA, 1862-1926

3028 CELLETTI, Rodolfo: Discografia
secondo del Bauer in Musica e Dischi,
IX (No. 82, July 1953): 16 ((7))

3029 CELLETTI, Rodolfo: Records in Record News, II/11 (July 1958): 406 [From
Musica e Dischi]

THIBAUD, JACQUES, 1880-1953

3030 BARBIER, Jean-Joel: Enregistrements
de M. Long et J. Thibaud in Revue
Musicale, No. 245 (1959): 34-37 ((-))

3031 Discographie J. Thibaud in Disques,
VI/59 (September-October 1953): 586-
587 ((5))

THIRIET, MAURICE, 1906-

3032 Discographie in Courrier Musical de
France, No. 7 (1964): 194 ((-))

3033 Discographie in SOLAR, Jean: Maurice
Thiriet. Paris: Ventadour, [1957]: 44
(Collection "Musiciens d'aujourd'hui")
((-))

TIBBETT, LAWRENCE, 1896-1960

3034 WHELAN, Robert: Lawrence Tibbett
(discography) in Record News, V/5
(January 1961): 165-170 ((-)); Addenda:
Record News, V/7 (March 1961): 258-
260 ((-))

TISNÉ, ANTOINE, 1932-

3035 Discographie in Courrier Musical de
France, No. 42 (1973): 81 ((-))

TODUTĂ, SIGISMUND, 1908-

3036 Disques in Muzica, XX/9 (September
1970): 45 ((-))

TOLDRA, EDUARDO, 1895-1962

3037 Eduard Toldrà: compositor. III. Gra-
vacions in CAPDEVILA MASSANA,
Manuel: Eduard Toldrà. Barcelona:
Editorial Aedos, [1964]: 390-391
(Biblioteca biogràfica catalana, 38) ((-))

3038 Eduard Toldrà: director. VI. Grava-
cions in CAPDEVILA MASSANA,
Manuel: Eduard Toldrà. Barcelona:
Editorial Aedos, [1964]: [417] (Biblioteca biogràfica catalana, 38) ((-))

3039 Eduardo Toldrà: compositor. III.
Discos in CAPDEVILA MASSANA,
Manuel: Eduardo Toldrà: musico. Barcelona: Ediciones Unidas, [1972]: 333-
334 ((-))

3040 Eduardo Toldrà: director. VI. Discos
publicado in CAPDEVILA MASSANA,
Manuel: Eduardo Toldrà: musico. Barcelona: Ediciones Unidas, [1972]: 359
((-))

TOMÁŠEK, VÁCLAV JAN, 1774-1850

3041 Gramofonové desky in KÁDNEROVÁ,
Jiřina: Václav Jan Tomášek: 17. 4.

1774-3. 4. 1850: výběrová bibliografie
o živote a díle. Kladno: Kraj. knihovna,
1974: 6 (Edice KK Kladno. Bibliografie.
Malá řada, 40) (Krajská knihovna
Kladno. Bibliografie: Malá řada, 40)
((-))

TOMASI, HENRI, 1901-1971

3042 Discographie in Courrier Musical de
France, No. 10 (1965): 130 ((-))

TOMKINS, THOMAS, 1575 (ca.)-1656

3043 Discography in STEVENS, Denis:
Thomas Tomkins: 1572-1656. London:
Macmillan; New York: St. Martin's
Press, 1957: 203-204 ((-))

3044 Discography in STEVENS, Denis:
Thomas Tomkins: 1572-1656. New
York: Dover Publications, [1967]: 203-
204 ((-))

TORRESELLA, FANNY

3045 CELLETTI, Rodolfo: Discografia in
Musica e Dischi, XVII (No. 183, September 1961): 58 ((7))

TOSCANINI, ARTURO, 1867-1957

3046 Arturo Toscanini. [Copenhagen]:
Nationalmuseet, [1961]: 22 pp. (Det
National Diskotek Katalog, 5) ((3, 4, 7))

3047 Arturo Toscanini: a complete discography. [New York]: Radio Corporation of
America, RCA Victor Record Division,
1966: [64] pp. ((7))

3048 Toscaniniouská diskografie in BURIAN,
Karel Vladimír: Arturo Toscanini.
[Vyd. 1.] Praha: Supraphon, 1967: 63-
69 (Edice Lyra) ((-))

3049 CLOUGH, F. F., and G. J. CUMING:
Arturo Toscanini; diskography in
Gramophone Record Review, No. 62
(December 1958): 103-105 ((7)); Ad-
denda: Gramophone Record Review, No.
63 (January 1959): 224 ((-))

3050 Discografia in CORTE, Andrea della:
Toscanini: visto da un critico.—
[Torino]: ILTE, [1958]: [495]-513
(Biblioteca storica della ILTE) ((-))

3051 Discografia di Arturo Toscanini: in
lingua italiana e in lingua inglese. [1.
ed. Milano]: Musica e dischi, [1957]:
85 pp. ((1, 7))

3052 Diskographie in Collegium Musicum
1971 (No. 4): 13-16; 1972 (No. 8): 29
((1))

3053 Essai de discographie d'Arturo Toscanini in Disques, No. 88 (April 1957):

453-456; No. 89 (May-June 1957): 576-578 ((1, 5))

3054 A complete list of Toscanini recordings in EWEN, David: The story of Arturo Toscanini. [1st ed.] New York: Holt, [1951]: 127-133 (Holt musical biography series) ((–))

3055 A complete list of Toscanini recordings in EWEN, David: The story of Arturo Toscanini. Rev. and enl. ed. New York: Holt, [1960]: 127-133 ((–))

3056 Elenco completo delle incisioni di Arturo Toscanini publicata in Italia in EWEN, David: Storia di Arturo Toscanini. Bari: "Leonardo da Vinci" editrice, [1951]: [135]-138 ((–))

3057 Discography in HAGGIN, B. H.: Conversations with Toscanini. [1st ed.] Garden City, NY: Doubleday, 1959: 165-249 ((7))

3058 HUPKA, Robert: The recorded repertoire of Arturo Toscanini in ANTEK, Samuel: This was Toscanini. New York: Vanguard Press, [1963]: 186-192 ((1))

3059 Komplettes Schallplatten-Verzeichnis Toscanini in LEZUO-PANDOLFI, Amina: Toscanini: ein Leben für Musik. Zürich: Apollo-Verlag, [c1957]: 77-80 ((–))

3060 MARSH, Robert Charles: Toscanini on records: Part 1: 1920-1948 in High Fidelity, IV/10 (December 1954): 55-58 ((7))

3061 MARSH, Robert Charles: Toscanini on records: Part 2: With the NBC Symphony—1944/47 in High Fidelity, IV/11 (January 1955): 75-81 ((7))

3062 MARSH, Robert Charles: Toscanini on records: Part 3: With the NBC Symphony—1949/54 in High Fidelity, IV/12 (February 1955): 83-91 ((7))

3063 List of the Toscanini recordings in MARSH, Robert Charles: Toscanini and the art of orchestra performance. [1st ed.] Philadelphia: Lippincott, [1956]: 108-192 ((7))

3064 List of the Toscanini recordings in MARSH, Robert Charles: Toscanini and the art of orchestral performance. Westport, Conn.: Greenwood Press, [1973, c1956]: 108-192 ((7))

3065 The Toscanini recordings in MARSH, Robert Charles: Toscanini and the art of conducting. New, rev. ed. New York: Collier Books, [1962]: 111-232 (Collier Books) ((7))

3066 MATZNER, Joachim: Das Phännomen Toscanini; aus der Diskografie in fono forum 1961 (No. 11, November): 9 ((–))

3067 MAYES, Stanley H.: Toscanini in Camden in Hill and Dale News, No. 28 (December 1965): 86-87 ((7))

3068 STONE, Ralph: Toscanini and the BBC Symphony—commercial recordings in Le Grand Baton, IV/2-3 (May-August 1967): 37 ((7))

3069 VEGETO, Raffaele: Discografia in Convegno di studi toscaniniani, Florence. 1967: La lezione di Toscanini. Firenze: Vallecchi, 1970: [347]-366 ((1))

3070 VEGETO, Raffaele: Discografia completa e cronologica delle musiche incise da Arturo Toscanini in Discoteca, No. 68 (February-March 1967): 41-56 ((1, 5, 7))

TOSTI, FRANCESCO PAOLO, SIR, 1846-1916

3071 CELLETTI, Rodolfo: Si vous l'aviez compris... Tosti e le romanze da salotto; nota discografica in Discoteca, No. 35 (August-September 1963) 24-25 ((–))

TOVEY, DONALD FRANCIS, 1875-1940

3072 Tovey discography in Recorded Sound, No. 59 (July 1975): 460 ((1, 7))

TRAXEL, JOSEF

3073 KNÖDLER, Otto: Aus der Diskografie in fono forum 1961 (No. 8, August): 14 ((–))

TREMAIN, RONALD
See listing for FARQUHAR, DAVID

TRIO PASQUIER

3074 Discographie in Courrier Musical de France, No. 17 (1967): 58 ((–))

TRÖTSCHEL, ELFRIED

3075 In memoriam; Elfried Troetschel, soprano in Record News, III/1 (September 1958): 30-31 ((–))

TRUMPET MUSIC

3076 GHITALLA, Armando: A selected discography in American Record Guide, XXIV/6 (February 1958): 245 ((–))

TSCHEREPNIN, ALEXANDER
See CHEREPNIN, ALEKSANDR NIKOLAEVICH

TSJAIKOFSKI, PETER ILLICH
See CHAĬKOVSKIĬ, PETR IL'ICH

TURINA, JOAQUÍN, 1882-1949

3077 Discografía in SOPEÑA IBÁÑEZ,
Federico: Joaquín Turina. 2d ed. corr.
y aumentada. Madrid: Editora Nacional, 1956: 139-145 (Libros de actu-
alidad intelectual, 25) ((-))

TURNER, EVA

3078 CAMERON, Norman: Eva Turner in
Gramophone, No. 149 (October 1935):
181-182 ((-))

3079 RICHARDS, J. B.: The recordings of
Eva Turner in Record Collector, XI/2
(February 1957): 45-47 ((3, 6, 7)); Addenda: Record Collector, XI/8 (August
1957): 183-184 ((3, 7))

3080 Unpublished records in 78 RPM, No. 5
(April 1969): 1-6 ((3, 7))

ULTRAPHON RECORDS
See listings for JANÁČEK, LEOŠ.
Prochazka, Jaroslav; MUSIC, CZECH

UNGER, HEINZ, 1895-1965

3081 Records by Dr. Heinz Unger in Disc,
II/5 (Winter 1948): 35 ((-))

URLUS, JACQUES, 1867-1935

3082 RIEMENS, Leo: Jacques Urlus in
Gramophone, No. 177 (February 1938):
406-408 ((7))

UTRECHT STATE UNIVERSITY
See listing for ELECTRONIC MUSIC.
Gramophone records on electronic
music

VALEN, FARTEIN, 1887-1952

3083 Discography in KORTSEN, Bjarne:
Fartein Valen life and music. Oslo:
J. G. Tanum, 1965- v. 2: 200 ((-))

VALERO, FERNANDO

3084 CELLETTI, Rodolfo: Fernando Valero
in Musica e Dischi, VIII (No. 72, September 1952): 21 ((5))

3085 CELLETTI, Rodolfo: Fernando Valero—
il tenore dai balzi sel vaggi in Musica e
Dischi, XVII (No. 177, March 1961): 76
((7))

VALLIN, NINON

3086 BARNES, H. M.: The records in Record
Collector, VIII/3 (March 1953): 55-65
((3, 7))

VANCEA, ZENO, 1900-

3087 DRĂGONI, Constantin V.: Disques in
Muzica, XX/6 (June 1970): 47 ((-))

VAN DYCK, ERNST MARIE HUBERT, 1861-
1923

3088 DENNIS, J.: Ernest Marie Hubert Van
Dyck: the records in Record Collector,
V/2 (February 1950): 32 ((-)); Addenda:
Record Collector, V/4 (April 1950): 78
((-))

3089 FREESTONE, John: [Van Dyck Pathés]
in Gramophone, No. 339 (August 1951):
52 ((-))

VARÈSE, EDGARD, 1883-1965

3090 Discographie d'ensemble in CHARBON-
NIER, Georges: Entretiens avec Edgard
Varèse. Paris: P. Belfond, [1970]: 169
(Collection Entretiens) ((-))

3091 Edgard Varèse—a discography; published and recorded works in Stereo
Review, XXVI/6 (June 1971): 66 ((-))

3092 Discographie in OUELLETTE, Fernand:
Edgard Varèse. New York: Orion
Press, [1968]: 241-242 ((-))

3093 Discographie in OUELLETTE, Fernand:
Edgard Varèse. Paris: Seghers, 1966:
257-258 ((-))

3094 ROY, Jean: Discographie in Revue
Musicale, No. 267 (1969): 30 ((-))

3095 Discographie in VIVIER, Odile: Varèse.
[Paris]: Éditions du Seuil, [1973]: 188
((-))

3096 WEBER, J. F.: An Edgard Varèse discography in Association for Recorded
Sound Collections Journal V/1 (1973):
30-37 ((5))

3097 WEBER, J. F.: Edgard Varèse. Utica,
NY: Weber, 1975: 13 pp. (Discography
series, 12) ((5, 7))

VARNAY, ASTRID, 1918-

3098 Diskographie in Collegium Musicum
1973 (No. 1-2): 5 ((-))

3099 Diskographie in WESSLING, Berndt
Wilhelm: Astrid Varnay. Bremen:
Schümemann, 1965: 122 ((-))

VASILESCU, ION

3100 FROST, Ana: Discographie in Muzica,
XXI/2 (February 1971): 44 ((-))

VAUGHAN WILLIAMS, RALPH, 1872-1958

3101 CLOUGH, F. F., and G. J. CUMING:
List of recordings in KENNEDY,
Michael: The works of Ralph Vaughan
Williams. London; New York: Oxford
University Press, 1964: 725-746 ((-))

3102 CLOUGH, F. F., and G. J. CUMING:
Discography 1963-1971 in The Music
yearbook, 1972-3. Ed. Arthur JACOBS.
London: St. Martins; Macmillan, 1972:
151-160 ((-))

3103 CUMING, G. J.: Ralph Vaughan Williams in Gramophone, No. 233 (October 1942): 61 ((-))

3104 List of gramophone records in PAKEN-
HAM, Simon: Ralph Vaughan Williams:
a discovery of his music. London:
Macmillan; New York: St. Martin's
Press, 1957: 195-197 ((-))

3105 List of recorded works in YOUNG,
Percy M.: Vaughan Williams. London:
D. Dobson, 1953: 228-231 (Contemporary
composers) ((-))

VERDI, GIUSEPPE, 1813-1901

3106 Dílo G. Verdiho na deskách Supraphon
in BACHTIK, Josef: Giuseppe Verdi:
život a dílo. [1. vyd.] Praha: Státní
hudební vydavatelství, 1963: 384-387
(Hudební profily, 11) ((-))

3107 [[BAPTISTA, J. A.: Discografia seleccionada de Verdi e Wagner in Arte
Musical, XXIX/23 (1964): 623-640]]

3108 BURKE, C. G.: The LP records of
Giuseppe Verdi in High Fidelity, II/1
(Summer 1952): 41-46 ((-))

3109 Werkverzeichnis (mit Schallplattenhin-
weisen in CHERBULIEZ, Antoine:
Giuseppe Verdi: Leben und Werk.
Zürich: A. Müller, [1949]: 207-211
(Meister der Musik im 19. und 20.
Jahrhundert) ((-))

3110 DE SCHAUENSEE, Max: Discography;
Verdi—Shakespeare in Musical America, LXXXIV (January 1964): 14-15, 56
((-))

3111 Discografia in GIANOLI, Luigi: Verdi.
[2. ed. interamente riv. Brescia]: La
Scuola editrice, [1961]: 261-267 ((-))

3112 Verdi on records in HUMPHREYS,
Dena: Verdi: force of destiny. New
York: Holt, [1948]: 323-331 ((-))

3113 Discographie in MALRAYE, Jena:
Giuseppe Verdi l'homme et son oeuvre.
Liste complète des oeuvres, discographie. [Paris]: Seghers, 1965: [179]-
187 (Musiciens de tous les temps, 24)
((-))

3114 [[MARINELLI, C.: Noterella discografica verdiana in La Fiera Letteraria,
1951, April 22]]

3115 OSBORNE, Conrad L.: The collector's
Verdi in High Fidelity, XIII/10 (Octo-
ber 1963): 37-66, 146-156 ((-)); XIII/12
(December 1963): 90-97 ((-))

3116 OSBORNE, Conrad L.: Verdi on microgroove in High Fidelity, X/1 (January
1960): 46-49, 95-100 ((-))

3117 A selected discography from Great
Britain and America in PETIT, Pierre:
Verdi. London: J. Calder, [1966]: 185-
190 (Illustrated Calderbook) ((-))

Aïda

3118 Discographie comparée in Harmonie,
No. 32 (December 1967): 68-71 ((-))

Un ballo in maschera

3119 LORD HAREWOOD: Un ballo in maschera in Opera, XXII/4 (April 1971):
287-302 (Opera on the gramophone, 30)
((1))

3120 VEGETO, Raffaele: Discografia in
Verdi, I (1960): 15-46 ((5))

Don Carlos

3121 EARL OF HAREWOOD: Don Carlos in
Opera, IX/5 (May 1958): 292-299
(Opera on the gramophone, 5) ((-))

Falstaff

3122 ROSENTHAL, Harold: Verdi's Falstaff
in Opera, XXI/5 (May 1970): 384-394
((5)); Addenda: Opera, XXI/8 (August
1970): 727 (Opera on the gramophone,
27) ((-))

La forza del destino

3123 BOLLERT, Werner: Diskografie in fono
forum 1970 (No. 5, May): 287 ((5))

3124 EARL OF HAREWOOD: La Forza del
Destino in Opera, XIII/10 (October
1962): 655-664 (Opera on the gramophone, 10) ((-))

3125 VEGETO, Raffaele: Discografia in
Verdi, II (1961-1966): 30-67 ((1, 5))

I Lombardi. Qui posa il fianco...Qual
voluttà transcorre

3126 VEGETO, R.: Nota discografica in
Discoteca, No. 55 (November 1965): 38-
39 ((-))

Nabucco

3127 ROSENTHAL, Harold: Nabucco in
Opera, XXIII/3 (March 1972): 207-217
((1)); Addenda: Opera, XXIII/6 (June
1972): 580 (Opera on the gramophone,
32) ((1))

Otello

3128 BLYTH, Alan: Otello in Opera, XX/2
(February 1969): 101-112 (Opera on the
gramophone, 22) ((1))

3129 [[BRUUN, Carl L.: Otello: a discography in Record Collector, IV/ (February
1949): 31-37]]

Requiem

3130 Discographie comparée in Harmonie,
No. 13 (January 1966): 79-83 ((-))

3131 MARCUS, Michael: Dis besprochenen
Aufnahmen in fono forum 1967 (No. 3,
March): 112 ((-))

3132 Requiem de Verdi in Diapason, No. 146
(April 1970): 36-39 ((-))

Rigoletto

3133 [[PUGLIESE, Giuseppe, and Rodolfo
CELLETTI: La discografia in Boletin In-
stituto Studia Verdiani, III/7 (1969):
177-245]]

Rigoletto. Bella figlia dell'amore

3134 BRUUN, Carl L.: The Rigoletto quartet
on records in Record Collector,
XII/10-11 (November-December 1958):
238-256 ((4)); Addenda: Record Collector, XIII/4-5 (June-July 1960): 110-113
((-))

Simon Boccanegra

3135 EARL OF HAREWOOD: Verdi's Simon
Boccanegra in Opera, XVI/12 (December 1965): 855-862 (Opera on the
gramophone, 16) ((-))

La Traviata

3136 BOURGEOIS, Jacques: Discographie
comparée in Harmonie, No. 35 (March
1968): 68-71 ((-))

3137 Les enregistrements in Diapason, No.
140 (October 1969): 32 ((-))

3138 JEFFERSON, Alan: La Traviata in
Opera, XXIII/6 (June-July 1972): 504-

512 ((1)); XXIII/7 (August 1972): 697-
708 (Opera on the gramophone, 33) ((-))

La Traviata. E strano! Ah! forsé lui,
sempre libera

3139 CELLETTI, Rodolfo, and Raffaele
VEGETO: Nota discografica in Discoteca, No. 43 (September 1964): 29-30
((1))

Il Trovatore

3140 BOLLERT, Werner: Diskografie in fono
forum 1964 (No. 4, April): 138 ((-))

Il Trovatore. Il balen del suo sorriso

3141 VEGETO, Raffaele: Nota discografica
in Discoteca, No. 47 (January-February
1965): 28-29 ((-))

Il Trovatore. Di quella pira

3142 GUALERZI, Giorgio: Discografia in
Discoteca, No. 17 (February 1962): 35-
36 ((-))

VERLET, ALICE

3143 WILE, Raymond: The Edison disc recordings of Alice Verlet in Association
for Recorded Sound Collections Journal,
III/2-3 (Fall 1971): 53-56 ((3, 6, 7))

VIDU, ION, 1863-1931

3144 Discografie in COSMA, Viorel: Un
maestru al muzicii corale Ion Vidu.
Bucureşti: Editura Muzicală a Uniunii
Compozitorilor di R. P. R., 1965: 239-
[240] ((-))

VIENNA PHILHARMONIC
See WIENER PHILHARMONIKER

VIENNA SCHOOL

3145 PFLUGER, Rolf: Diskographie der
Wiener Schule in Osterrichische
Musikzeitschrift, XXIV/5-6 (May-
June 1969): 353-364 ((-))

VIENNA SYMPHONY ORCHESTRA
See WIENER SYMPHONIKER

VILLA-LOBOS, HEITOR, 1887-1959

3146 Discografia de Villa-Lobos in Brasil
Musical, No. 27 (September-October
1948): 21 ((-))

3147   Discografia in FRANÇA, Eurico
Nogueira: Villa-Lobos: síntese crítica
e biográfica. 1. ed. [Rio de Janeiro:
Museu Villa-Lobos, 1970]: 57-123 ((-))

3148   Discoteca Villa Lobos in MARIZ,
Vasco: Heitor Villa Lobos. [Rio de
Janeiro]: Serviço de Publicações,
[author's pref. 1949]: [154]-157 ((-))

3149   [[[Discography] in MARIZ, Vasco:
Villa-Lobos; life and work of the Bra-
zilian composer. 2d rev. ed. Washington: Brazilian-American Cultural Institute, 1970: 78-84]]

3150   Relação de gravações de obras de
Villa-Lobos in MURICY, José Candido
de Andrade: Villa-Lobos: uma inter-
pretação. [Rio de Janeiro]: Ministerio
de Educaçã o e Cultura, Serviço de
Documentação, [1961]: 163-177 (Cole-
çãdo "Vida brasileira") ((-))

3151   Rio de Janeiro. Museu Villa-Lobos:
Villa-Lobos em discografia. [Rio de
Janeiro: Museu Villa-Lobos], 1965:
28 pp. ((-))

VIOL MUSIC

3152   Discography in ARAZI, Ishaq: D'amore
con amore in American String Teacher,
XIX/4 (1969): 7-10, 19.

VIOLA MUSIC

3153   BEAUMONT, François de: Viola-
Diskographie. [n.p.]: Bärenreiter-
Verlag, 1973 ((-))

VIOLIN

3154   A sampling of violin recordings in
BALLANTINE, Bill: The violin; an in-
troduction to the instrument. New
York: Watts, 1971: 116-121 ((-))

VIOLIN MUSIC

3155   The phonograph and the violin in
BACHMANN, Alberto: An encyclopedia
of the violin. New York; London: D.
Appleton & Co., 1925. New York: Da
Capo, 1966: 312-320; [No record num-
bers] ((-))

3156   CREIGHTON, James: Discopaedia of
the violin, 1889-1971. [Toronto; Buf-
falo]: University of Toronto Press,
[1974]: xvi, 987 pp. ((3, 4, 5, 6))

VIOLINISTS, VIOLONCELLISTS, ETC.

3157   Verzeichnis der Schallplattenaufnahmen des Autors in BAECHI, Julius: Von

Boccherini bis Casals: Essais über 17
Meistercellisten und die Entwicklung
des Cellospiels mit einem Anhang zur
Geschichte des Violoncellos. [Zürich:
Panton-Verlag, 1961]: 91 ((-))

3158   Co si poslechnout z desek in BUDIŠ,
Ratibor: Housle v proměnách staletí.
1. vyd. Praha: Supraphon, 1975: 143-
146 ((-))

3159   Schallplattenverzeichnis in HARTNACK,
Joachim W.: Grosse Geiger unserer
Zeit. München: Rütten & Loening, 1967:
320-326 ((-))

Swedish

3160   [[ENGLUND, Björn: Swedish violinists:
1907-1955, by Björn Englund & Tage
RINGHEIM. Stockholm: [National Mu-
seum], 1973: 42 pp. (Nationalfonoteteks
diskografier, 504)]]

VIOLONCELLISTS
See listings for VIOLINISTS, VIOLON-
CELLISTS, ETC.

VIVALDI, ANTONIO, 1678-1741

3161   BELLINGARDI, Luigi: Discografia di
Antonio Vivaldi in GIAZOTTO, Remo:
Antonio Vivaldi: catalogo delle opere a
cura di Agostino GIRARD. Torino: ERI,
1973: [527]-545 (Collana di monografie
per servire alla storia della musica
italiana) ((-))

3162   BENI, Pietro: Discographie in PIN-
CHERLE, Marc: Vivaldi. Paris: Le
Bon plaisir, [1955]: [237]-241 (Amour
de la musique) ((-))

3163   BERRI, Pietro: Indice discografico
vivaldiano. Milano: G. Ricordi, 1953:
35 pp. ((-))

3164   BERRI, Pietro: Tutti i dischi di Vivaldi
incisi nel mondo in Musica e Dischi,
VI (No. 44, April 1950): 9 ((-)); Appendix: Musica e Dischi, VII (No. 58, July
1951): 4 ((-)); VIII (No. 66, March
1952): 12 ((-))

3165   Discographie de base in CANDÉ, Roland de: Vivaldi. Paris: Éditions du
Seuil, 1967: 185-186 ((-))

3166   Discographie in GALLOIS, Jean: Antonio Vivaldi. Lyon: Éditions et Impr.
du Sud-Est, 1967: 112-114 (Collection
Nos amis les musiciens) ((-))

3167   Discographie de Vivaldi in MARNAT,
Marcel: Antonio Vivaldi: l'homme, son
milieu et sa musique. Paris: Seghers,
1965: [161]-180 (Musiciens de tous les
temps, 19) ((-))

Concertos, Bassoon & String Orchestra

3168   A discography of bassoon concerti in
SEIDLER, Richard David: A survey of
the bassoon concerti of Antonio Vivaldi.
[Austin, TX]: University of Texas,
1960: 85 ((-))

Concertos, Violin

3169   Record album collections of Vivaldi
violin concertos in MARTIN, Arlan
Stone: Vivaldi violin concertos: a handbook. Metuchen, NJ: Scarecrow Press,
1972: 275-277 ((-))

Il cimento dell'armonia e dell'inventione. No. 1-4

3170   [Diskografie] in fono forum 1971 (No.
10, October): 774 ((-))

3171   SCHWEIZER, Gottfried: [Diskografie]
in fono forum 1966 (No. 2, February):
55 ((-))

VLACH QUARTET

3172   ECKSTEIN, Pavel: Diskografie in fono
forum 1962 (No. 12, December): 29 ((-))

VOCAL MUSIC

3173   CHARPENTREU, Simonne: Veillées en
chansons; des disques et des thèmes.
Paris: Éditions ouvrieres, 1958:
101 pp. ((-))

3174   MILLER, Philip L.: Reissues of vocal
music in High Fidelity, VIII/6 (June
1958): 71-78 ((-)); VIII/7 (July 1958):
65-71 ((-))

3175   MILLER, Philip L.: Vocal music. New
York: Knopf, 1955: 381 pp. (The guide
to long-playing records, 2)

VON MATACIC, LOVRO

3176   GLUTH, Walter: Diskografie in fono
forum 1961 (No. 10, October): 14 ((-))

VUATAZ, ROGER, 1898-

3177   Discographie in Schweizerisches
Musik-Archiv: Roger Vuataz: né le 4
janvier 1898. Zürich: Archives musicales suisses, 1970: 30 ((-))

VYCPÁLEK, LADISLAV, 1882-1969

3178   Skladby na gramofonových deskách in
SMOLKA, Jaroslav: Ladislav Vycpálek:
tvůrčí vývoj. [1. vyd.] Praha: Státní
nakl. krásné literatury, budby a umění,
1960: 242 ((-))

3179   Skladby Ladislava Vycpálka na gramofonových deskách Supraphon vabcedním
pořadí in SVOBODOVÁ, Marie: Národní
uměnec Ladislav Vycpálek (23.2.1882-
4.1.1969) Úplná bibliografie. 1. vyd.
Praha: Měst. knihovna, rozmn., 1973:
39-41 (Ediční řada Hudebaího a divadelního odboru) ((-))

WAGNER, RICHARD, 1813-1883

3180   BAGAR, Robert C.: Wagner on records.
New York: Four Corners, 1942: 95 pp.
((-))

3181   [[BAPTISTA, J. A.: Discografia seleccionada de Verdi e Wagner in Arte
Musical, XXIX (1964): 623-640]]

3182   Grammophon-Aufnahmen berühmter
Orchester und Sänger in BARTICH,
Robert: Richard Wagner. Kopenhagen:
Bartich, 1923: [10]-15 [Omits record
numbers] ((-))

3183   BLAUKOPF, Kurt: Richard Wagners
Bühnenwerke auf Schallplatten. Dis-
cographische Hinweise in International
Wagner Bibliographie. 1945-1955.
Edited by Herbert BARTH. Bayreuth:
Edition Musica, 1956: 30-35 ((-))

3184   FAVRE, Georges: Richard Wagner par
le disque. Paris: Durand, 1958: 90 pp.
((-))

3185   Discographie in GALLOIS, Jean: Richard Wagner. Lyon: Éditions et imprimeries du Sud-est, [1962]: 121-122
(Collection Nos amis les musiciens)
((-))

3186   HINTON, James: Wagner on microgroove. Part 1: 1831-1859 in High Fidelity, V/2 (April 1955): 73-85 ((-))

3187   HINTON, James: Wagner on microgroove. Part 2: 1867-1882 in High Fidelity, V/6 (August 1955): 64-69 ((-))

3188   Wagner en discos in JACOBS, Robert
Louis: Wagner: su vida y su obra.
Buenos Aires: Editorial Schapire,
[1942]: 279-285 ((1))

3189   KAŃSKI, J.: Wagner na płytach gramo-
fonowych in Ruch Muzyczny, VII/11
(1963): 17 ((-)); VII/13 (1963): 18-19
((-)); VII/14 (1963): 18 ((-)); VII/16
(1963): 19 ((-)); VII/19 (1963): 18 ((-))

3190   MARINELLI, Carlo: Discografia wag-
neriana in Rassegna Musicale, XXXI/3
(1961): [259]-285 ((-))

3191   Discographie in MATTER, Jean: Wagner: l'enchanteur. Neuchâtel: Éditions
de la Baconnière, 1968: [272]-281 ((-))

3192   WITOLD, Jean: Catalogue complet et
discographie des oeuvres de Richard

Wagner in Richard Wagner. [Paris?]:
Hachette, [c1962]: [279-299] (Collection Génies et réalites)

Operas

3193 GLASS, Herbert: The Wagner operas on
microgroove in High Fidelity, XI/11
(November 1961): 57-60, 132-138 ((-))

3194 OSBORNE, Conrad L.: The Wagner
operas on records; a discography in
High Fidelity, XVI/11 (November 1966):
78-82, 122-124, 145-156 ((-)); XVI/12
(December 1966): 26-28, 32, 42, 46-50
((-)); XVII/1 (January 1967): 44-48
((-))

3195 [[[Discography] in WILLIAMSON, Audrey: Wagner opera. London: J. Calder,
1962: 184-192]]

Der fliegende Holländer

3196 Discographie in Phono, IV/2 (Winter
1957-1958): 4-5 ((-))

3197 MANN, William: Wagner's Der fliegende Holländer in Opera, XVII/2
(February 1966): 89-96 (Opera on the
gramophone, 17) ((-))

Die Meistersinger von Nürnberg

3198 Discografia in L'Approdo Musicale, I/2
(April-June 1958): 102-104 ((-))

3199 ROSENTHAL, Harold: Die Meistersinger in Opera, VIII/2 (February
1957): 82-88 (Opera on the gramophone,
1) ((-))

3200 VIVIAR: The Mastersingers of Nurenberg: the quintet (Act 3) in Record Collector, V/12 (December 1950): 284-286
((-))

Parsifal

3201 VIVIAR: Richard Wagner's "Parsifal"
on gramophone records in Record Collector, VII/4-5 (April-May 1952): 77-
119 ((3, 4, 6))

Der Ring des Nibelungen

3202 [[Discography in LEYNS, Bert: Richard
Wagners Musickdrama Der Ring des
Nibelungen. Leuven: De Monte, 1972:
104-105]]

3203 PUGLIESE, Giuseppe: Schede in Discoteca, No. 138 (March 1974): 16-19;
[Omits record numbers] ((5))

Der Ring des Nibelungen. Das Rheingold

3204 BLYTH, Alan: Das Rheingold in Opera,
XXV/10 (October 1974): 865-873 (Opera on the gramophone, 36) ((1))

Der Ring des Nibelungen. Siegfried

3205 BLYTH, Alan: Siegfried in Opera,
XXII/12 (December 1971): 1041-1047
((1)); XXIII/1 (January 1972): 25-30
(Opera on the gramophone, 31) ((-))

Der Ring des Nibelungen. Die Walküre

3206 BLYTH, Alan: Die Walküre in Opera,
XXI/9 (September 1970): 826-836 ((-));
XXI/10 (October 1970): 927-930 ((-));
Addenda: Opera, XXII/2 (February
1971): 160-162 (Opera on the gramophone, 28) ((1))

3207 HERZFELD, Friedrich: [Diskografie]
in fono forum 1966 (No. 12, December):
630 ((-))

Der Ring des Nibelungen. Die Götterdämmerung

3208 ROSENFELD, V. V.: Goeterdaemmerung in Record Collector, III/3 (March
1948): 37-43 ((-)); III/8 (September
1948): 151-154; III/10 (October 1948):
170-174 ((-)); III/11 (November 1948):
192-195 ((-)); III/12 (December 1948):
210-215 ((-))

3209 VIVIAR: The finale of Wagner's Goeterdaemmerung on gramophone records in
Record Collector, XIII/7-8 (September-
October 1960): 173-178 ((3))

Tristan und Isolde

3210 [[Discography in LANDEGHEM, Wilfried van: Richard Wagner: Tristan und
Isolde. Gent: Werkgroep Musiektheater
Gent, 1972: 20 pp.]]

3211 [[ROBBINS-LANDON, H. C.: Eine vergleichende Discographie in Phono,
VIII/1]]

3212 VIVIAR: Isolde's "Liebestod" on
gramophone records in Record Collector, IX/7 (December 1954): 165-170
((1, 3))

WAGNER, WIELAND, 1917-1966

3213 Discographie de Bayreuth depuis 1951
in GOLÉA, Antonie: Entretiens avec
Wieland Wagner. Paris: Pierre Belfond, 1967: 215-216 ((-))

3214 Discographie von Bayreuth seit 1951 in
GOLÉA, Antonie: Gespräche mit Wieland Wagner. Salzburg: SN Verlag,
Salzburger Nachrichten, 1968: 149-150
((-))

WALCHA, HELMUT

3215 Diskografie in fono forum 1961 (No. 12,
December): 14 ((-))

WALKER, EDYTH, 1867-1950

3216 WILE, Raymond: The Edison disc recordings of Edyth Walker in Association for Recorded Sound Collections
Journal, III/2-3 (Fall 1971): 57 ((6, 7))

WALLBERG, HEINZ

3217 Diskographie in Phonoprisma (January-
February 1966): 23 ((-))

WALLNÖFER, ADOLF, 1854-1946

3218 DENNIS, J.: Adolf Wallnoefer in Record
Collector, XIX/3-4 (June 1970): 87-88
((-))

3219 WIMMER, Wilhelm: Adolf Wallnöfer in
Record Collector, XIV/11-12 (n.d.):
277-278 ((-))

WALTER, BRUNO, 1876-1962

3220 BOONIN, Joseph M.: Bruno Walter;
discography in Musical America,
LXXXII (April 1962): 20-21 ((5))

3221 CLOUGH, F. F., and G. J. CUMING:
Bruno Walter; discography in Gramophone Record Review, No. 70 (August
1959): 718 ((-)); Errata: Gramophone
Record Review, No. 71 (September
1959): 824 ((-))

3222 Frankfurt am Main. Deutsches Rundfunkarchiv. Sender Hinweisdienst
Musik: Bruno Walter: 1876-1962; 10.
Todestag. Frankfurt am Main: Deutsches Rundfunkarchiv, 1972: 30 leaves
((1, 7))

3223 Diskographie in Collegium Musicum
1971 (No. 2): 20 ((-))

3224 Discographie in GAVOTY, Bernard:
Bruno Walter. Genève: Éditions R.
Kister, 1956: [32] (Les Grands inter-
prètes) ((-))

3225 MANN, Carl-Heinz: Aus der Diskografie in fono forum 1961 (No. 10, October):
29 ((-))

3226 MARSH, Robert C.: The heritage of
Bruno Walter; a discography in High
Fidelity, XIV/1 (January 1964): 44-48,
102-109 ((7))

3227 PICKETT, David A.: A Bruno Walter
discography: part one; commercial recordings, issued discs only. Berkeley:
Bruno Walter Society and Sound Ar-
chive, 1973: 28 pp. ((7))

3228 Ricordo di Bruno Walter in Musica e
Dischi, XVIII/3 (March 1962): 18 ((-))

WALTER, GUSTAV

3229 FREESTONE, John: Collectors' corner
in Gramophone, No. 356 (January 1953):
193 ((-))

WALTON, SIR WILLIAM TURNER, 1902-

3230 [[CLOUGH, F. F., and G. J. CUMING:
Discography in HOWES, Frank Stewart:
The music of William Walton. London;
New York: Oxford University Press,
1965: 219-228]]

3231 Discografia de William Walton in Brasil Musical, No. 26 (July-August 1948):
22-23 ((-))

3232 GREENFIELD, Edward: Walton by
Walton on record in Gramophone XLXIX
(May 1972): 1866 ((-))

WAND, GÜNTER, 1912-

3233 Schallplattenaufnahmen von Günter
Wand in Günter Wand, Gürzenich-
kapellmeister, 1947-1974. Köln:
Wienand, 1974: 54-55 ((-))

WARLOCK, PETER
See HESELTINE, PHILIP

WARREN, LEONARD, 1911-1960

3234 Diskographie in Collegium Musicum
1971 (No. 10): 28 ((-))

3235 [[ROSENTHAL, Harold: [Leonard War-
ren] in Gramophone, No. 373 (July
1954): 54]]

WEBER, KARL MARIA FRIEDRICH ERNST,
FREIHERR VON, 1786-1826

3236 APPEL, Richard G.: Carl Maria von
Weber's recorded works in Phonograph
Monthly Review, I/2 (November 1926):
3-4 ((-))

3237 [[[Discography] in LAUX, Karl: Carl
Maria von Weber. Leipzig: P. Reclam,
1965: 291-293]]

3238 SVOBODA, Sestavil O.: Nahráv ky z
díla C. M. v. Webera na deskách Supraphon in BURIAN, Karel Vladimír: Carl
Maria von Weber. Praha: Supraphon,
t. PG 3, 1970: 290-291 (Hudební profily,
19) ((-))

WEBERN, ANTON VON, 1883-1945
See also BERG, ALBAN. Nijman,
Julius...

3239 Discographie in Revue Musicale, No.
298-299 (1975): 135-136 ((-))

3240 Grammofonispelninger in Nutida Musik,
VIII/1 (1964-1965): 35 ((-))

3241 Discographie in KOLNEDER, Walter:
Anton Webern. Rhein: P. J. Tonger,
1961: 193 (Kontrapunkte, 5) ((-))

3242 Weberns Musik auf Schallplatte in
KRELLMANN, Hanspeter: Anton
Webern in Selbstzeugnissen und Bild-
dokumenten. Reinbek (bei Hamburg):
Rowohlt, 1975: [147] (Rowohlts Mono-
graphien, 229) ((-))

3243 Discographie et bibliographie som-
maires in ROSTAND, Claude: Anton
Webern: l'homme et son oeuvre. Paris:
Seghers, 1969: [189] (Musiciens de tous
les temps, 40) ((-))

3244 ROY, Jean: Discographie in Diapason,
No. 100 (October 1965): 39 ((-))

3245 Bibliography and discography in WILD-
GANS, Friedrich: Anton Webern. London: Calder & Boyars, 1966: 181-182
((-))

3246 Bibliography and discography in
WILDGANS, Friedrich: Anton Webern.
New York: October House, [1967]:
181-182 ((-))

WEDEKIND, ERIKA

3247 RIEMENS, Leo: Erika Wedekind in
Record Collector, VI/8 (August 1951):
176-188 ((-))

WEEL, LIVA, 1897-

3248 ANDREASEN, Axel: Liva Weel og
grammofonen: en discografi. København: [Axel Andreasen, Hothers plads
23/1], 1973: 84 pp. ((3, 4, 6, 7))

WEILL, KURT, 1900-1950

3249 PRAWY, Marcel: Diskografie in fono
forum 1962 (No. 6, June): 11 ((-))

WEINGARTNER, FELIX, 1863-1942

3250 PANIGEL, Armand, and HENRY-
JACQUES: Félix Weingartner; une
discographie in Disques, No. 1 (January 15, 1948): 35 ((-))

WEISS, EDWARD
See listing for BUSONI, FERRUC-
CIO. Åhlén, Carl-Gunnar: Ferruccio
Busoni (1866-1924)

WEISS, JOSEPH

3251 BENKO, Gregor: Joseph Weiss—
discography in Antique Records (October 1974): 9 ((3, 7))

WEISSENBERG, ALEXIS

3252 COSSÉ, Peter: Diskografie in fono
forum 1972 (No. 12, December): 1067
((-))

WEISSMANN, FRIEDER

3253 PORTE, J. F.: Dr. Weissmann in
Gramophone, V/2 (August 1927): 93-94
((-))

WELLER QUARTET

3254 KRAUS, Gottfried: Diskographische
Angaben in fono forum 1966 (No. 9,
September): 440 ((-))

WERICH, JAN, 1905-

3255 Diskografický soupis in CINCIBUS,
Josef: Gramofonová deska a Jan
Werich: historické úvahy v rozmarném
tónu. [1. vyd.] Praha: Státní hudební
vydavatelství, 1964: 32-37 (Edice kul-
turně osvětového odboru, 125) ((7))

WERNER, JEAN-JACQUES

3256 Discographie in Courrier Musical de
France, No. 47 (1974): 123 ((-))

WHIDDEN, JAY

3257 WALKER, Steve: The Jay Whidden discography in Talking Machine Review,
No. 4 (June 1970): 112-116 ((3, 6, 7));
No. 5 (August 1970): 156 ((3, 6, 7)); No.
6 (October 1970): facing page 157 ((3,
6, 7)); No. 8 (February 1971): 232 ((3,
7))

WHITE, CAROLINE

3258 BISHOP, G. K.: Collector's corner in
Gramophone, No. 191 (April 1939): 496
((-))

WHITEHILL, CLARENCE, 1871-1932

3259 MORAN, W. R.: The recordings of
Clarence Whitehill in Record Collector,
XXII/10-11 (April 1975): 247-263;
[Includes notes on playing speeds] ((3,
4, 6, 7))

WIELE, A. VAN DE

3260 Discographie in Diapason, No. 150
(October 1970): 5 ((–))

WIENER, JEAN

3261 Discographie de Jean Wiener in Courrier Musical de France, No. 52 (1975):
165 ((–))

WIENER PHILHARMONIKER

3262 Schallplatten in GRASBERGER, Franz:
Die Wiener Philharmoniker bei Johann
Strauss. Wien: Verlag Brüder Rosen-
baum, [c1963]: 82-83 ((–))

3263 PFLUGER, Rolf: Diskographie der
Wiener Philharmoniker in Österrei-
chische Musikzeitschrift, XXII/2-3
(February-March 1967): 153-167 ((–))

WIENER SOLISTEN

3264 SCHWINGER, Wolfram: Diskografie in
fono forum 1963 (No. 5, May): 187 ((–))

WIENER SYMPHONIKER

3265 [[SCHREIBER, Wolfgang: Die Wiener
Symphoniker in Muscalia, I/1 (September 1970): 30-43]]

WILEY, CLIFFORD ALEXANDER

3266 WALSH, Jim: The George Alexander
discography [includes recordings made
under the names Alexander Wiley and
George Alexander] in Hobbies, LXI
(October 1956): 33, 37 ((7))

WILHELM, MARGARTHE

3267 WILHELM, P.: Discography in Record
News, II/12 (August 1958): 425-427 ((5))

WILLAN, HEALEY, 1880-1968

3268 Sound recordings—Enregistrements
sonores in BRYANT, Giles: Healey
Willan catalogue. Ottawa: National Library of Canada, 1972: 135-143 ((1))

WILSON, STEUART

3269 [[List of Decca records in STEWART,
Margaret: English singer; the life of
Steuart Wilson. London: Duckworth,
1970: 287]]

WINDGASSEN, WOLFGANG

3270 NYS, Carl de: Discographie Windgassen
in Diapason, No. 191 (November 1974):
18 ((–))

3271 Diskographie in WESSLING, Berndt W.:
Wolfgang Windgassen. Bremen: Schünemann, 1967: 120 ((–))

WINKELMANN, HERMANN, 1849-1912

3272 DENNIS, J.: The records in Record
Collector, VII/6-7 (June-July 1952):
128 ((–)

3273 FREESTONE, John: Collectors' corner
in Gramophone, No. 356 (January 1953):
193 ((–))

WITKOMIRSKA, WANDA

3274 Records in Polish Music, X/2 (1975):
[19] ((–))

WOLF, HUGO, 1860-1903

3275 BLAUKOPF, Kurt: Discographische
Notizen zu Hugo Wolf in Österrichische
Musikzeitschrift, XV/2 (February
1960): 110-111 ((–))

3276 Discographie in Revue Musicale, No.
298-299 (1975): 101 ((–))

3277 KRAUS, Gottfried: Diskografie der
erwähnten Aufnahmen in fono forum
1972 (No. 12, December): 1072 ((–))

3278 [[LANGEVIN, Gilbert: Hugo Wolf;
l'oeuvre posthume in Musicalia, I/1
(September 1970): 45-53]]

3279 Discographie in ROSTAND, Claude:
Hugo Wolf l'homme et son oeuvre.
Paris: Seghers, 1967: [191] (Musiciens
de tous les temps, 36) ((–))

3280 WEBER, J. F.: Hugo Wolf complete
works. Utica, NY: Weber, 1970: 34 pp.
(Discography series, 2) ((–))

3281 WEBER, J. F.: Hugo Wolf. Utica, NY:
Weber, 1975: iv, 86 pp. (Discography
series, 2) ((3, 4, 5, 6, 7))

WOOD, SIR HENRY J., 1869-1944

3282 GOODBODY, Terence E.: Sir Henry J.
Wood in Gramophone, II/9 (February
1925): 326-327 [Omits record numbers]
((–))

3283 Recorded works by Sir Henry Wood and
the New Queen's Hall Orchestra in
Phonograph Monthly Review, I/3 (December 1926): 114 ((–))

WOODHOUSE, VIOLET GORDON

3284 HUGHES, E. A., and A. E. COOBAN: Violet Gordon Woodhouse: a discography in Recorded Sound, No. 41 (January 1971): 727-729 ((1, 3, 4, 6, 7))

WOODWIND INSTRUMENTS

3285 Discography in HILTON, Lewis B.: Learning to teach through playing; a woodwind method. Reading, MA: Addison-Wesley Pub. Co., 1970: 47-49 ((-))

WOYTOWICZ, STEFANIA

3286 SPINGEL, Hans Otto: Diskografie in fono forum 1963 (No. 1, January): 14 ((-))

WUNDERLICH, FRITZ

3287 Diskographie in Collegium Musicum 1971 (No. 10): 17-19 ((-))

3288 HERZFELD, Friedrich: Aus der Diskografie in fono forum 1962 (No. 1, January): 27 ((-))

XENAKIS, IANNIS, 1922-

3289 Recordings in BOIS, Mario: Iannis Xenakis: the man and his music; a conversation with the composer and a description of his works. London: Boosey & Hawkes Music Publishers, 1967: 38-39 ((-))

3290 Schallplatten in BOIS, Mario: Iannis Xenakis: der Mensch und sein Werk. Bonn: Boosey & Hawkes, 1968: 49 ((-))

3291 Discographie de Xenakis in Harmonie, No. 33 (January 1968): 25 ((-))

3292 FLEURET, Maurice: List of works with discography in Music and Musicians, XX (April 1972): 27 ((-))

3293 HOOGLAND, Claes: Yannis Xenakis på skiva in Nutida Musik, XV/2 (1971-1972): 51 ((-))

3294 ROY, Jean: Discographie in Revue Musicale, No. 267 (1969): 30-31 ((-))

YANKS, BYRON
See JANIS, BYRON

YAW, ELLEN BEACH

3295 ALTAMARINO, Antonio: An Ellen Beach Yaw discography in Record Collector, X/7 (December 1957): 153-160 ((1, 3, 7))

3296 FREESTONE, John: Collectors' corner in Gramophone, No. 360 (May 1953): 316 ((-))

YSAŸE, EUGÈNE, 1858-1931

3297 Gramophone recordings by Eugene Ysaÿe for the Columbia Gramophone Company, New York in YSAŸE, Antoine: Ysaÿe: his life, work and influence. London: W. Heinemann, [1947]: 245 ((-))

3298 Essai discographique in YSAŸE, Antoine: Eugène Ysaÿe. Bruselles: Editions Ysaÿe, 1972: 218-224 ((1))

ZADORA, MICHAEL VON
See listings for BUSONI, FERRUCCIO. Åhlén, Carl-Gunnar: Ferruccio Busoni (1866-1924); Discography in Busoni's pupils play Busoni compositions

ZANELLI, RENATO

3299 SAAVEDRA, Oscar, and W. R. MORAN: The records in Record Collector, VII/9 (September 1952): 204-207 ((3, 6, 7))

ZARZUELAS

3300 [[WEINSTOCK, H.: The world of the zarzuela in Saturday Review (May 28, 1955): 33]]

ZBINDEN, JULIEN FRANÇOIS, 1917-

3301 Discographie in Julien-François Zbinden: liste des oeuvres—Werkverzeichnis. Zürich: Schweizerisches Musik-Archiv, 1974: 4 ((-))

ZECHLIN, DIETER

3302 Diskographie in Medium Schallplatte, No. 12 (No. 3, 1969): 16 ((-))

ZENATELLO, GIOVANNI, 1876-1949

3303 [[HARDWICK, K. [Discography] in Record News, I/8 (February 1950)]]

3304 HUTCHINSON, Tom, and Clifford WILLIAMS: The records in Record Collector, XIV/5-6: 112-143 ((1, 3)); Addenda: Record Collector, XIV/7-8: 173-174 ((-))

3305 [[PHILLIPS, R.: Giovanni Zenatello in
      Record Collector, IV/ (February 1949):
      25-30]]

ZIMMERMANN, BERND ALOIS

3306 Schallplatten in ZIMMERMANN, Bernd
      Alois: Intervall und Zeit: Aufsätze u.
      Schriften z. Werk. Schott, 1974: 153-
      154 ((-))

ZONOPHONE RECORDS

See listings for CARUSO, ENRICO.
Drummond, Canon H. J.: The seven
Zonophone records; Freestone, John,
and H. J. Drummond: A Caruso
anniversary

ZUKERMAN, PINCAS, 1948-

3307 Zukerman discography in Records and
      Recording, XVI/ 8 (May 1973): 22 ((-))

INDEX

Note: References are to entry numbers, not page numbers. (Numbers appearing in parentheses indicate the volume in the numbered series of that specific entry.)

Åhlén, Carl-Gunnar, 24, 76, 525, 975, 1246, 1324, 1670, 2104, 2105, 2153, 2253, 2543, 2840, 2848
Abraham, Gerald, 360
Aerts, Karel, 1331
Affelder, Paul, 449, 450, 1087, 2732
Aguettant, Robert, 647
Ahlers, N., 1826
Alder, Caine, 1395
al-Hifní, Muhmūd Ahmad, 2559
Alice Marie, Sister, 637
Allen, Vic, 2307
Allorto, Riccardo, 695, 1269
Allvard, Didier, 41
Alonso, José Montero. See Montero Alonso, José
Altamarino, Antonio, 3295
Alvarez Coral, Juan, 2490
Amat, Carlos Gómez. See Gómez Amat, Carlos
America in the making, 1173
Amico, Fedele d', 603
Amor de la musique, 448, 2586, 3162
Amy, Dominique, 2353
Anderson, Harry L., 1242, 1614, 1615, 2234, 2496, 2540
Anderson, William Robert, 976
Andersson, Ingvar, 362
Andreasen, Axel, 1334, 2616, 3248
Andriessen, Hendrik, 1088
Andriessen, Johan, 2381
Angé-Laribé, Michel, 1849
Angoff, Charles, 707, 708
Annibaldi, Claudio, 2276
Anson, George, 253
Antek, Samuel, 3058
Antología de escritores y aristas montañeses, 73
Antonová, Jana, 2453
Apollo editions (A-162), 2049
Appel, Richard G., 269, 280, 3236
Appleton, Jon H., 963
Aprahamian, Felix, 856, 2992
Arazi, Ishaq, 3152
Archetti, Enzo, 1897

Archives de la musique enregistrée UNESCO. Ser. A: Musique occidentale (1), 658
Ardoin, John, 536
Argument-Sonderbände (5), 960
Armitage, Merle, 1158, 1159, 1160, 2912, 2913
Armstrong, F., 2836
Armstrong, William H., 3002
Arnold, Elliott, 2733, 2734
Arnold, Heinz Ludwig, 857
Arntsen, Ella, 1992
Artistas españoles contemporáneos (6), 2231; (34), 1285; (56), 1004
The Art of the conductor, 1475
Arts, a third level course, 119
Artsay, Aida Favia. See Favia-Artsay, Aida
Ashman, Mike, 395, 427, 432, 469, 913, 1667 2520, 2791
Asow, Erich Hermann Müller von. See Müller von Asow, Erich Hermann
Atlantis-Musikbücherei, 181, 486
Augé-Laribe, Michel, 1849
Autrey, R. L., 1555
Aylward, Derek, 1764

Bachmann, Alberto, 3155
Bachtik, Josef, 3106
Badura-Skoda, Paul, 1052
Baechi, Julius, 3157
Bäck, Sven-Erik, 137
Bagar, Robert C., 438, 3180
Baignères, Claude, 1577
Bălan, George, 1703
Ball, Charles H., 1993
Ballantine, Bill, 1071, 2297, 3154
Ballif, Claude, 339
Balzer, Jürgen. 831
Baptista, J. A., 3107, 3181
Barbaud, Pierre, 1301, 1302
Barbier, Jean-Joel, 1658, 3030
Barbier, Pierre-E., 2398, 2535, 2600
Barbour, Harriot Buxton, 1994
Barford, Philip, 93, 94
Bărgăuánu, Grigore, 1622